The
Fishing in Print

Also by Arnold Gingrich

The Fishing in Print

A Guided Tour Through Five Centuries of Angling Literature

Arnold Gingrich

*Some of the best
fishing is done not
in water but in print.*
—Sparse Grey Hackle

Winchester Press

All quotations are credited in context. Certain larger quoted portions, while also credited in context, are for copyright purposes additionally credited below, with thanks to the authors and publishers concerned:

In Chapter 3 the section called "Angling in Walton's Day" by A. J. McClane is taken from *McClane's Standard Fishing Encyclopedia,* copyright © 1965 by Holt, Rinehart and Winston, Inc. Used by permission of the author and Holt, Rinehart and Winston, Inc.

In Chapter 11, the sections called "Fancy Flies," "The Old Master," "A Fish Story," "Action Upstream," "The Dry Fly" and "The Modern Fly" are taken from *Quill Gordon* by John McDonald, copyright © 1947, 1972 by John McDonald. Used by permission of the author and Alfred A. Knopf, Inc.

In Chapter 11, the section called "The Quest for Theodore Gordon" is taken from *Fishless Days, Angling Nights* by Sparse Grey Hackle, copyright © 1971 by Alfred W. Miller. Used by permission of the author and Crown Publishers, Inc.

In Chapter 15, the two sections called "There *Is* a Royal Coachman" and "Three Secrets of the Salmon," by Preston J. Jennings, are taken from articles published in the July and October 1956 issues of Esquire, copyright © 1956 by Esquire, Inc. Used by permission of Adele Marie Louise Jennings and the publisher.

*To Kay, Jay and Jane
in memory of Dear Sonny
(Lalla Reynolds Biays, 1883-1968)*

The assistance is gratefully acknowledged of Bayard Schieffelin and Walter Zervas of the New York Public Library and of Mrs. Jed Braun of the Esquire Magazine staff. Helpful suggestions from Gene Anderegg, William Humphrey, Nick Lyons, Col. Henry Siegel and William Steinkraus are also appreciated.

Contents

1.

We Go
a-Fishing in Print

*A*s Sparse Grey Hackle says, some of the best fishing is to be found not in water but in print. It follows that some of the best fishing partners are to be found not in life but in literature.

I know there are some things I've read that come to mind more often while I'm fishing than anything I can remember that anybody ever said beside me on stream or pond.

A couple of them that have come to mind quite often were cited in the pages of *The Well-Tempered Angler,* almost a decade back, and I'm sure they'll go on cropping up in my fishing memories and reflections as long as I'm able to hobble or creep or even be wheeled to streamside.

One was the '98 "Complaint of a Bastard" — Thomas Bastard, to be precise, and the ground of his complaint was that "fishes decrease, and fishers multiply." The year was 1598. So the grumbling about increasing fishing pressures, in consequence of the population explosion, is not exactly a latter-day phenomenon.

The other was the passage from Andrew Lang's *Angling Sketches* called "Thirty Years Ago." That was a complaint too, in a sense, as its burden was the difference between the fishing then and that of thirty years before. But its "now" was 1890 and I'm sure that patient enough dig-

ging through the old books and journals could unearth a similar complaint, at thirty-year intervals, or roughly a generation apart, back to the
time of Thomas Bastard, and probably — if only the books could be
found — long before. The complaints yes, but not the beauty of the
language in which this one was couched. I've heard it so often in my
mind's ear, since I first read it sometime in the 1930s, that I can almost
mumble it to myself, like saying one's beads:

. . . even then, thirty years ago (1860), the old stagers used to tell us
that the water was overfished," said Lang, in effect, recalling his boyhood
in the South of Scotland, and quoting how they grumbled: "'Tis gone,
'tis gone: not in our time will any man . . . need a cart to carry the
trout he has slain." And the passage went on, in words that I could almost recite like so much poetry: "They are all gone now, the old allies
and tutors in the angling art. The companions of those times are scattered, and live under strange stars and in converse seasons by troutless
waters. But, except for the scarcity of fish, the scene is very little altered,

and one is a boy again, in heart, beneath the elms. . . . However bad the sport, it keeps you young, or makes you young again, and you need not follow Ponce de Leon to the Western wilderness, when, in any river you knew of yore, you can find the Fountain of Youth."

I used to say to myself, savoring that one as if it were a memory of my own, and not just something I remembered reading, "What wouldn't I give for a whole bookful of things like that?"

I've been wrestling with the answer off and on ever since, and what you're holding in your hands now is as near as I've come to it. Of course it isn't a whole bookful of passages like that. Andrew Lang himself couldn't come up with more than a couple, in a long lifetime of trying, and very few better fishing writers ever lived.

Walton came closest, of course, but even Walton (can't be quoted entire.) Yet there may be a clue, in something Lang said about Walton, to a good way to go about extracting the desired essence from a lot of angling writings. It was in the preface to his own edition of *The Compleat Angler,* in 1896, that Andrew Lang said: "To write on Walton is, indeed, to hold a candle to the sun. Had Montaigne been a fisher, he might have written somewhat like Izaak, but without the piety, the perfume and the charm."

We can do without the piety, I should think, but the perfume and the charm—yes, that's the two-way stretch with which to test the samples, to see if they warrant inclusion in a book of memorabilia.

I don't mean that we should go about with a divining rod that twitches only over Literature with a capital L. For one thing, there isn't all that much—it'd be a very slender volume. From Walton in the past to Haig-Brown in the present, you can almost count on your two hands the truly literary eminences between. That's a meager showing, for a span of over three centuries. But a book can fall considerably short of measuring up as a literary masterpiece, and still contain the wherewithal to enchant the angler. Let it diffuse the whiff of authenticity, that is to the fisherman the perfume of credence, and let it exude a modicum of charm, to endow things as they are with an aura of things as they ought to be at best, and you convey that sense of recognition value that makes the fisherman nod his head, and maybe touch his temple, as if to say, "I must remember this."

Over the years, whenever I've felt that little tingle in the hairs on the back of my neck, as I encountered an original thought or observation in a fishing book, I've turned the corner of the page down. It's my way of saying, "I must remember this," and it's a habit that dealers and serious book collectors find unendearing. But it's my way of evaluating fishing books, which I've always really wanted more for reading purposes than for mere "collecting." I wanted to read them, in the first place, for the sake of anything I might find in them worth remembering, at a later moment of actual fishing, and I turned the corners down whenever I came across anything memorable, presumably so I could go back and look it up in case I forgot it. How I could find it, if I forgot it, seems somehow never to have occurred to me.

My logic in this respect is of a piece with that of the old Irishman who said, "My boy, you should learn to cut your fingernails with your left hand, because you never know when you might lose your right hand."

But you and I could take crazier fishing trips, I imagine, than if we were to set out right now and start fishing those turned-down corners like so many pockets in a tumbling mountain stream.

We might get skunked, but that's no novelty to anglers. And there's always the chance that before we're through we might be glad I long ago began that messy habit of dog-earing books. And unlike most fishing trips, at least we haven't far to go.

Otherwise, the analogy to a fishing trip is pretty good. Entering the room in the house that was once called my office, we crawl through thickets of rod cases and fly boxes until we come upon a veritable spate of books. And there we go a-fishing.

2.
The Age of the Dame

T he oldest book I have, older even than any of my fiddles, is a copy of Rondelet's *Histoire des Poissons*, printed at Lyon in 1558. It was originally two volumes, but they were put together in one of those sumptuous eighteenth-century tooled-morocco bindings, which is in turn enclosed in a slipcase that also has a tooled-morocco spine. It would look at home, alongside books similarly housed, in a place like the Morgan Library, but among my books it's as incongruous a sight as a monocle with a mackinaw jacket, or a top hat with snowshoes.

Needless to say, it hasn't a single turned-down page corner, because it's so obviously the kind of book you hesitate to handle without putting gloves on first. (Needless also to say, I didn't buy this book; it was given to me in commemoration of an anniversary.) But if this had been an ordinary reading copy, such as I usually try to get of all the fishing books I buy, I doubt that I'd have turned down more than one or two corners anyway. Properly speaking, it isn't even a fishing book; just a book about fish. There are ten of them, of course, for every book there is about fishing. But with very few exceptions, they are of limited interest to the angler. Since one of the exceptions is a glorious one, we'll get around to it in due course, and give it all the time it takes. But we won't tarry long with Rondelet. He was preceded by Belon in 1553 (whose name survives on French menus, standing for those big oysters, almost the size of our Chincoteagues) and by Silviani in 1534. He was contemporary, and acquainted, with Jacques Sylvius and Conrad Gessner, along with whom he was cited a couple of times by Walton over a hundred years later.

But although I dutifully read it through at the time I got it, 1958, I don't honestly remember much in it that would be worth the bother of translating.

Well, there was a fairly amusing passage about Aristotle's belief that fish had no sex organs, because he couldn't see any signs of them, and it gave me pause because I couldn't remember ever before coming across a medieval reference to Aristotle that wasn't respectful almost to the point of worship.

All right, if you like, we'll take the time for just that bit, and then we really ought to get started.

My running, not to say horseback, translation, makes no effort to match the old French with correspondingly spelled English:

Aristotle is of this opinion, that fish are without genitals . . . no fish has them, neither inside nor outside, neither does any other creature without feet, nor serpents. Thus they utilize the same conduit that ejects their ordure from their bodies, making it serve also for engendering. This he says in the third book of his history of animals. And in the fourth, he says again that fish have no genitals, nor do serpents, but that they have two conduits, one on either side of the backbone, descending from the diaphragm, which are joined together at the top, and joined again below, as they reach the hole where the excrement is expelled. These conduits at appropriate times are full of semen. That is the opinion of Aristotle, which can be disproved with the naked eye. For dolphins have genital members inside their bodies, long as a finger, which Aristotle himself forgets to have remarked in another place, for in the beginning of the third book, he puts the dolphin among those creatures having inner genitals. Sea-cows too, and whales, have genital organs, and a genital member. But no fish has a protruding member, for that would interfere with their swimming, besides getting chilled by the water. That is why it was necessary that those creatures deprived of them by nature should have them inside and covered over, and not only the males but also the females have them, though differently placed. The females have them at the matrix corners; the males at the base of the belly, near the bladder. Still other differences between the male and female generative organs, principally in size, for the male's are very small and the female's very large, for in those of the female a great body is stored, comparable to a second womb, whereas in the male a small quantity of semen carries much strength. These same spermatic vessels are in other ways different from ours, both in the much greater number of sperm cells, as with the dolphin they are stored up, through an infinity of little veins and arteries, and this is done by nature with a purpose, to keep the semen ready prepared, for the semen must be released suddenly and quickly, otherwise with the fish it would impede their movements and upset their respiration, so the semen must be at the ready, to be shot out fast, which is also why the conduits which carry it to the genital member must be so short. Those which have lungs and genitals have a genital member accommodated to the length of the matrix column of their females. The more closely the animals are joined together in the generative act, the shorter their members, and the less closely the longer, as with asses, horses, cattle and savage beasts, of which animals the females receive the males on their backs, so that the hot semen with no loss of the vigor it contains shall be thrust forthwith to the very mouth of the matrix. For this cause the whales, which by the enormous size of their bodies cannot be closely coupled, must have a gigantic member. I have seen the penis of a whale so big that, being carried by a tall man on his shoulder, from there it reached the ground; you can from that imagine what its size becomes with awareness of the female's desire to receive it. . . . This member does not exist among fish, which agitate and press together their bodies, but not to inject the semen, but only to spread it over the expelled eggs. . . .

After further consideration of the mating habits and equipment of those fish which bear their young live, and not from eggs, such as the dolphin, the sea-cow and the whale, and nourish their young with their milk, Rondelet again takes issue with Aristotle:

Experience shows that some fish have teats, such as the whales and the sea-cows, and generally speaking all those which engender from semen without eggs, and which nourish their young with milk. . . . I have seen on the coast at Bayonne great quantities of whale milk, and dolphins too give milk, whence it follows that they have teats. For the young cannot be fed milk except through teats. Thus says Aristotle. All animals have teats that conceive within themselves another animal, and thrust it forth, like man, the horse and those cetaceous creatures, like the whale and the dolphin, and the sea-cow, all of which also have teats and give milk. Besides, the dolphin engenders another animal, because it has two teats, not up above but down below, and it has no nipples, or manifest teat-buttons, like the four-footed beasts, but two little streams or tubes, one on each side from which the milk falls, that the young may suck. There you have what Aristotle says: that not only the dolphins, but also the whales and the sea-cows, have no nipples, for nature has diligently foreseen that there should be no protuberance whatsoever to impede their swimming, or their other movements in the water. In these mammary parts, fish differ from terrestrial creatures. In place of the teats that the woman has on her breast and the elephant has farther down the torso and the dog has the length of its belly, fish have them only down by the genital parts, and close to the excremental hole. The teats of all are of the same substance and nature, of several veins and arteries that are swelled by the milk, for the young to receive by mouth. In this way does Aristotle explain his assertion that all fish are without genitals, while in another place conceding them to the dolphin, and also he several times deprives all fish of teats, then writes that the cetacean order, with the dolphin as example, is provided with them, for which read the fourteenth chapter of the second book of his whole history of the animals. But it must be noted that Aristotle, properly speaking, never puts the whale, the porpoise and the dolphin, and all those which breathe through lungs, in the category of fish, as true marine animals, nor yet in that of terrestrial beasts, but rather in a separate order that participates in the characteristics of both of them.

The amateur angling scholar isn't going to find anything very rewarding in any of the pre-Walton fishing books. Collectors may find them nice to have, just as rarities for their shelves, and conversation pieces for colloquies with other collectors. There are only a handful anyway, compared to the flow that came after Walton. Old Izaak himself is as easy to read as today's paper, but his predecessors are like the meat in the less accessible parts of the lobster. It's there if you want to dig for it, but unless you're practically starved, it's hardly worth the trouble.

On the other hand, if we have any feeling that we ought to start with first things first, we'll have to back up a couple hundred years, and go back to the Dame.

Dame Juliana Berners is to angling literature as Chaucer is to English literature, representing to all practical intents and purposes the very beginning. Of course they both had predecessors, but it's something of a feat of scholarship to figure out what they're saying, once you've gone to the trouble of looking them up. Chaucer's predecessors are familiar to students; as high school kids we had to struggle with Langland's *Piers Plowsman,* which I very much doubt one in a thousand found worth the effort, and in college *Beowulf* proved at first surprised glance to be every bit as unfathomable as Latin.

As for Juliana's predecessors, the hitch there is that we don't even know who they were. She speaks of "books of credence," but without naming one. You gather, from the general tone and attitude with which she discusses this "merrie disport," throughout *The Treatyse of Fysshynge wyth an Angle,* that the sport had already acquired traditions, by the early- to mid-fourteenth century time of her writing, and was not some new-fangled thing that she and her contemporaries had just dreamed up, like gin rummy or Monopoly in our day. But she doesn't cite a single example.

For that matter, we don't even know who she was, or for sure that the author of *The Treatise* was a she. As for *The Book of St. Albans,* in which *The Treatise* first appeared, her name was given there as the author of the portion on hunting, and had been also in the previous edition in 1486, as Dame Julyans Barnes. But when Wynkyn de Worde added the fishing treatise, for the later edition, he didn't give it any specific by-line, and the assumption was simply made that the same author had done both the hunting and the fishing treatises. But that was a hasty assumption, as careful reading of both the treatises soon gives reason to suspect. The hunting one is full of admonitions on the order of "listen to your dame," whereas not one word of the fishing treatise makes even oblique reference to the author's gender. It could just as well have been written by a man.

English is a baffling language, to all those who weren't born in its ambiance, but this is one of its most annoying aspects. If a thing is written in French or German, or Italian or Spanish, you know from the difference in various word endings, after only a sentence or so, whether it was written by a male or a female, but English never differentiates.

As for Dame Juliana's being an abbess of a convent, or indeed every other fact about her, everything dates from the eighteenth century, when a couple of antiquarians gave her an engaging and colorful *persona,* which may very well have been authentic, but in no way strengthened the link with which only tradition had bound her to the authorship of *The Treatise.*

Still, it's a fascinating story, and that's undoubtedly why it has been so generally accepted. As Major Hills said in 1921, in his invaluable *A History of Fly Fishing for Trout,* "I shall treat her as author until a better claimant appears, for it is awkward to have to cite an anonymous book."

There is no better place to get the whole story of Dame Juliana and the treatise than in John McDonald's 1972 volume, *Quill Gordon,* with which he merged everything he had written about both Theodore Gordon and Juliana Berners in his two previous books, *The Complete Fly Fisherman: The Notes and Letters of Theodore Gordon* (1947) and *The Origins of Angling* (and a new printing of *The Treatise of Fishing with an Angle*) in 1963. As I said of this latter volume, at the time it came out, it is one of the most intense and perceptive feats of angling scholarship ever performed over the centuries in which fishing has been written about. And anybody who catches the fever of wanting to know all there is to be known about Dame Juliana and the treatise will find it richly worthwhile to go back to that earlier volume, even though *Quill Gordon* does contain the essence of the story.

For our present purposes, John McDonald's simplified version, with its explanatory footnotes, is so much easier to read than the black-letter facsimile of the original that was featured in previous reprintings, that we will do well to take from him. Here, then, for some of "the perfume and the charm," hark to the inimitable Dame, putative though she may be.

"What are the means and cause to bring a man into a merry spirit?" Truly, in my simple judgment, it seems to me, they are good and honest sports and games in which a man's heart takes pleasure without any repentance. Then this follows—that good and honorable recreations are the cause of man's fair old age and long life. Therefore, I will now choose among four good sports and honorable pastimes, that is to say, among hunting, hawking, fowling, and fishing, particularly angling with a rod or a pole, a line, and a hook. . . . If a man lacks physicians or doctors, he shall make three things his doctors or physicians, and he will never have need of more. The first of them is merry thought. The second is work in moderation. The third is a good diet of pure foods and suitable drinks. First, then, if a man wishes to be merry and have a glad spirit, he must avoid all contentious company and all places of disputes and quarrels, where he might have a cause of melancholy.[3] And if he will have a labor which is not excessive, he must then arrange for himself, for his heart's pleasure—without care, anxiety, or trouble—a merry occupation which may rejoice his heart and his spirit in a respectable manner. And if he wishes to be moderate in diet, he must avoid all places of debauchery, which is the cause of overindulgence and sickness, and he must withdraw himself to a place of sweet and hungry[4] air, and eat nourishing and digestible foods.

I will now describe the said four sports or games to find out, as well as I can, which is the best of them; albeit, the right noble Duke of York, lately called the Master of Game,[5] has described the joys of hunting, just as I think to describe (of it and all the others) the griefs. For hunting, to my mind, is too much work. The hunter must run all day and follow his hounds, laboring and sweating very painfully. He blows on his horn till his lips blister; and when he thinks it is a hare, very often it is a hedgehog. Thus he hunts, and when he comes home in the evening, rain-beaten, sorely pricked by thorns and with his clothes torn, wet-shod, befouled, some of his hounds lost, some crippled[6]—such griefs happen to the hunter and many others which, for fear of the displeasure of those that love it, I dare not report in full. Truly, it seems to me that this is not the best recreation or sport of the four mentioned.

Reaching the conclusion, after describing the other two sports mentioned, that "It seems to me that hunting, hawking and fowling are so toilsome and unpleasant that none of them can succeed in bringing a man into a merry frame of mind," she opts for fishing:

Undoubtedly then, it follows that it must needs be the sport or game of fishing with an angle-rod—for every other kind of fishing is also right toilsome and unpleasant, often causing men to be very wet and cold, which many times has been seen to be the main cause of sickness and sometimes of death. But the angler can have no cold nor discomfort nor anger, unless he be the cause himself, for he cannot lose more than a line or a hook, of which he can have plenty of his own making, or of other men's making, as this simple treatise will teach him; so then his loss is no grievance. And he can have no other grievances, unless some fish breaks away from him when he[12] is on his hook, in the landing of that same fish, or in any case, he does not catch him. This is no great hardship, for if he fails with one, he cannot fail with another, if he does as this treatise which follows will instruct him—unless there are no fish in the water where he is angling. And yet, at the very least, he will have his wholesome and

[3] An excess of black bile in the body, a pathological condition which could produce all manner of dangerous ailments—as well as a gloomy frame of mind.
[4] Hunger-producing, conducive to a hearty appetite.
[5] Edward of Norwich, second Duke of York, 1373–1415, translator of the book called *The Master of Game.*
[6] *Surbatted*, bruised in the feet, footsore from too much running on rough ground.
[12] The fish. Fish are masculine in this treatise.

merry walk at his own ease, and also many a sweet breath of various plants and flowers that will make him right hungry and put his body in good condition. He will hear the melodies of the harmony of birds. He will also see the young swans or cygnets following their brood swans, the ducks, the coots, the herons, and many other birds with their broods, which seems to me better than all the noise of hounds and blasts of horns and other amusements that falconers and hunters can provide, or the sports that fowlers can make. And if the angler catches the fish with difficulty, then there is no man merrier than he is in his spirits.

The treatise itself ends with this charge:

You that can angle and catch fish for your pleasure, as the above treatise teaches and shows you: I charge and require you in the name of all noble men that you do not fish in any poor man's private water (such as his pond, or tank, or other things necessary for keeping fish in) without his permission and good will. And that you be not in the habit of breaking any men's fish traps lying in their weirs and in other places belonging to them, nor of taking the fish away that is caught in them. For after a fish is caught in a man's trap, if the trap is laid in the public waters, or else in such waters as he rents, it is his own personal property. And if you take it away, you are robbing him, which is a right shameful deed for any noble man to do, a thing that thieves and robbers do, who are punished for their evil deeds by the neck and otherwise when they can be discovered and captured. And also if you do in the same manner as this treatise shows you, you will have no need to take other men's fish, while you will have enough of your own catching, if you care to work for them. It will be a true pleasure to see the fair, bright, shining-scaled fishes outwitted by your crafty means and drawn out on the land. Also, I charge you, that you break no man's hedges in going about your sports, nor open any man's gates without shutting them again. Also, you must not use this aforesaid artful sport for covetousness, merely for the increasing or saving of your money, but mainly for your enjoyment and to procure the health of your body and, more especially, of your soul. For when you intend to go to your amusements in fishing, you will not want very many persons with you, who might hinder you in your pastime. And then you can serve God devoutly by earnestly saying your customary prayers. And in so doing, you will eschew and avoid many vices, such as idleness, which is the principal cause inciting a man to many other vices, as is right well known. Also, you must not be too greedy in catching your said game,[127] as in taking too much at one time, a thing which can easily happen if you do in every point as this present treatise shows you. That could easily be the occasion of destroying your own sport and other men's also. When you have a sufficient mess, you should covet no more at that time. Also you should busy yourself to nourish the game in everything that you can, and to destroy all such things as are devourers of it. And all those that do according to this rule will have the blessing of God and St. Peter. That blessing, may He grant who bought us with his precious blood!

[127] The quarry, i.e., the fish. The writer of the treatise proper does not use game in this sense.

As for the books of credence mentioned, I never found any other clues than these: there was a manuscript treatise mentioned by Robert Blakey in *Historical Sketches of the Angling Literature of All Nations* (1856) as having been found among the remains of the library belonging to the Abbey of St. Bertins, at St. Omer, which was supposed to have been written about the year 1000; and W. J. Turrell, in *Ancient Angling Authors* (1910), said that Aelfric's *Colloquy,* written by Aelfric the Abbott about the end of the tenth century to teach his pupils Latin, with the Latin translation beneath each Anglo-Saxon line, was the oldest English treatise on fishing.

Beyond providing two abbotts to strengthen the likelihood of the supposition that an abbess could have written the treatise contained in *The Book of Saint Albans,* these are of no interest.

Of the handful of known books between Dame Juliana in 1496 and Walton and Cotton in 1676, I would have found only a couple worth extended mention. One is *The Arte of Angling* (1577), and the other is the long poem *The Secrets of Angling,* by John Dennys (1613), whom Walton wrongly identified as Jo Davors (a credible mistake, considering the orthography of the time, as Jno could easily be read as Jo), though he later came to be known as the angler's "glorious John."

The others are *A Booke of Fishing with Hook and Line* by Leonard Mascall (1590), *Hawking, Hunting, Fouling and Fishing* by W(illiam) G(ryndall) (1596), *Certaine Experiments Concerning Fish and Fruite* by John Taverner (1600), *A Discourse of the General Art of Fishing with an Angle* by Gervase Markham (1614), *The Art of Angling* by Thomas Barker (1651), and *Northern Memoirs* by Richard Franck (written in 1658 but first published in 1674).

The first-mentioned of all of these, the 1577 volume, *The Arte of Angling,* has had something of a *succès de scandale* for the light it shed on the question of Walton's "plagiary," the charge first and most loudly raised by Richard Franck away back in honest Izaak's own lifetime. Walton had long been considered completely absolved of any borrowings beyond those sanctioned by the very liberal literary practices of his day. But the charge was raised again with a vengeance as recently as 1954, when Carl Otto von Kienbusch, a longtime stalwart of New York's Anglers Club, unearthed in London the one known copy of the anonymous and previously unknown book *The Arte of Angling.* Major Hills, long gone (he died in 1938), didn't have to contend with the awkwardness of dealing with an anonymous work, but it is interesting to speculate on how he might have voted on the question raised by von Kienbusch and his editor, Gerard Eades Bentley, in their Introduction and Preface, respectively, to the limited facsimile edition which von Kienbusch generously had printed in December 1956 by the Princeton University Library. (My own guess is that John Waller Hills would have voted a straight Walton ticket.)

To me, thinking about the whole affair again after the lapse of almost a decade, the most astonishing thing of all is not what von Kienbusch and Bentley tried to pin on poor old Walton but that in England, land of antiquarians beyond all others, this little sixteenth-century book could have escaped being recorded anywhere at all. If an upset like that can happen, after almost four hundred years, perhaps there is still a chance that some of Juliana's lost "books of credence" may yet come to light.

The Arte of Angling is, in general structure, the exact prototype of the 1653 first edition of *The Compleat Angler,* being a series of episodes in dialogue form, with two characters, Piscator and Viator, the former undertaking the instruction of the latter. After the first edition, Walton changed his Viator to Venator and added a third character, Coridon. Cotton, on the other hand, when he wrote Part Two for the fifth edition of *The Compleat Angler* in 1676, loyally stayed with the original two characters of the first edition, Piscator and Viator. (Maybe the first edition was all he had at Beresford, when he sat down to write Part Two in ten days.)

I'm still inclined to remain steadfastly Waltonian, but I'm open-minded enough about it to be perfectly willing to trot out the parallel passages, of the number and nature of which so much has been made, between *The Arte of Angling* and *The Compleat Angler,* and let you judge for yourself.

In a 1958 second printing of *The Arte of Angling,* Bentley replaced his original Preface to the limited edition with a more extended essay, *The Context of the Arte of Angling,* and cites two striking parallel passages:

In the first edition of his *Compleat Angler* Walton gives directions for keeping gentles:

Take a piece of beasts liver and with a cross stick, hang it in some corner over a pot or barrel half full of dry clay, and as the Gentles grow big, they wil fall into the barrel, and scowre themselves, and be alwayes ready for use whensoever you incline to fish; and these Gentles may be thus made til after

Michaelmas: But if you desire to keep Gentles to fish with all the yeer, then get a dead *Cat* or a *Kite,* and let it be fly-blowne, and when the Gentles begin to be alive and to stir, then bury it and them in moist earth, but as free from frost as you can, and these you may dig up at any time when you intend to use them; these wil last till *March,* and about that time turn to be flies.

Seventy-six years before, the unknown author of *The Arte of Angling* had published his directions for keeping gentles:

Of a peece of a beastes liuer, hanged in some corner ouer a pot, or little barrell, with a crosse sticke and the vessell halfe full of red Clay, and as they waxe big, they will fall into that troubled clay, and so scoure thē, that they will be readie at all times, these you may make vntill Alhallontide, frō time to time, & then a Cat, a Bussard, or a dead swan, ful blowen, and buried in the earthe, you shall there haue all Winter suche ientils, as you shall kill when others goe without, and they will laste vntill Marche, and then flie.

Similarly Walton gives directions for the preparation of malt bait for taking roach:

Get a handful of well made Mault, and put it into a dish of water, and then wash and rub it betwixt your hands til you make it cleane, and as free from husks as you can; then put that water from it, and put a smal quantitie of fresh

water to it, and set it in something that is fit for that purpose, over the fire, where it is not to boil apace, but leisurely, and very softly, until it become somewhat soft, which you may try by feeling it betwixt your finger and thumb; and when it is soft, then put your water from it, then take a sharp knife, and turning the sprout end of the corn upward, with the point of your knife take the back part of the husk off from it, and yet leaving a kind of husk on the corn, or else it is marr'd; and then cut off that sprouted end (I mean a little of it) that the white may appear, and so pull off the husk on the cloven side (as I directed you) and then cutting off a very little of the other end, that so your hook may enter, and if your hook be small and good, you will find this to be a very choice bait either for Winter or Summer, you sometimes casting a little of it into the place where your flote swims.

The instructions for the making of malt bait in order to take roach in the little book of 1577 read:

You must take a hādful of well made malt, &'rub it betweene your hands in a fair dish of water to make thē as clean as you may, the in a small vessel of water, seeth thē simpering wise, vntil they be somewhat softe, whiche you shall discerne by feeling of one of them between your finger and your thumbe, then take them off and dreane the water from them, thē must you haue a fine knife, and sharp, turning vp ye sprout ende of the corne vpward, and with the point of your knife, take of the backe part or houske first, leauing another houske notwithstanding, or else all is marred, then cut off that sprouted end a little, that the white may appeare, and so pull off the houske, on the clouen side, as afore, and then cutte off a little of the nether end, so putting it on your hook, which must be very fine, made of card wyre, and couer the point of your hooke in the cleft of your malt corne, beard & all, then thrust out betwene your finger and thumbs end, the white of ye corn a little, that the fish may see it.

In all fairness, I have to admit that *The Arte of Angling* bears very nearly as much resemblance to the first edition of Walton's work as that simple first edition itself bears to the greatly expanded fifth edition, where Cotton's part appears for the first time.

But I still can't go along with the conclusion, reached by von Kienbusch and Bentley, that *The Arte of Angling* bears the same relation to *The Compleat Angler* that a preliminary sketch might bear to a finished painting, and that it therefore compels the assumption that it served Walton, wholly and simply, as a source book.

Of course Walton and all his predecessors borrowed most liberally from each other, sometimes with credit but more often without. Bentley and von Kienbusch are both fully aware of this, and realize how all the writers before Charles Cotton leaned heavily on Dame Juliana's list of twelve flies. They are even ready to condone the parallel passages cited by Bentley above, as being within the loose literary practice of the time. But the sticking point, for Bentley, is the fact that where all the other writers before Walton followed the general form of the treatise, Walton alone took the dialogue form, and even the names of the two characters, straight out of *The Arte of Angling*.

I must admit that I had not seen Bentley's later essay, but only his original preface, when I touched on this question in *The Well-Tempered Angler*. There I pointed out that Mascall, Gryndall, Dennys, Markham and Barker had all repeated Dame Juliana's list of flies, though Barker had added some of his own, and that Markham had simply cannibalized all preceding works on the subject. Walton did acknowledge indebtedness to Barker, more fully in his first edition, where he said he was following him "without much variation" than in the fifth edition where he said he was following him "with a little variation." But Walton followed Markham in some of his errors, as well as some of his borrowings.

Many of Walton's editors cited dialogues of the sixteenth century as patterns for *The Compleat Angler*'s form, *Herabaschius' Husbandry* (1577) and *A Treatise on the Nature of God* (1599) being the ones most frequently cited. And the fact that Walton acknowledged foreign sources, such as Rondelet and Gessner, who wrote in France and in Germany a century before him, always seemed to me to weigh heavily in his favor, as he would not have had to worry about them, as he might have about a contemporary such as Barker, whose *Art of Angling* preceded his *Compleat Angler* by only two years; they would not have been around to plague him if he quoted them without credit.

So I came to the conclusion that, even if *The Arte of Angling* does, admittedly, whistle the selfsame tune Walton picked up in *The Compleat Angler*, still it is his own orchestration of it, so to speak, his weaving of it into a garland of imperishable beauties, that has given it its immortality. As I said of him at the time, "he gave angling not a how-to book of enduring utility, though even that could be said of Cotton's part, but the greatest literary idyll that any language has ever bestowed on any sport. In this respect it may still be said of him, as Andrew Lang said in the nineties: 'He is not so much unrivalled as absolutely alone. Heaven meant him for the place he filled, as it meant the cowslip and the mayfly.' And, in spite of latter-day revelations, Lang's can still stand as the last word, since it is only reasonable to concede, with him, that '*The*

Compleat Angler, the father of so many books, is the child of a few.' As to Walton's borrowings, it is perhaps not over-charitable to regard them as we do Shakespeare's. In that sense, we could say again, as Lang said, that Walton is 'indebted to none but his maker and his genius.'"

Hmm. Well. Yes, I guess I still feel that way. But I must say I hadn't reflected, until now, that "the child of a few" is a remarkably polite way of saying bastard, because who else is the child of more than one? And it is also discomfiting to remember that G. E. M. Skues wrote, in a letter to Patrick Chalmers, that Izaak Walton was "a miserable old plagiarist who owed what he knew about fishing to a lady, to Dame Juliana, in fact, of the first part, and, of the second, to 'that good young gentleman' Charles Cotton."

Bentley, in his essay in the 1958 edition of *The Arte of Angling,* is much less severe in his indictment of Walton:

"Clearly Walton took the general plan and structure of *The Arte of Angling* for his famous book; he took from it the names of the two principal characters in his first edition; and he also took, almost verbatim, his instructions for the cultivation of gentles and the preparation of malt bait. Like other writers of genius, Walton transformed what he borrowed. The anonymous author of *The Arte of Angling* had little of Walton's discursive charm, and his book has none of the idyllic quality of *The Compleat Angler,* or of its effective allusiveness."

(I wish now that I had read that sooner. Mr. Bentley, as prosecutor of the charge against Walton, actually seems to me to present Walton's side of the case better than I did as his self-appointed defender.)

But the great interest to me in the Bentley essay, aside from the embarrassment of finding that it says pretty much what I said about Walton's virtues, only rather better, is that he goes on to throw out some fascinating clues about the possible identity of the unknown author of *The Arte of Angling.* I've never much cared for mystery stories, except literary mysteries, like "Who was the dark lady of the sonnets?" and "Who killed Christopher Marlowe?" To me the most exciting mystery story I've ever read is Leslie Hotson's little Nonesuch Press volume, in which he tells how, looking for something else entirely, he stumbled onto the account, in some Elizabethan tax rolls, of how Kit Marlowe actually met his death at the hands of one Ingraham Frazer. Nothing had been known of Marlowe's death, before that moment, beyond the legendary line that he had been "stabbed in the eye and died swearing."

Bentley "almost" identifies the author of *The Arte of Angling* as Alexander Nowell, the Dean of St. Paul's, who was widely known as an angler, and whose life, at several points, seemed to fit exactly the inner evidences of the unknown author's identity as indicated by references to his travels, places of residence, etc. But, like a big fish breaking off, just at the moment of extending the net for him, the Dean of St. Paul's "got away," because, it turns out, he fished the wrong rivers.

A pity, because the excitement, as Bentley builds the case for his "candidacy," is almost unnerving. As one piece after another seems to fit together like a jigsaw puzzle, and you're just getting ready to cheer the splendid exploit of "landing" such a prize *persona,* to justify Bentley's contention that "this unknown writer of 1577 was no plodder and no amateur," then the letdown comes with a whopping thud, and, for me at least, a genuine sense of anguish.

The least one can do, under the circumstances, is hasten to agree with Bentley that *The Arte of Angling* is "of higher literary quality than any of the other early angling books except Walton's."

So, here let us insert a more or less random sample:

VIATOR: Well, now to your matter again.

PISCATOR: To return yet, for all that, the same Almighty God hath not so avenged the fall and offence of man that he should be altogether over pressed with careful travail, but hath spiced man's pains with delight, pastime, and recreation, many ways: in the finding, winning, or ending of his labors, whereof the fisher, falconer, and hunter are well able to report. And, as the same Almighty hath not made all kind of living creatures upon earth to be but one, but divided them into beasts, fowls, fishes, and worms [reptiles], and they of diverse sorts in every kind, so hath he given to sundry men, sundry minds; some in this, and some in that to have pleasure. For if all his living creatures should have been of one sort, as all fishes, all beasts, or all fowls, so had loathsomeness and waste hurt appetite and pleasure. But now to speak more particularly and to our purpose. As in fishing, fowling, and hunting there is degrees both of costs, pains, pleasures, and profits, so what cost, pain, pleasure, or profit the hunter or hawker hath, as I am not skillful in either of them, so do I leave such as would know to the sundry tongues that doth write of them both at large. Neither do I purpose so to speak unto you of fishing as severally to tell of all the cost, pain, pleasure, or profit that is in that marvelous and wonderful science.

VIATOR: No, friend Piscator, I come not therefor; only, I pray you, speak of angling.

PISCATOR: So I will, as of that pleasure that I have always most recreated myself withal, and had most delight in, and is most meetest for a solitary man, and is also of light cost. Yet do I not intend to make myself so skillful unto you in the art of angling as to leave out nothing that might be said, no more than you shall find me to contemn that which hath been put in print heretofore. For this I know: that both time, place, kind [nature], and custom is not so known unto me but that I may want in any of the four, yea, and in all, to say that may be said. But what I do know by report, by reading, or by experience, by myself at home or abroad, I will, God willing, not hide it from you; and if you can learn more of any others, or that at this time I shall forget or hereafter find any more knowledge, take that for advantage. And this I tell you plain: that the covetous and greedy man (for avoiding spoil)[35] may not be allowed in this fellowship; neither may the sluggard sleepy sloven be seen in this science; neither the poor man, lest it make him poorer and beg his bread to his fish; the angry man, also, and the fearful man, with the busybody, must tarry at home, and rather hunt or hawk.

VIATOR: Why then, I pray you, what gifts must he have that shall be of your company?

PISCATOR: 1. He must have faith, believing that there is fish where he cometh to angle. 2. He must have hope that they will bite. 3. Love to the owner of the game.[36] 4. Also patience, if they will not bite, or any mishap come by losing of the fish, hook, or otherwise. 5. Humility to stoop, if need be to kneel or lie down on his belly, as you did today. 6. Fortitude, with manly courage, to deal with the biggest that cometh. 7. Knowledge adjoined to wisdom, to devise all manner of ways how to make them bite and to find the fault. 8. Liberality in feeding of them. 9. A content mind, with a sufficient mess, yea, and though you go home without. 10. Also he must use prayer, knowing that it is God that doth bring both fowl to the net and fish to the bait. 11. Fasting he may not be offended withal, but acquaint himself with it, if it be from morning until night, to abide and seek for the bite. 12. Also he must do alms deeds; that is to say, if he meet a sickly poor body or doth know any such in the parish that would be glad of a few to make a little broth withal (as often times is desired of sick persons), then he may not stick to send them some or altogether.[37] And if he have none, yet with all diligence that may [be, he] try with his angle to get some for the diseased person. 13. The last point of all the inward gifts that doth belong to an angler, is memory, that is, that he forget nothing at home when he setteth out, nor anything behind him at his return.

VIATOR: Why, man, if he have an angle and baits, what need any more? And a small memory will serve for those two.

I know we weren't going to spend much time with the pre-Wal-tonians, but before we leave them it occurs to me that, just in case you should want to come back to this period and do a little browsing, it might be nice if we set up some sort of "leave-behind" before we go.

Westwood, for instance, thought the John Dennys poem *The Secrets of Angling* (1613) was the best thing before Walton, and from his own 19th-century point of view say it as the best thing, but for Walton, about

---

[35] *for avoiding spoil:* in order to avoid despoliation, the behavior of a game-hog.
[36] *Love to the owner of the game:* he must be no poacher.
[37] *altogether:* the whole catch.

angling, literarily speaking. Of course in Westwood's day *The Arte of Angling* (1577) was unknown. He didn't have any way of knowing that the qualities of an angler, as detailed by Dennys—and as turned into prose by Gervase Markham in *The Pleasures of Princes* (1614) and *Country Contentments* (1631)—both stemmed from the unknown 1577 volume.

In any case, here is the Dennys version:

THE QUALITIES OF AN ANGLER

Bvt ere I further goe, it shall behoue
To shew what gifts and qualities of minde
Belongs to him that doth this pastime loue;
And what the vertues are of euery kinde
Without the which it were in vaine to proue,
Or to expect the pleasure he should finde,
    No more than he that hauing store of meate
    Hath lost all lust and appetite to eate.

For what auails to Brooke or Lake to goe,
With handsome Rods and Hookes of diuers sort,
Well twisted Lines, and many trinkets moe,
To finde the Fish within their watry fort,
If that the minde be not contented so,
But wants great gifts that should the rest support.
    And make his pleasure to his thoughts agree,
    With these therefore he must endued be.

The first is Faith, not wauering and vnstable,
But such as had that holy *Patriarch* old,
That to the highest was so acceptable
As his increase and of-spring manifolde
Exceeded far the starres innumerable,
So must he still a firme perswasion holde,
    That where as waters, brookes, and lakes are found,
    There store of Fish without all doubt abound.

For nature that hath made no emptie thing,
But all her workes doth well and wisely frame,
Hath fild each Brooke, each Riuer, Lake and Spring
With creatures, apt to liue amidst the same;
Euen as the earth, the ayre, and seas doe bring
Forth Beasts, and Birds of sundry sort and name,
    And giuen them shape, ability, and sence,
    To liue and dwell therein without offence.

The second gift and qualitie is Hope,
The anchor-holde of euery hard desire;

That hauing at the day so large a scope,
He shall in time to wished hap aspire,
And ere the Sunne hath left the heau'nly cope,
Obtaine the sport and game he doth desire,
    And that the Fish though sometime slow to bite,
    Will recompence delay with more delight.

The third is Loue, and liking to the game,
And to his friend and neighbour dwelling by;
For greedy pleasure not to spoile the same,
Nor of his Fish some portion to deny
To any that are sicklie, weake, or lame,
But rather with his Line and Angle try
    In Pond or Brooke, to doe what in him lyes,
    To take such store for them as may suffice.

Then followeth Patience, that the furious flame
Of Choller cooles, and Passion puts to flight,
As doth a skilfull rider breake and tame,
The Courser wilde, and teach him tread aright:
So patience doth the minde dispose and frame,
To take mishaps in worth, and count them light,
    As losse of Fish, Line, Hooke, or Lead, or all,
    Or other chance that often may befall.

The fift good guift is low Humilitie,
As when a lyon coucheth for his pray
So must he stoope or kneele vpon his knee,
To saue his line or put the weedes away,
Or lye along sometime if neede there be,
For any let or chance that happen may,
    And not to scorne to take a little paine,
    To serue his turne his pleasure to obtaine.

The sixt is painefull strength and courage good,
The greatest to incounter in the Brooke,
If that he happen in his angry mood,
To snatch your bayte, and beare away your Hooke.
With wary skill to rule him in the Flood
Vntill more quiet, tame, and milde he looke,
    And all aduentures constantly to beare,
    That may betide without mistrust or feare.

Next vnto this is Liberalitie,
Feeding them oft with full and plenteous hand,
Of all the rest a needfull qualitie,
To draw them neere the place where you will stand,
Like to the ancient hospitalitie,
That sometime dwelt in *Albions* fertile land,

But now is sent away into exile,
Beyond the bounds of *Issabellas* Ile.

The eight is knowledge how to finde the way
To make them bite when they are dull and slow,
And what doth let the same and breedes delay,
And euery like impediment to know,
That keepes them from their foode and wanted pray,
Within the streame, or standing waters low,
    And with experience skilfully to proue,
    All other faults to mend or to remoue.

The ninth is placabilitie of minde,
Contented with a reasonable dish,
Yea though sometimes no sport at all he finde,
Or that the weather proue not to his wish.
The tenth is thankes to that God, of each kinde,
To net and bayt doth send both foule and Fish,
    And still reserue inough in secret store,
    To please the rich, and to relieue the poore.

Th' eleauenth good guift and hardest to indure,
Is fasting long from all superfluous fare,
Vnto the which he must himselfe inure,
By exercise and vse of dyet spare,
And with the liquor of the waters pure,
Acquaint himselfe if he cannot forbeare,
    And neuer on his greedy belly thinke,
    From rising sunne vntill a low he sincke.

The twelth and last of all is memory,
Remembring well before he setteth out,
Each needfull thing that he must occupy,
And not to stand of any want in doubt,
Or leaue something behinde forgetfully:
When he hath walkt the fields and brokes about,
    It were a griefe backe to retvrne againe,
    For things forgot that should his sport maintaine.

Here then you see what kind of quallities,
An *Angler* should indued be with all,
Besides his skill and other properties,
To serue his turne, as to his lot doth fall:
But now what season for this exercise,
The fittest is and which doth serue but small,
    My Muse vouchsafe some little ayd to lend,
    To bring this also to the wished end.

It would be too tedious to repeat the list of the angler's virtues still

another time, just to show how Gervase Markham contented himself
with turning the Dennys list into prose. For that, a much shorter sample
will suffice, and we can let Dennys go on for a few more stanzas, to show
the context from which Markham took the angler's proper garb.

HIS SEUERALL TOOLES, AND
WHAT GARMENT IS FITTEST.

And let your garments Russet be or gray,
Of colour darke, and hardest to descry:
That with the Raine or weather will away,
And least offend the fearefull Fishes eye:
For neither Skarlet nor rich cloth of ray
Nor colours dipt in fresh Assyrian dye,
  Nor tender silkes, of Purple, Paule, or golde,
  Will serue so well to keepe off wet or cold.

In this aray the *Angler* good shall goe
Vnto the Brooke, to finde his wished game;
Like old *Menaleus* wandring to and fro,
Vntil he chance to light vpon the same,
And there his art and cunning shall bestow,
For euery Fish his bayte so well to frame,
  That long ere *Phoebus* set in Westerne fome,
  He shall returne well loaden to his home.

OBIECTION.

Some youthfull Gallant here perhaps will say
This is no pastime for a gentleman.
It were more fit at cardes and dice to play,
To use both fence and dauncing now and than,
Or walke the streetes in nice and strange Aray,
Or with coy phrases court his Mistris fan,
  A poore delight with toyle and painfull watch,
  With losse of time a silly Fish to catch.

What pleasure can it be to walke about,
The fields and meades in heat or pinching cold?
And stand all day to catch a silly *Trout*,
That is not worth a teaster to be sold,
And peraduenture sometimes goe without,
Besides the toles and troubles manifold;
  And to be washt with many a showre of rayne,
  Before he can returne from thence again?

More ease it were, and more delight I trow,
In some sweet house to passe the time away,
Amongst the best, with braue and gallant show,
And with faire dames to daunce, to sport and play,
And on the board, the nimble dice to throw,
That brings in gaine, and helps the shot to pay,
    And with good wine and store of dainty fare,
    To feede at will and take but little care.

THE ANSWERE.

I meane not here mens errours to reproue,
Nor do enuie their seeming happy state;
But rather meruaile why they doe not loue
An honest sport that is without debate;
Since their abused pastimes often moue
Their mindes to anger and to mortall hate:
    And as in bad delights their time they spend,
    So oft it brings them to no better end.

Indeed it is a life of lesser paine,
To sit at play from noone till it be night:
And then from night till it be noone againe,
With damned oathes, pronounced in despight,
For little cause and euery trifle vaine,
To curse, to brawle, to quarrell, and to fight,
    To packe the Cardes, and with some cozning tricke,
    His fellowes Purse of all his coyne to picke.

Here a paragraph will suffice, to show the extent of Markham's fidelity. From *The Pleasures of Princes* (1614), here is how Markham prosified the Dennys poem, first published only the year before, 1613, though presumably written as far back into the sixteenth century as *The Arte of Angling* (1577):

OF THE ANGLERS APPARRELL, AND INWARD QUALLITIES.

Touching the Anglers apparrell (for it is a respect as necessary as any other whatsoever) it would by no meanes be garish, light coloured, or shining, for whatsoever with a glittering hue reflecteth upon the water, immediately it afrighteth the Fish, and maketh them flie from his presence, no hunger being able to tempt them to bite, when their eye is offended; and of all Creatures there is none more sharpe sighted then Fishes are. Let then your apparrell be plaine, and comely, of darke colour, as Russet, Tawny, or such like, close to your body, without any new fashioned slashes, or hanging sleeves, waving loose, like sayles, about you, for they are like Blinks which will ever chase your game farre from you: let it for your owne health, and ease sake, be warme, and well lyned, that neyther the coldnesse of the ayre, nor the moystnesse of the water may offend you; keepe your head, and feet dry, for from the offence of them springeth Agues, and worse infirmities.

Now for the inward qualities of the mind, albe some Writers reduce them into twelve heads, which indeed whosoever injoyeth cannot chuse but be very compleat in much perfection, yet I must draw them into many more branches. The first, and most especiall whereof, is, that a skilfull Angler ought to bee a generall Scholler, and seene in all the liberall Sciences, as a *Gramarian*, to know how eyther to Write or discourse of his Art in true tearmes, eyther without affection or rudenesse. He should have sweetnesse of speech, to perswade, and intice others to delight in an exercise so much laudable. Etc., etc.

Markham's *A Discourse of the General Art of Fishing with an Angle,* which he first embodied in *The Pleasures of Princes* (1614) and later included in *Country Contentments* (1631), is hardly worth going to much trouble to look up, whereas John Dennys is not only more rewarding but much more accessible. *The Secrets of Angling* was reissued, in facsimile from the 1883 Westwood reprint, by Freshet Press in 1970, and is a delightful little volume to own. With it, and the Princeton Library facsimile of *The Arte of Angling* (1577), and either of John McDonald's new printings of *The Treatise of Fishing with an Angle,* whether from *The Origins of Angling* (Doubleday, 1963) or *Quill Gordon* (Knopf, 1972), you're ready for Walton himself.

3.
The
Time of Walton

There's a very real risk that we might lose you here. Good men have been known to get lost in the nearly four hundred editions of *The Compleat Angler*, never to be heard from again. There are even two books about the editions of *The Compleat Angler*, to which I refer you at your own risk. The first is the standard, Peter Oliver's *A New Chronicle of The Compleat Angler*, published by the Paisley Press in New York in 1936, which has been considered indispensable to all serious collectors of Izaak Walton, since dealers' offerings of the various Walton editions are usually identified by their "Oliver numbers" (just as Mozart's compositions are identified by their K numbers), and the newer and more complete one is Bernard S. Horne's *The Compleat Angler 1653–1967*, published by the University of Pittsburgh Press in 1970. Since then, the Horne number has begun to show up along with, though not yet to the extent of supplanting, the Oliver number in dealers' listings.

Typical of the difficulties that seem to be an inherent part of the challenge and charm of book collecting, even the guide books are characteristically hard to find. You probably have to go to a dealer to find an Oliver, and now even a Horne, because the assumption always is

that such books are for the few, and hence are never printed in more
than very limited numbers. Both books are highly infectious—I've
known people to be sent off the deep end by both of them, and I suppose, for the well heeled, it's as happy a way to go as any.

So far, I've been able to survive possession of copies of both Oliver
and Horne, without succumbing to the collector's itch. But I confess I
can't look long in either without at least a tingling little intimation of it. I
have around a dozen different copies of *The Compleat Angler,* between
the office and the house, but I've never even bothered to make a list of
them, and that, along with the fact that I've read them all, shows that
I'm not a collector.

My favorite, and I suppose the only real collector's item among them,
is the 1847 first American edition, of which the anonymous by-line of
"the American editor" concealed the identity of the Rev. George Washington Bethune. John McDonald sent it to me, feeling that he shouldn't
keep it after finishing his work on Bethune for inclusion in his 1972 volume, *Quill Gordon,* not regarding himself as a serious collector and assuming that I was, and I have since sent it on to the Museum of
American Fly Fishing, in Manchester, Vermont, which I consider a
more suitable place of safekeeping for it than any of my cluttered
shelves.

The most sumptuous is the two-volume Sir Harris Nicolas edition of
1836, which I have only in its 1860 printing, but between the number of
the illustrations and the length and extent of the commentaries, the
overall effect is one of feeling that the overture overwhelms the opera.
To only a slightly lesser degree the same is true, of course, of the
Bethune, but you forgive it the more readily because Bethune is so interesting in his own right. One of his footnotes, for instance, grew and
swelled so much that it became, and remains, one of the best single
pieces of writing ever done on angling in America. (In fact, if you
equate Thad Norris to American fishing with Walton to the English,
then Bethune becomes his Berners, and all from a footnote tucked away
in a corner of the first American edition of *The Compleat Angler.*)

But for "the perfume and the charm," I most enjoy reading Walton in
a replica of the little first (1653) edition. I have a couple, here again one
at home and one at the office, and I have a habit of dipping into them
for stimulation the way in an earlier age a man might have paused, for a
moment, from whatever occupation, for an almost absent-minded pinch
of snuff. I can open one of them, almost anywhere the pages pull apart,

and just "inhale" a page or two, and be transported on a trip to never-never land, east of now and west of nowhere.

More or less the same is true of the pocket-size 1759 Moses Browne edition, produced at the suggestion of Dr. Johnson, and the first to be printed after Walton's death in 1683. Moses Browne, like so many of Walton's subsequent editors, was a cleric, and he began the practice, so long followed, of praising the book in spite of its being about fishing rather than because of it. But you forget all that, assuming you open the book far enough in to miss any of the prefatory matter, and engage old Izaak himself. The mood is idyllic, the setting pastoral, and to me the magic is always instant. I can be down in the dumps, or worried sick about something, and reaching for Walton is at least as soothing, and a little more lasting, than the momentary surcease found by the more routine means of reaching for a cigarette. Here, for example, is a purely random dip into its pages.

(Book opens to passage about otters, where it says "kill them right merrily" including the cubs.)

. . . And, I can tell you, there is brave hunting this water-dog in Cornwall; where there have been so many, that our learned Camden says there is a river called Ottersey, which was so named by reason of the abundance of Otters that bred and fed in it.

And thus much for my knowledge of the Otter; which you may now see above water at vent, and the dogs close with him; I now see he will not last long. Follow, therefore, my masters, follow; for Sweetlips was like to have him at this last vent.

VENATOR: Oh me! all the horse are got over the river, what shall we do now? shall we follow them over the water?

HUNTSMAN: No, Sir, no; be not so eager; stay a little, and follow me; for both they and the dogs will be suddenly on this side again, I warrant you, and the Otter too, it may be. Now have at him with Kilbuck, for he vents again.

VENATOR: Marry! so he does; for, look! he vents in that corner. Now, now, Ringwood has him: now, he is gone again, and has bit the poor dog. Now Sweetlips has her; hold her, Sweetlips! now all the dogs have her; some above and some under water: but, now, now she is tired, and past losing. Come, bring her to me, Sweetlips. Look! 'tis a Bitch-otter, and she has lately whelp'd. Let's go to the place where she was put down; and, not far from it, you will find all her young ones, I dare warrant you, and kill them all too.

HUNTSMAN: Come, Gentlemen! come all! let's go to the place where we put down the otter. Look you! hereabout it was that she kennelled; look you! here it was indeed; for here's her young ones, no less than five: come, let us kill them all.

PISCATOR: No: I pray, Sir, save me one, and I'll try if I can make her tame, as I know an ingenuous gentleman in Leicestershire, Mr. Nich. Segrave, has done; who hath not only made her tame, but to catch fish, and do many other things of much pleasure.

HUNTSMAN: Take one with all my heart; but let us kill the rest. And now let's go to an honest ale-house, where we may have a cup of good barley wine, and sing 'Old Rose,' and all of us rejoice together.

VENATOR: Come, my friend Piscator, let me invite you along with us. I'll bear your charges this night, and you shall bear mine to-morrow; for my intention is to accompany you a day or two in fishing.

PISCATOR: Sir, your request is granted; and I shall be right glad both to exchange such a courtesy, and also to enjoy your company.

THE THIRD DAY

VENATOR: Well, now let's go to your sport of Angling.

PISCATOR: Let's be going, with all my heart. God keep you all, Gentlemen; and send you meet, this day, with another Bitch-otter, and kill her merrily, and all her young ones too.

VENATOR: Now, Piscator, where will you begin to fish?

PISCATOR: We are not yet come to a likely place: I must walk a mile further yet before I begin. Etc., etc.

Well, that one backfired. I'm glad my old friend Hermann Deutsch of New Orleans wasn't around to be triggered by it into one of those hour-long diatribes against either Walton or Audubon that were always brought on by so much as an oblique reference to either of their now-sainted names. The fact that there are organizations named after both of them, the Izaak Walton League and the National Audubon Society, brought out the worst in him, and he could go on almost indefinitely about the bloodthirst of both of them.

Nothing is perfect, and Hermann knew it as well as anybody, but his ire against Walton was raised, retroactively, ever after he acquired a pet girl-otter, named Joshua, for which (he would have said for whom) he developed such a fatuous fondness that at great expense he built a separate swimming pool for her, right beside his own, and there came a time when that otter was poisoned, by persons unknown. Not long after that, Hermann died, from one of the three fatal diseases with which he had been walking around for a long time. I have since then begun to hope that there isn't a heaven, as no corner of it would have remained safe for Izaak Walton. After fifty-four years as a reporter known for getting his man, Hermann would have hunted him down and dispatched him merrily, in Joshua's ambiguous name.

Another try is indicated. This time, the book opens to one of Walton's tales of wonders, and note how scrupulously credited this one is:

But before I proceed further, I am to tell you, that there is a great antipathy betwixt the Pike and some frogs: and this may appear to the reader of Dubravius, a bishop in Bohemia, who, in his book "Of Fish and Fishponds," relates what he says he saw with his own eyes, and could not forbear to tell the reader. Which was:

"As he and the Bishop Thurzo were walking by a large pond in Bohemia, they saw a Frog, when the Pike lay very sleepily and quiet by the shore side, leap upon his head; and the Frog having expressed malice or anger by his swollen cheeks and staring eyes, did stretch out his legs and embrace the Pike's head, and presently reached them to his eyes, tearing with them, and his teeth, those tender parts: the Pike, moved with anguish, moves up and down the water, and rubs himself against weeds, and whatever he thought might quit him of his enemy; but all in vain, for the Frog did continue to ride triumphantly, and to bite and torment the Pike till his strength failed; and then the Frog sunk with the Pike to the bottom of the water: then presently the Frog appeared again at the top, and croaked, and seemed to rejoice like a conqueror, after which he presently retired to his secret hole. The Bishop, that had beheld the battle, called his fisherman to fetch his nets, and by all means to get the Pike that they might declare what happened; and the Pike was drawn forth, and both his eyes eaten out; at which when they began to wonder, the fisherman wished them to forbear, and assured them he was certain that Pikes were often so served."

I told this, which is to be read in the sixth chapter of the book of Dubravius, unto a friend, who replied, "It was as improbable as to have the mouse scratch out the cat's eyes." But he did not consider, that there be Fishing-frogs, which Dalmatians call the Water-devil, of which I might tell you as wonderful a story; but I shall tell you that 'tis not to be doubted but that there be some Frogs so fearful of the Water-snake, that when they swim in a place in which they fear to meet with him, they then get a reed across into their mouths; which, if they two meet by accident, secures the Frog from the strength and malice of the snake; and note, that the Frog usually swims the fastest of the two.

And let me tell you, that as there be Water and Land-frogs, so there be Land and Water-snakes. Concerning which take this observation, that the Land-snake breeds and hatches her eggs, which become young snakes, in some old dunghill, or a like hot place; but the Water-snake, which is not venomous, and as I have been assured by a great observer of such secrets, does not hatch, but breeds her young alive, which she does not then foresake, but bides with them, and in case of danger will take them all into her mouth and swim away from any apprehended danger, and then let them out again when she thinks all danger to be past; these be accidents that we Anglers sometimes see, and often talk of.

But whither am I going? I had almost lost myself, by remembering the dis-course of Dubravius. I will therefore stop here; and tell you, according to my promise, how to catch this Pike.

His feeding is usually of fish or frogs; and sometimes a weed of his own, called pickerel-weed, of which I told you some think Pikes are bred; for they have observed, that where none have been put into ponds, yet they have there found many; and that there has been plenty of that . . . etc., etc.

Well, this is Walton the wide-eyed believer, ready to credit anything strange and wonderful that he has ever either heard or heard tell of, and his own best example of what he elsewhere terms the angler's honest credulity. An engaging creature, surely, and he tells the tales well. But let's take another random dip into the river of Walton's words. This time the book opens to a more typical stretch, full of the eating and drinking and singing with which the idyll is replete:

Come, I thank you, and here is a hearty draught to you, and to all the Brothers of the Angle wheresoever they be, and to my young brother's good fortune to-morrow. I will furnish him with a rod, if you will furnish him with the rest of the tackling: we will set him up, and make him a fisher. And I will tell him one thing for his encouragement, that his fortune hath made him happy to be scholar to such a master; a master that knows as much, both of the nature and breeding of fish, as any man; and can also tell him as well how to catch and cook them, from the Minnow to the Salmon, as any that I ever met withal.

PISCATOR: Trust me, Brother Peter, I find my Scholar to be so suitable to my own humour, which is to be free and pleasant and civilly merry, that my resolution is to hide nothing that I know from him. Believe me, Scholar, this is my resolution; and so here's to you a hearty draught, and to all that love us and the honest art of Angling.

VENATOR: Trust me, good Master, you shall not sow your seed in barren ground; for I hope to return you an increase answerable to your hopes: but, however, you shall find me obedient, and thankful, and serviceable to my best ability.

PISCATOR: 'Tis enough, honest Scholar! come, let's to supper. Come, my friend Coridon, this Trout looks lovely; it was twenty-two inches when it was taken; and the belly looked, some part of it, as yellow as a marigold, and part of it as white as a lily; and yet, methinks, it looks better in this good sauce.

CORIDON: Indeed, honest friend, it looks well, and tastes well: I thank you for it, and so doth my friend Peter, or else he is to blame.

PETER: Yes, and so I do: we all thank you: and when we have supped, I will get my friend Coridon to sing you a song for requital.

CORIDON: I will sing a song, if anybody will sing another, else, to be plain with you, I will sing none. I am none of those that sing for meat, but for company: I say,

> " 'Tis merry in hall,
> When men sing all."

PISCATOR: I'll promise you I'll sing a song that was lately made, at my request, by Mr. William Basse; one that hath made the choice songs of the "Hunter in his Career," and of "Tom of Bedlam," and many others of note; and this, that I will sing, is in praise of Angling.

CORIDON: And then mine shall be the praise of a Countryman's life. What will the rest sing of?

PETER: I will promise you, I will sing another song in praise of Angling to-morrow night; for we will not part till then; but fish to-morrow, and sup together: and the next day every man leave fishing, and fall to his business.

VENATOR: 'Tis a match; and I will provide you a song or a catch against then, too, which shall give some addition of mirth to the company; for we will be civil and as merry as beggars.

PISCATOR: 'Tis a match, my masters. Let's e'en say grace, and turn to the fire, drink the other cup to whet our whistles, and so sing away all sad thoughts. Come on, my masters, who begins? I think it is best to draw cuts, and avoid contention.

This is Walton the merry old soul, as ready with a toast or a song as an anecdote. Such a blithe and genial spirit as seems to pervade *The Compleat Angler* all the way through is oddly out of joint with the previously quoted line of Piscator's "God . . . send you . . . another Bitch-otter, and kill her merrily, and all her young ones too." Another old friend is as biased in Walton's favor as Hermann Deutsch was against him. I wish I had thought, at the time, of trying to bring them together, for what would surely have been a memorable encounter. It's too late now, but it wouldn't have been in 1967, when Hermann and I were having breakfast on a fixed morning each month in the Rose Room at the Algonquin. That's when Kenneth Rexroth, whom I've known since his teens and my twenties, wrote: "Baron von Hügel loved to repeat that an abiding sweetness of temper was one of the prerequisites for sanctity in the canonization process by which the Vatican decides a person is a saint. It may sound outrageous to say that Izaak Walton wrote one of the Great Books — and that about catching fish — because he was a saint, but so it is."

It would be just as outrageous to try to deny that *The Compleat Angler* is one of the Great Books, because of a couple of bloodthirsty lines about a Bitch-otter and her pups.

But it is strange, how violently Walton rubs people one way or the other. Rexroth's "saint" is a mighty extreme to set against Skues's "miserable old plagiarist."

My own memory of *The Compleat Angler,* after the countless times I've dipped into it, and probably some score or more times that, in different copies that I've come upon of the various editions, I've found myself once again reading it all the way through, is still so dominated by the one, to me at least, "mighty line" about the silent silver streams that it's worth hunting that passage down again now, to see how it stands up.

Looking for it in one of my little replicas of the 1653 first edition, I find it readily, but am surprised to find that it is not, at least in this edition, a silver stream at all. It comes by way of preface to the quoting of a poem by Sir Henry Wotton, the second of two fishermen whom Walton cited, as being worthy of compare, with the fishermen-saints Peter, James and John. (The first was that same Dr. Nowell, Dean of St. Paul's and maker of the Catechism, whom Bentley tried to "nominate" as the author of *The Arte of Angling* [1577]).

The passage begins:

My next and last example shall be that undervaluer of money, the late Provost of Eton College, Sir Henry Wotton (a man with whom I have often fish'd and convers'd), a man whose forraign imployments in the service of this Nation, and whose experience, learning, wit and cheerfulness, made his company to be esteemed one of the delights of mankind; this man, whose very approbation of Angling were sufficient to convince any modest Censurer of it, this man was also a most dear lover, and a frequent practicer of the Art of Angling, of which he would say, "['Twas an imployment for his idle time, which was not idly spent;] for Angling was after tedious study "[A rest to his mind, a cheerer of his spirits, a divertion of sadness, a calmer of unquiet thoughts, a Moderator of passions, a procurer of contentedness, and that it begot habits of peace and patience in those that profest and practic'd it.]"

Sir, this was the saying of that Learned man; and I do easily believe that peace, and patience, and a calm content did cohabit in the cheerful heart of Sir Henry Wotton, because I know, that when he was beyond seventy years of age he made this description of a part of the present pleasure that possest him, as he sate quietly in a Summers evening on a bank a fishing; it is a description of the Spring, which because it glides as softly and sweetly from his pen, as that River does now by which it was then made, I shall repeat unto you.

He goes on to give the poem, beginning,

This day dame Nature seem'd in love:
The lustie sap began to move;
Fresh juice did stir th'imbracing vines,
And birds had drawn their Valentines.
The jealous Trout, that low did lye,
Rose at a well dissembled flie;
There stood my friend with patient skill
Attending of his trembling quil.

Maybe I've mistaken the passage, but the line ". . . it glides as softly and sweetly from his pen, as that River does now by which it was then made" seems close but still far from the remembered great line of "These silent silver streams which we now see glide so quietly by us."

It's hard to believe that this is a line which later underwent, in the changes of the subsequent editions, such a butterfly-from-caterpillar transubstantiation to that later line.

I even remember, now that I come to think of it, an earlier line, in a poem by Sir John Suckling, published fifteen years before the first (1653) edition of *The Compleat Angler:*

A silent silver stream ran softly by

Now *that's* a lot closer, it seems to me, than the first edition's line is to the "silent silver streams" one that I have always remembered so well as being "the loveliest line in Walton." Now that I can't find it in the first edition, I know it will haunt me until I do track it down.

We can go on, but don't be surprised, no matter how far on we may meanwhile meander, if I suddenly shout "Eureka," and tell you where I've finally found it.

As for the bloodthirsty line about the otters, I do think that unless you happen to be as hipped on otters as an object of affection, as poor Hermann Deutsch obviously was, the line is artistically justified. Certainly the ground was laid for it early on, when Piscator said that he hated otters perfectly, because they loved fish so well. So the dispatching of the otters, in the subsequent sense, becomes a *crime passionel,* for which due allowance has always had to be made.

I know I will go to almost any length to avoid even the accidental death of a trout that I've tried to release, that crosses me up by going belly over and head down some eight or ten feet out of my grasp, after I'd thought I had him safely out of shock and ready to be trusted to straighten up and swim right. Many's the wet ass I've earned, going after such fish, and it's a long time since I have killed one to be kept for eating. But I did, in the old days on the Upper Beaverkill, when Patti or Al McClane would tell me to bring back X many nine-inchers, to be pan-fried for a specific occasion. I killed them quickly, breaking their necks by bending their heads back sharply, and I suppose it could be said that I did it "right merrily," as I went about filling such an order. I must say I looked forward to the moment when, the order filled, I wouldn't have to keep any more, and could resume putting them back. But I filled it first.

And even today, I'll kill a chub or sucker or any other trash fish I pull out of one of our trout ponds, not because I have anything against them—I'd let them live in the open river—but simply because they are unfair competition for the oxygen in our ponds that I feel should be preserved exclusively for the captive trout with which we have them stocked.

And while I wouldn't kill a muskrat, and have a nodding acquaintance with one that haunts our ponds, I sure as hell would kill him if he were a mink. Muskrats are vegetarians, and won't prey on little fish. But a mink's as bad as an otter, in this respect, and I know that given the chance I wouldn't hesitate to dispatch one, if I saw him loose among our fish.

So on this count, as on the one of "plagiary," I wind up more Waltonian than not.

But maybe it's time to leave Walton anyway. If you love him, you'll read him on your own, probably again and again and year after year, and if you don't, I despair of being able to make you like him, by random sampling, any better than you do.

But before we go, I've found a "close but not quite" for my remembered "silent silver streams" line:

Look, under that broad *Beech tree* I sate down when I was last this way a fishing, and the birds in the adjoining Grove seemed to have a friendly contention with an Echo, whose dead voice seemed to live in a hollow cave, near to the brow of that Primrose hil; there I sate viewing the Silver streams glide silently towards their center, the tempestuous Sea, yet sometimes opposed by rugged roots, and pibble stones, which broke their waves, and turned them into some: and sometimes viewing the harmless Lambs, some leaping securely in the cool shade, whilst others sported themselves in the cheerful Sun; and others were craving comfort from the swolne Udders of their bleating Dams. As I thus sate, these and other sights had so fully possest my soul, that I thought as the Poet has happily exprest it:

I was for that time lifted above earth;
And possest joyes not promis'd in my birth.

The line reads the same in the 1653 first edition, and the fifth edition (1676); others I haven't checked. It's the same in the second Moses Browne edition (1759—I don't have the first, of 1750), and in the Bethune American first edition (1847). The odd switch is that the word "center" occurs in the 1653 edition, while the British spelling "centre" crops up in the American edition.

But somewhere, in some one of my copies of *The Compleat Angler,* I know I'll find the line as I first gave it above, because obviously I didn't dream it up. (The thought occurs to me that maybe I simply remembered it that way. But I didn't, and if I find it "my way," I'll stick it in here somewhere.)

But rather than devote any further space to any additional delvings in Walton for more examples of "the perfume and the charm," I'd rather use it for a sample of what I consider the best thing ever written about old Izaak from an angler's viewpoint. That's the "afterpiece" that Al McClane wrote, as a supplementary note to my own entry on Walton, for the first edition of *McClane's Standard Fishing Encyclopedia* in 1965.

ANGLING IN WALTON'S DAY

"And before you begin to angle, cast to have the wind on your back, and the sun, if it shines, to be before you, and to fish down the stream; and carry the point or top of your rod downward, by which means the shadow of yourself, and rod too, will be the least offensive to the fish; for the sight of any shade amazes the fish, and spoils your sport, of which you must take a great care." This quaint, yet entirely modern, advice is one of the many practical observations made by Izaak Walton. Even though he breathed in an atmosphere of troubled times, his cut-crystal words have been ringing through the dimness of time for centuries. Most of the world still thought it was standing on a flat, immovable platform when the serious business of fly fishing began. This first text, *A Treatyse of Fysshynge wyth an Angle,* was credited to a woman in the year 1496. Dame Juliana Berners not only preceded Walton, but her technically detailed work stood the test of time and shaped much of Izaak's early learning. Whether she was the "Lady Prioress of Sopwell" or a mere fiction matters little, as the volume was a well-spring of information.

Heat treating and hollow-built rod construction were well known to Berners, and she set down very precise instructions for both. The hollow-built rod, however, had none of the serious implications of greater power for less weight, but existed solely as a means of disguising the rod, "so that no man will know the errand on which you are going." Angling was in her day a game of questionable amusement, and by hiding the rod sections inside a crop or walking stick one could look like anything but an angler in the received sense of the word. This explains the protracted maundering to herself over the sports of hunting, hawking, and fowling—the hunter must blow his lips to a blister, while the hawker's hawk pays no attention to him, and the fowler must be out in the coldest and most inclement weather. Even Walton had to reaffirm the virtues of being an angler by starting off his book with a few quick jabs at the three manly amusements. The difference between Berners and Walton, however, is that Izaak created a popular habit.

On any Saturday in the year 1653, holiday seekers funneled out of the city's maw to breathe in the hills and plains and the dying sunsets. Izaak Walton was, of course, one of the country-goers and he went from Fleet Street to the rivers around London, usually in partnership with a pastry cook by the name of Thomas Barker. The tackle they carried was far from crude. Their hazel and ash fly rods were long, carefully tapered, and light enough to be fished with one hand. Tom bought his rod at Charles Brandon's tackle shop, and Izaak used one made by John Margrave, whose store was at the sign of the three trout in St. Paul's churchyard. They were earthbound among a mass of quiet folk, and in the warm sun their faces shone with perspiration. It was twenty miles to the River Lea at Wareham. But the "May butter" was on the water—that great hatch of green drakes which fattens a trout to bursting. As the sun rose above the trees, Walton's rod threw a long shadow across the green paths ahead.

New readers to *The Compleat Angler* are usually bewildered by the fact that his book is written in dialogue form. We expect a direct monologue in our angling works, but in Walton's day there was time to wet now-dried Elizabethan prose, and it is a pity really that words are perishable. As the two men walked to their river, the tremendous secret of an honest life was unfolded. Izaak's literary harvest was merely the shreds of these conversations, for he was by nature a profoundly inquisitive man. Even in reading him as the practical fisherman we find none of the dull stuff chronicled by scholars in the years following. To this day, nobody has written a more finely detailed study in the art of using live baits. Walton's eloquence lagged only when the subject of fly fishing became too pressing, and here he turned to his friend, Charles Cotton.

Cotton would be on the River Dove that day, fishing with Captain Henry Jackson. Their fly rods came from Yorkshire and were made of eight sections of seasoned fir and willow. The fir was used in the first three butt pieces, and, lacking ferrules, the end of each section was beveled to fit the other and then wrapped around with silk thread. In winters, when they didn't go grayling fishing, the windings could be removed and the pieces stored in a dry place. But Cotton seldom put his rods away—he was casually lethal in his approach, a practiced hand of great skill. His companion would be sitting in the meadow grass with a bag of feathers and hairs, building copies of insects on hooks that he had armed the night before. Jackson was a keen fly tyer and he worked his miracles with blunt, seamy hands—camel's hair, bright bear hair, and the beard of a black cat were spun ever so carefully.

Their play has been told against a thousand backdrops and will be told against a thousand new ones before the curtain finally falls. A Green Drake settling to the water, a flash of gold, and then a trout dashing toward his shelter of weed before threshing against the pliant rod. Cotton knew how to keep a fish from this dangerous retreat, and even though he may have angled for reasons different from Walton's, his talents helped lubricate the machinery of Izaak's philosophy. The reader is left to bob impotently on a river of words if he looks to *The Compleat Angler* for supernatural aid in the capture of fishes. Yet, the fundamentals of angling are here. In a practical sense, tools used for fly fishing were productive of excellent results. The fly line of 1653 was made of horsehair and it was tapered. A horse's tail isn't long enough to make twelve or fifteen feet of line, so equal lengths of hair were twisted and then knotted together by using a Water Knot. Each one of these line sections was known as a link. Walton used a somewhat heavier line than Cotton because he angled differently. Cotton built a light front taper of two hairs for two links next to the hook, three hairs for the next three links, four hairs for the next three links, and so on up the line. He concluded that such a taper would fall much better and straighter and with greater accuracy. The horsehair line was so light that the angler was forced to sink part of it in order to keep the fly in the water when a strong wind blew. Cotton's taper shows us that fly fishing had become a great deal more sporty since Dame Berners' day. She advised the two-hair taper for perch and twelve hairs for trout. Walton's disciple was not given to idle boasting when he set down his mark of ability: "He that cannot kill a trout of twenty inches with two, deserves not the name of angler." A 20-inch trout is, of course, a good 3 pounds, and it would be no mean feat to subdue a brown trout of this size on two hairs.

The average tensile strength of horsehair is less than that of raw nylon monofilament. It is somewhat stiffer and has a greater elongation than nylon—stretching about 30 percent. Horsehair diameters range from .010 to .006, or 1X to 4X, with a tensile strength of 1.7 to 0.9 pounds. White, or "glass-colored," hair proved consistently stronger than dark-colored hairs. Charles Cotton probably fished with a tippet testing about 2½ pounds. Remember, the angler couldn't let his fish run, so a two-hair trout was no easy mark.

The real problem in line building was finding the right horse. Walton's ideal was a lock of round, clear, glass-colored hair without scabs or galls. The hairs had to be of equal diameter so that they would stretch at the same ratio and have an equal breaking strain. This parallels the problem of our modern line

builder in getting a finish that stretches at the same ratio as the raw line inside. Unless the elongation is identical, the line simply stretches away from its
outside protective cover and it cracks apart. But oil and plastic finishes weren't
used in those days; finishing usually consisted of dyeing the line some color for
purposes of camouflage. Berners in a truly feminine fashion believed there was
a color for every situation and gave instructions for dyeing lines red, green,
yellow, blue, brown, and whatnot. Walton decided that most of this was unnecessary and advised a nearly transparent line with just a slight greenish tinge.
"And for dying your hairs, do it thus: Take a pint of strong ale, half a pound
of soot, and a little quantity of the juice of Walnut-tree leaves, and an equal
quantity of allum; put these together in a pot, pan, or pipkin, and boil them
half an hour; and having so done, let it cool; and being cold, put your hair into
it, and there let it lie; it will turn your hair to a kind of water or glass colour, or
greenish, and the longer you let it lie, the deeper coloured it will be; you might
be taught to make many other colours, but it is to little purpose; for doubtless
the water colour, or glass coloured hair, is the most choice and most useful for
an Angler; but let it not be too green." This agrees with the choice of many experts today.

Walton went through an evolution of rods, starting with simple, painted,
two-piece sticks—many of which he made himself—to eight- and ten-piece rods
built by more clever hands. As his friendship with Cotton sprung to mushroom
intimacy—the young disciple providing a temple for his prophet in the Dove
fishing cottage—Izaak became steeped in fly-fishing lore. In his first edition,
Walton recommends Charles Brandon, Mr. Fletcher, or Dr. Nowel as suppli-
ers; he next made a marginal note on the value of tackle in his second edition,
and finally there appears on the reverse leaf of Cotton's part of the fifth edition
in 1676, a memorandum to the effect that one may be fitted with the best
fishing tackle by John Margrave. Before you suspect Walton of whimsy, realize
that this change kept pace with his new interest.

Actually, the length of a fly rod was determined by the width of the river one
fished. It had to be long enough to make a cast near midstream. The standard
length for trout fishing was fifteen to eighteen feet, and if no wind was
blowing, the angler would employ about half that length of line. When the
wind blew, Walton and Cotton fished the quick fly, which required using a line
as long as the rod, "wherein you are always to have your line flying before you
up or down the river as the wind serves." One evening after a rain, Charles
Cotton stood in a whistling wind and played his Green Drake over the surface,
catching thirty-five very great trout. Five or six large fish broke off, even
though he tried them on three hairs.

This same method of fly fishing occurs to almost every generation of anglers
as a novel departure from orthodox casting, but actually it is the oldest way of
getting a natural or artificial fly to feeding fish. Using a long fly rod, a short but
light line, and a long leader, the modern angler turns his back to the wind and
lets his bivisible flap in the breeze, lowering it to the surface where he thinks
the trout might be. There is absolutely no drag and the fly dances like a live
insect.

Cotton had a self-conscious elegance that led him directly through his narrative minus those touches of unexpected detail that marked Izaak Walton's style.
Walton had never been yoked by the harness of royalty—his soul was un-

marked by artifice as the face of his milkmaid was unmarked by modern paint. Not only did they write differently, but they fished differently. Without a wind, Walton and Cotton whipped their lines back and forth, but basically they had two different styles of angling. Walton was a short-line artist—"Now you must be sure not to cumber yourself with too long a line, as most do"—and he much preferred the rustic art of dibbling. Cotton was for his day a long-line caster—"to fish fine and far off, is the first and principal rule for trout angling"—and, indeed, with a fifteen-foot rod he was working thirty to thirty-five feet away from his quarry.

The sometimes-wealthy Cotton could afford such luxury, because the problem with a reelless rod and long line was in landing the fish. A gentleman angler would hire some rubber-handed fellow to take the line in for him. This is what he meant when he said in his discussion on line length, "Every one that can afford to angle for pleasure has somebody to do it for him." It also explains why the art work of that period frequently depicted an angler taking his fish with the help of an assistant. Landing nets were used a great deal, but even a long-handled one served very poorly when the angler couldn't release the line at the critical moment.

Dibbling with both the natural and the artificial fly was probably the most common method of catching trout, and the technique is as effective today as it was then. The dibbler usually works very close to his fish by crawling or knee-walking along the bank. At a place where he knows the trout are, or ought to be, such as an undercut, the pool below a footbridge, a weed bed, or boulder, he cautiously pokes his rod out over the water and drops his fly to the surface. A minimum of rod and line will show if the angler is crafty. Perhaps he'll watch the float of this fly, but the skilled dibbler plays by sound, keeping himself well out of sight. Of course, the fly will float beautifully, as there is no drag from the line and no more than an inch of leader will touch the river. Walton liked this method and well he should—country boys have taken billions of trout this way in the past 300 years.

You would be blessed to breathe the nights in that little stone house on the Dove, when copper mugs finished their rattling courses around the black marble table, and our two anglers waded into the bottomless pool of fly patterns. Walton described his "jury of flies likely to betray and condemn all the Trouts in the river" in his first edition, and they were almost exactly the same twelve patterns recommended by Dame Juliana Berners 157 years before. Fly fishing had changed very little in that period; less than a dozen other works on angling had been published. A feather or two had changed in some of the dressings, but the Dun, Stone, Moore, Shell, and Wasp flies, for instance, were still identical. In fact, Berners' descriptions of certain patterns give us the origin of the March Brown, Black Gnat, Alder, Stonefly, Whirling Dun, and the fly that was "discovered" in our Ozark Mountains, the Woolly Worm. Being a comparative neophyte in fly fishing, Walton allowed that there were other patterns that would kill as well, and promised to correct or add to his list in future editions. But on the Sow, the Tame, the Derwent, and the ever glorious Lea, these twelve simple flies served him well. Cotton brought such technical embellishments to fruition in the fifth edition, with his "Instructions how to Angle for a Trout or Grayling in a Clear Stream." Here we find the Cowdung, Green Drake, Stonefly, and many others which are either new patterns or versions of old ones. It is noticeable that Cotton escaped from the use of wools in his fly bodies; almost all of these patterns require dubbed under fur. In his Blue Dun, for instance, he suggests that the angler "comb the neck of a black greyhound, and the down that sticks in the teeth will be finest blue you ever saw." His two favorite flies were the Stonefly and the Green Drake, and he observed that "the trout never feeds fat, nor comes into his perfect season, till these flies come in." This, of course, is as true today as it was then.

Although Walton's instructions on fly tying were sketchy by modern standards, he had the professional tyer's approach in stressing the right proportion between material and hook size and strongly urged that his pupil see a fly made by "an artist in kind." Furthermore, he advised that the angler study aquatic insect life and carry a bag of tying materials at the streamside so that he could make imitations of whatever flies might be hatching. Cotton elaborated on this point and also advised that the angler open the trout's stomach to learn what the fish was feeding on. The beginning fly fisher of today can profit immeasurably by this same advice.

Hooks in the fifteenth century were made from needles. The smallest ones were made from embroiderers' needles, while tailors' and shoemakers' needles were used for larger fish. Commercial hook making was established as a business in that period between Berners' and Walton's time, but many fly tyers continued to make their own hooks, as prescribed by Dame Juliana. "You must place the square headed needle in a red hot charcoal fire until it becomes the same color as the fire. Then take it out and let it cool and you will find that it will be tempered for filing. Then raise its barb with your knife and sharpen its point. Then temper it again or else it will break in the bending. When the hook is bent, beat the hind end flat and file it smooth for the purpose of binding the line to it. Place it in the fire until it barely glows. Then quench it in water and it will become hard and strong."

Eyed hooks were unknown in Walton's day, so when making flies the tyer used a line of one, two, or three horsehairs to serve as a snell. This was secured to the hook first, and then the fly was dressed over it; whenever more than one hair was necessary, there was always some question whether they should be twisted or left untwisted. Cotton decided that the untwisted way was better "because it makes less show in the water," but he wisely observed the twisted hairs to be stronger. Hair twisting was a semi-mechanical procedure, in that the angler used a stand having a perforated arm which held the hairs at the upper end, while a turning weight at the lower end made the necessary twists.

Although dry-fly fishing is considered by many students of angling history as a modern innovation, floating flies were used as much as sunken flies in Walton's era. Dry-fly fishing did not exist as a definitive method; the idea was to put the fly over a trout, "angling on top," and then either drift or retrieve it back, floating or wet. Although very few fly patterns other than the popular palmer-tied flies had hackles, most of them had dubbed fur bodies which were picked out, or "bearded," making the small steel needle hooks very buoyant. Walton was much more concerned with presentation, a point that is not nearly so well exploited today: "When you fish with a fly, if it be possible, let no part of your line touch the water, but your fly only; and be still moving your fly upon the water, or casting it into the water, you yourself being always on the move downstream." Walton preferred to fish with three hairs next to his hook for this reason: there was no line left to give to a large trout after he struck, as the fly dangled on the surface directly below his rod point. Not having a reel (contrary to the art work in many later editions), he was "forced to tug for't," and a strong link of hair meant the difference between success and failure. Only a few salmon fishermen of the seventeenth century used reels, and these were crude wood cylinders that were much too heavy for trout fishing.

Walton admitted to throwing his rod in the river when he couldn't play a large fish, tactics which earned him a trout nearly one yard long and whose picture was traced and hung at Rickabie's place, the George, in Ware. Purist Cotton found this innocent directness uncomfortable in print and censored him thus: "I cannot consent to his way of throwing in his rod to an overgrown trout, and afterwards recovering his fish with his tackle. For though I am satisfied he has sometimes done it, because he says so, yet I have found it quite otherwise." Actually, fly fishers of the day fastened their lines to the rod tops with waxed silk and in Isaak's south country rivers there must have been a few large trout that demanded more than fifteen feet of line.

—A.J.MCC.

Since then, McClane has done another note on Walton, which will undoubtedly have shown up in the new edition of his *Encyclopedia,* on the various spellings of the first name. It's *Izaak* in all the early editions, until Bethune made it *Isaac* on the title page of the first American edition in 1847. McClane points out that it was *Isaac* on Walton's birth, marriage and death certificates, and on his grave in Winchester Cathedral, which Susan McClane photographed, as documentation of her father's note on the subject.

Oddly enough, Bethune also broke away from the older spelling of *Compleat,* for his edition. But although the title page of the first edition (1653) had the older form, *Compleat,* all the running page headings of that edition read Complete. Isn't it ironical, to think of the multitudinous *Compleat Thises and Thats* that we might have been spared, but for a typesetter's whimsy in spelling the word that way on Walton's first title page, whence it spawned a thousand derivations?

But now that it is time to pass on from Walton to Cotton, I'm afraid I have to delay our departure just one more time—I'm reminded of the apology of England's second Charles, to the courtiers around his death bed, for "being such an unconscionably long time a-dying"—because, in case you care, I have finally found that "silent silver streams" line. The reason I had such a time finding it is that it is not in all the editions, but as given in the fifth (1676) edition, it is undoubtedly one of the best known and most often quoted passages of all. Here it is, from Chapter Five in Part One:

And now, Scholar, I think it will be time to repair to our angle-rods, which we left in the water, to fish for themselves; and you shall choose which shall be yours; and it is an even lay, one of them catches.

And, let me tell you, this kind of fishing with a dead-rod, and laying night hooks, are like putting money to use; for they both work for the owners, when they do nothing but sleep, or eat, or rejoice; as you know we have done this last hour, and sat as quietly and as free from cares under this sycamore, as Virgil's Tityrus and his Meliboeus did under their broad beech-tree. No life, my honest Scholar, no life so happy and so pleasant, as the life of a well-governed angler; for when the lawyer is swallowed up with business, and the statesman is pre-venting or contriving plots, then we sit on cowslip banks, hear the birds sing, and possess ourselves in as much quietness as these silver streams, which we now see glide so quietly by us. Indeed, my good Scholar, we may say of angling, as Dr. Boteler said of strawberries, "Doubtless God could have made a better berry, but doubtless God never did": And so, if I might be judge, "God never did make a more calm, quiet, innocent recreation, than angling."

Actually, that passage also serves well as a demonstration of how Walton built in extra detail, from one edition to another. Here is how it read in the first (1653) edition, where the passage was in Chapter Four, instead of Five:

PISC: Well, my loving Scholar, and I am pleased to know that you are so well pleased with my direction and discourse; and I hope you will be pleased too, if you find a *Trout* at one of our Angles, which we left in the water to fish for it-self; you shall chuse which shall be yours, and it is an even lay, one catches.

And let me tell you, this kind of fishing, and laying Night-hooks, are like put-ting money to use, for they both work for the Owners, when they do nothing but sleep or eat or rejoice, as you know we have done this last hour, and sate as quietly and as free from cares under this *Sycamore,* as *Virgils Tityrus* and his *Meliboeus* did under their broad *Beech* tree: No life, my honest Scholar, no life so happy and so pleasant as the Anglers, unless it be the Beggars life in Summer; for then only they take no care, but are as happy as we Anglers.

The essence of the passage is there, but still to come are not only the silent silver streams but also the lawyer with his business and the states-man with his plots, along with Dr. Boteler's strawberries and the calm quiet and innocence of angling.

There, I feel better, though at the risk of having tried your patience, but I do think there couldn't be a nicer note on which to leave Father Izaak at last.

4.
Cotton Is Forever

S aint and sinner, Walton and Cotton. Books, like politics, can make strange bedfellows. The Rev. George Washington Bethune, editing the first American edition of *The Compleat Angler* in 1847, took such joy in writing his long Bibliographical Preface, signed only "by the American Editor," with "Some Notices of Fishing, and Books on Fishing, Before Walton," that it is comical to see how he almost winces when he comes to the task of introducing Part Two:

"The friendship which our venerated Walton had for Cotton, besides his being the author of the following amusing and excellent treatise, will naturally lead the reader to desire a better knowledge of him; but, it must be confessed, that the duty laid upon the Editor, is by no means so pleasant as he could wish."

Distasteful though he found it, he discharged the duty manfully, and even with sympathetic grace. Despite his very evident bias, Bethune gives as good an account of Cotton as you're likely to find. Of Cotton's best known poem, *Scarronides or Virgil Travestie*, a Mock Poem of Virgile's aeneid, in English Burlesque, Bethune says "The Scarronides has very little of wit, nothing, indeed, beyond drollery, and that of the lowest kind." Of this production and its kin, the exaggeration of Lu-

45

cian's Dialogues, Bethune endorses Sir John Hawkins's strictures as not too severe: "In all of them we meet such foul imagery, such obscene allusions, such offensive descriptions, such odious comparisons, such coarse sentiment, and such filthy expressions, as could only proceed from a polluted imagination, and tend to excite loathing and disgust." Pointing out that the later editions of *Virgil Travestie* abound more in gross allusions than the first, "which shows the reverse of compunction," Bethune nevertheless quotes Cotton's excuse, given in the Epilogues to Lucian, for such "trumpery," though adding that it "but condemns him the more." Still, he does quote it, and I for one find it as charming as Skues's "little brown wink under water":

In the precious age we live in,
The people are so lewdly given,
Coarse heapen trash is sooner read,
Than poems of a finer thread.

*   *   *   *   *   *   *   *

Yet he is wise enough to know,
His muse however sings too low
(Though warbling in the newest fashion)
To work a work of reformation;
And so writ this (to tell you true)
To please himself as well as you.

Though not in the least beguiled by such cheerful effrontery, Bethune is generous in his judgment of Cotton's part of *The Compleat Angler:* "It is certainly very far inferior to Walton's in simplicity, beauty and moral feeling; but it is as far superior in its display of the art. Cotton felt himself upon his best behavior when he wrote it, and anxious to please his adopted father by conforming to his tastes, in which he very well succeeded. The wit is subdued and so gracefully pleasant, unmixed with any gross alloy, that we wish he had written always in the same strain." And Bethune concedes that there are "truly beautiful sentiments breathed through The Stanzes Irreguliers, which are prefixed to the second part of the Angler, and *Contentation,* which is subjoined to this sketch." Some portions of each should suffice in support of that concession:

From *Contentation*

Excess of ill got, ill kept self,
   Does only death and danger breed;
Whilst one rich worldling starves himself,
   With what would thousand others feed.

By which we see that wealth and power,
   Although they make men rich and great,
The sweets of life do often sour,
   And gull ambition with a cheat.

Nor is he happier than those,
   Who in a moderate estate,
Where he might safely live at ease,
   Has lusts that are immoderate.

Woman, man's greatest woe or bliss,
   Does ofter far, than serve, enslave,
And with the magic of a kiss,
   Destroys whom she was made to save.

We call that sickness which is health,
   That persecution which is grace,
That poverty which is true wealth,
   And that dishonor which is praise.

A very little satisfies
   An honest and a grateful heart;
And who would more than will suffice,
   Does covet more than is his part.

That man is happy in his share,
　　Who is warm clad, and cleanly fed;
Whose necessaries bound his care,
　　And honest labor makes his bed.

Who with his angle and his books
　　Can think the longest day well spent,
And praises God when back he looks,
　　And finds that all was innocent.

This man is happier far than he,
　　Whom public business oft betrays,
Through labyrinths of policy
　　To crooked and forbidden ways.

It is content alone that makes
　　Our pilgrimage a pleasure here;
And who buys sorrow cheapest takes
　　An ill commodity too dear.

But he has fortune's worst withstood,
　　And happiness can never miss;
Can covet nought but where he stood,
　　And thinks him happy where he is.

From *Stanzes Irreguliers*

Oh, my beloved nymph, fair Dove:
Princess of rivers! how I love
　　upon thy flow'ry banks to lie;
And view thy silver stream,
When gilded by a summer's beam!
　　And in it all thy wanton fry,
　　　Playing at liberty;
And, with my angle, upon them
　　The all of treachery
I ever learnt, industriously to try.

Lord! would men let me alone,
What an over-happy one
　　Should I think myself to be,
Might I in this desert place
(Which most men in discourse disgrace),
　　Live but undisturb'd and free!
Here, in this despis'd recess,
　　Would I, maugre winter's cold,
And the summer's worst excess,

Try to live out to sixty full years old;
  And all the while,
  Without an envious eye
  On any thriving under fortune's smile,
Contented live, and then contented die.

As Bethune mentions in a footnote, Cotton did not live out his life to
"sixty full years old," but died, at fifty-seven, in 1687. He is the outstanding exception to the well-known and often-celebrated longevity of
anglers.

In many ways, Cotton seems closer to our time than Walton. He is
much more direct, has no protestations of false modesty—in speaking of
mastery he comes right out and says, "I think myself a master in
this"—and except for the length of rod imposed by his lack of a reel,
everything he says about trout fishing is as validly applicable today as it
was three centuries ago. It's very hard to think of another fishing treatise that would pass such a test.

As for his notorious licentiousness, in our own unbuttoned age what
was regarded as unbridled license in Bethune's Victorian times would
probably seem pretty weak tea today. I haven't been able to lay hands
on a copy of *Scarronides*, but such poems of Cotton's as I have been able
to find seem about as daring as Tennyson's *Maud*. Here are a matched
pair of sonnets:

ALICE

Alice is tall and upright as a pine,
White as blanched almonds or the falling snow,
Sweet as are damask roses when they blow,
And doubtless fruitful as the swelling vine.

Ripe to be cut and ready to be pressed,
Her full-cheeked beauties very well appear;
And a year's fruit she loses every year,
Wanting a man to improve her to the best.

Full fain she would be husbanded; and yet,
Alas, she cannot a fit laborer get
To cultivate her to his own content.

Fain would she (God wot) about her task,
And yet (forsooth) she is too proud to ask,
And (which is worse) too modest to consent.

MARGARET

Margaret of humbler stature by the head
Is (as it oft falls out with yellow hair)
Than her fair sister, yet so much more fair
As her pure white is better mixed with red.

This, hotter than the other ten to one,
Longs to be put unto her mother's trade,
And loud proclaims she lives too long a maid,
Wishing for one to untie her virgin zone.

She finds virginity a kind of ware
That's very, very troublesome to bear,
And being gone she thinks will ne'er be missed:

And yet withal the girl has so much grace,
To call for help I know she wants the face,
Though, asked, I know not how she would resist.

I look between those lines in vain for any glimpse of a lurking monster. There's nothing there that could possibly, to any but the most rabid Women's Liberationist, be deemed to border on the unspeakable. The same applies, I feel, to this one:

TO COELIA

When, Coelia, must my old day set,
   And my young morning rise
In beams of joy so bright as yet
   Ne'er bless'd a lover's eyes?
My state is more advanced than when
   I first attempted thee:
I sued to be a servant then,
   But now to be made free.

I've served my time faithful and true,
   Expecting to be placed
In happy freedom, as my due,
   To all the joys thou hast:
Ill husbandry in love is such
   A scandal to love's power,
We ought not to misspend so much
   As one poor short-lived hour.

Yet I think not, sweet, I'm weary grown,
   That I pretend such haste;

Since none to surfeit e'er was known
  Before he had a taste:
My infant love could humbly wait
  When, young, it scarce knew how
To plead; but grown to man's estate,
  He is impatient now.

Though the attribution to Cotton of the authorship of a volume called *The Compleat Gamester* is dubious, he was indisputably the author of a treatise on gardening, and for a time at least his was the preferred translation of Montaigne's essays. Surely these are solid enough accomplishments to counterbalance the "trumpery" of his burlesque efforts, quite apart from his lasting fame as the author of the first known essay on fly fishing.

John McDonald, who is to angling scholarship of our time the counterpart of what Bethune was to his era, feels that the only reason Cotton's treatise is seldom read any longer by anglers is due to its "archaic overlay." He means the aping of Walton's pastoral dialogue form with frequent digressions for displays of the courtesies of the gentry. (One of these I love, though; it's about breakfast: Cotton preferred a pipe of tobacco and a glass of ale.) For McDonald agrees with Bethune, that Cotton was as much inferior to Walton in the pure pastoral (in which, after all, Walton has never had a peer in all literature) as he was his superior in the art of fly fishing. McDonald has therefore, in his 1972 volume, *Quill Gordon*, done the same service for Charles Cotton that he earlier performed, in *The Origins of Angling* (1963), for the Dame Juliana Berners *Treatise of Fishing with an Angle*—made it completely intelligible, in angling terms, for the modern reader, explaining his purpose as follows:

"To bring him back into the mainstream of active angling literature, I have therefore performed an unprecedented—and for some Waltonians, perhaps, unforgivable—piece of editing. I have extracted from Cotton's Part II of *The Compleat Angler* the essentials of fly-fishing, eliminating all 'extraneous' material. . . . If I am therefore Cotton's most drastic editor, I think I am also in another aspect his most faithful. For in the text I have extracted, I have been more sparing than other Walton-Cotton editors in editing his original text (provided by the Beinecke Rare Book and Manuscript Library of Yale University), making only alterations that seemed imperative, such as corrections of obvious printer's errors and occasional changes in punctuation.

"One of the peculiar charms of fly-fishing is that although it changes, even from day to day, it is accompanied by a literature that at its best is always fresh and informative about nature and the angler—a quality it doubtless derives from the experience that is everlasting in our ties to the natural earth."

And I, as an inveterate Cotton fan, can do no more at this late date for his memory and reputation than to direct you to John McDonald's *Quill Gordon,* published in 1972 by Alfred A. Knopf, with the earnest hope that as a fellow angler you will there read the Cotton essay in its stripped-down form, practically to the point of committing it to memory, beginning with what McDonald terms "the most celebrated instruction in the sport"—those five most valuable words ever uttered about trout—"fish fine, and far off."

5.

Venables and Chetham

After Cotton, the deluge. Where there had been only a handful, or let's say armload, of fishing books—under a dozen—before *The Compleat Angler,* they began to appear by the score, and soon by the hundreds, and now, of course, by the thousands. Qualitatively, however, the eighteenth century was a let down from the seventeenth, both in terms of literary and instructional value. But for the poet John Gay and the two Bowlkers, father and son, it's hard to name an eighteenth century angling figure of any real stature. Almost any decade in the two subsequent centuries has been more rewarding, both in new ideas and in felicities of expression, than that whole century was. You look in vain for characters as colorful as both Walton and Cotton were in their very different ways, or as solidly informative as both Barker and Venables were, or as interesting as even a crazy coot like Richard Franck.

Venables, just before Cotton, and Chetham, just after, are both worth reading, though neither is very memorable, but after them, for a good fifty years, there's hardly anything that wouldn't bore you blind. It's odd, too, because the period was one of great advance in tackle, when rods shortened as reels came into general use, and lines and leaders changed from horsehair to silk and gut. The actual fishing was getting better, but the writing about it was worse. I must have dozed and nodded over a dozen angling guides, wasting time that I would rather, and better, have devoted to rereading Venables.

The trouble is, nobody reads Venables any more, the way they still read Walton and Cotton, and I suppose the explanation is simply that he stuck too close to the business at hand, in writing about fishing, and didn't meander, as they did. *The Experienced Angler* appeared first in 1662, and ran through five editions, so when Walton offered it as part three of his fifth (1676) edition, along with the addition of Cotton for the first time as part two, he was really offering a known commodity, as is indeed indicated by the near-servile flattery with which he greets Venables in welcoming him to the volume. He practically presents

Venables as the past master, and himself as a sort of eternal apprentice. For this one occasion, the title of *The Compleat Angler* was changed to *The Universal Angler,* and it might have been expected, particularly since both Walton and Venables had been published by Richard Marriott before, that the team thus assembled might remain intact. But though Walton and Cotton were thereafter as entwined as their initials on the title page of part two (and over the door of Cotton's fishing cottage on the Dove) so that most of the hundreds of later editions of *The Compleat Angler* carry their names as a joint by-line, Venables left their company as suddenly as he had joined it.

Venables had not written his portion, as Cotton had, to order for this occasion, so his part did not conform to the dialogue style which Walton had adopted from the start, and Cotton had so sedulously aped. The result was that of the book's three parts, Walton's was mostly marvelous, almost magical, talk and fairly routine and commonplace fishing, whereas in Cotton's almost the exact reverse was the case, with the fishing nearly as superior to Walton's as the dialogue was inferior; but Venables, as if with his back turned to the other two, was all fishing and virtually no talk. Once past his introductory remarks, Venables never strays from the point, which is solidly instructional.

After a rather perfunctory performance of the usual grand tour of the other pastimes, which every angling writer after Dame Juliana had seemed to consider compulsory, Venables contents himself with this brief recap of the Dame's philosophy:

The Minds of *Anglers* being usually more calm and composed than many others, especially *Hunters* and *Folkners,* who too frequently lose their delight in their passion, and too often bring home more of melancholy and discontent than satisfaction in their thoughts; But the *Angler,* when he hath the worst success, loseth but a Hook or Line, or perhaps (what he never possessed) a Fish, and suppose he take nothing, yet he enjoyeth a delightfull walk by pleasant Rivers, in sweet Pastures, amongst odoriferous Flowers, which gratifie his Senses and delight his Mind; which Contentments induce many (who affect not *Angling*) to choose those places of pleasure for their Summers Recreation and Health.

He adds the consideration that:

The Cheapness of the Recreation abates not its pleasure, but with rational persons heightens it; and if it be delightful, the charge of Melancholy falls upon that score, and if Example (which is the best proof), may sway any thing, I know no sort of men less subject to Melancholy than *Anglers;* many have cast off other Recreations and embraced it, but I never knew any Angler wholly cast off (though occasions might interrupt) their affections to their beloved Recreation; and if this art may prove a *Noble, brave rest* to my mind, 'tis all the satisfaction I covet.

He has but one favor to ask the reader, and after that he gets right down to the business at hand:

I have one Request for my self; which is, that thou apply not what is spoken concerning clear and swift Rivers, to slow or more dark coloured waters, nor the contrary: and if some passages do appear at first view as if contradictory, read them again, and take them in their most moderate and reconcileable sense, but force them not to clash by thy Interpretation, which of themselves intend it not; proposing only (from different grounds and reasons) to a further discovery, make particular instances and deductions from general Rules; But withal remember that every general rule admits of particular exceptions, and so thou hast my full scope and mind. To write so as to be plainly understood by every dull capacity, were to prostitute this pleasant Art, and render it contemptible; I desire chiefly to speak, so as to give Ingenuity liberty and scope to exercise it self; and also to provoke others to correct Errors, and out of their own experience to supply defects, and thereby make this delightful Art compleat and perfect, which would be very great content and satisfaction to thy well wishing Friend.

He is a friend indeed, this Col. Robert Venables, and I wish his friendship had been longer and more actively cultivated by the generality of anglers. He was suffered to go out of wide circulation, as Cotton never was, after getting the supreme vantage point of inclusion in *The Compleat Angler.* Cotton's part was never dropped, except in the facsimile replicas of the little 1653 first edition, and from Moses Browne in 1750 on down to our own day, the main line of Walton's editors took pains to keep Cotton in and Venables out. When you remember how many of them, especially of the earlier editions, were clergymen first and editors second, it is all the more remarkable that the dissolute and reprobate Cotton should have been retained and Venables dropped.

Unadorned though his narrative is with anecdotal and allusive discursiveness, I love its language, with its echoes of the King James version as a constant and graceful continuum, such as in the flourish of that phrase "which of themselves intend it not."

The fishing is good. His advice is everywhere sound and sensible, as witness:

When you come first to the River in the morning, with your Rod beat upon the bushes or boughs which hang over the water, and by their falling upon the water, you will see what sorts of Flies are there in greatest numbers; if divers sorts and equal in number, try them all, and you will quickly find which they most desire. Sometimes they change their Flie (but its not very usual) twice or thrice in one day; but ordinarily they seek not for another sort of Flie, till they have for some days even glutted themselves with a former kind, which is commonly when those Flies die and go out. Directly contrary to our *London* Gallants, who must have the first of every thing, when hardly to be got, but scorn the same when kindly ripe, healthful, common and cheap: but the Fish despise the first, and covet when plenty, and when that sort grow old and decay, and another cometh in abundantly, then they change; as if Nature taught them, that every thing is best in its own proper season, and not so desirable when not kindly ripe, or when through long continuance it beginneth to lose its native worth and goodness.

Venables is right; trout generally will take more readily near the end of any hatch than at its very beginning. Why they have this "wait and see" attitude I can't imagine, but in general they do seem to like the hatch better when it is "kindly ripe." And beating the bushes before you start is still a good idea. And so is this:

The first fish you catch, take up his belly and you may then see his stomach; it is known by its largeness and place, lying from the Gills to the small Guts; take it out very tenderly (if you bruise it, your labour and design are lost) and with a sharp knife cut it open without bruising, and then you find his food in it, and thereby discover what bait the fish at that instant takes best, flies or ground baits, and so fit them accordingly.

Of course to the Simon-pure catch-and-release fly fishermen of today such advice is unspeakable not only for its countenancing of such a thing as ground bait but for its premise of killing the first fish caught, just to see what else, other than your fly, he may have been taking. For even those who shrink from the idea of killing a trout for any reason, there is a way to follow the age-old advice of examining the stomach-content of the first fish caught. This is by the use of a stomach-pump, called the Aymidge, which can be had for three dollars, plus fifty cents for air carriage, from Dermot Wilson in England. (Address: The Mill, Nether Wallop, Stockbridge, Hampshire.) It's a "pipette" or suction pump, which at the gentle squeeze of a bulb, after insertion in the trout's mouth, harmlessly draws out the contents of the stomach. The latter are far less damaged than by the old marrow spoon, beloved of

Skues and Hewitt forty years ago—in fact, often some of the insects are still alive.

As pointed out by Major Hills and by Horace Hutchinson, half a hundred years back, Venables was the first angling author to entertain the idea of casting the fly upstream instead of down. This, which from Stewart's time on became, for the last half of the nineteenth century, such an absolute fetish, should have earned Venables much greater renown than he has ever enjoyed. True, he only raised the idea for consideration, without actually advocating it, but as a "first" it is distinguished enough, in the light of its later importance, to have given him a much more distinguished position than he has commonly been accorded in the hierarchy of significant figures in the annals of angling.

Here is the relevant passage:

Fish are frighted with any the least sight or motion, therefore by all means keep out of sight, either by sheltring your self behind some bush or tree, or by standing so far off the Rivers side, that you can see nothing but your flie or flote; to effect this, a long Rod at ground, and a long Line with the artificial flie may be of use to you. And here I meet with two different opinions & practices, some always cast their flie & bait up the water, and so they say nothing occurreth to the Fishes sight but the Line: others fish down the River, and so suppose (the Rod and Line being long) the quantity of water takes away, or at least lesseneth the Fishes sight; but the other affirm, that Rod and Line, and perhaps your self, are seen also. In this difference of opinions I shall only say, in small Brooks you may angle upwards, or else in great Rivers you must wade, as I have known some, who thereby got the *Sciatica,* and I would not wish you to purchase pleasure at so dear a rate; besides, casting up the River you cannot keep your Line out of the water, which we noted for a fault before; and they that use this way confess that if in casting your flie, the line fall into the water before it, the flie were better uncast, because it frights the fish; then certainly it must do it this way, whether the flie fall first or not, the line must first come to the fish or fall on him, which undoubtedly will fright him: Therefore my opinion is, that you angle down the River, for the other way you traverse twice so much, and beat not so much ground as dowwards.

Given the vagaries of the English climate and the ignorance of such a thing as waders, the old colonel's raising of the specter of Sciatica is less fogeyish than it may sound, but the very fact that he mentions wading at all is startling—the usual mental picture of seventeenth-century anglers is of lolling at the water's edge, under a tree, and certainly not of what we call wading wet. The other hazard mentioned, that of "lining" the fish, also has a curiously modern sound in this quaint context.

But equally surprising is Venables's advice about positioning yourself in relation to the sun and the moon, which most of us grew up thinking we had first got from Bergman:

Keep the Sun (and Moon, if Night) before you, if your eyes will endure it, (which I much question) at least be sure to have those Planets on your side, for if they be on your back, your Rod will with its shadow offend much, and the Fish see further and clearer, when they look towards those Lights, than the contrary; as you may experiment thus, in a dark Night if a man come betwixt you and any light, you see him clearly; but not at all if the light come betwixt you and him.

This shows an experience and an evident liking of night fishing that is also unusual for that time. About all I remember of Chetham now is his distaste for all-night fishing, which he equated with "idle poaching fellows." Cotton too, as I recall, complained bitterly of the nocturnal activities of poachers. As for Walton, his written nights were always so filled with songs and toasts and the comings and goings of hostesses and serving wenches that it is hard to think of a single night fishing reference.

I feel guilty about moving on with no more than this almost side-swiping reference to James Chetham and his *Angler's Vade Mecum* (1681) but the book doesn't seem to fall readily to hand (it might have been one of those which I had in such dilapidated condition that I finally had them rebound, in which case I'll have to look in another section of the shelves for it, out of the area where it would normally show up). But the fact that I can't remember another word of it, beyond that one poaching reference, makes me doubt that you would feel repaid for any more time out to take hunting it down.

Of course, for that matter, I feel guilty about this whole damn manner that I seem, thus far at least, to have stuck us with, for even the most casual and easygoing of strolls through angling literature.

I know all I suggested at the outset was that we take a little fishing trip in print, and that I never promised that it would be encyclopedic. But at least I led you to believe that we would tour my own shelves, and gee whop if I can't find, or don't make an earnest effort to locate, all the books, then you're certainly entitled to feel that this is a hell of a way to run even the most vicarious of fishing trips.

What this country needs, I suppose, even more than say a good five-dollar Cuban cigar, is a one-volume equivalent of Robb's *Notable Angling Literature* and Hills's *A History of Fly Fishing for Trout* and Blakey's *Historical Sketches of the Angling Literature of All Nations* and Marston's *Walton and Some Earlier Writers on Fish and Fishing* and Radcliffe's *Fishing from the Earliest Times,* and if you had that you could get your money back right now and take off on your own.

But all we've got is Goodspeed and Wetzel, and they both cover only American books, and up to around a hundred years ago all the most interesting stuff came from overseas, meaning in almost every instance England. For this present century I'd be willing to agree that almost the reverse is true, but not much earlier.

Still, the kind of book I'm thinking of, that would really do justice to the best fishing in print, is one that only two Americans could do, at least that I know of, and I somehow doubt that either of them ever will. One is John McDonald, of course, whose three books to date constitute the most solid structure of angling scholarship yet erected on this side of the ocean. But although he has now retired from *Fortune,* where he was for a long time one of the editors, I doubt that he will ever feel like buckling down to such a monumental job of work. That he could do it is unquestionable, but that he ever will is doubtful. The only other one who could do it, that I know of, is Austin Hogan, who right now has more of a leg up on a definitive history of American fly fishing than anybody else. But aside from being plagued by health problems for years, he is now so bogged down with the curatorship of the Museum of American Fly Fishing, up in Manchester, Vermont, that it is hard to see how he will ever have time enough to do anything else.

Based on his latest book, *Nymphs,* Ernest Schwiebert could also do the job. As he has shown there, and indeed as was evident as far back as *Matching the Hatch* (1955), no amount of detail deters him, and his ability to assimilate it and make it palatable to the reader is impressive. The historical section of *Nymphs* is already the nearest equivalent we have to a full-fledged history of fly fishing, and it's by no means confined to America either.

For a long time I'd have pooh-poohed the idea that Ernie would stay home from far-flung fishing trips long enough to get any sort of book done, but his astonishing productivity of the last couple years gives that old assumption the lie. For almost eighteen years after *Matching the Hatch,* which he wrote when he was virtually a schoolboy, it seemed impossible to get another book out of him, and then in little more than a twelvemonth he came up with three! In *Salmon of the World,* which he both wrote and illustrated, *Remembrances of Rivers Past,* and *Nymphs,* he produced a more formidable body of work than any other American angling writer has matched in anything less than a decade. So that Schwiebert could do it is apparent, and that he will do it is to be hoped.

It could be both a reference work, comparable in scope if not in sheer bulk with *McClane's Standard Fishing Encyclopedia,* and at the same time it could be a book that could be read right through with enjoyment, and reading it would constitute the nearest thing to a degree, in mastery of our angling heritage. As for writing it, that would make Schwiebert's position absolutely impregnable as the leading angling author of our time.

Who knows but what if he should do it for Winchester Press, as he did his *Nymphs,* maybe we could even work out a deal whereby they'd let you turn in your copy of *this,* assuming you'd kept this one reasonably clean, as a trade-in on a really definitive work on the subject.

The operative word there is "work," I very much fear, and unless I stop horsing around and come up with some semblance of it, you'd be entirely justified in quitting me cold and deciding that it would be quicker to wait for Schwiebert.

All right, your remonstrance has done me a world of good, and I stand duly warned now, and I feel sure that I won't give you any more trouble. I'd always heard that traveling together was a terrible test of patience, even between old friends, and maybe we've just had our first proof of it.

But I'll really try to find the book now—let's see, it was Chetham, wasn't it?—and I'll let you at the good spots with a minimum of interference from me. Unless—well, no, I'm not reneging, but it just occurred to me—wouldn't it be funny if it turns out I haven't *got* a Chetham, and that's why I can't remember another word of it beyond that one reference to night fishing and poaching? But I must have one, somewhere around here, and I'll find it. I remember John McDonald always mentioning Chetham, as one of his favorites among the significant roadmarks of our angling past, so it stands to reason I must have it, and I seem to remember seeing one once or twice while looking for something else, combing through what Vincent Starrett once termed the "orderly chaos" of my shelves.

While we're waiting for Chetham to show up, I suppose the least I could do by way of amends is to offer you something to gnash on, while I look.

Well, here's something I found in Blakey:

LINES WRITTEN ON A PANE OF GLASS, IN AN INN, IN SOMERSETSHIRE

Here lies Tommy Montague,
Whose love for Angling daily grew;
He died regretted, while late out,
To make a capture of a trout.

EPITAPH

Anglers promised, when I died,
That they would, each spring-tide,
Daily morn and evening come,
And do the honors of my tomb;
Having promised—pay your debts,
Anglers here strew violets.

Hey, all's well, I did find it—and it was rebound, apparently it was a practically disintegrated copy of the 1681 edition, and in the plain covers I had a few of those old books rebound in, I couldn't tell them apart, so I twice picked up Best's *Art of Angling* and both times overlooked Chetham beside it.

Now that we've got it, what'll we do with it? Looks dull as ditch water, if you ask me. Still I said I'd give you the good parts and butt out and shut up, so I will.

Well, here for instance:

20. Let him that would be a compleat Angler, spend some time in Angling in all sorts of Waters, Ponds, Rivers, swift and slow, stony, pebly, gravelly, sandy, muddy, chalky, and slimy; and observe the differences in the Nature of the Soils and Ground on which they run or stand; and likewise the Nature and Humour of each particular Fish, Water and Bait, by which he'll become a perfect and judicious Artist, and be able to take Fish wherever he Angleth, and will find much difference between swift, slow, and standing Waters.

Likewise let the Angler observe when he takes store of Fish, the Age of the Moon, the Temperature of the preceding Night, and the darkness, brightness or windiness of it; season and nature of the Morning and Day, together with the Temperature of the Air, Water and Wind, and all other precedent, concomitant, natural or adventitious Advantages, that could any ways conduce to his Sport, and likewise on the contrary all things he finds to be Obstacles and Obstructors of his pastime, and enter them methodically in a Book, with the day of the Month, etc. Hereby, with a little practice, he'll be able to raise Conclusions for the improvement of this Art.

21. In all sort of Angling, be sure to keep out of Fishes sight, and as far off the Rivers bank as possible, unless you Angle in a muddy water, and then you may approach near the water.

22. Several Countries alter the time, and almost the manner of Fishes breeding, but doubtless of their being in season, as in the River *Wye,* in *Monmouthshire, Salmon* are in season from *September* to *April;* but in the *Thames, Trent,* and most other Rivers, they are in season almost all the six hot Months.

23. Gather or get all sorts of Materials, to make Anglerods on, as the Hazle, Blackthorn and Yew switches, etc. at the Winter Solstice, or, at least, between the last day of *November,* and the 20 day of *December;* because all sort of Wood then is most tough and freest from Sap; it not ascending with that vigour into the Ball and Branches, by season of the coldness of the Weather, and the Suns small stay on our Horizon, which renders its influence feeble.

24. Trouts, Salmons, Pikes, Pearches and Eels have large mouths, and their Teeth therein, but most other Fish have their Teeth in their Throat.

25. When you Angle for Pearch, Chub, Tench, Carp, Dace, Bream, Gudgeon and Ruff, and have hooked one who after makes his escape, you'll not often have any great Sport at that standing for one or two hours space next after such misfortune, because he's so affrighted, that he chases his fellows out of that place; therefore after some trial, you must remove your self, and Angle at some other Standing.

Don't look at me. Address any complaints to John McDonald. He's the one who finds Chetham fascinating. I never did.

But while you were looking at that exhibit, I stole a peek at the preceding page and found this curious entry:

Keep the Sun (and Moon, if Night) before you, if your Eyes will endure it, at least, be sure to have those Planets on your side, for if they be on your Back, both your self and Rod, will, with its shadow offend much, and the Fish see farther and clearer, when they look toward those Lights, than the contrary; as you may experiment thus: In a dark Night, if a man come between you and any Light, you see him clearly, but not at all, if the Light come betwixt you and him.

Hmm. Word for word, except one "between" instead of Col. Venables' two "betwixts"—and Venables wrote nineteen years ahead of Chetham.

So the seventeenth century ended as it began, with Chetham stealing from Venables as Gervase Markham had earlier stolen from John

Dennys and Leonard Mascall has stolen, although along with everybody else, from the Dame.

But here's another slice of Chetham:

Next follow Ointments and Receipts, which I have read and been informed of, by several knowing Anglers, and are practised for the better furtherance of this Sport; and some have such confidence, that they affirm they'll not only allure, but even compel Fish to bite. Part of the following Receipts I have Experienced, and though I found them in some measure advantagious to my Recreation, yet far from so high a degree, as has been pretended to me: Nevertheless I shall present you with them; and if you'll be at the expence and labour of a Tryal, you may elect those for your daily use, which on your own Experience you find to be the best: And the first shall be one highly commended by Monsieur *Charras*, (Operator and Apothecary Royal to the present French King, *Lewis* the Fourteenth) in his *Pharmacopoeia*, printed at London, Part the Second, f.245.

1. Take Man's Fat and Cat's Fat, of each half an Ounce, Mummy finely powdred three Drams, Cummin-feed finely powdred one Dram, distill'd Oyl of Annise and Spike, of each six Drops, Civet two grains, and Camphor four Grains, make an Ointment according to Art; and when you Angle anoint 8 Inches of the Line next the Hook therewith, and keep it in a Pewter box, made something taper: And when you use this Ointment, never Angle with less than 2 or 3 hairs next Hook, because if you Angle with 1 Hair, it will not stick so well to the Line; but if you will mix some of this Oyntment, with a little *Venice* Turpentine, it will then stick very well to your Line; but clog not your Line with too much on at a time.

2. Take Gum-Ivy, and put thereof a good quantity into a Box made of Oak, (such as Apothecaries use of White-wood, and long for Pills) and chafe and rub the inside of the Box with this Gum, and when you Angle put 3 or 4 Worms therein, letting them remain but a short time, (for if long it kills them) and then take them out, and Fish with them, putting more in their stead, out of the Worm-bag and Moss; and thus do all Day.

One thing I must say for Chetham, he's generous to a fault, having crammed his little book to a total of 326 pages, apparently with the omnivorous aim of cramming into it everything that everybody else had written on the subject to his 1681 date.

Before we leave him, I suppose we might as well have a look at his earlier-mentioned thoughts on night fishing:

1. In the Night usually the best Trouts bite, and will rise ordinarily in the still Deeps; but not so well in the Streams. And although the best and largest Trouts bite in the Night, (being afraid to stir, or range about in the Day time;) yet I account this way of Angling both unwholsom, unpleasant and very ungentiel, and to be used by none but Idle pouching Fellows. Therefore I shall say nothing of it, only describe how to lay Night Hooks; which, if you live close by a River side, or have a large Moat, or Pond at your House, will not be

unpleasant, sometimes to practice. But as for Damming, Groping, Spearing, Hanging, Twitcheling, Netting, of Firing by Night, I purposely omit them, and them esteem to be used only by disorderly and rascally Fellows, for whom this little Treatise is not in the least intended.

We probably ought not to leave the seventeenth century without at least some mention of J(ohn) S(mith), who wrote *The True Art of Angling,* published in 1696 and frequently reissued. It was, in fact, one of the ten all-time bestsellers, among fishing books cited by Robb in *Notable Angling Literature,* so I know I must have read it some nine or ten years back, but not a word of it has stayed with me, as at least a little of Chetham had, so I'll take a chance on skipping it if you will, since it doesn't seem to show up even among the rebound volumes. That probably means I didn't bother to get a copy for myself, but just read it in the library.

Besides, this is beginning to seem to me more and more like a real fishing trip, with hundreds of casts between every least semblance of a strike.

Still, there may be some consolation in the thought that our luck can only improve. But I have to admit, right now, that those rare moments of "the perfume and the charm" seem oasis-like in their distances apart.

6.
Gay,
Bowlker and Best

"When we leave them," said Major Hills of the seventeenth century writers, "we leave the reign of the book, and come to that of the manual."

Manuals to me are something best left to mechanics. They aren't meant to be read, only to be referred to, in moments usually of emergency, when you don't want one word more than it takes to tell you clearly what it is you have to know in a hurry. The more a manual tells you that you don't have to know, and aren't trying to find out, the more exasperating it is. And if it's out of date, and applies only to gear or tackle of another mode than yours, then it's useless and can be thrown away as casually as last month's newspaper.

A book, by contrast, can be treasured for the very irrelevancies that would make a manual infuriating. As long as you and I haven't the least interest or intention of smearing our flies with some disgusting gunk, we can read a passage like one of those we just found in Chetham and deem it quaint and curious. "Man's Fat and Cat's Fat," for outlandish instance. And there is a little tingle of interest added by the note that the mess comes highly commended by the Apothecary of Louis XIV "the present French King." And I know I'm driven to at least the shadow of a smile by a sentence like "clog not your Line with too much on at a time."

But that passage would cease to seem very amusing if it were all we could find when, with a degree of urgency, we went looking for a treatment for, say, snakebite.

For my reading purposes, manuals are a blank, and my shelves are void of them. They flourished, beginning with Howlett's *The Anglers Sure Guide* (1706), and I remember trying to plow through a number of them, when I was making a conscientious effort to cover the period in preparing the entry on angling literature for *McClane's Standard Fishing Encyclopedia,* but I never found one that I wanted to give shelf room, before Bowlker in 1747 and Best in 1787.

Since the eighteenth century was the first to lay any great stress on the attractions of scenery, and really the first to establish any really general vogue for travel for its own sake, or for no more serious purpose than a change of scenery and atmosphere, this dearth of any emphasis on the more picturesque aspects of angling is surprising. Maybe, since the eighteenth century was also that of the enlightenment, and the age of reason, anything so obviously unreasonable and unregimented as angling seemed momentarily out of joint with the prevailing spirit of the times. I know a lot of people who would be quick to agree to the premise that a rise of reason equates to a decline in angling.

But the premise is flawed. The lacuna in noteworthy and memorable angling literature in that period was not accompanied by a corresponding gap in either the popularity or the progress of the sport itself. Quite the contrary is the case. Angling flourished and increased as never before. It's just that the better they did it, apparently, the less they felt like talking about it.

Or maybe we're thrown back on the cynical Shavian concept that "those who can't, teach." In this century, with improved tackle, their results were so much better that they had less fishing time left over for that "contemplative" aspect of angling that is the chief ingredient of Walton's glory. The average angler's "basket" was certainly heavier in this period than in the earlier time.

It's a little like what they say of the eminently successful Swiss, "happy nations have no history." Maybe it takes frustration, and difficulty in attaining the object of the game, to engender good angling literature. Perhaps that's the irritation of the oyster that produces the pearl. In other words, the worse the fishing, the better the stories about it.

Well, it's a bizarre theory, but maybe we might do worse than bear it in mind, as we go along, prospecting in print, for "the perfume and the charm."

Meanwhile, I know no better voice to invoke, to dispel the "deadly 'ush" of this momentary lull, than John Gay's. The author of *The Beggar's Opera*, considering the worldwide popularity of *The Three Penny Opera* Kurt Weill quarried from it, should be much more famous in our time than he is. But for everybody who smiles knowingly at the sound of even the first notes of *Mack the Knife*, it's only the occasional bookish angler who ever heard of John Gay.

Two things have always prejudiced me in his favor. One was the purely fortuitous happenstance that of the two best graduation presents that I ever got, the one for high school graduation in 1921, was the lovely Claud Lovat Fraser edition of *The Beggar's Opera*. (The other was Kreisler's Red Seal recording of *Rondino*, for grammar school in 1917.)

Even more important, in giving his name a sunny association in my memory since boyhood, is somewhere having stumbled across the wording of his epitaph:

Life is a jest,
  And all things show it;
I thought so once,
  And now I know it.

Can your feelings be anything but kindly toward anybody who can leave this vale of tears with an exit line so deft as that?

Anyway, look to John Gay's *Rural Sports* (1720) for just about the only elegance to lend any tone to the angling of his time. The best known passage, of course, is the familiar:

Around the steel no tortur'd worm shall twine,
No blood of living insect stain my line;
Let me, less cruel, cast feather'd hook,
With pliant rod athwart the pebbled brook,
Silent along the mazy margin stray,
And with fur-wrought fly delude the prey.

But I like even better the corollary passage, about the clothing of the feather'd hook:

To furnish the small animal, provide
All the Gay hues that wait on female pride;

Let nature guide thee — sometimes golden wire
The shining bellies of the fly require;
The peacock's plumes thy tackle must not fail,
Nor the dear purchase of the sable's tail.
Each gaudy bird some slender tribute brings
And lends the glowing insect proper wings.
Silks of all colors must their aid impart,
And every fur promotes the fisher's art.

To my mind, a little of that goes a long way toward giving a good name to a sport. I can see how it might influence a body to become an angler, or even a fly-tier, who was none.

I hate to leave John Gay so soon, and for two cents I'd hang around for an hour, just letting him go on, as so much music to my ears, but a hundred other acts must be waiting their turn, so we'll press on.

By mid-century we come to Bowlker, an evolving classic, begun by the father Richard, with the 1747 edition of *The Art of Angling or the Complete Fly Fisher,* and this one qualifies, not merely as manual but as book. I say "evolving" because the son Charles went on with the subsequent improved and enlarged editions, until almost the century's end, and the book was enormously influential. You could, for translation into current or at least recent terms, say that the Bowlker was the Bergman of its day. Hills, in fact, deemed it as, among purely fishing books, the most successful ever published. The "purely" was how he got around Walton, since the Walton part of *The Compleat Angler* is as much philosophy as fishing.

Bowlker is juicier than the typical manual of the time, but generalizations about it are hazardous, as it had so many editions, after the first by Richard and the second, by his son Charles, that it came to be almost institutional rather than personal, and some of the later editions take a very patronizing attitude toward the earlier ones. For instance:

Whatever merit we may attribute to the Author, his condition in life and circumscribed course of reading, prevented the possibility of his acquiring correct information on literary subjects; and it has been found expedient to *omit the puerilities of an antiquated and obsolete philosophy,* to make room for extracts from modern writers, *more useful and interesting.*

The italics are mine, of course, but the by-line is still Charles Bowlker's, and the attitude seems far from filial. There is, however, this tempering afterthought:

Every science has its rules and axioms, and the following hortatory remarks will be deemed *of sufficient importance to be retained:*

Patience is ever allowed to be a great virtue, and is one of the first requisites for an angler.

In your excursion to or from fishing, should you overheat yourself with walking, avoid small liquors and water as you would poison; a glass of wine, brandy, or rum, is more likely to promote cooling effects, without danger of taking cold.

Whenever you begin to angle, wet the ends of the joints of your rod, to make them swell, which will prevent their loosening: and if you happen, with rain or otherwise, to wet your rod, so that you cannot pull the joints asunder, turn the ferrules round in the flame of a candle, and they will easily separate.

An angler should always be careful to keep out of sight of the fish, by standing as far from the bank as possible; but muddy water renders this caution unnecessary.

A judicious angler should observe that his amusement must be avoided in a strong east or cold north wind, as both are unfriendly to sport. Also, after a long drought; in the middle of days that are excessively hot and bright; when there has been a white frost in the morning; in days of high wind; in places where they have been long washing sheep; upon the sudden rising of clouds that precede rain; and on days following dark, windy nights.

In ponds, angle near the fords where cattle go to drink; and in rivers, angle for Bream in the deepest and most quiet parts; for Eels, under trees hanging over banks; for Chub, in deep shaded holes; for Perch, in scours; for Roach, in winter, in the deeps, at all other times where you angle for Perch; and for Trout in quick streams.

When you have hooked a fish, never suffer it to run out with the line; but keep the rod bent, and as nearly perpendicular as you can; by this method the top plies to every pull the fish makes, and you prevent the straining of the line.

Never raise a large fish out of the water by taking hold of the line, but either put a landing net under it, or your hat. You may, in fly-fishing, lay hold of the line to draw the fish to you, but this must be done with caution.

The silk for tying on hooks and other fine work must be very small; use it double, and wax it with shoemaker's wax; should the wax be too stiff, temper it with tallow.

If for strong fishing you use grass, which, when you can get it fine is to be preferred to gut, remember always to soak it an hour in water before using; this will make it tough, and prevent it from sinking.

Before fixing the loop of gut to the hook, in order to make a fly, singe the end of it to prevent its drawing; do the same with hair, to which at any time you whip a hook.

Make flies in warm weather only, for in cold the waxed silk will not draw.

In rainy weather, or when the season for angling is over, repair whatever damage your tackle has sustained.

Never regard what bunglers and slovens tell you, but believe that neatness in your tackle, and a masterly hand in all your work are absolutely necessary.

As dry feet are conducive to health, we have copied an excellent receipt for the angler's use, which will render boots or shoes completely water-proof: "drying oil, one pint; bee's wax, two ounces; turpentine, two ounces; burgundy pitch, one ounce. — Melt these over a slow fire, and then add a few drachms of essential oil of lavender or thyme; with this your boots or shoes are to be rubbed with a brush, either in the sun, or at some distance from the fire. The application must be repeated as often as the boots become dry again, until they are fully saturated."

Lastly, those who value health will not begin the delightful recreation of angling till March; although, in some years, if the weather be open and mild, February may afford more diversion.

Bowlker on salmon has a more modern sound than some writers more than a century later:

All fishermen agree that they never find any food in the stomach of this fish. Perhaps during the spawning time they may entirely neglect their food; and that they return to the sea lank lean, and come from it in good condition.

In most places, the artificial fly is the only bait used, being far superior to any other.

There is scarcely any time unless when it thunders, or when the water is thick with mud, but you may chance to tempt the Salmon to rise to an artificial fly. But the most propitious and critical moments are undoubtedly when, clearing after a flood, the water has turned to a light whey, or rather brown colour; when the wind flows pretty fresh, approaching almost to a mackarel gale, (if not from the north,) against the stream or course of the river; when the sun shines through showers, or when the cloudy rock runs fast and thick, and at intervals the fine blue ether from above. In these situations of the water, and of the weather, you may always depend upon excellent sport.

Nobody has ever said it better, either before Sir Humphrey Davy or even after William Scrope himself.

He's also sound and perceptive on trout:

In general the Trout prefers clear, cold, and briskly-running waters, with a stony or gravelly bottom; it swims with rapidity, and, like the Salmon, springs occasionally to a very considerable height in order to surmount any obstacle in its course. It generally spawns in October, and at that time gets among the roots of trees, and under large stones, in order to deposit its eggs, which are far less numerous than those of other fish; yet the Trout admits of very considerable increase, owing, no doubt, to the circumstance of most of the voracious kind of fishes avoiding waters of so cold a nature as those which Trout delight to inhabit; and their increase would be still greater, were they not themselves of a voracious disposition, frequently preying upon each other.

It is when he comes to the pike that his sense of wonder takes on almost Waltonian proportion:

The voracity of the Pike is commemorated by all ichthyological writers; it has been poetically styled the wolf of fishes, and tyrant of the watery plain; and, in fact, in proportion to its strength and celerity, it is the most active and ravenous of fresh water fish. It will attack every fish less than itself, and has been known to choke itself in attempting to swallow one of its own species which proved too large a morsel. It is immaterial of what species the animal it pursues appears to be, all are indiscriminately devoured; so that every fish owes its safety to its minuteness, its celerity, or its courage; nor does the Pike confine itself to feed on fish and frogs, it will draw down water rats and young ducks as they are swimming about, and even attack the legs of persons who are bathing. "I have been assured (says Walton) by my friend Mr. Seagrave, who keeps tame otters, that he has known a Pike, in extreme hunger, fight with one of his otters for a Carp that the otter had caught, and was then bringing out of the water." A Mr. Plott, of Oxford, has recorded the following highly singular anecdote. "At Lord Gower's canal at Trentham, a Pike seized the head of a swan as she was feeding under water, and gorged so much of it as killed them both; the servants, perceiving the swan with its head under water for a longer time than usual, took boat, and found both swan and Pike dead."

On flies, Bowlker is excellent, and here his "house-cleaning" tendency can only be applauded. From the cumulative confusion of the constant cannibalizing of each other's lists by the older writers, from Mascall and Markham on down, Bowlker took a new departure and with imitation as the aim, threw out "the antiquated and the obsolete" and those instances where the same flies had been confused under different names. Between Cotton and Ronalds, and the dawn of an entomological approach, Bowlker is the one main landmark. With a colored frontispiece, that remained the one constant of all the varied editions that carried the name of Charles, *Bowlker's Art of Angling* became the most dependable beacon the eighteenth century afforded the fly-tier.

One other constant, and a graceful one, is the volume's ending, carried as late as even the edition of 1839:

SIGNS OF RAIN

Forty reasons for not accepting the invitation of a friend to make an excursion with him.

by the Late DR. JENNER.

1. The hollow winds begin to blow,
2. The clouds look black, the glass is low;
3. The soot falls down, the spaniels sleep,
4. And spiders from their cobwebs peep.
5. Last night the sun went pale to bed,
6. The moon in haloes hid her head;
7. The boding Shepherd heaves a sigh,
8. For see a rainbow spans the sky:
9. The walls are damp, the ditches smell.
10. Closed is the pink-eyed pimpernel.
11. Hark how the chairs and tables crack,
12. Old Betty's joints are on the rack;
13. Loud quack the ducks, the peacocks cry;
14. The distant hills are seeming nigh.
15. How restless are the snorting swine,
16. The busy flies disturb the kine;
17. Low o'er the grass the swallow wings;
18. The cricket, too, how sharp he sings;
19. Puss on the hearth, with velvet paws,
20. Sits wiping o'er her wisker'd jaws.
21. Thro' the clear stream the fishes rise,
22. And nimbly catch th' incautious flies.
23. The glow-worms, numerous and bright,
24. Illumed the dewy dell last night.
25. At dusk the squalid toad was seen,

26. Hopping and crawling o'er the green;
27. The whirling wind the dust obeys,
28. And in the rapid eddy plays;
29. The frog has changed his yellow vest,
30. And in a russet coat is drest.
31. Though June, the air is cold and still,
32. The mellow black-bird's voice is shrill.
33. My dog, so alter'd in his taste,
34. Quits mutton-bones on grass to feast;
35. And see you rooks, how odd their flight,
36. They imitate the gliding kite,
37. And seem precipitate to fall,
38. As if they felt the piercing ball.
39. 'Twill surely rain, I see, with sorrow,
40. Our jaunt must be put off to-morrow.

We have now completed our undertaking; and having led our readers through a regular course of instruction, founded on experience, teaching the true art of making artificial and selecting natural baits, with a plain and comprehensive account of the best mode of so arranging all the necessary appendages of the art, as to secure to the adventurous fisherman the pleasures of his favourite amusement, in all seasons, regularly as they succeed each other; we take leave of our readers and pupils by quoting an extract from "Songs of the Chase."

> "The Angler envies no man's joys
> But his who gains the greatest sport;
> With peace he dwells far from the noise
> And bustling grandeur of a court."

The other outstanding eighteenth-century angling author, based on number of editions and influence, is Thomas Best, whose *Art of Angling* ran through four editions before the century's end. He is heavily derivative, particularly from Bowlker, both with and without credit, and since Bowlker remained in print, it is hard from this later viewpoint to understand how the many duplications could have avoided embarrassment. But Best is a better stylist than Bowlker, and like Walton, though of course to a lesser degree, he embellished what he took. He has a great fondness for poetry, both his own and other peoples', and uses it for emphasis, whenever he has made a point in prose that he wants to give especial stress. Often these are short Latin quotes, or longer ones from Gay, Pope, Dryden and Thomson, and sometimes they're his own.

Reading Best before, or instead, of reading Bowlker he seems most engaging, and consistently entertaining if not profound. But reading him after Bowlker it is disconcerting to find how often he merely *is* Bowlker, although, as Father Izaak said of his own use of Barker, "with a little variation." Often the addition of poetry is the only difference. Since he is most punctilious about crediting Mr. Gay, Mr. Thomson, Mr. Pope and Mr. Dryden, and even Mr. Drayton (though Drayton had been dead a hundred years) and making frequent mention of Mr. Walton and occasionally Mr. Bowlker, it becomes a parlor sport to read him just to see how many places he *doesn't* mention Mr. Bowlker. Here are two, in one paragraph:

As dry feet are very necessary to health, I have copied an excellent receipt for the angler's use. . . .

(He doesn't say where he copied it, but all Bowlker said was, "As dry feet are conducive to health, we have copied an excellent receipt for the angler's use, which will render boots or shoes completely water-proof.")

. . . that will prevent his boots or shoes letting in water. Take a pint of linseed oil, with half a pound of mutton suet, six or eight ounces of bees-wax, and a half-penny worth of rosin; boil all these in a pipkin together, and then let it cool till it be lukewarm; take a little hair brush, and lay it on your boots; but it is much better to be laid on the leather before the boots are made, and brushed with it once over when they are; as for your old boots and shoes, you must brush them with it when they are dry. As I am now acting the part of physician, let me advise you, whenever you are out in the heat of summer a fishing, and are thirsty, never to drink water, as the consequences arising from such an indiscretion may prove fatal; but either take a little brandy or rum out with you, in a wicker bottle, or wait till you come to some house where you can have a little; the effect it has of quenching the thirst, and cooling the body, are instantaneous.

But it's late in the day to start boggling about parallel passages, when for the previous two hundred years theft rampant had been standard practice among angling authors, and Best is more fun to read than many. Here's a place where he does quote Bowlker directly:

GREY-DRAKE

Found in general where the Green-drake is, and in shape and dimensions perfectly the same, but almost quite another colour, being of a paler and more livid yellow; and green and ribbed with black, quite down his body, with black shining wings, diaphanous and very tender. It comes in, and is taken after the

Green-drake, and when made artificially, as directed in part the 2d, for the month of May, kills fish very well; the following curious account of it, from *Bowlker,* cannot fail to amuse the reader.

"I happened to walk by the river side at that season of the year when the *May-flies* (he means the grey sort) which are a species of the *Libella,* come up out of the water, where they lie in their husks, for a considerable time, at the bottom or sides of the river, near the likeness of the *Nymph* of the small common *Libella,* but when it is mature, it splits open its case, and then, with great agility, up springs the new little animal, with a slender body, four blackish veined transparent wings, with four black spots on the upper wings, and the under wings much smaller than the upper ones, with three long hairs in its tail. The husks, which are left behind, float innumerable on the water. It seemed to me a species of *Ephemeron;* and I imagined it was the same insect described by *Goedart* and *Swammerdam,* but a few days convinced me the contrary; for I soon found them to be of a longer duration than theirs. The first business of this creature, after he is disengaged from the water, is flying about to find out a proper place to fix on, as trees, bushes, etc. to wait for another surprising change, which is effected in a few days. The first hint I received of this wonderful operation, was seeing the *Exuviae* hanging on a hedge: I then collected a great many, and put them into boxes, and by strictly observing them, I could tell when they were ready to put off their husks, though but so lately put on. I had the pleasure to shew my friends one that I held on my hand all the while it performed this great work. It was surprising to see how easily the back part of the fly split open, and produced the new birth, which I could not perceive partakes of any thing from its parent, but leaves head, body, wings, legs, and even its three-haired tail behind on the case. After it has reposed itself awhile, it flies with great briskness to seek its mate. In the new fly a remarkable difference is seen in their sexes, which I could not so easily perceive in their first state, the male and female being then much of a size; but now the male was much the smallest, and the hairs in his tail much the longest. I was very careful to see if I could find them engendering; but all that I could discover, was, that the males separated, and kept under cover of the trees, remote from the river; hither the females resorted, and mixed with them in their flight, great numbers together, with a very brisk motion of darting or striking at one another, when they met, with great vigour, just as house flies will do in a sunny room: this they continued to do for many hours, and this seemed to be their way of coition, which must be quick, and soon performed, as they are of so short a duration. When the females were impregnated, they left the company of the males, and sought the river, and kept constantly playing up and down on the water. It was very plainly seen that every time they darted down, they ejected a cluster of eggs, which seemed a pale blueish speck, like a small drop of milk, as they descended on the water; then, by the help of their tail, they spring up again, and descend again; and thus continue till they have exhausted their stock of eggs, and spent their strength, being so weak that they can rise no more, but fall a prey to the fish; but by much the greater numbers perish on the waters, which are covered with them: this is the end of the females; but the males never resort to the rivers, as I could perceive; but after they have done their office, drop down, languish, and die under the trees and bushes. I observed that the females were most numerous, which was very necessary, con-

sidering the many enemies they have during the short time of their appearance, for both birds and fish are very fond of them, and no doubt under
the water they are food for small aquatic insects. What is further remarkable in
this surprising creature, is, that in a life of a few days, it eats nothing, seems to
have no apparatus for that purpose, but brings up with it, out of the water,
sufficient support, to enable it to shed its skin, and to perform the principal end
of life with great vivacity. The particular time when I observed them very
numerous and sportive, was on the 26th of May, at six o'clock in the evening. It
was a sight very surprising and entertaining to see the rivers teeming with innumerable, pretty, nimble, flying insects, and almost every thing near covered
with them. When I looked up into the air, it was full of them, as high as I could
discern; and being so thick, and always in motion, they made almost such an
appearance as when one looks up and sees the snow coming down; and yet this
wonderful appearance, in three or four days after the last of *May,* totally disappeared."

In Part the Second, *The Complete Fly-Fisher; or, Every Man His Own Fly-
Maker,* Best gives forty-seven fly patterns, along with their emergence
dates and varying characteristics, together with the dubbings for them.
(Bowlker's famous colored frontispiece plate gives thirty.) In addition to
the "flies proper for each month," that emerge on given dates over the
fly-fishing season, from March to the end of September, he gives four
palmers as standard hackles to be tried first, before the angler knows

which specific fly to try, and may be generally relied upon throughout the season. While not calling them nymphs, he clearly intimates that they represent a developing or interior form of insect.

There have been various disputes, whether the *palmers* should be made with wings or not, all exceedingly idle and futile, therefore I dare venture to say they should not, nor will I ever recant from what I aver, until some one can assure me for a truth, that they have seen a caterpillar, or worm, with wings; a species of which they certainly are. No one as yet has ever given an account how to make the *palmer-worms,* but what has been so erroneous, dark, and unintelligible, that it would be impossible for a *tyro* in the *art* of *angling* to make either head or tail of it.

. . . These *palmers* (as I said before) being taken every month in the year, when I come to treat of the flies proper for each month, I shall not take any notice again of the four which I have set down, for that would be totally unnecessary; but the others that deviate in their size and dubbing from the general rule, will be fully expressed.

The angler should always try the *Palmers* first, when he fishes in a river that he is unaccustomed to; and even in that which he constantly uses, without he knows what fly is on the water, and they should never be changed till he does: the only way to come to the true knowledge of which, he must observe an old established rule laid down for that purpose; and as it is poetically described by Mr. *Gay,* I shall give it him in that dress.

> Mark well the various seasons of the year,
> How the succeeding insect race appear;
> In this revolving moon one colour reigns,
> Which in the next the fickle trout disdains.
> Oft have I seen a skilful angler try
> The various colours of the treach'rous fly;
> When he with fruitless pain hath skimm'd the brook,
> And the coy fish rejects the skipping hook,
> He shakes the boughs, that on the margin grow,
> Which o'er the stream a waving forest throw;
> When if an insect fall, (his certain guide)
> He gently takes him from the whirling tide;
> Examines well his form, with curious eyes,
> His gaudy vest, his wings, his horns and size:
> Then round his hook the chosen fur he winds,
> And on the back a speckled feather binds;
> So just the colours shine through ev'ry part,
> That Nature seems to live again in art.

In his opening chapter, "A Description of Fishes, according to Natural History, with the best Methods of breeding, feeding, etc.," he comes to the following close:

Having mentioned that fishes are exposed to numerous enemies, I shall conclude this chapter by giving the reader a poetical enumeration of them.

> A thousand foes the finny people chace,
> Nor are they safe from their own kindred race:
> The Pike, fell tyrant of the liquid plain,
> With rav'nous waste devours his fellow train,
> Yet, howsoe'er with raging famine pin'd,
> The Tench he spares, a salutary kind.
> Hence too the Pearch, a like voracious brood,
> Forbears to make this gen'rous race his food;
> Tho' on the common drove no bound he finds,
> But spreads unmeasur'd waste o'er all the kinds,
> Nor less the greedy Trout and gutless Eel,
> Incessant woes, and dire destruction deal.
> The lurking Water-Rat in caverns preys;
> And in the weeds the wily Otter slays.
> The ghastly Newt, in muddy streams annoys;
> And in swift floods the felly Snake destroys;
> Toads, for the shoaling fry, forsake the lawn;
> And croaking Frogs devour the tender spawn.
> Neither the habitants of land nor air,
> (So sure their doom) the fishy numbers spare!
> The Swan, fair regent of the silver tide,
> Their ranks destroys and spreads their ruin wide;
> The Duck her offspring to the river leads,
> And on the destin'd fry insatiate feeds;
> On fatal wings the pouncing Bittern soars,
> And wafts her prey from the defenceless shores;
> The watchful Halcyons to the reeds repair,
> And from their haunts the scaly captives bear:
> Sharp Herns and Corm'rants too their tribes oppress,
> A harrass'd race, peculiar in distress;
> Nor can the Muse enumerate their foes,
> Such is their fate, so various are their woes!

In his last chapter, devoted to "Prognostics of the Weather; independent of the Barometer, extracted from the best Authorities," he gives the various determinants to enable the angler "to form a judgment of the change of weather, on which his sport entirely depends."

Among the various signs of rain, here are the "Signs of the Change of Weather from the Animal Creation":

So long as the swallows fly aloft after their prey, we think ourselves sure of a serene sky; but when they skim along near the ground, or the surface of the water, we judge the rain is not far off, and the observation will seldom fail. In the year 1775, a drought of three months continuance broke up at the summer solstice: the day before the rain came upon us, the swallows flew very near the ground, which they had never done in the fine weather.

In the mountainous country of Derbyshire, which goes by the name of the *Peak*, the inhabitants observe, that if the sheep wind up the hills in the morning to their pasture, and feed near the tops, the weather, though cloudy and drizzling, which is very frequently the case in those parts, will clear away by degrees, and terminate in a fine day; but if they feed in the bottoms, the rains will continue and increase.

Dogs grow sleepy and stupid before rain, and shew that their stomachs are out of order by refusing their food and eating grass, that sort which is hence called dog's grass; this they cast up again soon afterwards, and with it the foulness that offended their stomachs. Water fowl dive and wash themselves more than ordinary; and even the fish in rivers are affected, because all anglers agree, that they never bite freely when rain is depending. Vide part Ist, Rule 16th, Flies, on the contrary, are particularly troublesome, and seem to be more hungry than usual; and toads are seen in the evening, crawling across the road or beaten path, where they seldom appear but when they are restless with an approaching change.

Before any considerable quantity of rain is to fall, most living creatures are affected in such sort, as to render them some way sensible of its approach, and of the access of something new to the surface of the earth, and of the atmosphere. Moles work harder than ordinary, they throw up more earth, and sometimes come forth; the worms do so too; ants are observed to stir about, and bustle more than usually for some time; and then retire to their burrows before the rain falls. All sorts of insects and flies are more stirring and busy than ordinary. Bees are ever on this occasion in fullest employ; but betake themselves all to their hives, if not too far for them to reach, before the storm arises. The common flesh-flies are more bold and greedy: snails, frogs, and toads, appear disturbed and uneasy. Fishes are sullen and made qualmish by the water, now more turbid than before. Birds of all sorts are in action: crows are more earnest after their prey, as are also swallows and other small birds, and therefore they fall lower and fall nearer to the earth in search of insects and other such things as they feed upon. When the mountains of the north begin to be capped with fogs, the moor-cocks and other birds quit them, fly off in flocks, and betake themselves to the lower lands for the time. Swine discover great uneasiness; as do likewise sheep, cows and oxen, appearing more solicitous and eager in pasture than usual. Even mankind themselves are not exempt from some sense of a change in their bodies.

I looked in vain, here as well as in the Addenda where there were more Signs from Animals, for the one that Al McClane taught me, many years ago in Iceland. We were on our way to a new pool to try, when Al suggested we stop for lunch.

"No fishing for the better part of an hour, anyway," he said, and when I wondered how he could tell he said, simply, "Cows are lying down." Sure enough, though I hadn't noticed before, they were, and sure enough, a half hour later, while we were eating, we sat out a sharp (and I would have said a sudden) thunderstorm. When it was over, Al said "Now the fish will bite," and sure enough, they did.

Why this simple rule should have escaped inclusion in all the weather prognostics with which the various angling manuals of the eighteenth century were generally bedecked, I have no idea. But in the almost twenty years since then, I have yet to see an exception to this simple four-word rule.

Better than Best, except for the poets (and the extent to which Best is Bowlker), I seem unable to trot out for your delectation, as representative of that age of enlightenment, the eighteenth century, and it seems a skimpy haul. I keep thinking I ought to do better.

And yet, in angling terms, it really wasn't the age of enlightenment. Except for tackle improvement, there was no great breakthrough, no sudden revelation that opened up untold vistas of new knowledge, and a multitude of avenues of innovation. It was only with Ronalds, well on into the nineteenth century, that the first bird sang in the darkness, ushering in the dawn of angling enlightenment.

But we don't have to wait that long, in poking about on the bookshelves, to find fairer rewards than in anything we have come across since Walton. The nineteenth century as a whole offers an embarrassment of choice, compared to the eighteenth, and for the first time, a lot of the good stuff is American.

I hope you'll have the feeling, as we move along, that we're starting to make up for some lost time, and that things are at last looking up a little.

I suppose we'd have had more sense of getting somewhere if I hadn't tried to stick to some semblance of respect for chronology. After all, we aren't preparing for an exam on the subject. But I figured we had to have at least rudimentary routine of form, and order, and progression, if only to keep from going in circles. True, it would have been a little more sporting if I'd warned you about that before we set out, but I just didn't think of it.

Maybe it's because I never have kept my books any way but helterskelter. My father dinged into me, when I was very young, "Form habits of order; a place for everything, and everything in its place." In lifelong reaction to that reiterated advice, you should see my office today.

Besides, you're a fisherman, or if you aren't it's very odd that you're still here. So you'll understand when I say, along with Odell Shepard (with whom we're going to spend some time) that "I shall be content to write the rambling, idle, quite unpractical sort of book about fishing that I myself like to read by the fire in winter when the brooks are sealed, or by the stream on drowsy noons—winding into and through the inexhaustible lore of angling as a lazy brook goes through a meadow where the grass is heavy and the reeds are high, pausing and deepening here and there but soon running free again with a glitter of sun on the stickle. There can never be too many books of that good, honest, and leisurely kind."

Well, yes, I see your point. "Good" and "honest" really are either-or terms.

But you do have to admit, don't you, that I'm batting .333 on those three qualifications of a book, taking them as a whole?

Well, anyway, we'll get on with it. That's a promise. And meanwhile, you can at least credit me with not having stiffed you into any of that Early Awful cast-iron dialogue (What ho, Piscator!) that too many books about fishing are much too full of.

7.

Ronalds and the New Era

From where I sit, there are twelve peaks of angling progress, and before we quit we will have climbed them all. To give them names, to serve chiefly as labels, since in some cases it's as much the matter of a moment, or a movement, as a man, they are Berners, Walton, Cotton, Ronalds, Stewart, Norris, Halford, Gordon, Skues, Mottram, Hewitt, Jennings.

U: Pretty peculiar list. Who's Mottram?

(Oh, so we *are* going to have dialogue, after all. Shows you how much attention anybody pays to me around here.)

Now wait. I didn't say these twelve were the greatest names in angling literature; in fact, in a couple of cases, pretty far from it. What I called them was "peaks of angling progress" and I see now I could have done better. Progress is a word I hate anyway, so I'll take it back. Probably I should have called them "influences," because what I'm thinking of, really, is twelve rocks that altered or deflected, or even reversed, the main stream of angling practice. You could say these are the ones that just happened to be the chief instruments of change. Like rocks in a stream, it's because of them—or after their time, if you prefer—that things took a different course.

This isn't to say that reading them necessarily gives us the best fishing in print. It's rather that, because they were in print, you and I fish today the way we do. I mean in actual practice, not just in talking or writing about it.

U: Oh.

If we likened the whole range, or course, or stream of angling literature to a college curriculum, you could say that these are the twelve "required reading" subjects, the ones we can't skip.

I grant you, it doesn't follow that they're the ones we have the most fun reading, or even that we will necessarily remember the longest and most fully. For sheer reading enjoyment I'll take Scrope, any day, ahead of Ronalds. Matter of fact, I can hardly *read* Ronalds, whereas I never tire of reading Scrope.

But it's because of Ronalds, largely, that you and I fish with the kinds of flies we use today, though I can't think of a single fly we owe Scrope. (Meg's Drawers, I seem to remember, was a fly Scrope talked about a lot, and I don't even know anybody who's ever seen one, let alone used it.)

For that matter, I'd much rather read Francis than Halford. Never cared too much for Halford simply as a writer, and the more he wrote the less I enjoyed him. But Francis I could go on reading indefinitely. Yet it's largely because of Halford rather than Francis that subsequent writings took the turn they did. And in the end, Halford, who followed him by almost twenty years, greatly influenced Francis. But Francis just happened to be a natural born writer, who could make anything he wrote sound good, and Halford happened not to be.

U: Why don't we start? If some of these writers are like spinach, that we're going to get because it's good for us, couldn't we sort of get it over with?

M: You know, I hate to bring this up, but it would be a touch more polite, really, if you said "resume" instead of "start." (Start, he says, for god's sake, when here I've been huffing and puffing and . . .)

All right, yes, we are headed for Ronalds now. But you know how it is with mountains; they're in sight, it seems, forever and yet for a long time they don't seem to be getting appreciably closer. So it's perfectly all right if we pick a few nosegays, here and there, as we go. Scrope, as it happens, is the other side of the mountain, but we'll be passing others on the way. There's Sir Humphrey Davy, for instance, and as I said, now all of a sudden there are a lot of them.

Speaking of dialogue, good and bad, Sir Humphrey Davy's is terrible. He was a distinguished scientist, his fame secure in another discipline, and by all accounts one of the most brilliant minds of his time, but he was betrayed by his fondness for Walton into casting *Salmonia or Days of Fly Fishing* into conversational form, and for such a bright man it was a stupid mistake. Seldom has dialogue so wooden and stilted been perpetrated, before the days of our early radio commercials (Gee, Mom, this steak is good. Tell me, Mom, what is the secret of its superior flavor? Why, Son . . .).

It's too bad, because despite his tin ear for dialogue, Sir Humphrey Davy wrote a lovely book, and he stands as the Berners of salmon fishing (taking Scrope as its Walton and Cotton combined). But maybe if you're braced for it, and expect it to be awful, it won't seem so bad, and if you can stand it, you're almost certain to succumb to its charm. It helps to remember that it was dictated from a bed of pain, in which the President of the Royal Society lay fatally ill. He died in 1829, the year after it was published. The first edition was anonymous, but all subsequent editions carried his name.

His preface, too, has a disarming candor, which I find helpful in making the dialogue go down:

> The conversational manner and discursive style were chosen as best suited to the state of health of the Author, who was incapable of considerable efforts and long-continuous attention; and he could not but have in mind a model, which has fully proved the utility and popularity of this method of treating the subject—*The Complete Angler*, by Walton and Cotton.

Explaining that the characters are of course imaginary, he concedes that "the sentiments attributed to them, the Author may sometimes have gained from recollections of real conversations with friends, from whose society much of the happiness of his early life has been derived."

But enough warm-up; now for the cold plunge:

FIRST DAY.
HALIEUS—POIETES—PHYSICUS—ORNITHER.

Introductory Conversation—Symposiac.
Scene, London.

PHYS.—Halieus, I dare say you know where this excellent trout was caught: I never ate a better fish of the kind.

HAL.—I ought to know, as it was this morning in the waters of the Wandle, not ten miles from the place where we sit, and it is through my means that you see it at table.

PHYS. — Of your own catching?

HAL. — Yes, with the artificial fly.

PHYS. — I admire the fish, but I cannot admire the art by which it was taken; and I wonder how a man of your active mind and enthusiastic character can enjoy what appears to me a stupid and melancholy occupation.

HAL. — I might as well wonder in my turn, that a man of your discursive imagination and disposition to contemplate should not admire this occupation, and that you should venture to call it either stupid or melancholy.

PHYS. — I have at least the authority of a great moralist, Johnson, for its folly.

HAL. — I will allow no man, however great a philosopher, or moralist, to abuse an occupation he has not tried; and as well as I remember, this same illustrious person praised the book and the character of the great Patriarch of Anglers, Isaac Walton.

PHYS. — There is another celebrated man, however, who has abused this your patriarch, Lord Byron, and that in terms not very qualified. He calls him, as well as I can recollect, "a quaint old cruel coxcomb." * I must say, a practice of this great fisherman, where he recommends you to pass the hook through the body of a frog with care, as though you loved him, in order to keep him alive longer, cannot but be considered as cruel.

HAL. — I do not justify either the expression or the practice of Walton in this instance; but remember, I fish only with inanimate baits, or imitations of them, and I will not exhume or expose the ashes of the dead, nor vindicate the memory of Walton, at the expense of Byron, who, like Johnson, was no fisherman: but the moral and religious habits of Walton, his simplicity of manners, and his well-spent life, exonerate him from the charge of cruelty; and the book of a coxcomb would not have been so great a favourite with most persons of refined taste. A noble lady, long distinguished at court for preeminent beauty and grace, and whose mind possesses undying charms, has written some lines in my copy of Walton, which, if you will allow me, I will repeat to you:

> Albeit, gentle Angler, I
>   Delight not in thy trade,
> Yet in thy pages there doth lie
> So much of quaint simplicity,
>   So much of mind,
>   Of such good kind,
>   That none need be afraid,
> Caught by thy cunning bait, this book,
> To be ensnared on thy hook.

---

* From Don Juan, Canto XII, Stanza CVI.
"And angling, too, that solitary vice,
    Whatever Izaac Walton sings or says:
The quaint old cruel coxcomb in his gullet
Should have a hook and a small trout to pull it."

Gladly from thee, I'm lured to bear
    With things that seem'd most vile before,
For thou didst on poor subjects rear
Matter the wisest sage might hear.
      And with a grace,
      That doth efface
  More labour'd works, thy simple lore
Can teach us that thy skilful *lines,*
More than the scaly brood *confines.*

Our hearts and senses, too, we see,
    Rise quickly at thy master hand,
And, ready to be caught by thee,
Are lured to virtue willingly.
      Content and peace,
      With health and ease,
  Walk by thy side. At thy command
We bid adieu to worldly care,
And joy in gifts that all may share.

Gladly, with thee, I pace along,
    And of sweet fancies dream;
Waiting till some inspired song,
Within my memory cherish'd long,
      Comes fairer forth,
      With more of worth,
  Because that time upon its stream
Feathers and chaff will bear away,
But give to gems a brighter ray.

And though the charming and intellectual author of this poem is not an angler herself, yet I can quote the example of her lovely daughters to vindicate fly-fishing from the charge of cruelty, and to prove that the most delicate and refined minds can take pleasure in this innocent amusement. One of these young ladies, I am told, is a most accomplished and skilful salmon fisher. And if you require a poetical authority against that of Lord Byron, I mention the philosophical and powerful poet of the lakes, and the author of

"An Orphic tale indeed,
A tale divine, of high and passionate thoughts,
To their own music chanted:"*

who is a lover both of fly-fishing and fly-fishermen. Gay's poem you know, and his passionate fondness for the amusement, which was his principal occupation in the summer at Amesbury; and the late excellent John Tobin, author of the Honey Moon, was an ardent angler.

PHYS. — I am satisfied with your poetical authorities.

---

* *The Friend,* page 303, by S. T. Coleridge.

HAL. — Nay, I can find authorities of all kinds, statesmen, heroes, and philosophers. I can go back to Trajan, who was fond of angling. Nelson was a good fly-fisher, and as a proof of his passion for it, continued the pursuit even with his left hand. Dr. Paley was ardently attached to this amusement; so much so, that when the Bishop of Durham inquired of him, when one of his most important works would be finished, he said, with great simplicity and good humour, "My Lord, I shall work steadily at it when the fly-fishing season is over," as if this were a business of his life. And I am rather reserved in introducing living characters, or I could give a list of the highest names of Britain, belonging to modern times, in science, letters, arts, and arms, who are ornaments of this fraternity, to use the expression borrowed from the freemasonry of our forefathers.

PHYS. — I do not find much difficulty in understanding why warriors, and even statesmen, fishers of men, many of whom I have known particularly fond of hunting and shooting, should likewise be attached to angling; but I own, I am at a loss to find reasons for a love of this pursuit amongst philosophers and poets.

HAL. — The search after food is an instinct belonging to our nature; and from the savage in his rudest and most primitive state, who destroys a piece of game, or a fish, with a club or spear, to man in the most cultivated state of society, who employs artifice, machinery, and the resources of various other animals, to secure his object, the origin of the pleasure is similar, and its object the same: but that kind of it requiring most art may be said to characterise man in his highest or intellectual state; and the fisher for salmon and trout with the fly employs not only machinery to assist his physical powers, but applies sagacity to conquer difficulties; and the pleasure derived from ingenious resources and devices, as well as from active pursuit, belongs to this amusement. Then, as to its philosophical tendency, it is a pursuit of moral discipline, requiring patience, forbearance, and command of temper. As connected with natural science, it may be vaunted as demanding a knowledge of the habits of a considerable tribe of created beings — fishes, and the animals that they prey upon, and an acquaintance with the signs and tokens of the weather and its changes, the nature of waters, and of the atmosphere. As to its poetical relations, it carries us into the most wild and beautiful scenery of nature, amongst the mountain lakes, and the clear and lovely streams that gush from the higher ranges of elevated hills, or that make their way through the cavities of calcareous strata. How delightful in the early spring, after the dull and tedious time of winter, when the frosts disappear and the sunshine warms the earth and waters, to wander forth by some clear stream, to see the leaf bursting from the purple bud, to scent the odours of the bank perfumed by the violet, and enamelled, as it were, with the primrose and the daisy; to wander upon the fresh turf below the shade of trees, whose bright blossoms are filled with the music of the bee; and on the surface of the waters to view the gaudy flies sparkling like animated gems in the sunbeams, whilst the bright and beautiful trout is watching them from below; to hear the twittering of the water-birds, who, alarmed at your approach, rapidly hide themselves beneath the flowers and leaves of the water-lily; and as the season advances, to find all these objects changed for others of the same kind, but better and brighter, till the swallow and the trout contend as it were for the gaudy May-fly, and till in pursuing your amusement in the calm and balmy evening, you are serenaded by the songs of the cheerful thrush and melodious nightingale, performing the offices of paternal love, in thickets ornamented with the rose and woodbine.

PHYS.—All these enjoyments might be obtained without the necessity of torturing and destroying an unfortunate animal, that the true lover of nature would wish to see happy in a scene of loveliness.

HAL.—If all men were Pythagoreans and professed the Brahmin's creed, it would undoubtedly be cruel to destroy any form of animated life; but if fish are to be eaten, I see no more harm in capturing them by skill and ingenuity with an artificial fly, than in pulling them out of the water by main force with the net; and in general when taken by the common fisherman, fish are permitted to die slowly, and to suffer in the air, from the want of their natural element; whereas, every good angler, as soon as his fish is landed, either destroys his life immediately, if he is wanted for food, or returns him into the water.

And here's a charming way to make a point that we have often encountered in the earlier angling writers:

[*Halieus leaves them fishing, and returns to the house; but soon comes back and joins his companions, whom he finds fishing below in the river.*]

HAL.—Well, gentlemen, what sport?

POIET.—The fish are rising everywhere; but though we have been throwing over them with all our skill for a quarter of an hour, yet not a single one will take, and I am afraid we shall return to breakfast without our prey.

HAL.—I will try; but I shall go to the other side, where I see a very large fish rising. There! I have him at the very first throw. Land this fish, and put him into the well. Now I have another; and I have no doubt I could take half a dozen in this very place, where you have been so long fishing without success.

PHYS.—You must have a different fly; or have you some unguent or charm to tempt the fish?

HAL.—No such thing. If any of you will give me your rod and fly, I will answer for it, I shall have the same success. I take your rod, Physicus.—And lo! I have a fish!

PHYS.—What can be the reason of this? It is perfectly inexplicable to me. Yet Poietes seems to throw as light as you do, and as well as he did yesterday.

HAL.—I am surprised, that you, who are a philosopher, cannot discover the reason of this. Think a little.

ALL.—We cannot.

HAL.—As you are my scholars, I believe I must teach you. The sun is bright, and you have been, naturally enough, fishing with your backs to the sun, which, not being very high, has thrown the shadows of your rods and yourselves upon the water; and you have alarmed the fish whenever you have thrown a fly. You see I have fished with my face towards the sun; and though inconvenienced by the light, have given no alarm. Follow my example and you will soon have sport, as there is a breeze playing on the water.

PHYS.—Your sagacity puts me in mind of an anecdote which I remember to have heard respecting the late eloquent statesman, Charles James Fox, who, walking up Bond Street from one of the club-houses with an illustrious personage, laid him a wager that he would see more cats than the Prince in his walk, and that he might take which side of the street he liked. When they got to the top, it was found that Mr. Fox had seen thirteen cats, and the Prince not one. The royal personage asked for an explanation of this apparent miracle, and Mr. Fox said, "Your Royal Highness took, of course, the shady side of the way, as most agreeable; I knew that the sunny side would be left to me, and cats always prefer the sunshine."

And, in a following passage, Sir Humphrey Davy injects a gentle dash of philosophy, with deliberate stress on Nature's sunnier side:

POIET. . . . I am much obliged to you for the hint respecting the effect of shadow, for I have several times in May and June had to complain of too clear a sky, and wished, with Cotton, for

A day with not too bright a beam;
A warm, but not a scorching, sun.

HAL.—Whilst we have been conversing, the May-flies, which were in such quantities, have become much fewer; and I believe the reason is, that they have been greatly diminished by the flocks of swallows, which everywhere pursue them: I have seen a single swallow take four, in less than a quarter of a minute, that were descending to the water.

POIET.—I delight in this living landscape! The swallow is one of my favourite birds, and a rival of the nightingale: for he cheers my sense of hearing; he is the glad prophet of the year—the harbinger of the best season; he lives a life of enjoyment amongst the loveliest forms of nature; winter is unknown to him; and he leaves the green meadows of England in autumn, for the myrtle and orange groves of Italy, and for the palms of Africa:—he has always objects of pursuit, and his success is secure. Even the beings selected for his prey are poetical, beautiful, and transient; the ephemerae are saved by his means from a slow and lingering death in the evening, and killed in a moment, when they have known nothing of life but pleasure. He is the constant destroyer of insects,—the friend of man; and, with the stork and the ibis, may be regarded as a sacred bird. His instinct, which gives him his appointed seasons, and teaches him always when and where to move, may be regarded as flowing from a Divine Source; and he belongs to the Oracles of Nature, which speak the awful and intelligible language of a present Deity.

But it is in fishing for salmon and sea trout that Sir Humphrey is at his best, and not least in conveying some sense of the difficulties of getting to the scene of the action, in the still primitive modes of transportation of his day, just before the age of steam:

FOURTH DAY.
HALIEUS—POIETES—ORNITHER—PHYSICUS.
Fishing for Salmon and Sea Trout.
Scene—Loch Maree, West of Rosshire, Scotland.
Time—Middle of July.

POIET.—I begin to be tired. This is really a long day's journey; and these last ten miles through bogs, with no other view than that of mountains half hid in mists, and brown waters that can hardly be called lakes, and with no other trees than a few stunted birches, that look so little alive, that they might be supposed immediately descended from the bogwood, every where scattered beneath our feet, have rendered it extremely tedious. This is the most barren part of one of the most desolate countries I have ever passed through in Europe; and though the inn at Strathgarve is tolerable, that of Auchnasheen is certainly the worst I have ever seen—and I hope the worst I shall ever see. We ought to have good amusement at Pool Ewe, to compensate us for this uncomfortable day's journey.

HAL.—I trust we shall have sport, as far as salmon and sea trout can furnish sport. But the difficulties of our journey are almost over. See, Loch Maree is stretched at our feet, and a good boat with four oars will carry us in four or five hours to our fishing ground; a time that will not be misspent, for this lake is not devoid of beautiful, and even grand scenery.

Once arrived at their boat, provided for them by the Laird of Braham, and installed at the inn which is "a second edition of Auchnasheen," their fishing begins:

POIET.—This is a fine river; clear, full, but not too large; with the two handed rod it may be commanded in most parts.

HAL.—It is larger than usual. The strong wind which brought us so quickly down has made it fuller; and it is not in such good order for fishing as it was before the wind rose.

POIET.—I thought the river was all the better for a flood, when clear.

HAL.—Better after a flood from rain; for this brings the fish up, who know when rain is coming, and likewise brings down food and makes the fish feed. But when the water is raised by a strong wind, the fish never run, as they are sure to find no increase in the spring heads, which are their objects in running.

POIET.—You give the fish credit for great sagacity.

HAL.—Call it instinct rather; for if they *reasoned*, they would run with every large water, whether from wind or rain. What the feeling or power is, which makes them travel with rain, I will not pretend to define. But now for our sport.

POIET.—The fish are beginning to rise; I have seen two here already, and there is a third, and a fourth; scarcely a quarter of a minute elapses without a fish rising in some part of the pool.

HAL.—As the day is dark, I shall use a bright and rather a large fly, with jay's hackle, kingfisher's feather under the wing, and golden pheasant's tail, and wing of mixed grouse, and argus pheasant's tail. I shall throw over these fish; I ought to raise one.

POIET.—Either you are not skilful, or the fish know their danger. They will not rise.

HAL.—I will try another and a smaller fly.

POIET.—You do nothing.

HAL.—I have changed my fly a third time, yet no fish rises. I cannot understand this. The water is not in good order, or I should certainly have raised a fish or two. Now I will wager ten to one, that this pool has been fished before to-day.

ORN.—By whom?

HAL.—I know not; but take my wager and we will ascertain.

ORN.—I shall ascertain without the wager if possible. See, a man connected with the fishery advances, let us ask him. There you see; it has been fished once or twice by one, who claims without charter the right of angling.

HAL.—I told you so. Now I know this, I shall put on another kind of fly, such as I am sure they have not seen this day.

POIET.—It is very small and very gaudy, I believe made with humming bird's feathers.

HAL.—No,—the brightest Java dove's hackle, kingfisher's blue, and golden pheasant's feathers, and the red feathers of the paroquet. There was a fish that rose and missed the fly—a sea trout. There, he has taken it, a fresh run fish, from his white belly and blue back.

POIET.—How he springs out of the water! He must be 6 or 7 lbs.

HAL.—Under five, I am sure; he will soon be tired. He fights with less spirit: put the net under him. There, he is a fine fed sea trout, between 4 and 5 lbs. But our intrusive brother angler (as I must call him) is coming down the river to take his evening cast. A stout Highlander, with a powerful tail,—or, as we should call it in England, *suite*. He is resolved not to be driven off, and I am not sure that the Laird himself could divert him from his purpose, except by a stronger tail, and force of arms; but I will try my eloquence upon him. "Sir, we hope you will excuse us for fishing in this pool, where it seems you were going to take your cast; but the Laird has desired us to stand in his shoes for a few days, and has given up angling while we are here; and as we come nearly a thousand miles for this amusement, we are sure you are too much of a gentleman to spoil our sport; and we will take care to supply your fish kettle while we are here, morning and evening, and we shall send you, as we hope, a salmon before night."

POIET.—He grumbles good sport to us, and is off with his tail: you have hit him in the right place. He is a pot fisher, I am sure, and somewhat hungry, and, provided he gets the salmon, does not care who catches it!

HAL.—You are severe on the Highland gentleman, and I think extremely unjust. Nothing could be more ready than his assent, and a keen fisherman must not be expected to be in the best possible humour, when he finds sport which he believes he has a right to, and which perhaps he generally enjoys without interruption, taken away from him by entire strangers. There is, I know, a disputed point about fishing with the rod, between him and the Laird; and it would have been too much to have anticipated a courteous greeting from one, who considers us as the representatives of an enemy. But I see there is a large fish which has just risen at the tail of the pool. I think he is fresh run from the sea, for the tide is coming in. My fly and tackle are almost too fine for so large a fish, and I will put on my first fly with a very strong single gut link and a stretcher of triple gut. He has taken my fly, and I hold him—a powerful fish: he must be between 10 and 15 lbs. He fights well, and tries to get up the rapid at the top of the pool. I must try my strength with him, to keep him off that rock, or he will break me. I have turned him, and he is now in a good part of the pool: such a fish cannot be tired in a minute or two, but requires from ten to twenty—depending upon his activity and strength, and the rapidity of the stream he moves against. He is now playing against the strongest rapid in the river, and will soon give in, should he keep his present place.

POIET.—You have tired him.

HAL.—He seems fairly tired: I shall bring him in to shore. Now gaff him; strike as near the tail as you can. He is safe; we must prepare him for the pot. Give him a stunning blow on the head to deprive him of sensation, and then make a transverse cut just below the gills, and crimp him, by cutting the bone on each side, so as almost to divide him into slices: and now hold him by the tail that he may bleed. There is a small spring, I see, close under that bank, which I dare say has the mean temperature of the atmosphere in this climate, and is much under 50°—place him there, and let him remain for ten minutes; then carry him to the pot, and before you put in a slice let the water and salt boil furiously, and give time to the water to recover its heat before you throw in another; and so proceed with the whole fish: leave the head out, and throw in the thickest pieces first.

PHYS.—Why did you not crimp your trout?

HAL.—We will have him fried. Our poacher prevented me from attending to the preparation; but for frying he is better not crimped, as he is not large enough to give good transverse slices.

POIET.—This salmon is a good fish, and fresh as you said from the sea. You see the salt-water louse adheres to his sides, and he is bright and silvery, and a thick fish; I dare say his weight is not less than 14 lbs., and I know of no better fish for the table than one of that size.

PHYS.—It appears to me that so powerful a fish ought to have struggled much longer: yet, without great exertions on your part, in ten minutes he appeared quite exhausted, and lay on his side as if dying: this induces me to suppose, that there must be some truth in the vulgar opinion of anglers, that fish are, as it were, drowned by the play of the rod and reel.

HAL.—The vulgar opinion of anglers on this subject I believe to be perfectly correct; though, to apply the word drowning to an animal that lives in the water is not quite a fit use of language. Fish, as you ought to know, respire by passing water, which always holds common air in solution, through their gills or bronchial membrane, by the use of a system of muscles surrounding the fauces, which occasion constant contractions and expansions, or openings and closings of this membrane, and the life of the fish is dependent on the process in the same manner as that of a quadruped is on inspiring and expiring air. When a fish is hooked in the upper part of the mouth by the strength of the rod applied as a lever to the line, it is scarcely possible for him to open the gills as long as this force is exerted, particularly when he is moving in a rapid stream; and when he is hooked in the lower jaw, his mouth is kept closed by the same application of the strength of the rod, so that no aerated water can be inspired. Under these circumstances he is quickly deprived of his vital forces, particularly when he exhausts his strength by moving in a rapid stream. A fish, hooked in a part of the mouth where the force of the rod will render his efforts to respire unavailing, is much in the same state as that of a deer caught round the neck by the lasso of a South American peon, who gallops forwards, dragging his victim after him, which is killed by strangulation in a very short time. When fishes are hooked foul, that is, on the outside of the body, as in the fins or tail, they will often fight for many hours, and in such cases very large salmon are seldom caught, as they retain their powers of breathing unimpaired; and if they do not exhaust themselves by violent muscular efforts, they may bid defiance to the temper and the skill of the fisherman. A large salmon, hooked in the upper part of the mouth in the cartilage or bone will sometimes likewise fight for a long while, particularly if he keep in the deep and still parts of the river, for he is able to prevent the force of the hook, applied by the rod, from interfering with his respiration, and by a powerful effort, can maintain his place, and continue to breathe in spite of the exertions of the angler. A fish, in such case, is said to be sulky, and his instinct, or his sagacity, generally enables him to conquer his enemy. It is, however, rarely that fishes hooked in the mouth are capable of using freely the muscles subservient to respiration; and their powers are generally, sooner or later, destroyed by suffocation.

POIET.—The explanation that you have just been giving us of the effects of playing fish, I confess alarms me, and makes me more afraid than I was before, that we are pursuing a very cruel amusement; for death by strangulation, I conceive, must be very laborious, slow, and painful.

PHYS.—I think as I did before I was an angler, as to the merciless character of field-sports; but I doubt if this part of the process of the fly-fisher ought so strongly to alarm your feelings. As far as analogies from warm-blooded animals can apply to the case, the death that follows obstructed respiration is quick, and preceded by insensibility. There are many instances of persons who have recovered from the apparent death produced by drowning, and had no recollection of any violent or intense agony; indeed, the alarm or passion of fear generally absorbs all the sensibility, and the physical suffering is lost in the mental agitation. I can answer from my own experience, that there is no pain which precedes the insensibility occasioned by breathing gases unfitted for supporting life, but oftener a pleasurable feeling, as in the case of the respiration of nitrous oxide. And in the suffocation produced by the gradual abstraction of air in a close room where charcoal is burning, we have the record of the son of a celebrated chemist, that the sensation which precedes the deep sleep that ends in death is agreeable. There is far more pain in recovering from the insensibility produced by the abstraction of air than in undergoing it, as I can answer from my own feelings; and it is, I believe, quite true, what has been asserted, that the pain of being born, which is acquiring the power of respiration, is greater than that of dying, which is losing the power.

Sir Humphrey's knowledge of flies, and of the breeding and life patterns of many insects, foreshadow the work of Ronalds. Given in conversational form, it is rather like whistling a tune that somebody else will have to take all the time and trouble and, above all, skill to orchestrate, but the outline of the music is none the less unmistakable. Greatly abridged, his animadversions on the transformations of winged insects, from maggot or grub to chrysalis or pupa, before achieving their final form ready for flight, almost amount to a blueprint for an entomological approach to the systematized study of anglers' flies. He even uses the term "nymphal" at one point. But he concludes with "I have not, however, the knowledge, or if I had, have not the time, to go through the lists of these interesting little animals—but . . . to study the organs and faculties of these various insect tribes, in their function of respiration, nutrition, and reproduction, would be sufficient for the labour of a life."

Sir Humphrey's fishing travels for salmon, trout and grayling, not only throughout the British Isles but Central Europe as well, were really formidable. He even caught, and gave one of the earliest angling accounts of, the fearsome *huchen* of the Danube basin, the vicious monster that is the real gangster of the *salmo* family.

The book's ending, on the ninth day, is gently and almost wistfully philosophical, though carefully concealing any hint of what Sir Humphrey must have known to be a mortal illness:

HAL.—But our horses are ready, and the time of separation arrives. I trust we shall all have a happy meeting in England in the winter. I have made you idlers at home and abroad, but I hope to some purpose; and I trust you will confess the time bestowed upon angling has not been thrown away. The most important principle, perhaps, in life is to have a pursuit—a useful one if possible, and at all events an innocent one. And the scenes you have enjoyed—the contemplations to which they have led, and the exercise in which we have indulged, have, I am sure, been very salutary to the body, and, I hope, to the mind. I have always found a peculiar effect from this kind of life; it has appeared to bring me back to early times and feelings, and to create again the hopes and happiness of youthful days.

PHYS.—I felt something like what you described, and were I convinced that in the cultivation of the amusement, these feelings would increase, I would devote myself to it with passion; but I fear, in my case this is impossible. Ah! could I recover any thing like that freshness of mind, which I possessed at twenty-five, and which, like the dew of the dawning morning, covered all objects and nourished all things that grew, and in which they were more beautiful even than in mid-day sunshine,—what would I not give? All that I have gained in an active and not unprofitable life. How well I remember that delightful season, when, full of power, I sought for power in others; and power was sympathy, and sympathy power. When the dead and the unknown, the great of other ages and of distant places, were made, by the force of the imagination, my companions and friends; when every voice seemed one of praise and love; when every flower had the bloom and odour of the rose; and every spray or plant seemed either the poet's laurel, or the civic oak—which appeared to offer themselves as wreaths to adorn my throbbing brow. But, alas! this cannot be; and even you cannot have two springs in life—though I have no doubt you have fishing days, in which the feelings of youth return, and that your autumn has a more *vernal* character than mine.

POIET.—I do not think Halieus had ever any season, except a perpetual and gentle spring: for the tones of his mind have been always quiet, it has been so little scorched by sunshine, and so little shaken by winds, that, I think, it may be compared to that sempivernal climate fabled of the Hesperides, where the same trees produced at once buds, leaves, blossoms, and fruits.

HAL.—Nay, my friends, spare me a little, spare my gray hairs. I have not perhaps abused my youth so much as some of my friends, but all things that you have known, I have known; and if I have not been so much scorched by the passions from which so many of my acquaintances have suffered, I owe it rather to the constant employment of a laborious profession, and to the exertions called for by the hopes, wants, and wishes of a rising family, than to any merits of my own, either moral or constitutional. For my health, I may thank my ancestors after my God, and I have not squandered what was so bountifully given; and though I do not expect, like our arch-patriarch, Walton, to number ninety years and upwards, yet, I hope, as long as I can enjoy in a vernal day the warmth and light of the sunbeams, still to haunt the streams—following the example of our late venerable friend, the president of the Royal Academy, Benjamin West, in company with whom, when he was an octogenarian, I have thrown the fly, caught trout, and enjoyed a delightful day of angling and social amusement, in the shady green meadows by the bright clear streams of the Wandle.

In all fairness, Davy really should be read like Scrope, as a whole and not in isolated bits like this. For one thing, it takes a while to get used to the awkwardnesses of the dialogue form, and become really engrossed in what he's saying. Once that happens, you realize that as a thinker he stands head and shoulders above anybody in the previous century of angling literature, and you find yourself wishing that his health, and all his other concerns, had permitted him to write more.

One who did write much more, and in the generation immediately following Sir Humphrey's, I never much cared for, though he has had a high reputation. That's the poet-angler Thomas Tod Stoddart. Not to profess a fondness for Stoddart is probably tantamount to admitting to a lack of liking for dogs. But his famous Angling Songs all seem too much like hymns to move me much.

Fresh and free the breezes blow,
   And the amber streams run gaily;
Forth, and warble as ye go,
   All ye anglers of the valley.

That's only a random verse, out of fifty-seven such songs, but it's typical. These and the angling poems of Thomas Doubleday, and all those
Border Ballads, etc., have always been a celebrated part of angling literature, but I've never been inclined to give them shelf-room. They're too
self-consciously joyful for my taste, but I've discharged whatever duty I
ought to feel toward them by at least giving them passing mention. So
consider them mentioned, and go warble if you've a mind to, but a very
little of this stuff goes a long way with me. It's not that I'm against
poetry, but simply that I feel it should be confined to thoughts that
can't be adequately expressed in prose, and such thoughts I've found
singularly scarce in that whole body of famous and mostly Scottish
angling minstrelsy of the early nineteenth century.

As against this blind spot in what I've always thought was a pretty
catholic taste for angling writings, I've invariably warmed to all quotes
of that earlier angler's song, by George Smith in *The Gentleman Angler*,
1726. I quoted the "old age" stanza myself, in *The Well-Tempered Angler*,
as one of the earlier testimonies to the longevity of fishermen as a sub-
species. In that instance, I was quoting from its citation in Eugene
Burns's 1952 volume, *An Angler's Anthology*, which without ever having
had a copy of *The Gentleman Angler* itself, I simply assumed to be
complete. Here is the way it appeared there:

THEN TO ANGLE WE WILL GO

Of all the Sports and Pastimes
  Which happen in the Year,
To Angling there are none, sure,
  That ever can compare;

We do not break our Legs or Arms
  As Huntsmen often do;
For when that we are Angling
  No Danger can ensue.

In Westminster the Gentlemen
  In Black their Conscience sell
And t'other Gentleman in Black
  Will sure reward them well.

A Client is a Gudgeon
  And freely takes the Bait
A Lawyer is a Jack, and
  For him does slyly wait.

Then you who would be honest,
  And to Old Age attain,
Forsake the City and the Town
  And fill the Angler's Train.

We meddle not with State Affairs
  Or for Preferment push;
Court places and Court pensions
  We value not a Rush.

For Health and for Diversion
  We rise by Break of Day,
While Courtiers in their Down-beds
  Sweat half their Time away.

And then unto the River
  In haste we do repair;
All Day in sweet Amusement
  We breathe good wholesome Air.

Through Meadows, by a River,
  From Place to Place we roam,
And when that we are weary,
  We then go jogging Home;

At Night we take a Bottle,
  We prattle, laugh and sing;
We drink a Health unto our Friends,
  And so God bless the King.

Then to Angle we will go, will go,
  To Angle we will go.

Then to my surprise, when I encountered it in Thomas Salter's *The Angler's Guide* (1814), I found that, assuming it was complete as quoted in Burns's anthology, and it carried no asterisks or dotted lines to indicate deletions, it had apparently both shrunk and stretched in the course of the next near-century.

In the Burns version, there are ten stanzas, but in Salter there are twelve. Yet the Burns quotation carries three stanzas that are omitted by Salter, who includes five more that were not included by Burns.

Salter credits only *Songs of the Chace*, noting that the tune is a familiar and evidently traditional one. He also makes clear, which the Burns version does not, that the chorus is repeated after each verse. With that much repetition intended anyway, surely we needn't boggle at adding a little more, by giving the complete Salter version below:

ANGLING WE WILL GO *Tune,—A Begging we will go.*

1.

Of all the sports and pastimes
  That happen in the year,
To Angling there are none, sure,
  That ever can compare.
        Then to Angle we will go, etc.

2.

We do not break our legs or arms,
  As Huntsmen often do,
For when that we are Angling
  No danger can ensue.
        Then to Angle, etc.

3.

Cards and dice are courtly games,
  Then let them laugh who win,
There's innocence in Angling,
  But gaming is a sin.
        Then to Angle, etc.

4.

Then you who would be honest,
  And to old age attain;
Forsake the City, and the Town,
  And fill the Angler's train.
        Then to Angle, etc.

5.

For health, and for diversion,
  We rise by break of day,
While courtiers in their down beds
  Sleep half their time away.
        Then to Angle, etc.

6.

And then unto the River
  In haste we do repair,
All day in sweet amusement,
  We breathe good wholesome air.
        Then to Angle, etc.

7.

Our constitution sound is,
  Our appetites are keen,
We laugh and bid defiance
  To vapours and the Spleen.
        Then to Angle, etc.

8.

The gout and stone are often bred
   By lolling in a coach,
But Anglers walk, and so remain
   As sound as any Roach.
            Then to Angle, etc.

9.

The Trout, the Pike, the Salmon,
   The Barbel, Carp, and Bream,
Afford good sport, and so the Perch
   And Tench will do the same.
            Then to Angle, etc.

10.

So let us now remember
   To praise the smaller Fish,
Bleak, Gudgeon, Roach, and Dace,
   Will garnish well a dish.
            Then to Angle, etc.

11.

Through meadows, by a river;
   From place to place we roam,
And when that we are weary
   We then go jogging home.
            Then to Angle, etc.

12.

At night we take a bottle,
   We prattle, laugh, and sing;
We drink a health unto our friends,
   And so God bless the King.
            Then to Angle, etc.

Anyway, it's a grand old song, I think, whether at ten, twelve, or as combined between these two versions, fifteen stanzas. I could even do with more, and wish I had a copy of *The Gentleman Angler,* to look it up and see if there are still others that both of these secondary sources skipped.

And while I'm wishing, I wish that Salter himself were half as much fun to read. But he isn't bad, though not very fanciful, and we really ought to spend some time with him, now that we're here, because he gives a very clear picture of the state of the art after Bowlker and before Ronalds. His first edition appeared in 1814, the year before Waterloo, and by 1825 he was into his sixth. That seems to be the one we have before us now.

(I've already warned you that you'll come across very few first editions as long as we're sticking to the books I've got at hand. I only got them for reading purposes in the first place—for eating on the spot, so to speak, as opposed to "collecting"—and always welcomed later editions, where the author had the chance to correct errata and add second thoughts.)

In his preface, Salter defines his aims and his limits:

In writing this Treatise on Angling, my pen has always been guided by a love of truth, and a sincere desire to improve an Art in which I so much delight;—and the publication of it proceeds wholly from a conviction that a plain practical Guide to the Art of Angling was wanted; for it is of little value to the learner to be told, that worms are a good bait for Carp, Gudgeon, etc.; or that Roach will take paste, Barbel—greaves; or that Jack and Pike are taken with a Gudgeon, Dace, or other small Fish; unless such information be accompanied with clear and practical rules how to bait the hook, at what depth to fish, what sized hook is proper to use, what kind and quality of ground-bait, how to make and cast it in, etc., for, in such minute (but necessary) information, most writers on Angling are, I conceive, very deficient. This information is particularly needed by the Juvenile Sportsman, as the old practitioner is, generally speaking, by no means communicative; and I have often witnessed the evasive answers of Old Anglers, when applied to on the subject: indeed, it is a very common practice for those who are masters of the Art, to discontinue Angling, and move away, when accosted by strangers or a novice. I have, also, been careful not to introduce any thing resting on mere theory, but to instruct the novice by rules drawn from actual practice, experience, and observation; arranged in the most plain and intelligible manner; and I feel highly gratified to find that my endeavours to supply such a work, have been so well received. In this Edition, the whole of the Treatise has been carefully corrected and revised; and much additional information, relative to Angling, has been introduced, as well as many new cuts and engravings to illustrate and embellish the subject: and to which is added, the Troller's Guide, a new and complete Treatise on Trolling, or the Art of Fishing for Jack and Pike. The only work written expressly on the art of taking Jack and Pike, by Angling, is called the Complete Troller, written and published about the year 1682, by the Rev. R. Nobbs; and as this healthy and delightful branch of Fishing is followed with avidity, and preferred, by many Anglers, to every other mode of Angling, and the Art itself having received many improvements since Mr. Nobbs wrote on the subject, it has been suggested to me, that a Treatise on Jack-fishing, written by a modern practical Troller, would be very acceptable to the lovers of Angling in general. In consequence of such opinions and suggestions (in which I fully coincide, as I cannot agree with the Rev. Moses Brown, or any other writer on this subject, that the Art had arrived at the highest state of perfection, under the esteemed Father of Anglers, Isaac Walton; seeing that that gentleman himself says, in his

Preface, that Angling is so like Mathematics, that it can never be fully learned), and having had much practice and experience in every method pursued in taking both Jack and Pike with the angle, with the advantage, also, of a residence, for several years, near one of the best Rivers in England for Trolling; I have presumed to offer my opinions and instructions, as a guide to those who may be desirous of learning how to take Jack and Pike in a fair, pleasing, and sportsman-like manner; and in order to prevent the possibility of misunderstanding the direction given for baiting the hooks, etc., I have illustrated those directions with cuts, executed under my own immediate inspection; and have, also, endeavoured to convey my instructions in so plain and concise a manner, that the juvenile and inexperienced Troller may clearly and promptly understand them; and I doubt not, if those directions are assiduously put in practice, the novice may be soon enabled to say,—

> I seldom to the Rivers went,
> But either Jack or Pike I took.

And I, also, flatter myself, that many who have had some practice in the Art of Trolling, will find, in this work, observations on the seasons and weather proper for Trolling, how to cast the baited hook in search, and divers other matters connected with, and relative to, Jack and Pikefishing, worthy their notice and attention.

A man little accustomed to arrange his ideas for the press, ought, perhaps, to make some apology for the imperfections of his style; but, as my desire has only been to convey plain practical rules in an Art with which I considered myself well acquainted, I trust my readers will pardon the manner for the matter.

> The Angler envies no man's joys,
>   But his, who gains the greatest sport;
> With peace, he dwells far from the noise
>   And bustling grandeur of a Court.

I thought, at first, that this last was still another stanza of *Angling We Will Go,* but apparently it's a verse from a different "Song of the Chace," as it has four beats to the line, where the other had only three.

Jack, as in Jack and Pike, seems to be the common English appellation for pickerel, as the context of the passage on the two fish soon makes clear:

SNAP-FISHING.

Snap-fishing for Jack and Pike is neither so scientific, gentlemanly, or sportsman-like a way of angling, as with the gorge or live-bait; nor does it afford so much amusement or profit; for, when the hook or hooks are baited, the Angler casts in search, draws, raises, and sinks his bait, until he feels a bite; he then strikes with much violence, and instantly drags or throws his victim, *nolens volens,* on shore, (and then almost wonders how the devil he came there,) which he is enabled to do, because the hooks used for the Snap are of the largest and strongest kind used in fresh-water fishing. But this hurried and unsportsman-like way of taking Fish can only please those who value the game more than the sport afforded by killing a Jack or Pike with tackle, which gives the Fish a chance of escaping, and excites the Angler's skill and patience, mixed with a certain pleasing anxiety, lest he escapes, and the reward of his hopes by killing the fish, which is the true sportsman's delight. Neither has the snapfisher so good a chance of success, unless he angle in a pond or piece of water, where the Jack or Pike are very numerous, or half starved, and will hazard their lives for almost any thing that comes in the way; but in rivers where they are well-fed, worth killing, and rather scarce, the coarse snap-tackle, large hooks, etc. generally alarm them: on the whole, I think it is two to one against the snap, in most rivers; and if there are many weeds in the water, the large hooks of the snap, by standing rank, are continually getting foul, damaging the bait, and causing much trouble and loss of time. Jack are also killed by the artificial bait, called a Devil, which should be about three inches long; they are kept ready fitted at the fishing-tackle shops.

TWO-HANDED, OR CROSS-FISHING

In the North of England, two-handed or cross-fishing is practised for Salmon, Trout, and also for Jack and Pike, though this method of fishing is but little practised elsewhere. Indeed, it can hardly be called fair fishing; and, as such, it is generally forbid by the proprietors of private waters, who seldom deny a sportsman a day's angling, under fair restrictions. This two-handed Snap-fishing for Jack and Pike is practised in the following manner:—take about forty or fifty yards of strong cord, sash, or jack line, and fasten each end to poles about seven or eight feet long; and on each pole fasten a large winch that will hold fifty yards of the strongest platted silk trolling-line; in the middle of the strong line (which is fastened to the poles) tie on a small brass or wooden pulley; then draw the trolling line from the winches, and pass it through the pulley; now, bait a snap-hook or hooks with a full-sized bait-fish, and fix it to the trolling-line, and all is ready to commence two-handed Snap-fishing. The parties managing the poles, proceed directly opposite each other, on the banks of rivers or other waters, and drop their baited hooks in places where they expect to find; and when they feel a bite, one strikes very smartly, and his companion then lowers or otherways manages his pole, so as to give him any or every assistance while killing and getting the Jack or Pike on shore. When the gorgehook is used in this way of fishing, it is then proper to have two pulleys fastened to the thick cord, near the centre of it, at about a yard apart; because, when one Angler feels a run, the other should immediately keep all still while the Fish pouches: this cannot be so well done when both lines pass through one pulley; and the Troller knows that if Jack or Pike are not well on the feed, they will throw or drop the bait from the least check or alarm; if there be only one pulley, then only one line should be used. In some places, the country people get a strong small rope or clothes line, and tie one or more snap-baited hooks to it, and take hold one at each end of the rope, and walk opposite each other, on the banks of small rivers and ponds, letting the baited hooks drag in the water, until they feel a bite; the one strikes and immediately drags the Jack on shore, the other person slacks the line he holds, while his companion is so doing.

Various other ways are practised for taking Jack and Pike, by night lines, trimmers, etc.; but such methods are justly reprobated by the true Angler who exercises his skill and art for amusement more than profit; therefore, I shall say but very little on this part of the subject. The trimmers mostly used in lakes, meers, broads, pools, and large ponds, are taken up from a boat; if the place be not too broad, you may get them with the drag hooks, or with a large stone, fastened to plenty of strong cord, being thrown over the trimmer line: these trimmers are made of strong thin hempen cord, with a hook tied to brass wire (but gimp is better) and wound on a large piece of flat cork, about five or six inches in diameter, with a groove to admit the line: the hook is baited with a Gudgeon, Roach, or some small Fish; you then draw as much line out as admits the bait to hang about a foot from the bottom. There is a small slit in the cork, that you pass the line in, to prevent it unwinding: as soon as the Jack or Pike seizes the bait, the line loosens, and runs from the groove of the cork free, and allows the Fish to retire to his haunt, and pouch at leisure.

TO TAKE JACK AND PIKE, WITH HOOK, BLADDER, OR BOTTLE.

Jack and Pike are also taken in lakes, and other large pieces of water, by baiting with a full-sized Dace, Gudgeon, or a Roach; nearly half a pound weight is best. Use strong snap-hooks, with two lengths of gimp, and two swivels, which must be fastened to about a yard of the stoutest platted silk trolling-line: then tie the line very secure to the neck of a large bladder, and launch it in the water with a brisk wind: if the Fish are on the feed, you will soon perceive the water agitated in the most violent manner; and, after an amusing and desperate struggle, the bladder will kill the heaviest Pike, provided your hooks and tackle are good. In Ramsey Meer, Huntingdonshire, there is an annual exhibition, called a bottle-race, and often much betting on the event of which bottle kills a Pike first: the baits and hooks are managed in the same manner as with a bladder; the bottle (a wine bottle) is used in place of a bladder; the line is tied round the neck. When several are so prepared, they are ranged in a row, and all launched at a given signal; and much amusement and delight is afforded the spectators, by the Jack and Pike dragging the bottles about, and often two come in contact. If the Fish feed well, which is generally the case, for this extensive piece of water abounds with Jack and very large Pike, some fasten their trimmer lines to large bricks, or heavy pieces of stone, or clods of earth, to prevent them being noticed, and throw them into the water.

SNARING, OR HALTERING, OF JACK AND PIKE.

In the Spring and Summer, Jack and Pike will frequently lie dozing near the surface of the water, especially in large ditches, connected with rivers and ponds, also among weeds; they are then taken in an unsportsmanlike manner, by making a running noose of wire gimp trolling-line, or treble-twisted gut fastened to a strong line and rod, or pole; the noose should be very carefully drawn over the Fish's head beyond the gills, then, with a strong jerk, he is securely caught; lift him out immediately. Fish may be taken, when found lying in a similar manner to that already described, by putting two or three strong hooks at the bottom of your line, and letting them sink under the Fish; then strike smartly, and you will generally be successful.

REMARKS ON THE NATURE, HAUNTS, HABITS, SHAPE, COLOUR, ETC. OF JACK AND PIKE

> Beware, ye flirting Gudgeons, Roaches fair,
> And all who breathe the lucid crystal of the lakes,
> Or lively sport, between the dashing wheels
> Of river mills; — beware; the Tyrant comes;
> Grim death awaits you in his gaping jaws,
> And lurks behind his hungry fangs.

SEE MCQUIN'S DESCRIPTIONS OF THREE HUNDRED ANIMALS.

Jack and Pike have a flattish head; the under jaw is something longer than the upper one; the mouth is extremely wide, the tongue very large, and studded with teeth, the lower jaw is set round with large crooked canine teeth; the expanse of mouth, jaws, and teeth, enables this merciless Fish to hold fast, and quickly destroy the victim that is so unfortunate as to come within its reach. The body of a Jack is long, and cased in very small hard scales, and, when they are in season, it is covered with a mucous or slimy substance; the back and upper part of the sides are of a greenish golden hue, and the belly of an indifferent white colour; the eyes are of a bright yellow, and sunk low in the sockets, but are so placed as to enable the Jack to look upwards, which should teach the Angler not to sink his bait too low in the water.

After Jack and Pike have fully recovered from spawning, they then have many beautiful spots on their bodies, of a bright white and yellowish colour; their tails and fins have also on them numerous dusky spots and waved lines. Jack and Pike, when on the feed, are as bold as they are voracious, attacking all kinds of Fish, except the Tench.

> Pike, fell tyrant of the liquid plain,
> With ravenous waste devours his fellow train;
> Yet, howsoe'er with raging famine pin'd,
> The Tench he spares, a medicinal kind;
> For when by wounds distress'd, or sore disease,
> He courts the salutary Fish for ease;
> Close to his scales the kind Physician glides,
> And sweats the healing balsam from his sides.
>
> — Pope.

When much distressed for food, they will seize the smaller of their own species, and also ducks, water-rats, mice, frogs, or any other small animal they can meet with: they will often seize a small Fish, which the Angler has hooked, while he is drawing it out of the water, leaping above the surface for that purpose. I have known many instances of their swallowing the leaden plummet that the Angler is taking his depth with; and once, while I was plumbing the depth (preparatory to fishing for Chub in the winter) with a folding plummet, having a No. 8 hook and a gut-line, a Jack of about two pounds immediately pouched my plummet; the hook, hanging over the side of this folding plummet, got sufficient hold of the Jack, that I held him, and soon killed and landed this hungry intruder.

Perch (the large ones especially) seem but little intimidated by the appearance of Jack or Pike, for they continue to swim about as before those tyrants appeared. The following singular circumstance occurred with my friend, Mr. R. Robinson, who laid a trimmer baited with a stone loach, which a Perch, of about half a pound weight, took and gorged; a Pike, then finding the Perch somewhat embarrassed, seized him, and attempted to pouch him; but the dorsal fin of the Perch stuck so fast across the throat of the Pike, that he could not extricate himself; by which means, Mr. R. secured both Perch and Pike. It is, however, different with other Fish, as they immediately swim or dart away with the greatest velocity, and the Eels suddenly sink and bury themselves in the mud, or lay close under thick and heavy beds of weeds.

It is generally supposed, that Jack will increase in weight something more than a pound in a year, for the first four or five years, and, during that time, continue to grow in length; but, after that period, they grow more in depth or breadth and thickness. Some writers on Natural History affirm that Pike will live two or three hundred years, and grow to the amazing size of a hundred

and fifty pounds, or more, and that they are so wonderfully prolific, as to produce more than a hundred and fifty thousand eggs in one roe. Of those circumstances, respecting the age, etc. of Jack and Pike, I must confess, I know but little; therefore shall say nothing more on the subject, leaving the curious to consult Natural History of fishes, etc. during unfavorable weather; but, instead thereof, will inform the Angler where he is likely to find both old and young, large and small Jack and Pike, so that he may avoid much loss of time and fruitless labour, when in search of them.

Jack and Pike are partial to quiet retired places where the water is rather shallow than deep, forming a bend or bay in rivers and large waters, and also removed from strong currents, especially if those bends or bays abound with their favorite weed, the pickerell, (on which they are said to feed,) also the candock or water lily, and the shore sides are shaded with tall sedgy sags. Among those sedges, Jack and Pike lay (especially during floods, heavy runs of water, and while the water is thick) a foot or two below the surface, with their noses just projecting from the sedges, looking up stream for what may come within their reach as food; therefore the Angler, when he trolls in thick heavy water, must try close in-shore.

Of course, this is pretty demotic, after the gentleman anglers of the previous centuries, and I think it's funny, how after deploring a method as unsporting, Salter goes on to give pretty precise instructions on just how not to do it. The grammar, too, is feebler than that to which the older writers have accustomed us; Salter invariably uses "lay" for "lie."

By his time, Salter says, "The London Angler has but seldom the pleasure of bringing home a dish of Trout caught in either the Thames or the Lea; for those rivers, however famous they may have been, at present contain very few; but those are very large and fat; some weighing more than ten pounds."

He goes on to point out that there are still many good trout streams within twenty miles of the metropolis, but they are all private property. "Yet here the Gentleman Angler is seldom refused a day's fair fishing." He then lists a number of them, from Carshalton to Uxbridge, and "at the latter place, the Angler may indulge himself in angling for Trout, by paying for board and lodging, at the Crown and Cushion or at the White Horse Inns."

The most killing way of angling for those large or old trout in the Thames and Lea, Salter says, he has found by long experience, is spinning a minnow, and he therefore gives "a very full and particular description of the method of fishing tackle and baiting hooks for so desirable a purpose."

After treating for a couple of pages the ways and means of fishing for

trout with live minnows, he passes to the previously mentioned "Devil,"
an artificial spinning bait for trout.

In treating on baits, to troll for Jack and Pike, in another part of this work,
some objections are made against using artificial baits; but, by no means do I
feel inclined to oppose the fictitious spinning Minnow in angling for Trout,
much less the Artificial Caterpillar or Devil, as they are generally called. This
artificial bait has nearly superseded every other of late years, and it is, most certainly, very attractive and killing, when used by the skillful and experienced
Angler for heavy Trout. These Devils, or Artificial Caterpillars, are made of
leather, silk, etc.; of various striped colours, and laced over with gold or brass,
and silver thread or wire; and the tail is the shape of a Fish's tail, made either
of silver or block tin. About this Devil bait are placed several small hooks, some
hanging loose, and others fastened to it. I have given an engraving of a Devil,
with seven hooks, which I consider the best way of placing hooks about it. To
fix those hooks, proceed as follows: take two hooks, size No. 10, tied to a short
piece of gut, and fasten them to the said Devil, so that they shall hang nearly
half way down its back, then two others of the same size, fixed so as to hang to
the bait's belly, reaching nearly to the tail; and now tie three hooks together,
the same size, and fix them to the Devil so that they may hang loose just below
the tail. There is a small brass staple, at the head of the bait, to which you
should fasten a very small box swivel, and to this swivel tie, neatly, a length of
choice single gut, and then fasten the single gut to a length of double twisted
gut by another box swivel, and loop the other end of it, to which you fix the
running line. (*See the Cut.*) – Note, the swivels are to enable you to spin the bait,
which so excites the old Trout, that they seem to lose their cunning, and rush
heedlessly to seize their prey.

You can spin a Devil to the greatest advantage from a bridge, or some other
eminence, especially when the wind is on your back. The top of your rod
should be somewhat lowered, and the bait kept in the middle of the stream or
current for some time, then let it drift further down the stream, 30 or 40 yards.
At the tail of a mill, whilst the wheel is turning round, is a very likely place for
Trout, both early and late; there drop in your bait, close to the apron of the
mill, and let it swim down some distance, and by playing it awhile, if any Trout
are on the feed, be assured they will take your bait; there is another and most
destructive way of fishing for Trout, called cross-fishing. (*See Trimmer Angling.*)

Note, the provincial Angler must not imagine that the London Angler is
disappointed of a dish of Trout for want of the necessary skill to take them:
neither should he too hastily jeer or challenge the Cockney sportsman, for the
fact is, that the greatest adepts, in the art of angling, are to be found among the
inhabitants of the metropolis. Although Trout are not so numerous near
London, as in the rivers northward or westward, yet there are several killed by
angling, every season, in the river Lea, weighing from three to more than ten
pounds each. Every other species of fresh-water Fish are found in the rivers
and waters within a few miles of the capital, and thousands are caught an-
nually, with the angle, from one ounce weight to Fish weighing more than
twenty pounds each. Here the most experienced and ingenious mechanics are
employed in furnishing the various tackle for the Angler's use. The tackle
shops also, for a few pence, supply him with different kinds of choice worms,

gentles, greaves, etc., for baits; and there are stage coaches going and coming every hour of the day, near several waters, frequented by hundreds who delight in angling; those facilities enable the London Angler to pursue his amusement of angling with very little trouble or expense, and with the best chance of improvement, from the number of his associates. Angling has ever been a favourite sport with the Londoners, or, at least, since the time the worthy and respected Father of Anglers, Isack Walton, wrote his admired work on Fish and Fishing; who, as a man, a writer, and an Angler, has left a name and character, that his fellow-citizens of London may well quote with pride and exultation. And I am highly pleased, and much gratified, to see that the Work on Fishing, of the venerable author, has been, of late years, republished, enriched, illustrated, and embellished in a manner worthy the subject, and equally creditable to the taste of the publisher, and the talent of the artist, displayed in the recent edition of Walton's "Complete Angler," sent forth to the public, by several spirited booksellers of the metropolis.

The last section of *The Angler's Guide* is devoted to fly fishing, and it states the case pretty clearly, as of about the midway point between Bowlker and Ronalds:

ARTIFICIAL-FLY FISHING, AND FLY-MAKING FOR TROUT, SALMON, &C.

"Silent along the mazy margin stray,
And with the fur-wrought fly delude the prey."

Fishing with an artificial fly is, certainly, a very pleasant and gentlemanly way of angling, and is attended with much less labour and trouble than bottom-fishing. The Fly-fisherman has but little to carry, either in bulk or weight; nor has he the dirty work of digging clay, making ground-baits, &c. &c. He may travel for miles, with a book of flies in his pocket, and a light rod in his hand, and cast in his bait, as he roves on the banks of a river, without soiling his fingers; it is, therefore, preferred by many to every other way of angling. Yet fly-fishing is not without its disadvantages, for there are many kinds of Fish that will not take a fly; whereas, all the different species which the fresh waters produce, will take a bait at bottom, at some season of the year; and it is also worthy of notice, that the Angler who fishes at bottom has many months and days in the year when the Fish will so feed; consequently he has frequent opportunities of enjoying his amusement, when the Fly-fisherman is entirely deprived of the chance of sport by very cold or wet weather, the Winter season, &c. Many good Jack and Pike are taken at Christmas; but, at that season of the year, neither Trout nor Chub are likely to rise for a fly, however skillfully made or thrown. Fly-fishing certainly partakes more of science than bottom-fishing, and, of course, requires much time, study, and practice, before the Angler can become anything like an adept at making or casting a fly; indeed, artificial-fly making is somewhat difficult to learn, but more difficult to describe. The young Angler would gain much more information on the subject, by attending a Fly-fisherman, while he is casting or making an artificial-fly; if he cannot avail himself of such knowledge, he must persevere, and strictly follow the directions I shall offer to his notice, in both making and casting a fly. There are many excellent Fly-fishermen who never trouble themselves to make a fly, yet kill Trout, in every Trout stream they fish, with flies bought at the London tackle-shops, where the Angler may get a fly made to any pattern, colour, or shape, he chooses; in truth, flies are now made so well at those shops, that it is not worth the Angler's trouble to make them. — Note. The artificial flies, sold at the fishing-tackle shops, are principally made from the directions given by Bowlker, of Shrewsbury; and, perhaps, have been but little improved during the last century: but, among the modern writers on Fly-fishing, the Angler may consult *Captain Williamson's Angler's Vade Mecum*, and *Bainbridge's Fly-Fisher's Guide*, probably, with some advantage.

I should, certainly, recommend the young Fly-fisherman, in the first instance, to purchase his artificial flies; but after some experience in the art, to make his own; and, to enable him to do so properly, I shall minutely describe the method of making them, and the materials of which they should respectively be formed, as will enable him, at all times, to supply himself, should he prefer making them to buying them at the tackle-shops; the Angler will then be enabled to imitate any fly that may be a killing one, where they are not to be purchased; this sometimes occurs when far from home. In purchasing artificial flies, it would be proper to apply for them at some respectable fishing-tackle-shop, that the novice may feel assured he will receive those for which he asks. The following will be proper to select: red and black palmers, red and black hackles, grouse-red and black ant-flies, the yellow may-fly or green-drake, stone-fly, small black gnat-flies, the red-spinner, and white-moth. Having purchased the above assortment of flies, the Angler should make himself well acquainted with their several forms, the number of wings, and every other particular, that he may be able to know every difference between the several kinds, thereby guarding against having flies imposed on him of a species different to what he may think proper to order. The flies above enumerated are all of established credit; their respective merits, the way and materials of which they are made, will be found under their different names. In many places, certain flies are preferred; the bean or thistle-fly has been considered a secret in some part of Wales, and much valued. There is a fly used very much at Watford, in Herts, called Harding's-fly, or the Coachman's; the merits of such flies experience will teach how to appreciate. — Note: make it an invariable rule to try a red or black palmer, first in the morning and last in the evening, when whipping for Trout, the other part of the day, winged flies. This is following nature, as Fish seek for food by instinct, expecting winged insects in the day time, and the palmer or caterpillar in the cool and damp of the mornings and evenings.

CONCISE DIRECTIONS FOR MAKING AN ARTIFICIAL FLY.

Take some fine silk, of the proper colour, and wax it well with bees' wax; then hold the bend of the hook between the forefinger and thumb of the left hand, and with the right give the silk two or three turns round the shank, and fasten it; then take a small feather, of the colour you intend the fly should be, strip off some of the fibres towards the quill, and leave a sufficient quantity for the wings, holding the point of the feather between your finger and thumb;

turn back most of the remaining fibres, and laying the point end of the feather upon the hook, give a few more laps round it with your silk, and fasten; then twirl the feather round the hook till all the fibres are wrapped upon it; which done, fasten and cut off the two ends of the feather; then, with dubbing of the proper colour twisted round the remaining silk, warp from the wings towards the bend of the hook, till the fly is the size required. Before the young artist tries his skill at dressing or making a fly, (suppose a green-drake,) he should carefully take an artificial one to pieces, and observe how it is formed.

Thus, having learnt how to apply his materials to the hook, the knowledge how to make the may-flies is first requisite to be understood; for these flies are of so much value to the Angler, that every one who wishes to excel in Fly-fishing, should learn how to make them as soon as possible. There are several persons in London who manufacture artificial flies for sale; and among those professed fly-makers, some, for a gratuity, will instruct the Angler in the whole art and mystery of fly-making. The manufacture of the green-drake, grey-drake, and stone-fly, in particular, should be well understood, as it is sometimes difficult to procure, or preserve the natural ones; and, moreover, a proficiency in the art of making these will enable any person to make a fly to any pattern, an art highly necessary, for it will often happen that Trout will refuse every fly you may have with you; and the only resource then is, to sit down and make one resembling, as much as possible, those which you may find flying about the spot.

> When artful flies the Angler would prepare,
> This task of all deserves his utmost care:
> Nor verse nor prose can ever teach him well
> What masters only know, and practice tell;
> Yet thus at large I venture to support,
> Nature best followed best secures the sport:
> Of flies the kinds; their seasons, and the breed,
> Their shapes, their hue, with nice observance heed:
> Which most the Trout admires, and where obtain'd,
> Experience will teach, or perchance some friend.

Thus sang Moses Brown, an old Piscator.

Unless I'm mistaken, we just heard a small but significant toot on the trumpet of angling history — I believe that's the first mention in print of the Coachman, which has of course since become the most widely used of all trout flies. Most of the books I've read attribute the Coachman's naming to Bosworth, Queen Victoria's coachman. Of course, when Salter first wrote the sentence in the foregoing, where the name is first used, Victoria was not only not yet Queen — she came to the throne in 1837 — she was not yet even born.

But the operative phrase, of all in the foregoing, is "This is following nature," and its corollary in the Moses Browne verse:

"Nature best followed best secures the sport."

(Why Salter always drops the final "e" in Moses Browne's name I don't know. But the old Piscator he means is the Reverend first editor of Walton after his lifetime, whose second edition, of 1759, we've already looked at. By the way, *he* calls it the seventh edition, instead of the second, which of course it is, since there were five in Walton's lifetime. So punctilious about everything, and so anxious to emphasize the authenticity of everything concerning his editions of Walton, it must have killed him to have Sir John Hawkins come along with *his* edition of Walton the next year, in which he ignored Moses Browne completely.)

At all events, the stage is now set for Ronalds. Although the aim of imitating nature was increasingly stressed, as noted here in the angling writings, confusion was confounded and compounded by the totally unsystematized hodgepodge of vernacular names for flies. Bowlker tried to clear this up, with his wholesale throwing out of obsolete and redundant dressings that had accumulated like barnacles on the main body of fly-fishing literature, but the real housecleaning of the Augean stables of fishing-fly nomenclature had to wait for Alfred Ronalds in 1836.

It's impossible to overstress the importance of Ronalds. Certainly he is the most significant figure in fly fishing after Cotton, whom he followed by a hundred and sixty years. And while *The Compleat Angler* was of course unique in its impact on the literary world, and will undoubtedly always remain so, it is safe to say that no single book ever had the revolutionary effect on the angling world—that is, the actual practice of angling, as opposed to the recording of its annals—of *The Fly-fisher's Entomology* in 1836.

Of course he had his forerunners. "There were great generals before Agamemnon." Two of them were mentioned by Salter in the last passage quoted, Capt. T. Williamson's *Angler's Vade Mecum* (1822) and George Cole Bainbridge's *Fly-fisher's Guide* (1816). And as Robb has pointed out, Ronalds was to a degree anticipated by George Scotcher's (c.1800), *The Fly-fisher's Legacy* and W. Carroll's *The Angler's Vade-mecum* (1818). And by the modesty of his own approach, in prefacing his fifth edition, you might have supposed that he was the least of the lot. (I have to borrow from Robb for this, because my Ronalds is the fifth edition, of 1856):

The Author of this little work entreats that it may be considered and judged as the labour, or rather the amusement, of an amateur; whose chief object has been to facilitate to the Tyro in the art, the making and choice of artificial flies, on a plan of elucidation derived from personal experience. Having himself sorely felt the inadequacy of mere verbal instructions to enable him to imitate the natural fly correctly, or even approximately, and the little utility of graphical illustrations unaccompanied by the principal requisite, *viz.* colour, he has been induced to paint both the natural and the artificial fly from nature, to etch them with his own hand, and to colour, or superintend the colouring of each particular impression. He therefore presumes to hope that he has succeeded in giving a useful collection of the leading flies for every month in the season, and that anyone, who may be led by it to a choice of flies from the stock of the manufacturer, or to the construction of his own, will not have cause to repent of having consulted the catalogue, chiefly composing the Fourth Chapter.

Never has so little presumption preceded such solid accomplishment. Ronalds drew 47 flies, coincidentally the same number as Bowlker's final list, but with one for the natural and another for the artificial, the number of drawings was doubled to 94. But more important than the drawings themselves, he did what hadn't been done before, he threw a bridge, so to speak, across between the practice of angling and the science of entomology. Without abandoning the vernacular names, he linked them for the first time with their technical or scientific names. True, he didn't accomplish this latter all in one fell swoop, and it wasn't until his fifth edition, in 1856—a span of twenty years—that he completed the process. But by correlating the angler's names with the scientific identifications, which had been around for a hundred years since Linnaeus but nobody had bothered to notice, he gave fly fishing for the first time a systematic and scientific basis of distinguishing one fly from another.

As a discovery, it was about as basic, and as simple, as the realization that the world is round instead of flat. Of course, it could conceivably be argued that since the sport of fly fishing and the science of entomology co-existed, somebody sometime would have thought of forging the connecting link between the two. But the point is that before Ronalds nobody did.

And fortunately Ronalds had the wit and the sense to play up the familiar and recognizable vernacular names, in tagging them with their counterparts in scientific terms. That afforded the bridge between the two worlds, without which the passage couldn't have been found.

While Ronalds's work has since been succeeded by considerable extension and amplification and a great deal of specialization, and in many ways corrected, still it can be maintained that in a sense it has never really been superseded. He has had a number of worthy successors, but while he has been supplemented by all of them he has been supplanted by none.

One of them, J. R. Harris, author of *An Angler's Entomology* (1954 although undated), which enjoys an advantage of color photography undreamed of in Ronalds's day, sums up the debt as well as anyone:

Up to the publication of Ronalds's *Flyfisherman's Entomology* in 1836 anglers were interested only in the superficial characteristics of flies—that is, in their general colour, size and habits. Before the appearance of Ronalds's great work, fishing authors used vernacular names only and gave, at the most, only superficial descriptions of the species about which they were writing. Their descriptions were generally combined with, or consisted merely of, descriptions of the artificial imitations, and the natural species was presumably recognized from the colour resemblance which it bore to its artificial counterpart. But Ronalds's book possessed the great advantage that the technical name was always subservient to the vernacular name. In recent books, and particularly in recent articles appearing in various periodicals, there is a tendency to overemphasize the importance of the technical name.

Ronalds had one other great advantage. In extension of that note of diffidence sounded in his preface, he didn't take a revolutionary stance and announce any violent rupture with the past. In advising the choice of flies, he echoed the advice of his elders, even his forefathers, in angling; he reiterated that the angler "would often do well to begin fishing with a Palmer as a stretcher, and the fly which *seems* most suitable for the day as a dropper . . . not changing these until he can discover what fly the fish are actually rising at. The Palmer is never totally out of season, and is a *good fat bait*. It should never be forgotten, that, let the state of the weather or the water (in respect of clearness) be what it may, success in fly-fishing very much depends upon showing the fish a good imitation, both in colour and size, of that insect which he has recently taken: an exact resemblance of the shape does not seem to be quite so essential a requisite as that of colour, since the former varies, according to the position of the insect either in or upon the water; but a small fly is usually employed when the water is fine, because the fish is then better enabled to detect an imitation, and because the small fly is more easily imitated. The resemblance of each particular colour, etc., is not required to be so exact as in the case of a large fly."

Sound, sane and soothingly sensible talk. Nothing there to "scare the horses," so to speak, and even the conservative British were more than ready to take the way that Ronalds pointed with such sweet reason.

8.

Scrope and Upstream with Stewart

Partner, it occurs to me, somewhat belatedly I'm afraid, that I'm not getting us very far very fast, on this printed-fishing trip that I inveigled you into.

I know I never said we'd cover all of angling literature, but I'm sure I led you to think we'd at least get from Hither to Yon. I may not have undertaken to exhaust every letter of the alphabet, but I certainly raised every expectation of getting farther than from say A to halfway through B.

Still, I wonder. Awhile back I said we had twelve points to keep in sight, like landmarks, or milestones, for our journey. I likened them to rocks that determined the course of the stream we're following.

Well, with Ronalds, we've just passed the fourth. Stewart coming up. And there are seven more, at various turns, beyond him. Mixed feelings about the practicability of this trip, and the competence of your self-engaged guide, are in order at this point.

Surely we both realize that the essence of a trip is that there be some limit to its duration, or else it becomes a residence. I know my own time isn't totally unlimited, and for feasibility as well as politeness, I certainly ought to assume that yours is even less so. But I'm torn, in the oldest

115

tug-of-war known to the soul of man, between a vague sense of duty and a very specific appetite for pleasure. Pretty obviously, one of them will have to yield to the other.

So here's what I think we ought to do from now on. I think we ought to spend less of our time on these "duty calls," the places where we're expected to put in an appearance, because it seems that invariably they turn out to be right next door to others where, unless I've misjudged you, we'd both be likely to have a great deal more fun.

To get back to something Sparse Grey Hackle said, in one of those countless introductions he's done for other people's fishing books—I forget which one because he's done so many, but this one was fairly recent—anyway, he had a phrase, about "this good talk, these engaging stories" as being the ingredient of fishing books that the dedicated angler can never get enough of—these and not a lot of "how-to" stuff. It may have been—yes, it was the recent Crown Sportsmen's Classics reprint of Howard Walden's *Upstream and Down* and *Big Stony,* and here's the passage:

> Only books like these survive as pinnacles of angling literature, timeless and unchanging, because they deal with those fundamentals of angling that are also timeless and unchanging—the fisherman and the fish. Books that deal with tackle and tactics and the endless, trivial detail of "how-to-do-it" proliferate like weeds and like weeds perish. They become out of date and are superseded as greenheart is displaced by bamboo and bamboo by glass fibers; as hair gives way to silk and silk to plastic filaments; as silkworm gut is superseded by nylon monofilament; and as the native brook trout yields his haunts to the European brown.

There's the veritable *cri de coeur* that distinguishes real angling literature from the ephemeral "literature" of a sales and promotional kind that you carry away by the bagfull from the vacation and outdoor shows.

Now if we'll simply keep that distinction clearly in mind, and apply it resolutely, I'll bet you anything we'll wind up playing, if not more, then at least better fish. All we have to do is decide to leave a lot to the manuals and the monthlies and just not worry about it.

For instance, here we are back in stride again, on our way to Stewart, exactly as planned, and

. . . *well, what do you know? here's Scrope.* (Pronounced of course as if it were spelled with two "o's" instead of one, but don't ask me why, except that as so often with English names it figures, like saying *Hume* for Home, and *Froom* for Frome, etc., etc. There was a title—Lord Scrope—for the eldest son in each generation, but our Scrope, William, never made it, and the line ended with him.)

To leave out Scrope, or even to slight him, in any book that purports to be about fishing, is like passing up the roast beef when you're at Simpsons in the Strand. Next to Walton himself, there's no more engagingly discursive and allusive angling writer in the language. For the feel of fishing, the sense of it, I almost said the taste of it, I know of no other to place him beside. Put me ashore on the desert island and along with *The Compleat Angler* I'll beg for only one other book and that's *Days and Nights of Salmon Fishing in the Tweed* (1843).

In fact, I wish we could cram it all in, right here. To quote an isolated passage of Scrope is to eat one peanut—it simply isn't possible. Oh, I know, there are bits and snippets out of Scrope in almost every angling anthology I've ever seen, but like a wine that doesn't ship, they lose something the minute they're taken out of context. The only way to get the inimitable flavor of Scrope is to take a whole hunk, that you can do almost at random, and count on its being so highly habit-forming that he who reads will want to rush right out and find the rest.

As so often happens with the great books, it has no companion volume in its field. Scrope wrote only one other, *The Art of Deer Stalking*, at which he was evidently just as accomplished as he was in the art of salmon fishing. Born in 1772, he succeeded his father, the Rev. Richard Scrope, in the possession—at age fifteen—of Castle Comb in Wiltshire, which was a part of the old Scrope estates. In 1852, his death ended the male line of the "ancient and once famous house of the Lord Scropes of Bolton." A friend of Sir Walter Scott's, he was actually more active as a painter than as a writer, and according to Sir Herbert Maxwell, who edited *The Sportsman's Library* in which both of Scrope's books were included, Scott made frequent mention of him in his journals and, in one instance, deemed him "one of the best amateur painters I ever saw—Sir George Beaumont scarcely excepted." Pointing out that it was unprecedented to include a second work by the same author in the limited list of *The Sportsman's Library* when so many other writers of the past, without whom it could hardly be considered thoroughly representative, still awaited inclusion, Sir Herbert wrote "It was hard to put them aside, yet Scrope has qualities which distinguish him from almost all other writers on sport." Scrope did the landscapes for his book on the

Tweed, which was also embellished by lithographs and wood engravings of paintings by five of the leading artists of the time, and when Dean Sage forty-five years later sought to attain the ultimate with the physical format of his book on the Restigouche, his avowed intention was to emulate Scrope's.

A random opening of my copy, possibly conditioned by frequency of use, brings us to Chapter III.

HOSTESS. Say what beast, thou knave thou.
FALSTAFF. What beast! Why, an otter.
HOSTESS. An otter, Sir John! Why an otter?
FALSTAFF. Why, she's neither fish nor flesh. A man knows not where to have her.

Before I enter upon the practical part of salmon fishing, I will just say a few words about my natural tendency to the sport, to the end that it may be evident that my maxims are not drawn from books, but originate in my own experience.

I declare, then, that I, Harry Otter, am by nature a person of considerable aquatic propensities, having been born under the sign of Aquarius, or Pisces,—it matters not which. My delight in water, however, has its limits, and extends only to external applications: the placid amusement of wading in a salmon river is very much to my taste—quite captivating. Showers, and even storms, if not of too long a continuance, are exceedingly refreshing to my person; but I must in candour admit that the decisive action of a water-spout may not possibly be so gratifying—*ne quid nimis.* Macintosh's invention I consider as wholly uncalled for, accounting it, as I do, an unpardonable intrusion to place a solution of Indian-rubber between the human body and a refreshing element. It is like taking a shower-bath under shelter of an umbrella.

Thus far I can extend; but desire me to drink water by itself, and I am your very humble servant. Had I been at a symposium of brandy and the said vapid element with that worthy Magnus Troil, he should not have drunk all the brandy himself, and put me off with the water, as he is recorded to have done to his very simple friend. I beg to say that I am not one of those two thousand patients who have been relieved by a *water cure,* administered by James Wilson, Esq., physician to his Serene Highness the Prince of Nassau, as advertised. Internally, in its pure state, I totally discard it. But I like the society of fish; and as they cannot with any convenience to themselves visit me on dry land, it becomes me in point of courtesy to pay my respects to them in their own element.

Next to wading in water, comes, I think, the pastime of trudging over bogs and fens—ground intimately allied to it, and which Colonel Hawker has made quite classical. This is a sort of debateable land, and the natural inhabitants of it reject you with most unequivocal signs of disapprobation. The redshank, the peewit, the curlew, and all their allies, scream and dart around you, inhospitable as they are, and tell you, as plainly as bills can speak, to sheer off, and not invade their premises. But we are a sort of Paul Pry, and love to persist responding now and then with our double barrel, which we more especially direct towards the ruff, snipe, wild duck, and teal—birds whose merit we particularly appreciate. Thus we are, as may be seen, of an amphibious nature, and respond to the fat knight's description, when he compared Hostess Quickly to our namesake. That this predilection for humidity is with me an instinct, may be seen from the following brief notice of my infant propensities.

When I was an urchin I stole off, and wandered up the stream that came winding through the verdant meadows of my native valley, till I arrived at the foot of the Castle Hill; following the little path that dived into a thicket, and wound round its base near the margin of the river: thence, amongst irregular clumps of thorn bushes, holly trees, and other wild wood, stopping a while to gather the cowslips and white violets that dappled the sunny slopes, I pursued my way through a tangled thicket, whose branches overhung the stream. I remember even now that the sunbeam glittered on the leaves, struck through the masses here and there, and pierced to the surface of the water, which shone in spots through the gloom like the fragments of a broken mirror: these lucid touches caught my childish fancy; but my favourite spot was not yet attained. Not until I had rounded the rib of the promontory on which stood the grey castle, and came to another face of it, did I obtain the object of my ramble. At this turn of the stream I found myself in a small lonely meadow sprinkled with cowslips, upon which opened two wooded valleys, each watered by a small stream, which at their junction washed out a deep hole; and at the foot of the hole a small gravel heap was thrown up, upon which grew the yellow iris, and some other vegetation. In Lilliput it would have been termed an island: so in truth it was. I know not how it happened,—unless, indeed, that I was strictly enjoined not to go near the water—but I had a decided propensity to establish my little person on this insular spot. For some time I was either very good, or very much afraid—it matters not which,—and the achievement was dubious. At length the demon of temptation appeared in the form of a dragon-fly, which, glancing from some branches that extended across the stream a little above, danced up and down in the air in all its gaudy trim, and at length settled on an iris, in this enchanted island. I stood enraptured on the bank with my arms outstretched, and my longing eyes fixed upon the beauty. It was irresistible—I could hold out no longer. So mustering up my naughty courage, and letting myself gently down the bank, I paddled through a little shallow water, till I actually set foot safely on the desired spot. Here I found that my love for the *Libellula* was not mutual; or, if it was, I may say,

"Love, free as air, at sight of human ties,
Spreads its light wings, and in a moment flies."

Even so did the dragon-fly; he and my hopes vanished at once. Nevertheless I showed a decided taste for an insular life, and sat down watching the trout rise on all sides, as happy as a king; and I might have remained there to this day, had not that killjoy Martha, who was blest with the care of me, and from whom I had escaped in the morning, come upon my trail. Infuriated she was (for the whole Xantippe possessed her). She sallied forth like another Ceres in quest of her lost child. Half frightened, half pleased, I could see her toiling up the hill. "Master Harry! Master Harry!" resounded shrilly through the woods and valleys; even now methinks her voice rings in my ears. In vain—

"Nor at the lawn, nor at the wood, was he."

But when at length she returned, "alla solinga valle," I stood confessed within the range of her animated optics. She declared her sentiments without reserve in very fluent language. I was an *obstropolous* brat; a perfect *damon* (demon), as fond of dabbling in water as a *sallymander*. I should catch it when she got hold of me, that I should. This being intelligibly explained, I thought I would delay that period as long as possible. To all this eloquence, therefore, answer made I none; but I believe I looked and felt rather oddly. At length, seeing her amble to and fro upon the banks, and perceiving that she had the hydrophobia strong upon her, I told her if she wanted me she must come and fetch me, as I was forbidden to go into the water. "Hang your imperance, I says, Master Harry, but I'll find one as shall fetch you in a twinkling!" So saying, the eloquent Martha suited the action to the word, and ran round the turn of the river, where it seems she knew the keeper was fishing, who, I believe in village phrase, "kept company with her." Down comes John, a good-natured fellow; tickles me with the point of his fishing rod in gamesome mood; makes two or three casts with his fly at me; and at length wades to me, and places me on the mainland at the gentle Martha's side. Peace was made, but without promise for the future.

Henceforth, when I could escape control, I divided my time between the water and the meadows: in warm weather the water, in cold the land possessed me. Then I began to tamper with the minnows; and, growing more ambitious, after a sleepless night full of high contrivance, I betook me at early dawn to a wood near the house, where I selected some of the straightest hazel sticks I could find, which I tied together and christened a fishing rod: a rude and uncouth weapon it was. I next sought out Phyllis, a favourite cow so called in order to have a pluck at her tail to make a line with. But Phyllis was coy, and withheld her consent to spoliation; for when I got hold of her posterior honours, she galloped off, dragging me along, tail in hand, till she left me deposited in a water-course amongst the frogs. The dairy-maid, I think, would have overcome this difficulty for me, had I not discovered that horse-hair, and not cow's tail, was the proper material for fishing lines; so the coachman, who was much my friend, plucked Champion and Dumplin, at my request, and gave me as much hair (black enough to be sure) as would make a dozen lines. For three whole days did I twist and weave like the Fates, and for three whole nights did I dream of my work. Some rusty hooks I had originally in my possession, which I found in an old fishing book belonging to my ancestors. In fact, I did not put the hook to the rod and line, but my rod and line to the hook. I next proceeded to the pigeon-house, and picking some coarse feathers, made what I alone in the wide world would have thought it becoming to have called a fly; but call it so I did, in spite of contradictory evidence. Thus equipped, I proceeded to try my skill; but exert myself as I would, the line had domestic qualities, and was resolved to stay at home. I never could get it fairly away from the hazel sticks; therefore it was that I hooked no fish. But I hooked myself three times: once in the knee-strings of my shorts, once in the nostril, and again in the lobe of the ear. At length, after sundry days of fruitless effort, like an infant Belial, I attempted that by guile which I could not do by force; and dropping the fly with my hand under a steep bank of the stream, I walked up and down trailing it along: after about a week's perseverance, I actually caught a trout. Shade of Izaak Walton, what a triumph was there! That day I could not eat, — that night I slept not. Even now I recollect the spot where that generous fish devoted himself.

As I grew up I became gradually more expert, and at length saved money sufficient to buy a real fishing rod, line, reel and all, quite complete. Down it came from London resplendent with varnish, and many cunning feats did I perform with it. About this time I learned to shoot; not that I was strong enough to hold a gun, but that the keeper put the said implement to his shoulder, when I took aim at larks and sparrows, and those sort of things, and pulled the trigger. So I waxed in years and wisdom. All the time I could steal from my lessons (for I was not quite a Pawnee) I spent in this edifying manner; at length I was fully initiated in all the mysteries of sporting by a relation, himself the prince of sportsmen, who took a fancy to me. The reason was as follows: —

In the depth of winter, the ground being smothered with snow, and the blast bitter, I followed him out a wild-fowl shooting. I was devoid of hat, an article that I looked upon as superfluous, and that I always lost or mislaid as soon as it was given me. Equipped I was in white cotton stockings; and my shoes, which were of the thinnest, I had tied to my feet with a string which passed over the instep. I could not put them up at heel with any comfort, because I had large chilblains there, which were broke. At length, after creeping a space on my gloveless hands and knees in the snow, and under cover of some sedge and willow bushes, up flew some wild ducks before my patron. "Quack, quack!" — down came one to his shot, and fell with a splash into the river. In I plunged after him like a Newfoundland dog: you might have heard the flounce in a still day at Chippenham, about six miles off. The duck not being dead, made a swim and a dive of it. Long and dubious was the chase; but in the end I descried his bill amongst the sedges, where he had poked it up to take a little breath. Making a dexterous snatch, I seized him underneath by the legs — Chinese fashion, with the exception of the pumpkin — and drew him loud quacking to the bank. When landed I squeezed my clothes a little, according to order; but I do not believe that I benefited my chilblains.

At a rather more advanced period of my life I used to make long fishing excursions, generally with prosperous, but occasionally with disastrous results. I remember well, when a pair of bait-hooks was to me a valuable concern, I hooked two large black-looking trouts in a deep pool at the same time. As I had to pull them several feet upwards against the pressure of the stream, my line gave way, and left me proprietor of a small fragment only. For some time I looked alternately at my widowed rod and my departed fish; which last were coursing it round and round the pool, pulling in opposite directions, like coupled dogs of dissenting opinions: *durum — sed levius fit patientiâ.* So I sat down with somewhat of a rueful countenance, and began to spin with my fingers some horse-hair which I had pulled that morning, at the risk of my life, from the grey colt's tail. This being done in my own peculiar manner, and my only remaining hook being tied on with one of the aforesaid hairs, I continued to follow my sport down the stream for about half a mile. After the lapse of a considerable time, I had occasion to cross bare-legged from one bank to the other. In my transit through the current, I found something like a sharp instrument cutting the calves of my legs. I scampered ashore, under the impression that I was trailing after me some sharp-toothed monster, perhaps a lamper eel; when, upon passing down my hand to ascertain the fact, I found to my great astonishment and delight that I was once more in possession of my lost line, hooks, fish, and all. The fish had fairly drowned each other, and, by a curious coincidence, were passively passing in the current at the time my legs stemmed it.

Originally I had what in Scotland is called a *poke* or bag to carry my trouts in. This being rather of a coarse appearance, I panted after a basket. One of my schoolfellows had exactly the thing; and I bargained for it by giving in return all my personal right in perpetuity to two young hawks. Proud of my acquisition, I set out with no small share of vanity, carrying my basket through the whole length of a neighbouring village, which was considerably out of the way. When I arrived at the happy spot where my sport lay, I was successful as usual. At length the declining sun admonished me of some ten miles betwixt me and home; so I resolved only to take a few casts in a dark and deep pool which was close at hand, and then to bend my course homeward. There I hooked a fine fish, which I was obliged to play for some time, and then, after he was fairly tired, to lift out with my hands, not having yet arrived at the dignity of a landing net. In stooping low to perform this process, the lid of my new pet basket, which from want of experience I had omitted to fasten, flew open, and two or three of my last-killed fish dropped into the deep water immediately before me. In suddenly reaching forward to secure these, round came my basket, fish and all, over my head, and fairly capsized me. With some difficulty, and even risk of drowning, I got my head above water, and my hand on the crown of a sharp rock. There I stood, streaming and disconsolate, casting a wistful look at the late bright inmates of my basket, which were tilting down the weeds through the gullet into a tremendous pool, vulgarly called Hell's Cauldron. Into that same pool with the ominous name had I myself very nearly passed, and thus had followed my hat, which was coursing about in the eddy or wheel of this fearful depth. Thus vanished before my eyes my whole day's sport, for dead fish immediately sink; and it was not without some skilful fishing up that my hat and I renewed our acquaintance. I have before observed that when I was quite an urchin I never wore a hat, or any covering over my hair; but as I grew older I thought it decorous to follow the fashion.

At another time, whilst still a *puer,* and only possessed of one single bait-hook, to my utter confusion I found that solitary hook had been swallowed by a duck, which a mass of sedges under the bank had concealed from my view. There we were, Mrs. Duck and I, dashing, swashing, and swattering down the stream; the duck all the time declaring his sentiments by the utterance of a fearful noise, and I endeavouring by every means in my power to prevent my only hook from being ravished from me by my feathered opponent. In the meantime a group of lasses, who were washing clothes at the river side, and were friendly to the bird, set upon me, first with their tongues, of the use of which they seemed to be in full possession, and latterly with their pails and watering pans; in consequence of which I was compelled to snap my line, and turn upon my fair tormentors. But let no boy of fourteen ever try to face a batch of lasses. In fine, I was terribly mauled, and did not feel my ears at all comfortable in their externals for a considerable time afterwards.

But enough of these idle anecdotes. The reader will now understand that I, Harry Otter, was an idle scamp. If he chooses to keep company with me in my rambles, he will, nevertheless, find no very particular harm in me, and I on my part shall be delighted to hold good fellowship with an indulgent brother of the craft.

CHAPTER IV

> "I in these flowery meads would be;
> These crystal streams shall solace me."

Much has been said by various humane persons about the cruelty of fishing; but setting aside that, according to the authority of the eminent author of *Salmonia,* and of Dr. Gillespie also, who, by-the-by, is professor of humanity at St. Andrews, fish seldom feel any pain from the hook. Let us see how the case stands. I take a little wool and feather, and, tying it in a particular manner upon a hook, make an imitation of a fly; then I throw it across the river, and let it sweep round the stream with a lively motion. This I have an undoubted right to do, for the river belongs to me or my friend; but mark what follows. Up starts a monster fish with his murderous jaws, and makes a dash at my little Andromeda. Thus he is the aggressor, not I; his intention is evidently to commit murder. He is caught in the act of putting that intention into execution. Having wantonly intruded himself on my hook, which I contend he had no right to do, he darts about in various directions, evidently surprised to find that the fly, which he hoped to make an easy conquest of, is much stronger than himself. I naturally attempt to regain this fly, unjustly withheld from me. The fish gets tired and weak in his lawless endeavours to deprive me of it. I take advantage of his weakness, I own, and drag him, somewhat loth, to the shore, where one rap at the back of the head ends him in an instant. If he is a trout, I find his stomach distended with flies. That beautiful one called the May-fly, who is by nature almost ephemeral, who rises up from the bottom of the shallows, spreads its light wings, and flits in the sunbeam in enjoyment of its new existence, no sooner descends to the surface of the water to deposit its eggs, than the unfeeling fish at one fell spring numbers him prematurely with the dead. You see, then, what a wretch a fish is; no ogre is more bloodthirsty, for he will devour his nephews, nieces, and even his own children, when he can catch them; and I take some credit for having shown him up. Talk of a wolf, indeed, a lion, or a tiger! Why these are all mild and saintly in comparison with a fish. When did any one hear of Messrs. Wolf, Lion, and Co. eating up their grandchildren? What a bitter fright must the smaller fry live in! They crowd to the shallows, lie hid among the weeds, and dare not say the river is their own. I relieve them of their apprehensions, and thus become popular with the small shoals.

When we see a fish quivering upon dry land, he looks so helpless without arms or legs, and so demure in expression, adding hypocrisy to his other sins, that we naturally pity him; then kill and eat him with Harvey sauce, perhaps. Our pity is misplaced,—the fish is not. There is an immense trout in Loch Awe in Scotland, which is so voracious, and swallows his own species with such avidity, that he has obtained the name of *Salmo ferox.* I pull about this unnatural monster till he is tired, land him, and give him the *coup de grace.* Is this cruel? Cruelty "should be made of sterner stuff." There is a certain spurious sort of humanity going about that I cannot understand. Thus I know a lady who will not eat game, because, she says, shooting is a cruel amusement; but she is very much addicted to fowls, and all domestic poultry, feeding them one day, and eating them up the next, with treacherous alacrity and amiable perseverance. It would be more candid in her, therefore, to say to us sportsmen, like the fox in the fable,—

"Go, but be moderate in your food;
A pheasant too might do me good."

"I once saw," says the learned and accomplished Dr. Gillespie, "one of these all-devouring fish in a curious predicament. In fishing, or rather strolling, within these few years, with a rod in one hand and a book in the other, so as to alternate reading and fishing, as the clouds came and went, I observed a great many June-flies, at which the fish were occasionally rising, and which at the same time were picked up by the swallows, as they skimmed over the surface of the still water. It so happened that a trout from beneath, and a swallow from above, had fixed their affections upon the same yellow-winged and tempting fly. Down came the swallow, and up came the open mouth of the fish; into which, in pursuit of his prey, the swallow pitched his head. The struggle was not long, but pretty severe; and the swallow was once or twice nearly immersed, wings and all, in the water, before he got himself disentangled from the sharp teeth of the fish." It is true that the trout had no intention of encountering the bird; but every one knows that pike will pull young ducks under the water, and devour them.

"The Tay trout," says John Crerar (I copy from his MS.), "lives in that river all the year round. It is a large and yellow fish, with a great mouth, and feeds chiefly on salmon spawn, moles, mice, frogs, &c. A curious circumstance once happened to me at Pulney Loch. One of my sons threw a live mouse into it, when a large trout took the mouse down immediately. The boy told me what had happened; so I took my fishing rod, which was leaning against my house close to the loch, and put a fly on. At the very first throw I hooked a large trout, landed it, and laid it on the walk: in two seconds the mouse ran out of its mouth, and got into a hole in the wall before I could catch it." Thus far John Crerar.

> "The mouse that is content with one poor hole
> Can never be a mouse of any soul."

I believe every author on the subject, from the time of dear Isaak Walton to the present day, has taken some pains to vindicate the amusement of angling. For this purpose they have quoted men eminent for humanity, illustrious for science, and famed for high achievement—philosophers, warriors, divines,—who have been dear lovers of the sport.[1] But does it require this vindication? For myself, far from being surprised that distinguished men have delighted in fishing, I only wonder that any man can be illustrious who does not practise either angling or field sports of some sort or another. They all demand skill and enterprise. If you ask me to reconcile angling to reason, you may possibly distress me. It is an instinct, a passion, and a powerful one, originally given to man for the preservation of his existence. The waters as well as the land yield forth their increase. In the joyless regions of the north, when the bear famishes on the iceberg, and the gaunt wolf howls amongst the snow-drifts, the miserable tenant of the land stalks along the desolate shores, and with his javelin, or hooks of bone, acquires by his rude skill a precarious subsistence for his family. Everlasting winter has stamped her iron foot upon the soil: the snow whitens all interminably, except where the blasts drive it from the face of the bleak rocks; and without this resource he must perish,—he and his sad family together. Even so it is ordained from above.

Thrice happy are we, who live in a more genial climate, and who inherit the instinct given to our less fortunate fellow-creatures, and exercise it not from hard necessity, but as a means of recreation. Man being thus evidently destined to fish, let us consider the style of thing that is likely to give him the most gratification.

When I read of the whale fishery, and of that animal running out a mile of rope, for an instant my thoughts were bent on the seas of Greenland; but I was taken aback by the frontispiece of Captain Scoresby's entertaining narrative, which represents his boat thrown aloft in the air by a playful jerk of a whale's tail, and all the crew tumbling seaward in very sprawling and unstudied attitudes. Now this is a sort of adventure which I do not covet myself, or recommend others to seek. In such case, perhaps, the heroes of the harpoon might be

---

[1] When Sir Humphrey Davy was at Gisburn, the late Lord Ribblesdale took him to see the celebrated Gorsdale Rocks, expecting they would astonish and interest him, and call forth some very learned remarks; but the great philosopher noticed only the stream beneath them, which he scrutinised minutely, saying he was sure there were no fish in it, or he should have discovered them.

caught at their descent by some ravenous shark; and unless people have a curiosity about the construction of that animal's intestines for the sake of scientific purposes, a visit to his interior would be useless, and I think imprudent. Besides, whale fishery is a sort of unsavory butchery, which does not suit all tastes. We will take leave, therefore, to discard it at once.

The truth is, that I like no sea fishing whatever, being of opinion that it requires little skill; neither do I enjoy sailing in the salt element, for very particular reasons relating to health. But my mind is full of solemn thoughts as I stand on the sounding shore, and see the gallant vessel pass away into the great desert of waters, till her misty hull rests lonely in the horizon. Then, as shades of night set in, and as she fades in the general gloom, I meditate on the perils of storm and battle, and all the adventurous scenes her crew may encounter, for good or for evil, – far, far away from the land of their affections.

> "Nos patriam fugimus, nos dulcia linquimus arva:
> Nos patriam fugimus."

No; the wild main I trust not. Rather let me wander beside the banks of the tranquil streams of the warm South, "in yellow meads of asphodel," when the young spring comes forth, and all nature is glad; or if a wilder mood comes over me, let me clamber among the steeps of the North, beneath the shaggy mountains, where the river comes raging and foaming everlastingly, wedging its way through the secret glen, whilst the eagle, but dimly seen, cleaves the winds and the clouds, and the dun deer gaze from the mosses above. There, amongst gigantic rocks, and the din of mountain torrents, let me do battle with the lusty salmon, till I drag him into day, rejoicing in his bulk, voluminous and vast.

But, alas! we run riot. Let me now set forth by what chance I became a fisher for salmon. Dining one auspicious day with a friend in London, after a sultry morning gratifying to nothing but a lizard or a serpent, – the town hot, still, and deserted, as the ruins of Pompeii, – we turned from the base thraldom to which we had subjected ourselves, and resolved to wander over the blue hills of Scotland; "for we had heard of *grouse-shooting*, and we longed to follow in the field some lusty *heath-cock*." It was Wednesday. On Friday we would depart, that was certain; for we were young and ardent. Our travelling means were not very rich: they consisted of a curricle with one horse (his companion having died lately), and a tilbury without any. But the next day there was to be a sale at Tattersall's, which all juveniles delight in; so away we went to the hammer, rejoicing in our *soi disant* judgment, and purchased two animals most indubitably of the horse species. My friend accommodated himself with a chestnut, I with a mottled grey; and it would be difficult to say which of the two had the best bargain.

Now it chanced that these two nags never had harness on their backs from the time of their foalhood; but this did not interest us in the least: they had it on soon at all events, all at the door of Thomas's Hotel, Berkeley Square. The chestnut shone as off-horse in the curricle, the grey was resplendent in the tilbury. As for the start, I cannot boast much of that – kicks, plunges, rearings to match. There was evidently some misunderstanding. My fellow-traveller, wheeling round in spite of curb or rein, passed me in an opposite direction. My thoughts were intent on Davies Street: the grey differed with me widely in opinion, and was ambitious of the Square; round which (if I may use the expression) he galloped with unnecessary haste, till he met my fellow-traveller at the bottom, and we passed each other in grand style, our nags being considerably animated by the lumbering of the wheels. Not once alone did this happen; and before our coursers could be gained over to our opinion, Charing Cross possessed the curricle, and Hanover Square could boast of the tilbury. Our skill might reasonably be questioned—our perseverance could not; for before midnight we rallied, and urged our reluctant beasts to the dulness of Stilton. From henceforth everything went on smoothly with them; except that the chestnut died of the distemper, and the grey fell out of a crazy boat into Loch Lomond, ran away some time afterwards, overturned the vehicle, broke my unfortunate servant's leg, and lamed himself for life.

We journeyed on to Selkirk in juvenile mood. From hence my friends went to Edinburgh, where I agreed to join them. And now comes the point—what made me, Harry Otter, a fisher for salmon? Why thus it was: I went forth, after my arrival at the aforesaid town, at the hour of prime. I asked no questions, for I cannot endure to hear beforehand what sort of sport I am likely to have. Sober truth is sometimes exceedingly distressing, and brings one's mind to a lull; it puts an end to the sublimity of extravagant speculation, which I hold to be the chief duty of a sportsman. So, as I said, I asked no questions; but I saw the river Ettrick before me taking her free course beneath the misty hills, and, brushing away the dew-drops with my steps, I rushed impatiently through the broom and gorse with torn hose and smarting legs, till I arrived at the margin of that wild river, where the birch hung its ringlets over the waters.

Out came my trusty rod from a case of "filthy dowlass." Top varnished it was, and the work of the famous Higginbotham: not he the hero of an hundred engines, "who was *afeard* of nothing, and whose fireman's soul was all on fire;" but Higginbotham of the Strand, who was such an artist in the rod line as never appeared before, or has ever been seen since. "he never joyed since the price of hiccory wood rose," and was soon after gathered to the tomb of his fathers. I look upon him, and old Kirby the quondam maker of hooks, to be two of the greatest men the world ever saw; not even excepting Eustace Ude, or Michael Angelo Buonarotti.

But to business. The rod was hastily put together; a beautiful new azure line passed through the rings; a casting line, made like the waist of Prior's Emma, appended, with two trout flies attached to it of the manufacture even of me, Harry Otter. An eager throw to begin with: round came the flies intact. Three, four, five, six throws—a dozen: no better result. The fish were stern and contemptuous. At length some favourable change took place in the clouds, or atmosphere, and I caught sundry small trout; and finally, in the cheek of a boiler, I fairly hauled out a two-pounder. A jewel of a fish he was—quite a treasure all over. After I had performed the satisfactory office of bagging him, I came to a part of the river which, being contracted, rushed forward in a heap, rolling with great impetuosity. Here, after a little flogging, I hooked a lusty fellow, strong as an elephant, and swift as a thunderbolt. How I was agitated say ye who best can tell, ye fellow tyros! Every moment did I expect my trout tackle, for such it was, to part company. At length, after various runs of dubious result, the caitiff began to yield; and at the expiration of about half an hour, I wooed him to the shore. What a sight then struck my optics! A fair five-pounder at the least; not fisherman's weight, mark me, but such as would pass muster with the most conscientious lord mayor of London during the high price of bread. Long did I gaze on him, not without self-applause. All too large he was for my basket; I therefore laid the darling at full length on the ground, under a birch tree, and covered over the precious deposit with some wet bracken, that it might not suffer from the sunbeam.

I had not long completed this immortal achievement ere I saw a native approaching, armed with a prodigious fishing rod of simple construction guiltless of colour or varnish. He had a belt round his waist, to which was fastened a large wooden reel or pirn, and the line passed from it through the rings of his rod: a sort of Wat Tinlinn he was to look at. The whole affair seemed so primitive; there was such an absolute indigence of ornament, and poverty of conception, that I felt somewhat fastidious about it. I could not, however, let a brother of the craft pass unnoticed, albeit somewhat rude in his attire; so, "What sport," said I, "my good friend?"

"I canna say that I hae had muckle deversion; for she is quite fallen in, and there wull be no good fishing till there comes a spate."

Now, after this remark, I waxed more proud of my success; but I did not come down upon him at once with it, but said somewhat slyly, and with mock modesty,—

"Then you think there is not much chance for any one, and least of all for a stranger like myself."

"I dinna think the like o' ye can do muckle; though I will no say but ye may light on a wee bit trout, or may be on a happening fish. That's a bonny little wand you've got; and she shimmers so with varnish, that I'm thinking that when she is in the eye o' the sun the fish will come aneath her, as they do to the blaze in the water."

Sandy was evidently lampooning my Higginbotham. I therefore replied, that she certainly had more shining qualities than were often met with on the northern side of the Tweed. At this personality, my pleasant friend took out a large mull from his pocket, and, applying a copious quantity of its contents to his nose, very politely responded—

"Ye needna fash yoursel' to observe aboot the like o' her; she is no worth this pinch o' snuff."

He then very courteously handed his mull to me.

"Well," said I, still modestly, "she will do well enough for a bungler like me."
I was trolling for a compliment.

"Ay, that will she," said he.

Though a little mortified, I was not sorry to get him to this point; for I knew I could overwhelm him with facts, and the more diffidently I conducted myself the more complete would be my triumph. So laying down my pet rod on the channel, I very deliberately took out my two-pounder, as a feeler. He looked particularly well; for I had tied up his mouth, that he might keep his shape, and moistened him, as I before said, with soaked fern to preserve his colour. I fear I looked a little elate on the occasion; assuredly I felt so.

"There's a fine fish now,—a perfect beauty!"

"Hout tout! that's no fish ava."

"No fish, man! What the deuce is it, then? Is it a rabbit, or a wild duck, or a water-rat?"

"Ye are joost gin daft. Do ye no ken a troot when ye see it?"

I could make nothing of this answer, for I thought that a trout was a fish;[1] but it seems I was mistaken. However, I saw the envy of the man; so I determined to inflict him with a settler at once. For this purpose I inveigled him to where my five-pounder was deposited; then kneeling down, and proudly removing the bracken I had placed over him, there lay the monster most manifest, extended in all his glory. The light, — the eye of the landscape, — before whose brilliant sides Runjeet Sing's diamond, called "the mountain of light," would sink into the deep obscure; — dazzled with the magnificent sight, I chuckled in the plenitude of victory. This was unbecoming in me, I own, for I should have borne my faculties meekly; but I was young and sanguine; so (*horresco referens*) I gave a smart turn of my body, and, placing an arm akimbo, said, in an exulting tone, and with a scrutinising look, "There, what do you think of that?" I did not see the astonishment in Sawny's face that I had anticipated, neither did he seem to regard me with the least degree of veneration; but, giving my pet a shove with his nasty iron-shod shoes, he simply said,

"Hout! that's a wee bit gilse."

This was laconic. I could hold no longer, for I hate a detractor; so I roundly told him that I did not think he had ever caught so large a fish in all his life.

"Did you, now? — own."

"I suppose I have."

"Suppose! But don't you know?"

"I suppose I have."

"Speak decidedly, yes or no. That is no answer."

"Well, then, I suppose[2] I have."

And this was the sum-total of what I could extract from this *nil admirari* fellow.

A third person now joined us, whom I afterwards discovered to be the renter of that part of the river. He had a rod and tackle of the selfsame fashion with the apathetic man. He touched his bonnet to me; and if he did not eye me with approval, at least he did not look envious or sarcastic.

"Well, Sandy," said he to his piscatorial friend, my new acquaintance, "what luck the morn?"

"I canna speecify that I hae had muckle; for they hae bin at the sheepwashing up bye, and she is foul, ye ken. But I hae ta'en two saumon, — ane wi' Nancy,[3] and the ither wi' a Toppy, — baith in Faldon-side Burn fut."

And twisting round a coarse linen bag which was slung at his back, and which I had supposed to contain some common lumber, he drew forth by the tail a never-ending monster of a salmon, dazzling and lusty to the view; and then a

---

[1] Salmon, salmon trout, and bull trout alone, are called *fish* in the Tweed. If a Scotchman means to try for trout, he does not say "I am going a *fishing*," but "I am going a *trouting*."

[It requires some courage to criticize the phraseology of such a master as Scrope, but let the stranger beware of applying the term "fish" to anything of less dignity than a salmon in Scotland. — Ed.]

[2] Suppose, in Scotch, does not imply a doubt, but denotes a certainty.

[3] A fly so called from Nancy Dawson, who was born on the Tweed, near little Dean Tower.

second, fit consort to the first. Could you believe it? One proved to be fifteen pounds, and the other twelve! At the sudden appearance of these whales I was shivered to atoms: dumbfoundered I was, like the Laird of Cockpen when Mrs. Jean refused the honour of his hand. I felt as small as Flimnap the treasurer in the presence of Gulliver. Little did I say; but that little, I hope, was becoming a youth in my situation.

I was now fairly vaccinated. By dint of snuff and whiskey, I made an alliance with the tenant of the water; and being engaged for that year to join my friends at Edinburgh, and go on a shooting excursion to the Hebrides and the north of Scotland, I resolved to revisit the Tweed the summer following.

It was the above incident that regulated my residence, in a great measure, for above twenty years of my life.

Major Hills, in *A History of Fly Fishing for Trout,* said it was "impossible to pass over Scrope, who, though he despised the trout, is too good to be left out. He is one of the very best." And James Robb, in *Notable Angling Literature,* echoed the opinion, adding that Scrope's name was "beloved wherever the literature of the salmon is known," and that he "occupies a place in the literature of angling which is not in danger of being superseded."

The big point to bear in mind about Scrope is that while it seems so effervescent and sparkly, it's not all superficial; Scrope is not all icing and no cake, not all froth and no ale beneath. It only seems that way, because he's so beguiling, but Scrope did at least as much for salmon fishing as Cotton before him had done for trout. Before Scrope people weren't even sure what the relation of the parr was to the salmon, and they used to catch them and keep them as if they were so many small trout. Scrope made it clear. (I'd forgotten, what Hills says, that Scrope despised trout, and don't feel much like believing it, even if I were shown that it is true—his enjoyment of those two trout in the sequence we just had seems to me to be up to anybody's; but it was fun to see again, which I'd also forgotten, how much he *did* despise water, which he considered fit for external use only; I'm with him there.)

Stewart, in a way, is Scrope in reverse. He harrumphs and snorts about being strictly utilitarian, in his approach to angling—even calls his book *The Practical Angler*—but Stewart too has a twinkle in his eye. He can't stay as school-teacherly as he professes to be in his preface.

Here again, no first edition for us. This turns out to be the fourth edition, 1863, as the book ran through an edition per year after its original appearance in 1857, demonstrating, as Stewart said in his note appended to the fourth edition's preface, "an amount of success which shows clearly that what the angling community now want, is not another amusing description of the pleasures of angling, but a book to teach them how to fish."

And while Stewart does, with a candid, no-nonsense and even rather combative assertiveness, undertake to straighten people out on the one right way to fish, that is, upstream, he does at the same time provide some amusing descriptions of the pleasures of angling.

If, however, on the one hand angling is looked upon with little favour by an unenlightened multitude, on the other hand there is no amusement to which those who practise it become so much attached. Nor do we think that anglers generally can fairly be accused either of stupidity, or, let us say, patience. They have certainly in their ranks a larger proportion of men of literature and science than can be found among the followers of any other field sport; and for the comfort of those who have not the much-despised gift of patience, we could point to a number of celebrated anglers, who are by no means celebrated as possessing this virtue, while numbers of the most patient followers of Izaak Walton are very far from having rivalled his success. Angling, when once embarked in by any person possessed of a reasonable amount of soul and brains, becomes a passion, and like other passions will grow and feed upon the smallest possible amount of encouragement. Fish or no fish, whenever opportunity offers, the angler may be found at the water-side. If this only went on in fine weather, people could understand it, but now-a-days, even in summer, the weather is not always fine; and when a man is seen standing in the water for hours in a torrent of rain, with benumbed hands and an empty basket, doubts of the individual's sanity naturally suggest themselves, mixed with feelings of pity for the terrible consequences in the way of colds, rheumatism, &c., which it is supposed must inevitably follow, but which don't. We have it from high medical authority, that rheumatism is more engendered by hot rooms and fires than by exposure, and as for the comfort of the thing, that is according to taste. It is surely better to have fresh air and exercise, even in wet, than to be spending the whole day in some country inn, yawning over some second-rate novel for the third time, the amusement agreeably diversified by staring out of the window at the interminable rain, by poking a peat-fire, and possibly by indulging in a superfluity of that institution of the country, pale ale.

> "Though sluggards deem it but an idle chase,
> And marvel men should quit their easy chair,
> The toilsome way and long long league to trace;
> Oh! there is sweetness in the mountain air,
> And life that bloated ease can never hope to share."

That angling is good for exercise is certain. That it is also good for amusement is equally certain; but the pleasure derived from the catching of fish, like that derived from other field sports, is more easily felt than described. There can be no doubt, that by the great majority of people an amusement is valued in proportion as it affords room for the exercise of skill—there is more merit, and therefore more pleasure, in excelling in what is difficult—and though we may astonish some of our readers, we assert, and shall endeavour to prove, that angling is the most difficult of all field sports. It requires all the manual dexterity that the others do, and brings more into play the qualities of the mind, observation, and the reasoning faculties. In shooting and hunting, the dogs do the observation and the reasoning part of the business, and the sportsmen the mechanical; but the angler has not only to find out where his fish are but to catch them, and that not by such a "knock-me-down" method as is practised upon some unfortunate blackcock or unwary hare, but by an art of deception. The angler's wits, in fact, are brought into direct competition with those of the fish, which very often, judging from the result, prove the better of the two.

Besides the mere pleasure of fishing, however, angling has more varied attractions than almost any other amusement. To the lover of nature no sport affords so much pleasure. The grandest and most picturesque scenes in nature are to be found on the banks of rivers and lakes. The angler, therefore, enjoys the finest scenery the country offers; and, whereas other sportsmen are limited to particular places and seasons, he can follow his vocation alike on lowland stream or highland loch, and during the whole six months in which the country is most inviting. From April, with her budding trees and singing birds, to May and June, with their meadows decked with the daisy and the primrose, and breezes scented with the hawthorn and wild thyme, and on to autumn, with her "fields white unto the harvest," he sees all that is beautiful—all that is exhilarating—all that is grand and elevating in this world of ours, which, whatever people may say, is not such a bad world after all, if they would only keep bleachfields and blackguards off the rivers' banks.

With this brief resume of some of the principal attractions of angling we must content ourselves. We have neither space, inclination, nor ability, to do justice to this branch of the subject. Furthermore, it is unnecessary, as the ground in this respect is already fully occupied; and if any one wishes to have all the joys of angling set forth in genuine old English style, let him read Izaak Walton, "being a discourse on fish and fishing not unworthy the perusal of most anglers." Here may be found a conglomeration of fertile meadows, crystal brooks, meandering streams, milk-maids' songs, and moral reflections, which must prove irresistible; and also, if a man of tender conscience, be able to satisfy himself that angling is not a cruel amusement, though it must be admitted that some of Izaak's injunctions, such as putting a hook "through a frog tenderly, as though you loved him"—seeing that the said tenderness is to be evinced, not for the sake of saving the frog's feelings, but of prolonging its wretched life—do savour a little of harshness, and seem to justify Lord Byron's lines:—

> "The quaint old cruel coxcomb in his gullet
> Should have a hook, and a small trout to pull it."

Never having had any scruples of this sort ourselves, we have not studied the subject, and therefore leave the defence of it to Walton and a celebrated Doctor of Divinity who has taken it in hand; but if any one has any scruples, or thinks angling slow and stupid, or has any other objections, let him keep clear of it by all means. There are plenty of anglers already, and every year adds to the list a number who are not to be deterred either by the sneers of this world, or by terror of the punishment, which, the poet thinks, should be reserved for the master, and we suppose for all his followers, in the next; and our purpose is not to make more anglers, but to make successful anglers of those unsuccessful at present.

But to get to his thesis, and the thing for which Major Hills cited him as one of the four most influential figures in the history of angling, here he is on the wisdom and advantage of fishing upstream:

In trouting with the minnow, worm, or natural fly, the angler has the real fish, worm, or insect, with which to entice the trout, but in fly-fishing he has, by means of a few feathers, to deceive the wary keen-sighted fish, and make it believe that his imitation is a natural fly either alive or dead. Any one will at once see that this is the more difficult, and that to prevail upon a trout to seize a reality does not afford room for the exercise of so much skill as to prevail upon the same trout to seize an imitation. Hence fly-fishing, in the same condition of water, requires more address than angling with the worm, or any other known method; and consequently, fly-fishing in a clear low water is, beyond comparison, the most difficult of all the branches of the angler's art, and should therefore rank highest as sport.

This, however, is not an art that can be learned in a day, or so easily as some seem to imagine. A beginner becomes enamoured of fly-fishing. For six weeks he grinds at Walton and all the other authorities upon the subject, and having equipped himself with all the paraphernalia for waging a war of extermination upon the finny tribe, he rolls his hat round with cast after cast of flies, which bear a far greater resemblance to bumble bees than river insects; and thus accoutred, sets out to put his acquired information in practice. Arrived at the river-side he finds his mistake: if the water be swollen, and of the dark porter colour so celebrated among anglers, he may be rewarded with the capture of a few trout; but if it be clear, he plies his lure to the terror and alarm of almost every trout in the water, and returns, if not with an empty basket, at least with a very light one, to confirm the prevailing opinion that it is of no use fishing when the water is clear. If this opinion were correct, it would limit the time when angling could be successfully practised to a few weeks in the season, and sometimes to a few days; but fortunately for the angler it is not correct, being merely the natural result of a mode of angling which ignores the habits and instincts of the trout. Trout are just as much inclined to feed when the waters are clear as when they are coloured. In a clear water they may be seen rising in immense numbers at the natural insect, showing that they are not inclined to starve in these circumstances.

When the water is of a dark colour, it conceals the angler from view, and disguises his tackle, and so he meets with fair sport. If the body of water, though clear, is sufficiently large to conceal him from the sight of the trout, as in Tweed, Tay, and other first-class streams, he may still meet with tolerable success. But in all our small rivers and waters, when they are low and clear, not one angler out of twenty meets with much sport, and the reason of it is, because the clearness of the water either allows the trout to see him, or enables them to detect the artificial nature of his lure; and to meet these difficulties as far as possible is the great object to be aimed at in fly-fishing.

The great error of fly-fishing, as usually practised, and as recommended to be practised by books, is that the angler fishes down stream, whereas he should fish up.

We believe we are not beyond the mark in stating that ninety-nine anglers out of a hundred fish down with the artificial fly; they never think of fishing in any other way, and never dream of attributing their want of success to it. Yet we are prepared to prove, both in theory and practice, that this is the greatest reason of their want of success in clear waters. In all our angling excursions we have only met one or two amateurs and a few professionals, who fished up stream with the fly, and used it in a really artistic manner. If the wind is blowing up, anglers will occasionally fish up the pools—(as for fishing up a strong stream they never think of it)—but even then they do not do it properly, and meet with little better success than if they had followed their usual method. They will also, if going to some place up a river, walk up, not fish up to it—their plan being to go to the top of a pool, and then fish it down, never casting their line above them at all.

We shall now mention in detail the advantages of fishing up, in order to show its superiority over the old method.

The first and greatest advantage is, that the angler is unseen by the trout. Trout, as is well known, keep their heads up stream; they cannot remain stationary in any other position. This being the case, they see objects above and on both sides of them, but cannot discern anything behind them, so that the angler fishing down will be seen by them twenty yards off, whereas the angler fishing up will be unseen, although he be but a few yards in their rear. The advantages of this it is impossible to over-estimate. No creatures are more easily scared than trout; if they see any object moving on the river's bank, they run into deep water, or beneath banks and stones, from which they will not stir for some time. A bird flying across the water, or the shadow of a rod, will sometimes alarm them; and nothing connected with angling is more certain than this, that if the trout see the angler, they will not take his lure. He may ply his minnow in the most captivating manner, may throw his worm with consummate skill, or make his flies light softly as a gossamer—all will be unavailing if he is seen by his intended victim.

The next advantage of fishing up we shall notice, is the much greater probability of hooking a trout when it rises. In angling down stream, if a trout rises and the angler strikes, he runs a great risk of pulling the flies straight out of its mouth; whereas, in fishing up, its back is to him, and he has every chance of bringing the hook into contact with its jaws. This, although it may not seem of great importance to the uninitiated, tells considerably when the contents of the basket come to be examined at the close of the day's sport; indeed, no angler would believe the difference unless he himself proved it.

Another advantage of fishing up is, that it does not disturb the water so much. Let us suppose the angler is fishing down a fine pool. He, of course, commences at the top, the place where the best trout, and those most inclined to feed, invariably lie. After a few casts he hooks one, which immediately runs down, and by its vagaries, leaping in the air, and plunging in all directions alarms all its neighbours, and it is ten to one if he gets another rise in that pool. Fishing up saves all this. The angler commences at the foot, and when he hooks a trout, pulls it down, and the remaining portions of the pool are undisturbed.

This is a matter of great importance, and we have frequently, in small streams, taken a dozen trout out of a pool, from which, had we been fishing down, we could not possibly have got more than two or three.

The last advantage of fishing up is, that by it the angler can much better adapt the motions of his flies to those of the natural insect. And here it may be mentioned as a rule, that the nearer the motions of the artificial flies resemble those of the natural ones under similar circumstances, the greater will be the prospects of success. Whatever trout take the artificial fly for, it is obvious they are much more likely to be deceived by a natural than by an unnatural motion.

No method of angling can imitate the hovering flight of an insect along the surface of the water, now just touching it, then flying a short distance, and so on; and for the angler to attempt by any motion of his hand to give his flies a living appearance is mere absurdity. The only moment when trout may mistake the angler's fly for a real one in its flight, is the moment it first touches the water; and in this respect fishing down possesses equal advantages with fishing up. But this is the only respect, and in order to illustrate this, we shall give a brief description of fly-fishing as usually practised down stream.

The angler, then, we shall suppose, commences operations at the head of a pull or stream, and throwing his flies as far as he can across from where he is standing, raises his rod and brings them gradually to his own side of the water. He then steps down a yard or two, repeats the process, and so on. Having dismissed the idea that the angler can imitate the flight of a living fly along the surface of the water, we must suppose that trout take the artificial fly for a dead one, or one which has fairly got into the stream and lost all power of resisting. A feeble motion of the wings or legs would be the only attempt at escape which a live fly in such a case could make. What then must be the astonishment of the trout, when they see the tiny insect which they are accustomed to seize as it is carried by the current towards them, crossing the stream with the strength and agility of an otter? Is it not much more natural to throw the flies up, and let them come gently down as any real insect would do?

In addition to drawing their flies across the stream, some anglers practise what is called playing their flies, which is done by a jerking motion of the wrist, which imparts a similar motion to the fly. Their object in doing this is to create an appearance of life, and thus render their flies more attractive. An appearance of life is certainly a great temptation to a trout, but it may be much better accomplished by dressing the flies of soft materials, which the water can agitate, and thus create a natural motion of the legs or wings of the fly, than by dragging them by jumps of a foot at a time across and up a roaring stream. Trout are not accustomed to see small insects making such gigantic efforts at escape, and therefore it is calculated to awaken their suspicions.

We believe that all fly-fishers fishing down must have noticed, that apart from the moment of alighting, they get more rises for the first few yards of their flies' course than in the whole of the remainder; and that when their flies fairly breast the stream they seldom get a rise at all. The reason of this is clear: — for the first few feet after the angler throws his flies across the stream they swim with the current; the moment, however, he begins to describe his semicircle across the water, they present an unnatural appearance, which the trout view with distrust. Experienced fly-fishers following the old method, who have observed this, and are aware of the great importance of the moment their flies alight, cast very frequently, only allowing their flies to float down a few feet, when they throw again. We have seen some Tweedside adepts fill capital baskets in this way; but, as we have before stated, it will only succeed when the water is coloured, or when there is a body of clear water sufficiently large to conceal the angler from view; and even then he may have much better sport by fishing up. The angler drawing his flies across and up stream will catch trout, and this is the strongest evidence that trout are not such profound philosophers as the notions of some would lead us to suppose. But though he does catch trout, they are in general the very smallest. Indeed, the advantages of fishing up are in nothing more apparent than in the superior size of the trout captured. We believe they will average nearly double the size of those caught with the same flies fishing down, and though generally not so large as those taken with the worm, they are not much behind them, and we almost invariably kill a few larger trout in a river with the fly than with the worm.

Though our remarks in this chapter have principally reference to angling in small rivers, where fishing up is *essential* to success, the same arguments hold good in every size or colour of water in a less degree, as, even though the trout cannot see the angler, the other advantages which we have mentioned are still in his favour.

If we were fishing a large river when it was dark-coloured, and required to wade deep, we should fish down, because the fatigue of wading up would, under such circumstances, become a serious drawback. In such a case we fish in the following manner: — Throwing our flies, partly up and partly across from where we are standing, we allow them to swim down a yard or two, when we cast again, never allowing them to go below that part of the stream opposite us. But though the angler gets over the ground as quickly this way, and casts as often, as if he were fishing up, yet he has not the same chance, because if a trout catches sight of his flies just as he is lifting them, their sudden abstraction may deter it from taking them on their again alighting; whereas in fishing up the angler casts a yard or two farther every time, so that every trout may see his flies at the moment they alight.

The reader must not suppose that fishing up is all that is necessary for success; on the contrary, the angler may throw his flies up stream, and know less of the art of fly-fishing, and catch fewer trout, than his neighbour who is fishing down. The mere fact of an angler throwing his flies up stream is no proof that he is a fly-fisher. Of those who fish down stream some catch more and some less, and in like manner with those fishing up, one may catch three times as many as another, depending upon the particular method they adopt; and unless the reader pays *strict* attention to the details which will be mentioned subsequently, we are afraid he will not derive much benefit. Fishing up is *much more* difficult than fishing down, requiring more practice, and a better acquaintance with the habits of the trout; and we believe that a mere novice would, in a large water, catch more trout by fishing down than up, because the latter *requires more nicety* in casting. But to attain anything like eminence in fly-fishing, the angler *must* fish up, and all beginners should *persevere* in it, even though they meet with little success at first, and they will be amply rewarded for their trouble.

The only circumstance in which fishing down has the advantage of fishing up, is when the water is so dark or deep that the fish would not see, or if they did see, would not have time to seize the flies unless they moved at a slower rate than the stream. We think that this rarely applies to angling for river trout, as when inclined to feed upon flies they are generally on the outlook for them; so that if the salmon-fisher were to throw his flies up stream, they would come down at such a rate that the salmon would never see them. Besides which, it is obvious that whatever salmon take the angler's fly for, they cannot take it for anything they have seen before, and therefore there is no reason for supposing they can detect anything unnatural in its motion.

We have devoted this chapter principally to the errors of fly-fishing as generally practised, and we hope we have succeeded in convincing the reader of the truth of our observations; but as we have frequently endeavoured in vain by *viva voce* demonstration to persuade anglers to fish up, we have no doubt numbers will adhere to their own way. As no amount of mere argument will convince such, we offer to find two anglers, who in a water suitable for showing the superiority of fishing up, will be more successful than any three anglers fishing down after the ordinary method.

We have just given the same reasons for fishing up stream as in our first edition, because upon this point there can be nothing new; and are as ready as ever to find anglers who are prepared to do battle on their behalf, on the terms just stated; but while one or two have come forward to dispute the theory, none have accepted our challenge and come forward to dispute the practice. One reviewer — the only objector we recollect of who gives a reason — says, "that so long as streams run down, carrying the food of the fish with them, so long should anglers fish down." This seems said purely for the sake of appearing to give a reason; and while his premises are undeniably correct, we entirely dissent from his conclusions. Streams certainly run down and carry the food of the trout with them, but along with that food they do not carry an apparition in the shape of an angler with rod and line upon the bank; and as nothing will familiarise them to such an apparition, we draw the conclusion that that apparition had better keep out of sight and fish up stream. Moreover, the fact that the natural food floats down is anything but a reason that the artificial lure in imitation of that food should be pulled up.

We must confess, however, that fishing up stream with fly has not been adopted by a large portion of the angling community, and that for various reasons. In spite of the strong manner in which we cautioned our readers about the difficulties of fishing up stream, numbers who read the arguments for it, and were struck with the soundness of the theory, thought they saw at a glance the cause of their previous want of success, and that in future the result would be different. Having equipped themselves à la *Practical Angler,* and even taken a copy of that excellent work in their pockets, they started with high hopes on their new career, but the result was not different, and after one or two trials with no better success, not a few have condemned fishing up stream as erroneous and ourselves as impostors; though we imagine the fault lies with themselves. We have met anglers fishing down stream — and this is no supposititious case, but one which we have seen over and over again — with a copy of this volume in their pockets, who complained that they had got everything herein recommended and were getting no sport. On pointing out to them that there was one important mistake they were committing, in fishing down stream instead of up, they stated that when they came to a pool they fished it up — that is to say, they first walked down the pool and showed themselves to the trout, and then commenced to fish for them.

> "The trout within yon wimplin' burn,
>   Glides swift, a silver dart;
> And safe beneath the shady thorn
>   Defies the angler's art."

John Younger objects to this as incorrect, but we rather think that Burns is right, and the angler wrong; as it is evident the poet alludes to a trout that has caught sight of the angler, and safe he is at least *pro tem.*, as our pupils, who first frighten the fish by walking down a pool-side and then fish it up, will find to their cost.

Others object to fishing up stream, as requiring too frequent casting, being too fatiguing, and because they have been accustomed to fish down, and would prefer fishing in that way, even though they do not catch so many trout. If any angler prefers catching five pounds weight of trout fishing down stream, to ten pounds weight fishing up, we may wonder at his taste, but it is no concern of ours. Our duty is to point out how most trout can be captured in a given time; and that is by fishing up stream, and such is now the method adopted by all the best fly-fishers of the day.

Those anglers who have adopted fishing up stream are principally those who were adepts in the old system, and who were possessed of all the nicety in casting and other knowledge so essential to successful up-stream fishing.

The art of fly-fishing—or fishing of any kind—may be summed up in knowing what to fish with, and how, when, and where to fish. We have rather transposed the arrangement, and taken part of the second division first, because it is necessary to establish whether the angler should fish up or down, before considering what he is to fish with, different tackle being necessary for the former method. In the subsequent chapters we shall return to the proper arrangement, and shall complete in its proper place the division already half finished.

Having shown the way that the purists of the south of England would shortly adopt, and then rigidify into a sacrosanct dogma, it may seem surprising that Stewart should himself be disinclined, beyond his advocacy of upstream fishing, to go any of the rest of the route toward purism. Hear him, for instance, on the matter of imitation, which of course was to become, a generation later, the main tenet of the purist methodology:

The practice of using artificial flies has undoubtedly had its origin in the necessity for imitating insects which cannot be used in their natural state. From the first rude attempt at fly-making of some ingenious angler, the art has gone on progressing, the number of imitations always increasing, and the prevalent opinion always being that, in order to fish successfully, the angler must use an imitation of one or other of the natural insects on the water at the time. In spite of the exertions of Mr. Wilson and Mr. Stoddart to inculcate an opposite theory, this opinion is still held by the great majority of anglers in Scotland, while in England it is all but universal.

Anglers holding these views rejoice in the possession of as many different varieties of flies as would stock a fishing book, all of which they consider imitations of so many real insects, and classify under the heads of the different months when these appear. They have a fly for the morning, another for noon, and another for the evening of every day in the year, and spend a great deal of time in taking off one fly, because it is a shade too dark, and a second because it is a shade too light, and a third to give place to the imitation of some insect which has just made its appearance on the water.

During the summer months it is supposed that the varieties of insects are reckoned by the thousand, and we have seen several dozens of different kinds on the water at one time, all of which are greedily devoured by the trout. Those anglers who think trout will take no fly unless it is an exact imitation of some one of the immense number of flies they are feeding on, must suppose that they know to a shade the colour of every fly on the water, and can detect the least deviation from it—an amount of entomological knowledge that would put to shame the angler himself, and a good many naturalists to boot. This opinion arises from the supposition that trout will not take anything readily unless they are accustomed to feed upon it, and consequently that they will not take a fly unless it has been on the water sufficiently long to allow them to become acquainted with it. Nothing can be more erroneous than this. Trout will take worms and grubs which they have never seen before. They will also take parr-tail readily, and they can never have seen it before; and in like manner with other things; and there is no reason why fly should be an exception.

We do not think it at all likely that trout can see the colour of a fly very distinctly. The worst light of all for seeing its colour is when it is placed between you and the sky, as the trout see it. And when the fly is rolled round by every current, and sometimes seen through the medium of a few feet of running water, the idea that they can detect its colour to a shade is highly improbable. Even granting they could, there is no reason for supposing they would reject it on that account. Flies of the same kind differ so much in colour that we could show the reader a May-fly almost black, and a May-fly almost yellow, and of all the intermediate shades.

It is singular inconsistency, that anglers, scrupulously exact about a shade of colour, draw their flies across and up stream in a way in which no natural insect was ever seen moving, as if a trout could not detect an alteration in the motion much more easily than a deviation in the colour of a fly.

The argument brought by anglers in support of these views is, that having fished unsuccessfully all the morning, they changed their flies and had good sport, or that when they were getting nothing they met with some celebrated local angler, who gave them the fly peculiar to the district, after which they met with success. We think that on most of these occasions the trout take better, not because the new fly is more to their liking, but because as the day advances they are more inclined to feed. We have frequently proved this by rechanging to our flies which at first proved unsuccessful, and have almost invariably found they were as killing as their predecessors. Other causes also operate. The thread of gut on which the fly is dressed is of more importance than the fly itself; and those professional anglers who haunt most southern streams, and

whose "fail-me-never" is the only fly suitable for the water—because they expect to be well paid for it—take care to have their flies dressed on fine gut.

Such a difference does the gut make, that if an angler will take two threads of
gut of the same thickness, but one of a glossy white colour, and the other clear
and transparent, and dress two flies upon them exactly alike, the fly dressed on
the clear gut will kill two trout for one which the fly dressed on the white gut
will. The shape of the fly will also make a great difference, and really practical
anglers, such as all those who make their living by it are, do not put a third of
the feathers on their flies that some town-made ones have.

We have frequently got flies, which, we were assured, were exact imitations
of some fly on the water at the time, and which the donors were certain would
kill more trout than any other, but on trying them we did not find them so
deadly as those we were using; and they killed quite as well, and sometimes
better, two months before the natural fly came on the water, or two months
after it was gone. We think it just possible that when a large fly, such as the
green drake, remains a long time on the water, trout may recognise it, and
when the waters are dark coloured and there is a strong breeze of wind, take
an imitation of it more readily than any other. But in our own experience we
have never found this to be the case; and though we have frequently tried this
fly—so celebrated on English streams—we have never found it nearly so deadly
as our usual flies, even when the water was coloured; and in clear water it failed
entirely, as all large flies will, for the obvious reason that their size enables the
trout to detect their artificial character. Furthermore, we have killed more trout
with this imitation in the month of May, before the real insects had made their
appearance, than in June, when the water was swarming with them, which we
ascribe to the circumstance that trout will take a larger fly in May than in June.

This opinion would not have been maintained so long, but that there is at
first sight a degree of plausibility about it, and that it does not to any great extent interfere with the successful practice of fly-fishing. What is meant for an
imitation of a particular fly may occasionally do good service; not because the
trout see any resemblance between it and the fly it is intended to imitate, but
because, if the size and colour are suitable, it will just kill as well as any other.
And we believe the angler who has a different fly for every day in the season
will kill nearly as many trout as the angler who adheres to three or four
varieties the whole season through; but he is proceeding upon an erroneous
principle, and losing both labour and time.

That trout sometimes take more readily flies of one colour than another is
certain, and the reason of their doing so affords room for a great deal of
ingenious speculation, but it is exceedingly difficult to ascertain satisfactorily.
We think that to some extent a certain colour is more deadly, because it is more
readily seen. In clear waters we have rarely found a black fly surpassed by any
other, and in such circumstances a black fly is very easily seen. In dark waters a
yellow-bodied fly, or one of dingy white colour, takes readily, being easily seen.
And on Tweedside, in the month of July, just after sunset, a bright yellow fly is
held in great repute, and such is more likely to attract attention than any other.
Mere caprice, however, and love of variety, may be the main reasons why the
trout prefer one colour to another.

A rule to be guided by on this point is of little use, as the angler can always
regulate the colour of his flies by practice; and in practice it has been proved

beyond doubt, that a black, brown, red, and dun-coloured fly, used together, and varied in size according to circumstances, will at any time kill as well, and even better, than the most elaborate collection arranged for every month in the year. If trout are at all inclined to rise, one or other of the above will be found inviting. It is quite clear that whatever the angler's opinion with regard to flies may be—whether he believes that he must have an imitation of some insect on the water at the time, that he must have a fly of the same colour as the majority of those on the water, or with ourselves holds neither of these opinions; if he has four flies such as those mentioned above, he cannot be very far off the mark, as these comprise all the leading colours of which insects generally are.

The opinion that it is necessary to imitate the particular fly on the water at the time has recently received the weight of Mr. Francis Francis' support, who in advocating what may be called the English theory gives a sort of side-swipe to Scotch anglers—the drift of his remarks being, that though a small assortment of flies may do well enough in Scotch streams where little fishing goes on and anglers count their takes by the dozen, it will not answer in the much-fished streams on the other side of the border, where anglers count their takes by the brace. If Mr. Francis' views as to an exact imitation being necessary in English streams be correct, which we very much doubt, he will require to find some other reason for its being unnecessary in Scotland than this. In comparing the severity of the fishing in Scotch and English streams, it must be borne in mind that the former are, as a rule, open to the public, and that the latter, as a rule, are preserved and fished only by a favoured few. If Mr. Francis will point out any stream in England, in which he thinks it worth while to throw a fly for trout, that is more and better fished than Tweed and its tributaries, we shall be very much surprised. And on behalf of Scotch anglers we repudiate with scorn the bare idea that it requires less skill to catch a Scotch trout than an English one, or that the former in any way receives an inferior education as regards flies, etc, to his English brother. In fact, we believe that in the before-mentioned streams the education of the inhabitants is as superior to that of the inhabitants of English streams as the education of the people of the one country is admitted to be to that of the other; and supposing the most accomplished believer in the English theory—ay, even Mr. Francis himself—engaged on a mile of Tweed along with twenty or thirty Galashiels weavers (by no means an unusual number), we question if his basket at the finish would illustrate very strongly the superiority of his theory and practice. We have met English anglers even in Scotland counting their takes by the brace, and not in much danger of going wrong in their reckoning either. Having relieved our feelings of this protest on behalf of Scotch anglers and Scotch trout, we must now consider what it is necessary to imitate, or what do trout take, or rather mistake, the artificial fly for. As before stated, we believe that, deceived by an appearance of life, they take it for what it is intended to imitate—a fly or some other aquatic insect. In proof of this, artificial flies are not of much use unless the trout are at the time feeding on the natural insect. And an artificial fly will kill twenty trout for one which the feathers composing it, rolled round the hook without regard to shape, will. Nay, more; a neatly-made, natural-looking fly will, where trout are shy, kill three trout for one which a clumsy fly will; and a fly with the exposed part of the hook taken off will raise more trout than a fly with the same left on. In the first case, the trout see no

resemblance in form to anything they are accustomed to feed upon, and, unless very hungry, decline to seize it. In the second case, the resemblance to nature not being so complete in the one fly as in the other, fewer trout are deceived by it. The third case shows that trout can detect that a hook is an unnatural appendage.

The great point, then, in fly-dressing, is to make the artificial fly resemble the natural insect in shape, and the great characteristic of all river insects is extreme lightness and neatness of form. Our great objection to the flies in common use is, that they are much too bushy; so much so, that there are few flies to be got in the tackle-shops which we could use with any degree of confidence in clear water. Every possible advantage is in favour of a lightly-dressed fly; it is more like a natural insect; it falls lighter on the water, and every angler knows the importance of making his fly fall gently, and there being less material about it, the artificial nature of that material is not so easily detected; and also, as the hook is not so much covered with feathers, there is a much better chance of hooking a trout when it rises. We wish to impress very strongly upon the reader the *necessity of avoiding bulky flies.*

The verbal encounter with Francis Francis is amusing, particularly in view of the more or less midwifely role that Francis was to play in the subsequent embodiment of Purism, which it would not be too fanciful to say was fathered by Stewart's upstream technique on the body of Ronalds's entomology. The offspring was, of course, that super-orthodox religion of dry-fly practice—only upstream and only the most precise imitation—of which Halford was to become the godhead, so

holy that his true name could hardly be whispered, but whose enthrone-
ment in the highest angling heaven was not established without a lot of
John-the-Baptist advance proselytizing by Francis Francis.

But that's anticipatory. Let us rather let Stewart have his summation:

Having in the preceding chapters expressed our opinion, that fly-fishing
should be practised up stream, and having mentioned the flies and tackle most
suitable for the purpose, we now request the reader's particular attention to the
remainder of the subject, as being the most important part of it.

The first point which falls under consideration is the casting of the line.
After having put up your rod, drawn off a sufficient quantity of line from your
reel, and fastened on your flies; before commencing, soak the line and flies in
the water for a few minutes, as it is no use fishing when the gut is dry, and
lying in rebellious curls upon the surface; and when, should a trout take any of
the flies, there is a great risk of its carrying them all away—dry gut being very
brittle and apt to break at the knots. When the line is thoroughly soaked, take
the rod in your right hand, raise it with sufficient force to make the line go to
its full length behind, and then pausing for a moment till it has done so, with a
circular motion of the wrist and arm urge the rod forward, rapidly at first, but
gradually lessening the speed, so that when it stops no recoil of the point will
take place. The whole motion of the rod in casting should be in the shape of a
horse-shoe; and care must be taken not to urge the flies forward, till they have
gone the full length behind, or you will be apt to crack them off. Many a
beginner who cracks off his flies pleases himself with the idea that some trout of
large dimensions has carried them away.

The line must be so thrown that the flies will fall first upon the water, and as
little of the line with them as possible. If you were to fish up a strong stream,
and allow the middle of your line to light first, before you could get it straight
and prepared for a rise, your flies would be almost at your feet, and should a
trout take one of them on their alighting—the most deadly moment in the
whole cast—the chances of hooking it would be exceedingly small. It is very
different if the flies light first; the line is then nearly straight from the point of
the rod to the flies, and the least motion of the hand is felt almost instantaneously. Again, in fishing nooks, eddies, and comparatively still water, at the
opposite sides of strong streams, if any of your line lights in the current it is
dragged down, and the flies no sooner touch the water, than they are drawn
rapidly away in a most unnatural manner, and without giving the trout time to
seize them should they feel inclined.

In order to make the flies light first, considerable force must be employed in
casting; and the rod must be kept well up; it should never be allowed to make a
lower angle with the water than from forty to forty-five degrees. It is upon this
point that beginners fail. Their unavailing efforts to get the line well out are entirely owing to their allowing the point of their rod to go too far down, and to
their stopping it too quickly, which makes the point recoil, and stops the line in
its forward motion. When the flies are just about alighting on the water, you
should slightly raise the point of your rod; this checks their downward motion,
and they fall much more softly.

The first advice given to beginners, in all treatises upon fly-fishing, is to acquire the art of throwing a long and light line. This practice of throwing a long line is the natural consequence of fishing down stream and for this method of fishing it is absolutely necessary—the advantage being, that the angler is farther away from the trout, and therefore less likely to be seen. As we have already shown, this can only be accomplished in a very limited and imperfect manner by throwing a long line, whereas fishing up secures the object perfectly.

In contradistinction to the maxim of throwing a long line, we advise the angler never to use a long line when a short one will, by any possibility, answer the purpose. The disadvantages of a long line are, that too much of it touches the water, and that it is impossible to throw it as it should be done, making the flies light first. It is also very difficult to throw it to any desired spot with certainty—to cast it neatly behind a stone or under a bank; besides which, more time is necessary to throw it, thus wasting that valuable commodity. The greatest objection to it, however, is its disadvantages in striking a trout; a long line lies curved in the water, and when the angler strikes, it is some time before the flies move; the line, in fact, requires to be straightened first. When they do move, it is slowly and without force, and there is little chance of hooking the trout. It is very different with a short line; in this case the line is almost straight from the point of the rod to the flies, and the least motion of the hand moves the latter immediately. We advise the angler who is using a long line, and raising but not hooking a number of trout, to shorten his line, and he will at once be struck with the difference. We have invariably found that the nearer we are to our flies the better we can use them, and the greater is our chance of hooking a trout when it rises.

The advantages of the second part of the maxim to throw a light line it is impossible to over-estimate. The moment the flies light—being the only one in which trout take the artificial fly for a live one—is the most deadly in the whole cast, and consequently it is of immense importance to make the flies light in a soft and natural manner. To accomplish this, and to throw with certainty to any spot wished, requires great practice and even the most practised angler can never make his flies fall so softly as an insect with outspread gauzy wings.

Thin gut, the necessity of which we have advocated so strongly, is exceedingly difficult to cast, as it has little weight to carry it forward, and therefore beginners should use moderately strong gut at first, and as they improve in casting reduce its size.

A difference of opinion exists as to whether a trout should be struck on rising; but in common with the great majority of anglers, we advocate immediate striking. When a trout takes a fly it shuts its mouth, and if the angler strikes then, he is almost sure to bring the hook into contact with its closed jaws. We have frequently watched the motions of trout on taking a fly, and when left to do with it what they choose, they very quickly expelled it from their mouths with considerable force; and we think that if the angler strikes even when the trout's mouth is open, he will have much better chance than by leaving it to hook itself. A trout on seizing an artificial fly is almost instantaneously aware that it is counterfeit, and never attempts to swallow it, very frequently letting it go before the angler has time to strike; so that it is of the utmost importance to strike immediately, and this is the reason why a quick eye and a ready hand are considered the most necessary qualifications for a fly-fisher. A trout first takes a fly, and then makes the motion which anglers term a rise, and which consists of their turning to go down; the angler therefore does not see the least break on the surface until the trout has either seized or missed the fly, so that he has already lost so much time, and should strike immediately.

Although it is impossible to strike too soon, it is quite possible to strike too hard. Some anglers strike with such force as to pull the trout out of the water, and throw it a considerable distance behind them. Now this is much too hard, and very apt with a small hook to tear it away from its hold, should it have any. Striking should be done by a slight but quick motion of the wrist, not by any motion of the arm. The angler should also take care to strike in the same direction as his rod is moving in at the time, for if he raises his rod, or otherwise alters its direction, the effect will not be nearly so immediate, and a moment is of the utmost importance in this matter.

One advantage of striking is, that should the trout miss the fly it rises at, the angler has still a chance of coming across it with some of the remaining ones. In a day's fishing we have frequently killed half a dozen trout hooked by the sides and other parts. And a trout hooked in this way always runs twice as hard as one hooked in the mouth. When hooked in the mouth, the strain that is kept on it prevents it from moving its gills, and suffocation ensues. This takes place sooner when the trout is drawn down a strong stream; so that the popular notion of pulling a trout down the water to drown it is correct, though the word is rather misapplied. If the trout is hooked by the outside of the body, the respiratory organs are left free, enabling it to run a long time; and when it does come to the side, the angler is disappointed at the small size of a fish which has been making such a desperate struggle.

In fishing up, the rise of a trout is by no means so distinct as in fishing down. They frequently seize the fly without breaking the surface, and the first intimation the angler gets of their presence is a slight pull at the line. The utmost attention is therefore necessary to strike the moment the least motion is either seen or felt. This is in some measure owing to the flies being in general a little under water, but principally to the fact that trout take a fly coming down stream in a quieter and more deadly manner than a fly going up. Seeing it going across and up stream, they seem afraid it may escape, make a rush at it, and in their hurry to seize, very frequently miss it altogether. It is very different in angling up stream: the trout see the fly coming towards them, rise to meet it, and seize it without any dash, but in a firm deadly manner.

When you hook a trout, if it is a small one and you are not wading, pull it on shore at once; if you are wading, it is better to act upon the maxim that "a bird in the hand is worth two in the bush," and come on shore before taking it off the hook, as it is very dangerous doing so when in the water. When you hook a large trout, which you cannot pull on shore at once, but require to exhaust previously, pull it down stream, as, in addition to choking it sooner, you have the force of the current in your favour. In playing a trout, do so as much as possible by keeping up with it by walking, and never let out line if you can avoid it. It is obvious that with a long line you cannot have the same command over it as with a short one; and take care never to allow your line to get slack, as, if you do, and the hook is not fixed, but merely resting on some bone, a thing which frequently occurs, the trout will throw it out of its mouth. To leave this point, in taking the trout out of the water do so with your hands, if you have not a landing-net; and never attempt lifting it by the line, or you are almost certain to pay dearly for your experience.

When you are approaching a pool which you intend to fish, if the water is clear do so carefully; you must recollect that the trout see you much more readily if you are on a high bank than if you are on a level with the water. For this reason keep as low down as possible, and always, if the nature of the ground will admit of it, stand a few yards from the edge of the water. If there is a ripple on the water you may meet with good sport in the still water at the foot of the pools, but if there is no wind, it is useless commencing till you come to where the water is agitated. If you do not intend fishing the lower part, do not walk up the side of it, as by so doing you will alarm the trout in that portion, and they may run up to the head of the pool for shelter, and frighten the others; but always come to the edge of the pool at the place where you intend to begin fishing. If the water is very low and the sun bright, it may be advisable to kneel in fishing a pool, in order to keep out of sight, and you must avoid allowing your shadow to fall upon the water above where you are standing.

First, as you approach, fish the side on which you are standing with a cast or two, and then commence to fish the opposite side, where you are to expect the most sport. For this reason you should always keep on the shallow side of the water, as the best trout generally lie under the bank at the deep side. After having taken a cast or two on the near side, throw your flies partly up stream and partly across, but more across than up, from where you are standing. You should throw them to within an inch of the opposite bank; if they alight on it so much the better; draw them gently off, and they will fall like a snow-flake, and if there is a trout within sight they are almost sure to captivate it. In this way your flies will fall more like a natural insect than by any other method.

After your flies alight, allow them to float gently down stream for a yard or two, taking care that neither they nor the line ripple the surface. There is no occasion for keeping them on the surface, they will be quite as attractive a few inches under water. As the flies come down stream, raise the point of your rod, so as to keep your line straight, and as little of it in the water as possible; and when they have traversed a few yards of water, throw again about a yard or two higher up than where your flies alighted the previous cast, and so on. Unless the spot looks exceedingly promising, you need not cast twice in one place if you do not get a rise, but if there is any quick turn in the water where there is likely to be a good trout, we frequently cast over it six or seven times in succession, just allowing the flies to alight when we cast again. When the current is strong, the trout may not see the fly at first, and so we cast repeatedly to make sure; and we have frequently, after casting unsuccessfully half-a-dozen times over the same place, caught a good trout at last. Move up the pool as quickly as you can, first taking a cast or two straight up on the side you are on, and then fishing the opposite side, and so on, until you finish the pool. Although it is about the edges of the pool you will generally get most trout, the main current must by no means be neglected; indeed in it you will frequently capture the best fish. By fishing in the way we have described, throwing a yard or two further up every cast, the flies may be brought in a wonderfully short space of time over every foot of water where a trout is likely to be.

Streams should be fished in exactly the same manner as pools; fishing the side you are on straight up, and the opposite side partly across and partly up. All quiet water between two streams, and eddies behind stones, should be fished straight up, and the flies just allowed to remain sufficiently long to let the trout see them; and in fishing such places care must be taken to keep the line out of the current. It is more difficult fishing streams than pools, as it requires greater nicety in casting; and on account of the roughness of the water it is not so easy to see a trout rise.

In fishing still water with no breeze upon it you should wait until the motion of the line falling has subsided, and then draw the flies slowly towards you; as, if they were allowed to remain stationary, the trout would at once detect their artificial nature.

Casting partly across and partly up stream, for a variety of reasons, is more deadly than casting directly up. The advantage of having a number of flies is entirely lost by casting straight up, as they all come down in a line, and it is only the trout in that line that can see them; whereas, if thrown partly across, they all come down in different lines, and the trout in all these lines may see them. In casting across, when the flies light, the stream carries them out at right angles to the line, and they come down the stream first, so that the trout sees the flies before the line; whereas, in casting straight up, if a trout is between the angler and the place where his flies light, the line passes over it before it sees the flies and may alarm it.

The moment the fly alights, being the most deadly of the whole cast, it is obvious that the oftener it is repeated the better, and therefore the angler should cast as frequently as possible, always allowing the flies to remain a few moments, in order to let the trout see them; but there is not much danger of casting too often, or even casting often enough, as the angler's arm will quickly rebel against it.

Rivers which can be commanded from bank to bank, either by wading or otherwise, constitute by far the most agreeable fishing; but if the river is so large that you cannot reach the opposite side, you must look for sport on the side you are on. And in this case, though you should neglect no spot where a trout may be lying, fish most carefully the part of the pool where the shallow merges into the deep, and where the current is moderately strong; fishing it in the same manner as you would do the opposite side, and always as you go up taking a cast or two straight up, as close to the edge as possible.

On all occasions cast your flies about a yard above where you think the trout are likely to be found, as if on alighting it attracts their attention, there is much less chance of their discovering its artificial nature at that distance. For the same reason, if you see a trout rise at a natural fly throw above it, and in general it will meet the fly half-way. If a trout rise and you miss it, cast again, and continue doing so until it ceases to rise; a small trout will frequently rise four or five times in succession; but the large well-conditioned fish are more wary, and if they miss once or twice will sometimes decline returning, however temptingly you may throw your flies.

A breezy day is generally considered favourable for fly-fishing, and no doubt it is so if the wind is blowing up stream; but it is equally likely that it may be blowing down—it generally blows either up or down, very seldom across—in which case the angler would be very much better without it. Because the wind is blowing down, the angler should on no account fish in the same direction, but must endeavour to cast against it as well as he can. He may, however, stand a little farther back from the water, and fish more nearly opposite to where he is standing than would otherwise be advisable. To cast against the wind, it is necessary to use great force, and immerse a considerable portion of the line in the water. If the wind is very strong, it is a great nuisance, no matter which way it is blowing, as it is sometimes almost impossible to keep the line in the water. In such circumstances it is impossible to fish the streams properly, and the angler should limit his operations to the pools, and should use thicker gut and a heavier casting-line, which will be found a great assistance to casting. It is in such a case that the thorough worthlessness of a supple rod becomes apparent.

As the trout seldom take fly readily for more than four or five hours in the forenoon, you must make the most of the time, fish quickly, walk over the intervening ground smartly, take the trout off the hook, and basket them as speedily as possible, and in every way economise time. If you ever see a professional angler at work when the trout are taking, watch him, and you will be able to form some idea of how expeditiously fishing may be done. As long as you are fishing, do it as if you expected a rise every cast; we have lost many a good trout in an inadvertant moment. If you are tired, or the trout are not taking, sit down and console yourself in some way or other. A late writer upon the subject suggests, that for this purpose the angler should carry a New Testament in his pocket, to which there can be no possible objection, but we rather think most anglers prefer spiritual consolation of a very different sort, coupled with sandwiches; there is a time for all things, and at noon we must admit having a preference for the latter method. It has moreover this advantage, that you will be the more able to fish properly when the trout begin to take again.

We have as yet said nothing about the adaptation of flies in point of size to the season of the year and the state of the water, because this subject is so intimately connected with the habits of the trout during the different fly-fishing months, that it is impossible to separate them, and we shall therefore discuss them together; but before commencing, we may remark, that a knowledge of the habits of the trout is the most necessary of all information to the angler. He may have the best tackle and the best flies, and be skilled in the art of throwing them lightly; but unless he knows where feeding trout are to be found, he will never achieve great success.

There you have pretty much the essence of Stewart. Bearing in mind that Stewart was as radical in his day, with his advocacy of a ten-foot rod, after the prevalence of rods two and three feet longer, as Lee Wulff was a century later in advocating a six-foot rod, virtually everything that Stewart says about tackle and tactics is basically right, and subject only to the modifications that improvement in the material components of rods, lines and leaders have since brought about.

It's a little horrifying to see how he practically recommends foul-hooking, as one of the advantages of the "ladder" of flies that all anglers of his time customarily employed, but still I'm old enough to recall Herman Christian doing the same thing, as he went down the Neversink jerking out one "double" after another, some of which had one trout hooked in the mouth and the other in the tail, and being reproved by Mr. Hewitt for having "the soul of a poacher." Since Mr. Hewitt was being rather conspicuously skunked, with his "stream-emptying" single-size 16 nymph at the time, while Christian went marching to glory with his pair of wet flies, I have the feeling that the ghost of Stewart, the "practical" angler, would have sided with Herman Christian and against Mr. Hewitt. But that's something we can come back to later.

Mr. Hewitt, who bragged of feeding an entire company of soldiers with fish in his youth, did finally outgrow the small boy's "how many" attitude to espouse the "how well" approach of the mature angler. But that's a concept that, far from expecting from an angler of Stewart's time, would actually have been hard to explain to him. His idea of par for the "practical" angler's daily average take was a matter of twelve pounds. Baskets like that would take us back, at least over here, to the days of Uncle Thad Norris and W. C. Prime, long before the thought of returning hooked trout to the water had ever been entertained.

And since that virtually is the time of Stewart, maybe it wouldn't be such a bad idea to take a look at the American side of the bookshelf, before we pursue the English angler's progress.

After all, since Norris and Prime were less than a century removed from this country's liberation from colonial status, they stand in relation to the shorter time-span of angling in America about where Walton and Cotton stood. With the foreshortening of perspective imposed by a difference of some four hundred years in the angling backgrounds of the two countries, England and the United States, Bethune could even play the role of their Juliana.

This is not to say that Prime was our Cotton, as indeed I do happen to feel that Norris *was* our Walton, but merely that Norris and Prime occupied a comparable time-spot, in relation to the beginnings of American angling as opposed to the British.

9.

America and Uncle Thad

I like to announce my prejudices beforehand, loud and clear, rather than let them sneak in the side door after our proceedings are under way.

So before I say anything at all about American angling, let me declare a prejudice or two, like so much dutiable stuff at the customs counter, so nobody can feel I've sneaked them in.

I don't like Prime. Nor do I much care for "Barnwell," Teddy Roosevelt's uncle. I find them both pompous, conceited, opinionated, and more than a little stuffy. And while Prime's garrulous tendency, his "logorrhea" if you like, his habit of getting, as Disraeli said of Gladstone, "inebriated with the exuberance of his own verbosity," is really not too much worse than Walton's finally became, still I find Walton's charming and Prime's almost maddening. And while Walton's piety was pronounced, Prime's seems to me overweening.

I'm probably just as unfairly biased against both Prime and Robert Barnwell Roosevelt as I always felt my friend Hermann Deutsch was against both Walton and Audubon.

And to allow you to make your own wind-allowances, every time I open my mouth about either Prime or "Barnwell," I suppose I ought to declare a few tendencies to go too far in another direction.

150

I adore Uncle Thad Norris, warmly admire and respect George Washington Bethune, and of course virtually worship Theodore Gordon. There's the one I'd call our Cotton, in counterpart to the role of Thaddeus Norris as the American Walton. And since I realize that I may easily get carried away whenever I get started on either of them, it's only fair to hoist a warning flag to indicate the imminence of some prejudice pro as well as con.

Among my own books, I find nothing American earlier than the Jerome Smith volume, *Natural History of the Fishes of Massachusetts, embracing a practical essay on Angling,* originally published in 1833, and reprinted by Freshet Press in 1970. This has been generally credited as the first essay on angling in America.

There were, of course, some earlier references to fishing, for food and for commerce, but this quite probably is the first thing devoted exclusively to sport-fishing, or angling for its own sake as a diversion, as opposed to fishing purely for considerations of commissary or commerce. I do recall, somewhere among my books, some John White sixteenth-century drawings, depicting the fishing activities of Seminole Indians in Florida, and I have seen, but don't have a copy of, an 1830 volume devoted to the history of what was certainly the first fishing club in the country, The Schuylkill Fishing Company which dated from pre-Revolutionary days in Philadelphia. But earlier than that there seems to be no angling literature worthy of the term. For that matter, I don't find the essay by Jerome V. C. Smith, M.D. particularly quoteworthy, though I suppose we could spare a moment for a sample of its style.

. . . round the casting line when wet, as it is inclined to do. Its distance from the end fly or stretcher is about three feet, but if bait is used, it should be at least double that distance. Its body or dubbing may be made of red worsted, mohair or floss silk, the last being neatest, and objectionable in all flies only on account of its greater liability to hold the water. Then comes the *hackle,* from the neck feathers of a white rooster dyed red, which is wound round the body, making a very simple *fly,* so called, but more resembling a caterpillar, as it will be observed it has no wings.

When three flies are used, there can be no better arrangement for them than the following. The first drop-fly, to be thirty inches from the stretcher, the gut only four inches long, and of the stoutest kind. The second drop-fly to be thirty-five inches from the first, and the gut eight inches long. The advantage of observing this fixed distance between the flies, is that of their all three coming in contact with the water in the ordinary position of the line after it is cast.

Highly as we appreciate it as a pleasing resource to the angler, and forming one object for the exercise of his skill, it is not intended to add to these remarks our own experience in the art of fly making; it will however be proper to state the names of those mentioned in the books on angling—where ample directions may be seen—of such as are said, and we have proved to be, *standard flies,* that is, such as are found to be good at all times and in all places. They are the palmer flies, namely, the red hackle, yellow hackle, grouse hackle, etc.; and wing flies, such as the green drake or may-fly, the march brown, and indeed any and all of that class of insects known by the name of phryganeae and ephemerae, to which may be added the grasshopper as well as beetles, "for there is hardly any insect that flies, including the wasp, the hornet, the bee and the butterfly, that does not become at sometime the prey of fishes."

If the angler has half a dozen of each of the palmers, as well as a small stock of the wing flies above alluded to, he may be considered well provided, particularly if he has also feathers and other materials to repair his loss in case either variety should be exhausted. The manufacture of flies is a very nice operation, and more suited to the delicate fingers of females, by whom they are principally made in England, Scotland, &c. The very best of them are but rude imitations of nature, but the practised eye will distinguish at a glance those that are made by rule, from those that are made by a novice in the art. From our own experience we have been of opinion that quite as much stress is laid upon the necessity of an infinite variety of flies as is consistent with fact; neither do we believe that the most killing will prove to be such flies, as at the time the trout happen to be taking. For on the contrary we have often noticed that a totally different fly may be used with success, and it may too, be unlike any insect in creation, for which reason, they seem to give it the preference. There are however certain general rules to be observed, such as a dark fly for a bright day, and a bright fly for a cloudy day; a small fly for calm water and a larger one for a rapid. The great difficulty in fly making is in the wings, nay, it is not only difficult but impossible to imitate with anything like truth to nature, those little reticulated gossamer transparencies, neither would the flies be any better if we could.

A judicious selection of feathers then is all that can be done; they have the advantage of any substance more delicate, which would not bear the use. The smaller the fly the more difficult it is to make, and this accounts for the artificial ones being so out of all proportion; though we do not believe they are any the worse for it. Indeed it would be a very difficult thing not only to procure a hook sufficiently small, but to make a fly so very minute as to be scarcely perceptible on the water. It frequently happens, in a calm time, that the surface is covered with an insect so small that they could not be perceived by the fish if it was at all agitated by the wind. At such times the trout are rising in all directions, apparently in sport, but upon examination they will be found to have fifty or more of these little specks collected in the throat. To imitate the size then is out of the question, the most we can do is to come as near as possible to the colors, and if we have nothing like it in our collection, to make one upon the spot, though it may be twenty times as large.

But enough of calms, the test of an angler's skill. The most showy and therefore the most killing salmon flies, resemble nothing which skims the air; after the body requiring great nicety in the operation of tying, they are principally made up of a mass of the most gaudy feathers possible; well arranged, gay and attractive as the butterfly, and intermingling their tints like the prismatic colors of the rainbow. Such are the Irish flies of Martin Kelly, some remarks upon which, taken from an English Magazine, we here subjoin, as they apply to fly fishing and fly making in general.

"I would recommend every man who aspired to be a first rate salmon fisher, or is likely to have frequent opportunities of enjoying that noble sport, to learn the art of fly *dressing*. The occupation is agreeable, and the pleasure of killing a salmon with those of one's own manufacture is infinitely greater than that afforded by doing so with the handy-work of any other artist. The dressing of an Irish fly is, it must be admitted, a tedious, and to do it neatly, rather a difficult operation, and requires not only practice in the mere mechanical part of the process, but likewise considerable judgment in the selection and adaptation of the component parts. Any man who has been taught to *tie* flies, may imitate a pattern correctly enough; but it is not so easy a matter, without a model, to select and mix a good wing, and choose the colors of the body, legs, head, &c., so as to make a judicious whole. The merely being able to tie a neat and pretty looking fly, is not sufficient; something more is wanting, and this something, most men whether regular tackle makers, or amateurs, want, and nothing but experience and careful and minute observation will supply the deficiency."

Having made this long *détour* from Childs' River, we now return to it, for the purpose merely of stating the numbers and size of the fish taken at one particular time. It was on the eighteenth of May 1829, that two persons—one of whom was an English gentleman, a "brother of the angle," to whom we are principally indebted for the small stock of practical skill we possess—took seventy fine sea-trout, weighing thirty-eight pounds. A number of the largest weighed about a pound and a half, but none over. They were nearly all taken with the fly, and most of them with three or four varieties of those standard flies already mentioned, namely, the red and yellow palmer or hackle, the march brown, and grouse hackle. The time on the whole was favorable, though the sun was out, the wind blowing up the river, mild and gentle.

There is another river which flows into Waquoit Bay, known by the Indian name of Quashnut. In its tide waters the sea-trout are sometimes collected in considerable numbers. It is at best however an uncertain place, and never can amount to much as a trout stream on account of the mill which obstructs their progress to its upper waters, to say nothing of the stealthy practice of seining, before mentioned. And here it may be remarked that the effect of a mill, as it respects the trout stream, depends very much upon its location. If it is high up and near the source, its operation is far less unfavorable to their annual upward tendency, as many instances might be adduced to prove, but if on the contrary, as in the instance of the stream last mentioned, the fall happens to be such that the mill is erected upon the lower waters, it proves an effectual barrier to their migrations, and they desert the stream for one more congenial . . .

Austin S. Hogan, angling historian and curator of the Museum of American Fly Fishing, in *American Sporting Periodicals of Angling Interest*, a selected check list and guide, prepared for and published by the museum, in Manchester, Vermont, lists the *American Angler's Guide*, published anonymously ("by an American angler") in 1845 by John J.

Brown, New York City tackle dealer and collector of angling books, as the first complete book on angling printed in America. I've never seen it, but remember that it was cited by Goodspeed's *Angling in America*, along with some angler's almanacs published by Brown for several years thereafter as being among the scarcest items of American angling literature. Since like the Jerome Smith volume its interest is almost entirely historical, I wouldn't go out of my way to look for it. Besides, it precedes by only a couple of years the masterful essay by "The American Editor," Bethune's Bibliographical Preface and Notes to the 1847 first American edition of *The Compleat Angler*, which I do consider "worth the journey," as the Michelin guides would put it. Certainly if we're talking in terms of angling literature, worthy of the name, then Bethune is the beginning, beyond a doubt.

Hogan points out, in the preface to his check list, a basic problem of American angling history, and offers a key to its solution:

The purpose of this check list is to open several doors. What little is in print concerning the history of angling in America, and particularly fly fishing, rests very insecurely on the textual material found in two books. These are Mary Orvis Marbury's *Favorite Flies and Their Histories*, a colorful, romantic and charming Victorian presentation, and Charles E. Goodspeed's *Angling in America*, which within its space limitations provides an excellent introduction to historic fishing as it developed within the framework of its literature. A third contribution might be mentioned—Charles Wetzel's introduction to his *American Fishing Books*, which also is bound firmly to the world of books. These three publications are necessarily limited in scope, but should be read by everyone who has more than a casual interest regarding their American past. Unfortunately, though Marbury, Goodspeed and Wetzel offer many hours of pleasurable and instructive reading, and within the last several decades a number of articles have appeared in magazines which might be termed regionally historical, the whole of our inquiries have scarcely touched the surface. There still remains a vast body of information which has never been collected. The basic source for the necessary research is the American sporting publication of which over three hundred were published before 1900. . . . Here is a literature that reflects the thinking and the lives of thousands of fishermen week by week and year by year for nearly a century and a half. So few American angling books have come on the market that there is no doubt sportsmen by choice are readers of the magazine and sporting newspaper.

The longest-lived of these was *Spirit of the Times*, which began in 1831 and, though it had little coverage of angling after 1861, continued up to the first years of this century.

A frequent contributor was the Englishman Henry William Herbert, London born and Eton and Cambridge educated, who came to this country the year *Spirit of the Times* was started, and wrote under the pseudonym Frank Forester. Although he adopted the pseudonym only because he felt that he was demeaning himself in writing for the *Spirit of the Times,* he retained it as the author of numerous sporting books and indeed became known under that by-line as the father of sport fiction in America. A suicide at fifty-one, in 1858, he was a colorful character on the sporting scene. (I always found his stuff unreadable, which is obviously another prejudice since he was wildly popular, though I can't conceive of any conscious basis for being prejudiced against him; but my shelves are devoid of so much as a line by Frank Forester.)

Hogan, based on better knowledge, apparently shares at least some of my antipathy to Forester, as he wrote me, in response to a query about him that he was "a very well-educated S.O.B. and an unethical bastard in dealing with publishers, and so disliked, they couldn't get more than a handful at the funeral. The first attempt at a Forester Memorial was almost a complete failure. (Donation: $1.00.) Not one contemporary author on the list. I have the original."

To revive an old slogan, such popularity must be deserved (I find that one-dollar sum total of the donation a fascinating touch), but I don't know enough about him to justify my comment. Hogan, however, is literally drenched with data and lore about the early American angling figures, and I wish he could be prevailed upon to embody between book covers his version of *Angling in America.*

John McDonald, in *Quill Gordon,* has dealt extensively with Bethune's unique contribution to American angling history, so it is to him that I next turn, to put "The American Editor" into the proper perspective, against the background of his time.

George Washington Bethune is distinguished in fly-fishing for having edited the earliest edition of Walton's *The Compleat Angler* in the United States (1847), and for having collected the first great library of fishing books in this country. In his edition of Walton he buried a long footnote on fly-fishing in his time, which seems to have been overlooked in discussions of early American commentary on the sport. It constitutes an essay on the subject, the earliest, I believe, of its kind.

Not much is known in detail about American fly-fishing before the Civil War. The first comprehensive work by an American was Thaddeus Norris's classic *The American Angler's Book* in 1864, which guided many angling writers, including Theodore Gordon, during the rest of that century. The late Charles

Eliot Goodspeed (*Angling in America*, 1939), a great bibliophile, introduced us to the evidences of American angling before Norris, but most of what we know about early American fly-fishing is drawn from three important books, all of them published in the 1840's: *The American Angler's Guide* (1845), compiled by John J. Brown, a New York tackle dealer; Bethune's edition of Walton; and Frank Forester's *Fish and Fishing* (London, 1849; New York, 1850).

Brown tells us that fly-fishing "finds but little favor in this country." Flies, he says, were "made to order or procured from England." But he adds a significant observation: If no satisfactory fly was available, it was the practice to "examine the waters and shake the boughs of the trees, to procure the latest insect . . . and imitate nature's handiwork on the spot."

Bethune's essay gives the argument of anglers of that time, with a few indigenous fly dressings. His language for natural and artificial flies is largely descriptive; he does not often give his flies artificial titles. One should keep in mind that Bethune, like all anglers of the period, was limited to fishing for Brook trout with the wet fly.

But it is to Bethune himself that we must turn, to get the contrast between his own style, shaped no doubt by his studies and his work as a Dutch Reformed clergyman, and that of Walton, and yet so carefully attuned to the nature of the work he was editing that he somehow seemed to be able, whenever he felt the need, to make it completely compatible with that of the older writer. Perhaps I am reading things into it that are not there, but I find particularly in the opening of his preface, a rhythm and a cadence that seems to me especially finely tuned and adapted to the matter at hand:

BIBLIOGRAPHICAL PREFACE,
by
THE AMERICAN EDITOR,
with
Some Notices of Fishing, and Books on Fishing,
Before Walton.

Every lover of books knows that he finds his best refreshment from closer study, in books themselves; and how likely he is to get a love for some one author, so as to read him again and again, liking him the better for his very faults, and thinking everything worth remark that throws light on his history, manner of life, means of knowledge, and standing among those who knew him in his own time. Such a love have I for dear old Iz. Wa., which fondness is not a little heightened by an inborn fondness for, perhaps some skill in his gentle, contemplative art. The stream side is ever dear to me, and I love to think of the times when I have trudged merrily along it, finding again in the fresh air and moderate exercise and devout looks upon nature, the strength of nerve, the buoyancy of heart and health of mind, which I had lost in my pent library and town duties; now I need but to open the pages of *The Complete Angler*, and the stream flows by my side, the birds sing for me, the "daisies, culverkeys, and ladysmocks" bloom, the bright trout leap, the finny spoils are won, and a quiet chat enjoyed with the Master and his Scholar under a wide tree shedding off the rain; or by the fire of the wayside Inn, while the hostess, "clean, handsome, and civil," is taking out "sheets smelling of lavender," for our beds, in a room that has "more than twenty ballads stuck against the wall;" or within the little shrine, *Sacrum Piscatoribus*, built by Cotton for his father, and "all true men who love quiet and go an angling." I trust that I have drunk enough of the old angler's spirit not to let such pastime break in upon better things; but, on the other hand, I have worked the harder from thankfulness to HIM who taught the brook to wind with musical gurglings, as it rolls on to the Great Sea.

It has been my wont at such times, to note down what I happened to find, giving greater zest to father Walton's quaint homilies, not in any hope that others would think it worth while to share my gatherings, but rather for my better memory and coming delight. The good publishers of this darling book, hearing of my little store, have asked me to put it at their disposal for your use, kind reader; and, as I count (with honest Shirley in his Angler's Magazine) "that a person has a mean soul that could die without disclosing anything he knows, that he might benefit or please his fellow-creatures," I have done as they wished. The whole work has been gone over; the several editions collated, some notes chosen from the various editors, and, as you will see, more added by myself. Of how much worth these last are, you shall judge; but you can never know what happy hours I have spent in preparing them, or how truly I wish they may be to your liking. A good and pious friend of mine (how good and pious I dare not say, for he will surely read what I write, and I would spare him a blush even at his own true praise) has told me that it was reading this book, which awakened the love of God in his heart; nor may we wonder, that such meek-hearted, cheerful strains of godly contentment should have been blessed to such an end; and I pray that a like blessing may go with your reading.

My first task shall be to give you some knowledge of books upon Angling, or rather fishing, before Walton. I say, rather books on *fishing;* for an angler, kind reader, is not a *fisherman,* who plies his calling for a livelihood, careless in what way he gets his scaly rewards. The name comes from *angle* or hook, for the true angler touches no net, but that with which he lands the heavy struggler hung on his tiny hair. He scorns to entrap by weir, or fyke, or wicker-pot, the finny people, when not bent on harm; but as they watch murderously for the pretty fly, the helpless minnow, or the half-drowned worm, he comes like a chivalrous knight to wreak upon them the wrong they would do, and slay them as they think to slay. For every one he kills a hundred lesser lives are saved, and the small fry shoot fearlessly along, where once they dared not to be seen, when he has drawn the tyrant of the brook from his long kept lair. As Franklin said to the cod in whose belly some small cod were found, so says the angler to his prey, "If you eat your kind, I will eat you." If skilful as he ought to be, the angler need fix no quivering life on his hook, but with feather and silk and downy dubbing, he makes a bait far more winning, that drops upon the curling water, or plays among the whirlpools, as though it were born for the frolic. When a trout chooses to prey upon what he thinks is weaker than himself, the angler ought not to be blamed for it. Neither does he love the sea for his pastime, nor to sit in a boat, or on a rock, or a quay, watching his cork for a nibble (forgive us, shades of Jo. Dennys and Iz. Walton, but, surely, we pigmies on your giant shoulders may see further than you!). His choice is the swift river, the rock-broken stream; and he walks hopefully on from one jutting cliff to another, making his fly fall lightly as a drop of snow on each turn of the wave, or under the out-eaten turf, or over the deep, dark pool. You have taken from him half his life "if his free breathing be denied" among the meadows, the glens, and the uplands. Nevertheless, we shall speak of fishing in any of the ways followed by those, who lived so much in the dark ages as to know nothing of the fly; yet enjoyed what the learned author of "L'Art de la Peche aux lignes volantes et flottantes, aux filets et autres instruments," calls by a rare melange of languages, "*Pisciceptologie.*"

Fisher, editor of the Angler's Souvenir, from a praiseworthy pride in his nominal ancestors, says the Saxon race were called *Anglo,* because of their skill with the *angle;* and truly they have earned such an honorable epithet, for the art is well carried out only among their descendants; though Kresz (aine) has written on artificial flies with rare cleverness for a Frenchman;* and it is worthy of remark, that Masaniello, vulgarly called The Fisherman of Naples, was an angler, who used "to catch small fish with a rod and hook."† We must, however, go further back than the *ultima Thule* of our Saxon lineage, for the first fisherman.

---

* There is a translation of this treatise in the Sporting Magazine, London, xxiii., xxiv., 1829.
† La professione di lui era di pescare pesciolini con la canna e con l'hamo. – Le Revoluzioni di Napoli dal Signor Alessandro Giraffi.

Gervase Markham, in his book of "Country Contentments" (A.D. 1631), speaking of angling, says: "For the antiquity thereof (for al pleasures, like Gentry, are held to be most excellent, which is most ancient), it is by some Writers sayd to be found out by *Deucalion* and *Pyrrha* his Wife after the general flood; others write that it was the invention of *Saturne,* after the peace concluded between him and his brother *Tytan;* and others that it came from *Belus* and sonne of *Nimrod,* who invented all holy and vertuous Recreations; and al these, though they savour of fiction, yet they differ not from truth, for it is most certaine that both *Deucalion, Saturne,* and *Belus,* are taken for figures of *Noah* and his Family, and the invention of the art of angling, is truly sayd to come from the sonnes of Seth, of whom Noah was most principall. Thus you see it is good as having no coherence with evil, worthy of use; inasmuch as it is mixt with a delightfull profit; and most ancient, as being the Recreation of the first Patriarkes."

Walton himself, speaking of the antiquity of angling (p. 32), quotes the opinion of Jo. Da* (as he calls the author of "The Secrets of Angling") thus: "Some say it is as ancient as Deucalion's Flood;" for in the poem (under the head of "The Author of Angling, Poetical Fictions"), the writer says, that urged by a lack of food for his starving family,

> "Then did Deucalion first this art invent
> Of angling, and his people taught the same.
>
> And thus with ready practice and inventive wit,
> He found the means in every lake and brook
>
> Such store of fish to take with little pain,
> As did long time this people now sustain."

But "others," adds our venerable father, "which I like better" (meaning Gervase Markham, see B.1, *first* edition), "say that Belus (who was the inventor of godly and vertuous Recreations) was the inventor of it; and some others say (for former times have had their disquisitions about it), that Seth, one of the sons of Adam, taught it to his sons, and that by them it was handed down to posterity. Others say, that he left it engraved on those Pillars which hee erected to preserve the knowledge of the mathematicks, musick, and the rest of those precious arts, which by God's appointment and allowance and his noble industry were thereby preserved from perishing in Noah's Flood." These were the same with the tables of stone engraved with sacred characters by the first Mercury, and translated, according. . . .

But it is in the footnotes that Bethune's love and knowledge of angling transform his style; there he seems to speak with two voices, in one type of comment, concerning a variorum reading or the attribution of a source to a given line or allusion, he is all deferential grace, the perfect scholar abnegating himself to the prime consideration of elucidation of the text, but when it comes, on another occasion, to a practical

---

* The name is noted only in the first edition.

question of applying angling skills to a local condition, he is all man of action and confident expertise, changing in a trice from abstract theorist to assertive pragmatist. He knows what works over here, and what doesn't, he seems to be saying, and in the moment of saying it, he seems to put on quite another persona, like a change of hats.

Here, for example, is the long footnote that stretched to nearly treatise length, and that John McDonald extracted to feature in *Quill Gordon* as the earliest essay on American fly fishing:

As has been before stated, the anglers of our day are divided into two schools, which may be conveniently distinguished as the *routine* and the *non-imitation*. The former hold that the trout should be angled for only with a nice imitation of the natural flies in season at the time, and that, therefore, the flies seen on the water, or found in the belly of the fish, are to be carefully imitated. To this school belong the older writers, from Venables down, and Taylor, Blaine, Hansard, South, Shipley, and Fitzgibbon, &c., &c. The *non-imitation* school (which reckons among its adherents Rennie, Professor Wilson, Fisher, of the Angler's Souvenir, &c., &c.), hold that no fly can be made so as to imitate nature well enough to warrant us in believing that the fish takes it for the natural fly; and, therefore, little reference is to be had to the fly upon which the trout are feeding at the time. "The fish," says Professor Rennie (*Alphabet of Angling*), "appear to seize upon an artificial fly, because, when drawn along the water, it has the appearance of being a living insect, whose species is quite unimportant, as all insects are equally welcome. The aim of the angler, accordingly, ought to be to have his artificial fly calculated, by its form and colors, *to attract the notice* of the fish, in which case he has a much greater chance of success than by making the greatest efforts to imitate any particular species of fly." Fisher (*Angler's Souvenir*) remarks, in the same strain: "Wherever fly-fishing is practised—in England, Scotland, Ireland, Wales, France, Germany, and America—it has been ascertained, from experience, that the best flies are those which are not shaped professedly in imitation of any particular living insect. Red, black, and brown hackles, and flies of the bittern's, mallard's, partridge's, woodcock's, grouse's, bald-coot's, martin's, or blue hen's feathers, with dubbing of brown, yellow, or orange, occasionally blended, and hackles, red, brown, or black, under the wings, are the most useful flies that an angler can use in daylight, on any stream, all the year through. For night-fishing in lakes, or long still ponds, no fly is better than a white hackle. The directions given in books to beat the bushes by the side of the stream, to see what kind of fly is in the water, and to open a fish's stomach to see what kind of fly the fish has been feeding on, are not deserving the least attention. The angler must be guided in his selection of flies by the state of the water—whether clear or dull, smooth or ruffled by a breeze; and also by the state of the weather, as it may be cloudy or bright. When the water is clear, and the day rather bright, small flies and hackles of a dark shade are most likely to prove successful, if used with a fine line and thrown by a delicate hand; but then it is only before eight in the morning and after six in the evening, from June to August, that the fish may be expected to rise. When the water, in such weather, is ruffled by a fresh breeze, larger hackles and flies of the same color may be used. When the water is clearing after rain, a red hackle, and a fly with a body of orange-colored mohair, dappled wings of a mallard or pea-fowl's feather, with a reddish brown hackle under them, are likely to tempt trout, at any time of day, from March to October. The old doctrine of a different assortment of flies for each month in the year is now deservedly exploded, for it is well known to practical anglers, who never read a book on the subject, and whose judgment is not biassed by groundless theories, that the same flies with which they catch most fish in April will generally do them good service throughout the season. The names given to artificial flies are for the most part arbitrary, and afford no guide (with one or two exceptions) for distinguishing the fly meant. Where the materials for dressing a dozen of flies are so much alike, that when they are finished there is so little difference in appearance, that one angler will give them one name and another another, it is absurd to affix to each an individual appellation."

On the other side, it is contended, that the non-imitation writers themselves admit, as experience compels them to do, that there must be an adaptation of *colors* in the fly, and also that certain flies will not be taken at some seasons which are freely taken at others. Nay, that though, when the fish are wantonly playful and hungry, they may rush at almost anything like an insect, when the water is clear, the day bright, and the fish coy, the angler who best imitates the natural fly of the time, and casts it with skill, "stands," to use the words of Mr. Blaine, "proudly conspicuous among his fellows."

For my own part (in common with most American anglers), I lean to the non-imitation theory, but would not carry it so far as to reject all the notions of the *doctrinaires*. The trout in our upland streams are more plentiful, and, clearly, less sophisticated than those with whom our transatlantic brethren are conversant. In a virgin stream (such an one as an artificial fly has never been cast upon, which the American fly-fisher sometimes meets with), the trout, if fairly on the feed, will take anything that is offered to them. I have, from mere wantonness of experiment, caught dozens from a still pool, at noon-day, with a *white miller;* and have rarely known a hackle, adapted to the water, and weather, and time of day, to fail. Hackles, in their several varieties, are the mainstays of the American angler, though not to the exclusion of winged flies. Thus, in the Long Island ponds and sea fed streams, hackles are almost exclusively used early in the season, followed, not supplanted by the far-famed Professor, the green drake, the grey drake, and the camlets. Indeed, a skilful angler, well acquainted with those waters, and disposed to give information, persisted in answering to all my questions about flies in their seasons, "hackle, hackle, hackle." He says: "I have found the plain, black hackle, the black and blue-bodied hackle, the dark red hackle, the bright red hackle, the yellow hackle, and the partridge and woodcock hackles, decidedly the most killing flies in all American waters at all seasons, keeping this in mind, that the later the season, the brighter and gaudier-bodied fly may be used successfully. I am not an admirer of *fancy flies*, nor have I seen them take many or large fish on Long Island. On the lakes in the interior of New York, I have been informed that this is not the case, but that peacock's eyes, drake wings, and even gaudy macaws kill well; but were I fishing for a wager, I would stick to the various hackles, unless it were for salmon or sea trout, in taking which I believe the fancy flies preferable."

Another skilful brother of the rod says, that (the present year) about the first of April, the trout on Long Island would take freely only the grey drake, made large for the tail and smaller for the drop; though he killed several with a gnat fly of brown body and black wings.

Yet another, and a friend on whose judgment much reliance is to be placed, writes his experience of the inland streams: "When I began to fish, I *bought* flies according to the season in which the seller said they were good, as did some of the books; but I soon found that nothing could be ascertained in this way, and that I could judge of a fly only by actual trial, as the trout are very capricious in their taste. By observing what fly was on the water, or by putting on three or four of different colors, I could decide what fly was to their taste, and keeping that fly so far as the wings were concerned, I could change the body of the fly according to circumstances. For my part, I believe that book knowledge will help an angler in this country very little, for the obvious reason that the seasons vary so much in different places. Our fly-fishing season includes May, June, July, and August; and as a general rule for May and June, I would use — 1. Drab bodies, with light or cream-colored wings. 2. Yellow bodies, with light or brown wings. 3. Red bodies, with light or brown wings. For July and August, red and brown flies." This is, of course, not to the exclusion of the palmers or wingless hackles.

My own experience on the inland streams is not much earlier than the end of April, and my practice is to observe the fly on the waters for my tail fly, and experiment with hackles on the drop. My favorite early flies are the March brown, stone, blue dun, and the cow dung; to be followed, as the season advances, by the green and grey drake, and later, the claret and red bodies, with light brown, sometimes more showy wings. For the hackles, the red hackle is the queen, — but a large coarse black or furnace hackle, *silver* ribbed, kills early: afterwards, the sorrel gold ribbed; in the summer, red and black hackles, small and very buzz. As a general rule, my flies grow *smaller* as the summer advances, for then the waters are lower and clearer, while the sky is brighter.

From all these opinions, the reader will see that the routine system is neither to be contemptuously rejected nor slavishly followed. There are flies that kill all the season; but the stone-fly will not tell in August, nor the claret body in April. Still, it cannot be doubted, that the trout, like men, have their caprices of appetite, and, except in the first few days of the May-fly, they may be as glad of a chance at a fly out of season, as an epicure would be of early green peas.

In this country, fly-fishing for trout is out of question before March, and, except on Long Island, before the middle of April, that is, after the chill of the snow freshets is gone, and when the streams, though full, are clear. After the first of September, a true-hearted angler will not wet a line in a trout stream. It will therefore be readily seen, as has been observed, that directions serviceable in Great Britain and Ireland, must be greatly modified to be of use among us, from the varieties of our climate, the character of our waters, and the habits of our aquatic insects. I shall, therefore, conclude the notes on this part of our subject by a list of flies furnished by an excellent brother of our gentle art, who relieves the labors of a life most zealously devoted to the best interests of his fellow-men, by occasionally fishing the head waters of the Susquehannah and Delaware, all the tributaries to which abound in trout. His particular haunts are the streams of Pike, Wayne, and Susquehannah counties in Pennsylvania, and of Sullivan and Broome in New York. To great skill at the stream side, he unites equal aptness in making his own flies from the means within his reach.

If, from the directions given, the reader should acquire a due proportion of my friend's art in making and using the flies recommended, he will have nothing to wish for but a heart equally at peace with God and man—and, when he goes a fishing,

> "A day with not too bright a beam,
> And a south-west wind to curl the stream."

It must not be supposed that these flies are all that may be used, but with those others, too well known to need description, a book well supplied according to the list, is all that the fly-fisher necessarily needs. The experienced angler will recognise some old and highly valued acquaintances.

No. 1. A tail, end, or stretcher fly, on a No. 4 (Limerick) hook. *Body*, light slate drab, wound with the smallest gold cord and a red hackle. *Wings*, the brown under feather of a peacock's wing. Its *tail* has a tuft of red worsted (or mohair); and its *head* is wound round with gold cord. This is so excellent a fly as to be known in some places as *The* Fly. It is good as a general fly throughout the season. Made on a No. 8 hook, it may be used as a drop-fly with much execution.

No. 2. For a tail-fly on No. 5, for a drop on No. 8. *Body*, first wound with yellow floss silk, then a thread of crimson, then in an opposite direction a thread of gold, with a slight yellow or red hackle at the head for legs. *Wings*, rather full of the brown wing feathers of the peacock, or the lightest brown wing feathers of the peacock, or the lightest brown wing of the turkey-cock. (This fly is my friend's own invention, and he pronounces it very good. It resembles the cow dung, except in the body, which is gayer.)

No. 3. A dropper on a No. 6 hook. Having attached the hook to the snell, take two pieces of stiff gut about 1/2 to 3/4 of an inch long, and, having soaked some pieces of fine gut, wind them round the stiff gut to make a *tail*, winding in three black hairs at the end, then bind this on the hook. The *body* is of peacock's herl; red hackle for *legs;* wings of a mottled wild duck's feather. An early fly.

No. 4. A dropper on a No. 9 hook. The *body*, of bright yellow floss silk, wound with gold and a red hackle. *Wings*, of the bright feathers on the breast of a wild pigeon, cut rather short, and dropping a little below the line of the hook. A most effective fly for May and June, indeed for the whole season. It may be varied in the color of the body by dubbing with red, &c.

No. 5. On a No. 8 hook. Resembles No. 2, with the wings of No. 4.

No. 6. A tail Palmer, on a No. 4 hook. *Body*, black mohair, with a little orange towards the *head;* wound with silver, and a strong black hackle from the tail of a Poland cock. A very killing fly, though it has a coarse look, and will tell effectively through the season, especially after a flood or windy days.

(N.B. The palmers, as is well known, may be varied. When the gold or silver thread is used, the black should be wound with silver, the red with gold or silver. The angler should be provided with a plentiful assortment, both as to color and size to suit the weather, time of day, and color of the waters. A red hackle wound with gold and silver on a dark brown dubbing, or without the tinsel, is the most killing of all the palmers. A short, thick, black hackle, wound lightly with silver over black, will kill in a bright sun at midsummer, on a fresh current or shaded pool, when nothing else will raise a fish.)

No. 7. A drop on a No. 8 or 9 hook. *Body*, black mohair, wound with silver, a small black hackle for legs; *wings* of a black cock's feather; tail tufted with two hairs.

This fly may be greatly varied.

No. 8. A dropper on a No. 9 hook. *Body,* red, floss silk, wound with gold; the head with a small black hackle; *wings,* brown wing of the peacock, or the domestic cock, or the dun wing of the pigeon, or the breastfeather of the cock pigeon; varying the complexion of the fly many ways.

No. 12. A dropper on a No. 9 hook. Body and wings like No. 13, with dark red hackles, round the head, for wings. Latter end of May, June, and beginning of July.

No. 13. A dropper on No. 8 hook. *Body,* a brownish, greenish, or yellowish brown, wound with a small red hackle about the head; *wings,* brown wing-feathers of a wild pigeon; *tail,* tufted with two hairs.

A beautiful and effective fly for May and June.

No. 14. A dropper on a No. 8 hook. *Body* thin, of brown floss silk, wound with gold, pale red hackle wound about the head; *wings,* a cock's reddish brown wing-feather. Good the whole season, but better in July and August.

No. 15. A tail-fly on a No. 2 hook. *Body* of crimson, wound with gold, and a red hackle; *wings* of a cock's blackish grey wing-feather.

It is an English prejudice to consider night fishing ungentlemanly, because resembling poaching; but as in this country there are no game laws, we may enjoy our delightful sport by moonlight, without such scruples. Old Barker used three palmers at night: a light fly (white palmer) for darkness; a red palmer *in medio;* and a dark (black) palmer for lightness. The best flies for moonlight fishing are the white, and brown, and cream-colored moths. The white are made: *Body,* white ostrich herl, and a white cock's hackle over it; the *wings* from the feather of the white owl. The brown: *Body,* dark bear's hair and a brown cock's hackle over it; *wings* from the wing-feather of the brown owl. Cream-colored moth: *Body,* fine cream-colored fur, with pale yellow hackles; wings, feather of the yellow owl of the deepest cream-color. To these add a black fly: *Body,* black ostrich herl, thickly wound with large black hackle; *wings,* the darkest wild goose wing-feather. The stone-fly also kills well at night. What fish are taken at night will generally be found to be large; and, therefore, the tackle should, as it may, be stouter than by day.

I end this notice of flies with a note from Hawkins: "The inutility of laying down precise rules for the color of the flies to be used on particular days, or hours of the day, must be obvious. Walton himself has humorously observed: 'That whereas it is said by many, that fly-fishing for a trout, the angler must observe his twelve several flies for twelve months of the year. I say, he that follows that rule shall be as sure to catch fish, as he that makes hay by the almanac, and no surer.' The directions contained in the following rhyme, respecting the color of flies as adapted to a certain time of day, are at least as useful as the others which have been published:

"'A brown red fly at morning grey,
A darker dun in clearer day;
When summer rains have swelled the flood,
The hackle red and worm are good;
At eve when twilight shades prevail,
Try the hackle white and snail;
Be mindful aye your fly to throw,
Light as falls the flaky snow." ' —*Am. Ed.*

For reasons I can't understand, McDonald's version in *Quill Gordon* omits the last paragraph and its dependent verse. Surely it couldn't have been because of a reference to a *worm* in the latter? Was it just a lack of space, a simple miscalculation of the logistics of getting the tailfeathers through the door? I can't decide which seems the more unlikely, but can't think of a third explanation for this odd truncation, so near the end. In the first case, shame on John McDonald; in the second, fie on Alfred Knopf. They left out the best part, like the man eating the martini glass, who threw the stem away.

I find Bethune's footnotes delightful, and would rather read *The Compleat Angler* in his edition, tiny though the type is in his footnotes, than any other, except the simple unadorned first edition in facsimile.

But what fun, in reading Piscator's plan to dress a big chub, "to make a good dish of meat," in Bethune's footnoted comment:

The chub of this country is the scorn and vexation of the angler, and, except when large, is by no means the shy fish that Walton and other English writers describe him to be; on the contrary, he is a bold biter, more ready than welcome at any bait offered to him. Palmer Hackle (*Hints on Angling and Angling Excursions in France,* &c., Lon., 1846, 8vo.), speaking of Walton's recipe for cooking the chub, suggests as an improvement that the chub be left out, in imitation of the Irish play bill which announced that the tragedy of Hamlet would be performed, the part of Hamlet omitted. Hackle also says that the chub in France has been known to reach a weight of ten pounds; but this is an enormous size. — *Am. Ed.*

And Bethune, on tackle, though quaint to our ears, is sound for his time, at least in this country, remembering the enormous time lag between the development of British fly fishing and ours over here:

As few persons in these days make their own rods, it may be well here to give some directions how to choose or order a rod to be made. A trout fly-rod should not be more than fourteen feet and a half at furthest; the *butt* solid, for you need weight there to balance the instrument, and your spare tips will be carried more safely in the *handle* of your landing-net. I use, in fishing streams, a light handle about four and a half feet long with a small net attached, which is more easily carried under the left arm, and answers every purpose. A rod in three pieces is preferred at the stream, but inconvenient to carry, and, if well made, four will not interfere materially with its excellence; i.e. the butt of ash, the first joint of hickory, the second of lance wood, and the tip of East India bamboo, or, as I like better, the *extreme* of the tip of whalebone *well* spliced on. The rod should be sensibly elastic down to the hand, but proportionately so, for if one part seem not proportionately pliant, the rod is weak somewhere. Every part should bear its share of the strain, or it will disappoint your hand in the cast of the fly or the play of the fish. In some rods there is what is called a double action, and such a one (the first I ever had) I used for years, and thought nothing could be better; but, on trying another stiffer (that is, the elasticity less, not at the further end, but nearer the hand), though at first rather awkward in the use of the novelty, I learned to like it better; and now believe it a mistake to have the rod so very pliant, as some young fly-fishers affect to like it. The proper elasticity is when a quarter of an ounce weight attached to the tip causes it to descend five feet below the horizontal line of a rod fourteen feet long. The entire *weight* of the rod should not exceed a *pound.* The rod should be procured at a well-established shop, where you may hope to have *thoroughly seasoned wood,* and the maker has a reputation to sustain. Use the plain *ferules* (if you use them at all, for a well-spliced rod is much better), always taking care to rub them with a tallow candle, that they may be drawn out easily again; but have *nothing shining* about the rod, as the flashing of the light will certainly scare the trout. Let your reel be not too large and a multiplier, *without* a *check* or *balance to the crank,* for the first will annoy you, besides being of no use, and the last make your reel turn faster than you think. A *click* may be added. Kelly is said to be the best rod-maker in Europe, but Conroy in New York can make one so good, that it will be your own fault if it be not successful.—*Am. Ed.*

And I know a lot of grown men, pretty good fishermen otherwise, who could still profit today by Bethune's advice to rub down their rods, to have *nothing shining* about them.

But leaving me loose with a copy of Bethune is a sure way to lose more time than we can afford, with Uncle Thad coming up, so I'll give over, but like a lawyer saying "Objection!" just for the record, not without recording my reluctance.

Reading Norris right after Bethune is tantamount to jumping all the way to Walton and Cotton right after reading Dame Juliana, though the *American Angler's Book* followed the 1847 first American edition of *The Compleat Angler* by only seventeen years. But although Norris's first edition came out only in 1864, he is believed to have finished it almost five years before that, but its publication was delayed by the outbreak of the Civil War. Certainly it is hard otherwise to account for his mighty second edition (over 700 pages) being ready to follow within a year, as it did.

To get his measure, hear him first on the kinds of anglers there are—not all the kinds he knows but just a couple of those he cites, and then his idea of a true angler:

There is the Fussy Angler, a great bore; of course you will shun him. The "Snob" Angler, who speaks confidently and knowingly on a slight capital of skill or experience. The Greedy, Pushing Angler, who rushes ahead and half fishes the water, leaving those who follow, in doubt as to whether he has fished a pool or rift carefully, or slurred it over in his haste to reach some well-known place down the stream before his companions. The company of these, the quiet, careful angler will avoid.

We also meet sometimes with the "Spick-and-Span" Angler, who has a highly varnished rod, and a superabundance of useless tackle; his outfit is of the most elaborate kind as regards its finish. He is a dapper "well got up" angler in all his appointments, and fishes much in-doors over his claret and poteen, when he has a good listener. He frequently displays bad taste in his tackle, intended for fly-fishing, by having a thirty dollar multiplying reel, filled with one of Conroy's very best relaid sea-grass lines, strong enough to hold a dolphin. If you meet him on the teeming waters of northern New York, the evening's display of his catch, depends much on the rough skill of his guide.

The Rough-and-Ready Angler, the opposite of the aforenamed, disdains all "tomfoolery," and carries his tackle in an old shotbag, and his flies in a tangled mass.

We have also the Literary Angler, who reads Walton and admires him hugely; he has been inoculated with the *sentiment* only; the five-mile walk up the creek, where it has not been fished much, is very fatiguing to him; he "did not know he must wade the stream," and does not until he slips in, and then he has some trouble at night to get his boots off. He is provided with a stout bass rod, good *strong* leaders of salmon-gut, and a stock of Conroy's "journal flies," and wonders if he had not better put on a *shot* just above his stretcher-fly.

The Pretentious Angler, to use a favorite expression of the lamented Dickey Riker, once Recorder of the city of New York, is one "that prevails to a great extent in this community." This gentleman has many of the qualities attributed by Fisher, of the "Angler's Souvenir," to Sir Humphrey Davy. If he has attained the higher branches of the art, he affects to despise all sport which he considers less scientific; if a salmon fisher, he calls trout "vermin;" if he is a trout fly-fisher, he professes contempt for bait fishing. We have talked with true anglers who were even disposed to censure the eminent Divine, who has so ably, and with such labor of love, edited our American edition of Walton, for affectation, in saying of the red worm, "our hands have long since been washed of the dirty things." The servant should not be above his master, and certainly "Iz. Wa.," whose disciple the Doctor professed to be, considered it no indignity to use them, nor was he disgusted with his "horn of gentles." But the Doctor was certainly right in deprecating the use of ground bait in reference to trout, when the angler can with a little faith and less greed soon learn the use of the fly.

The *Shad-roe Fisherman.*—The habitat of this genus (and they are rarely found elsewhere) is Philadelphia. There are many persons of the aforesaid city, who fish only when this bait can be had, and an idea seems to possess them that fish will bite at no other. This fraternity could have been found some years back, singly or in pairs, or little coteries of three or four, on any sunshiny day from Easter to Whitsuntide, heaving their heavy dipsies and horsehair snoods from the ends of the piers, or from canal boats laid up in ordinary—the old floating bridge at Gray's Ferry was a favorite resort for them. Sometimes the party was convivial, and provided with a junk bottle of what they believed to be *old rye.*

Before the gas-works had destroyed the fishing in the Schuylkill, I frequently observed a solitary individual of this species, wending his way to the river on Sunday mornings, with a long reed pole on his shoulder, and in his hand a tin kettle of shad-roe; and his "prog," consisting of hard-boiled eggs and crackers and cheese, tied up in a cotton bandana handkerchief. Towards nightfall, "he might have been seen" (as James the novelist says of the horseman), trudging homeward with a string of Pan Rock and White Perch, or "Catties" and Eels, his trowsers and coat sleeves well plastered with his unctuous bait, suggesting the idea of what, in vulgar parlance, might be called "a very nasty man."

But let us not turn up our scientific noses at this humble brother; nor let the home missionary or tract distributor rate him too severely, if he should meet with him in his Sunday walks; for who can tell what a quiet day of consolation it has been to him; he has found relief from the toils and cares of the week, and perhaps from the ceaseless tongue of his shrewish "old woman." If his sport has been good, he follows it up the next day, and keeps "blue Monday."

We have seen some very respectable gentlemen in our day engaged in fishing with shad-roe at Fairmount Dam. The bar even had its representative, in one of our first criminal court lawyers. He did not "dress the character" with as much discrimination as when he lectured on Shakspeare, for he always wore his blue coat with gilt buttons: he did not appear to be a successful angler. "Per contra" to this was a wealthy retired merchant, who used to astonish us with his knack of keeping this difficult bait on his hooks, and his skill in hooking little White Perch. Many a troller has seen him sitting bolt upright in the bow of his boat on a cool morning in May, with his overcoat buttoned up to his chin, his jolly spouse in the stern, and his servant amidship, baiting the hooks and taking off the lady's fish. The son also was an adept as well as the sire. Woe to the perch fisher, with his bait of little silvery eels, if these occupied the lower part of the swim, for the fish were all arrested by the stray ova that floated off from the "gobs" of shad-roe.

As we love contrasts, let us here make a slight allusion to that sensible "old English gentleman," the Admiral, who surveyed the north-west coast of America, to see, if in the contingency of the Yankees adhering to their claim of "fifty-four forty," the country about Vancouver's Island was worth contending for. He was an ardent angler, and it is reported, that on leaving his ship he provided stores for a week, which comprised of course not a few drinkables, as well as salmon rods and other tackle, and started in his boats to explore the rivers and tributaries, which, so goes the story, were so crammed in many places with salmon, that they could be captured with a boat-hook; and still with all the variety of salmon flies and the piscatory skill of the admiral and his officers, not a fish could be induced to rise at the fly. He returned to his ship disheartened and disgusted, averring that the country was not worth contending for; that the Yankees might have it and be _____; but it would be indecorous to record the admiral's mild expletive.

The *True Angler* is thoroughly imbued with the spirit of gentle old Izaak. He has no affectation, and when a fly-cast is not to be had, can find amusement in catching Sunfish or Roach, and does not despise the sport of any humbler brother of the angle. With him, fishing is a recreation, and a "calmer of unquiet thoughts." He never quarrels with his luck, knowing that satiety dulls one's appreciation of sport as much as want of success, but is ever content when he has done his best, and looks hopefully forward to a more propitious day. Whether from boat or rocky shore, or along the sedgy bank of the creek, or the stony margin of the mountain brook, he deems it an achievement to take fish when they are difficult to catch, and his satisfaction is in proportion. If he is lazy, or a superannuated angler, he can even endure a few days' trolling on an inland lake, and smokes his cigar, chats with the boatman, and takes an occasional "nip," as he is rowed along the wooded shore and amongst the beautiful islands.

A true angler is generally a modest man; unobtrusively communicative when he can impart a new idea; and is ever ready to let a pretentious tyro have his say, and good-naturedly (as if merely suggesting how it should be done) repairs his tackle, or gets him out of a scrape. He is moderately provided with all tackle and "fixins" necessary to the fishing he is in pursuit of. Is quietly self-reliant and equal to almost any emergency, from splicing his rod or tying his own flies, to trudging ten miles across a rough country with his luggage on his back. His enjoyment consists not only in the taking of fish: he draws much pleasure from the soothing influence and delightful accompaniments of the art.

With happy memories of the past summer, he joins together the three pieces of his fly-rod at home, when the scenes of the last season's sport are wrapped in snow and ice, and renews the glad feelings of long summer days. With what interest he notes the swelling of the buds on the maples, or the advent of the bluebird and robin, and looks forward to the day when he is to try another cast! and, when it comes at last, with what pleasing anticipations he packs up his "traps," and leaves his business cares and the noisy city behind, and after a few hours' or few days' travel in the cars, and a few miles in a rough wagon, or a vigorous tramp over rugged hills or along the road that leads up the banks of the river, he arrives at his quarters! He is now in the region of fresh butter and mealy potatoes—there are always good potatoes in a mountainous trout country. How pleasingly rough everything looks after leaving the prim city! How pure and wholesome the air! How beautiful the clumps of sugar-maples and the veteran hemlocks jutting out over the stream; the laurel; the ivy; the moss-covered rocks; the lengthening shadows of evening! How musical the old familiar tinkling of the cow-bell and the cry of the whip-poor-will! How sweetly he is lulled to sleep as he hears

"The waters leap and gush
O'er channelled rock, and broken hush!"

Next morning, after a hearty breakfast of mashed potatoes, ham and eggs, and butter from the cream of the cow that browses in the woods, he is off, three miles up the creek, a cigar or his pipe in his mouth, his creel at his side, and his rod over his shoulder, chatting with his chum as he goes; free, joyous, happy; at peace with his Maker, with himself, and all mankind; he should be grateful for this much, even if he catches no fish. How exhilarating the music of the stream! how invigorating its waters, causing a consciousness of manly vigor, as he wades sturdily with the strong current and casts his flies before him! When his zeal abates, and a few of the *speckled* lie in the bottom of his creel, he is not less interested in the wild flowers on the bank, or the scathed old hemlock on the cliff above, with its hawk's nest, the lady of the house likely inside, and the male proprietor perched high above on its dead top, and he breaks forth lustily—the scene suggesting the song—

"The bee's on its wing, and the hawk on its nest,
And the river runs merrily by."

When noon comes on, and the trout rise lazily or merely nip, he halts "sub tegmine fagi," or under the shadow of the dark sugar-maple to build a fire and roast trout for his dinner, and whiles away three hours or so. He dines sumptuously, straightens and dries his leader and the gut of his dropper, and repairs all breakage. He smokes leisurely, or even takes a nap on the green sward or velvety moss, and resumes his sport when the sun has declined enough to shade at least one side of the stream, and pleasantly anticipates the late evening cast on the still waters far down the creek. God be with you, gentle angler, if actuated with the feeling of our old master! whether you are a top fisher or a bottom fisher; whether your bait be gentles, brandling, grub, or red worm; crab, shrimp, or minnow; caddis, grasshopper, or the feathery counterfeit of the ephemera. May your thoughts be always peaceful, and your heart filled with gratitude to Him who made the country and the rivers; and "may the east wind never blow when you go a fishing!"

Though respectful of the tradition of fly fishing, and fully cognizant of its lore through thorough study of all the English writers up to the very year in which he writes, Uncle Thad peppers his pages nevertheless with Declarations of Independence, like this one on rods:

Few anglers, after having accustomed themselves, though only for a day, to casting with a light, pliant, one-handed rod as here described, are ever satisfied to resume a two-handed rod, or one of greater length and weight.

There are many highly-finished one-handed English fly-rods imported and sold by tackle stores, but they are too stiff, besides being heavier by one-third than is necessary, and so clogged with unnecessary mountings, reel-fastenings, ferules, wrappings, and varnish, that the purchaser is apt to abandon them after a few seasons' experience, for a rod of his own designing, or his own make.

The more weight or force applied to the tip of a well-proportioned fly-rod, the more the strain is thrown on the lower part; exemplifying the principle of Remington's bridge, in which the strain is longitudinal where the timbers are small, and transverse at the abutments.

The color of a rod, if not too light, is of little importance; it may be stained black or yellow; the latter color should never be produced by strong acids, which are apt to impair the strength of the wood. Dark woods, of course, require no staining. A neutral tint is imparted by one or two coats of common writing-fluid, of bluish tint.

Shellac, which is soluble in alcohol or ether, is generally preferred to copal varnish; it should be applied thin; the glare of the last coat should be removed from a new rod by sprinkling a little segar ashes on a wet rag, rubbing gently, and then wiping it off with clean water.

And this one on flies:

FLIES.— In giving a list of flies best adapted to American waters, I have done so without reference to the opinions of English writers, considering many of their rules and theories regarding flies inapplicable to our country. The observations here jotted down are rather the result of my own experience, as I have learned them on the stream and from members of our little club the "Houseless Anglers."

Much, perhaps most, of the theoretical knowledge of flies acquired by the reading angler, when he begins, is obtained from the writings of our brethren of the "Fast-anchored Isle." Every fly-fisher can read Chitty, Ronalds, Rennie, "Ephemera," and others, with interest and profit. Though I do not pretend to condemn or think lightly of their precepts, drawn from long experience of bright waters and its inmates, yet if followed without modification and proper allowance for climate, season, water, and insect life here as contrasted with England, the beginner is apt to be led into many errors, corrected only by long summers of experience. So he will come at last to the conclusion, that of the many flies described and illustrated in English books, or exhibited on the fly-makers' pattern-cards, a very limited assortment is really necessary, and many totally useless, in making up his book. He will also find, after the lapse of some years, that of the great variety with which he at first stored his book, he has gradually got rid of at least three-fourths of them, as he has of the theory of strict imitation, and the routine system, (that is, an exact imitation of the natural fly, and particular flies for each month), and settles down to the use of a half dozen or so of hackles and a few winged flies; and with such assortment, considers his book stocked beyond any contingency.

An extensive knowledge of flies and their names can hardly be of much practical advantage. Many a rustic adept is ignorant of a book ever having been written on fly-fishing, and knows the few flies he uses only by his own limited vocabulary. One of the most accomplished fly-fishers I ever met with has told me that his first essay was with the scalp of a red-headed woodpecker tied to the top of his hook. Notwithstanding all this, there is still a harmonious blending of colors or attractive hues, as well as the neat and graceful tying of a fly, that makes it killing.

He refuses to go more than a few steps of the way with Stewart:

The largest Trout love the shade of trees and bushes which overhang the bank, and it is only by the means just described that you can present your flies. It is customary to fish down stream, and there is much difference of opinion as to whether the general rule should be to cast directly down or across the water. In this the angler must be governed much by circumstances, and his own judgment. I prefer the diagonal cast, as presenting the flies in a more natural way, although the drop-fly may appear to play better, and set more at right angles with the leader, when drawing up against the stream.

When the wind is blowing up the stream, it becomes in a good degree necessary to fish across, if possible casting below the desired spot, and allowing the wind to carry the flies to the right place as they fall on the water. If, however, it blows strongly in the direction of the cast, care should be taken when putting on a fresh fly to moisten the gut to which it is attached, if it be a stretcher. Many flies are cracked off by neglecting this precaution.

The advice of English writers to fish *up stream*, or with the wind at one's back, in most cases cannot be followed; for our rough rapid streams in the first instance, and the thickly wooded banks in the other, which make it necessary to wade, ignore both rules. The force of the current in many a good rift would bring the flies back, and, as I have seen with beginners, entangle them in the legs of his pantaloons. It is only in a still pool, or where the current is gentle, that one is able to fish up stream with any degree of precision.

Nor will he go along with the "strict imitationists," though he is astonishingly anticipatory of the very essence of dry fly practice that was still in an emergent state even in England:

It seems to me that there is no more appropriate place than this to say a few words about the "routine" and "strict imitation system," which some English writers advocate so strenuously. The former, that is, certain flies for certain months, or for each month, is now considered an exploded theory by practical anglers who wish to divest fly-fishing of all pedantic humbug; for the fly that is good in April is killing in August, and the Red and Brown Hackle, the Coachman, Alder-Fly, and Brown Hen, will kill all summer.

For the theory of "strict imitation," there is some show of reason, but I cannot concede that Trout will rise more readily at the artificial fly which most closely resembles the natural one, for the fish's attention is first attracted because of something lifelike falling on the water, or passing over the surface, and he rises at it because he supposes it to be something he is in the habit of feeding upon, or because it resembles an insect or looks like a fly, not that it is any *particular* insect or fly; for we sometimes see the most glaring cheat, which resembles nothing above the waters or beneath the waters, a piece of red flannel, for instance, or the fin of one of their own species, taken greedily.

The marvel about Norris's fishing is not the ease and speed with which he filled his bucket—after all, he was fishing at a time when this country was still more wilderness than not, but that even then, before the ecological and environmental concerns of our troubled time had occurred to anybody, he was putting back many more fish than he kept, and urging his fellow anglers, too, to give some thought to the morrow.

In this, the contrast with Prime couldn't be greater. Though W. C. Prime's *I Go A-Fishing* (1873) was written a full decade after Norris finished his manuscript for the *American Angler's Book,* his attitude is Neanderthal compared to that of Uncle Thad. (I feel about the same, in comparing the style of their prose, but since that's not a sporting consideration I won't harp on it.) But let's, just for example, take two typical excerpts, and see the difference in their philosophies. Since he's the earlier, we'll start with Norris. Here's his chapter, "Fly-Fishing Alone":

With many persons fishing is a mere recreation, a pleasant way of killing time. To the true angler, however, the sensation it produces is a deep unspoken joy, born of a longing for that which is quiet and peaceful, and fostered by an inbred love of communing with nature, as he walks through grassy meads, or listens to the music of the mountain torrent. This is why he loves occasionally—whatever may be his social propensity indoors—to shun the habitations and usual haunts of men, and wander alone by the stream, casting his flies over its bright waters: or in his lone canoe to skim the unruffled surface of the inland lake, where no sound comes to his ear but the wild, flute-like cry of the loon, and where no human form is seen but his own, mirrored in the glassy water.

No wonder, then, that the fly-fisher loves at times to take a day, all by himself; for his very loneliness begets a comfortable feeling of independence and leisure, and a quiet assurance of resources within himself to meet all difficulties that may arise.

As he takes a near cut to the stream, along some blind road or cattle-path, he hears the wood-robin with its "to-whe," calling to its mate in the thicket, where itself was fledged the summer before. When he stops to rest at the "wind clearing," he recalls the traditional stories told by the old lumbermen, of the Indians who occupied the country when their grandfathers moved out to the "back settlements," and, as he ruminates on the extinction, or silent removal of these children of the forest, he may think of the simple eloquent words of the chief to his companions, the last he uttered: "I will die, and you will go home to your people, and, as you go along, you will see the flowers, and hear the birds sing; but Pushmuttaha will see them and hear them no more; and when you come to your people they will say, 'Where is Pushmuttaha?' and you will say 'He is dead:' then will your words come upon them, *like the falling of the great oak in the stillness of the woods.*"

As he resumes his walk and crosses the little brook that "goes singing by," he remembers what he has read of the Turks, who built their bowers by the falling water, that they might be lulled by its music, as they smoked and dreamed of Paradise. But when the hoarse roar of the creek, where it surges against the base of the crag it has washed for ages, strikes his ear, or he hears it brawling over the big stones, his step quickens, and his pulse beats louder—he is no true angler if it does not—and he is not content until he gets a glimpse of its bright rushing waters at the foot of the hill.

Come forth, my little rod—"a better never did itself support upon" *an angler's arm,*—and let us rig up here on this pebbly shore! The rings are in a line, and now with this bit of waxed silk we take a few hitches backward and forward over the little wire loops which point in opposite directions at the ends of the ferules, to keep the joints from coming apart; for it would be no joke to throw the upper part of the rod out of the butt ferule, and have it sailing down some strong rift. The reel is on *underneath,* and not on top, as those Bass-fishers have it, who are always talking of Fire Island, Newport, and Narragansett Bay.

What shall my whip be? The water is full, I'll try a red hackle, its tail tipped with gold tinsel; for my dropper, I'll put on a good sized coachman with lead-colored wings, and as soon as I get a few handsful of grass, to throw in the bottom of my creel, I'll button on my landing-net and cross over, with the help of this stick of drift-wood, for it is pretty strong wading just here. Do you see that rift, and the flat rock at the lower end of it which just comes above the surface of the water, and divides the stream as it rushes into the pool below? There's fishing in rift and pool both; so I'll begin at the top of the rift, if I can get through these alders. Go in, my little rod, point foremost; I would not break that tip at this time to save the hair on my head;—hold! that twig has caught my dropper—easy, now,—all clear—through the bushes at last.

When I was here last July, and fished the pool below, there was no rift above, the water hardly came above my ankles; now it is knee-deep; if there was less it would be better for the pool; but it makes two casts now, where there was only one last summer, and I have no doubt there is a pretty fellow by the margin of the strong water, on this side of the rock,—an easy cast, too,—just about eight yards from the end of my tip. Not there—a little nearer the rock. What a swirl! He did not show more than his back; but he has my hackle. I had to strike him, too, for he took it under water like a bait—they will do so when the stream is full. Get out of that current, my hearty, and don't be flouncing on top, but keep underneath, and deport yourself like an honest, fair fighter! There you are, now in slack water; you can't last long, tugging at this rate; so come along to my landing-net; it's no use shaking your head at me! What a shame to thrust my thumb under that rosy gill! but there is no help for it, for you might give me the slip as I take the hook out of your mouth, and thrust you, tail-foremost, into the hole of my creel. You are my first fish, and you know you are my *luck;* so I would not lose you even if you were a little fellow of seven inches, instead of a good half-pound. I imbibed that superstition, not to throw away my first fish, when I was a boy, and have never got rid of it. Now, tumble about as much as you please; you have the whole basket to yourself.

Another cast—there ought to be more fish there. He rose short,—a little longer line—three feet more will do it—exactly so. Gently, my nine-incher! Take the spring of the rod for a minute or so—here you are! Once more, now. How the "young 'un" jumps! I'll throw it to him until he learns to catch; there, he has it. No use reeling in a chap of your size, but come along, hand-over-hand; I'll release you. Go, now, and don't rise at a fly again until you are over nine inches.

Not a fly on the water! So I have nothing to imitate, even if imitation were necessary. Take care! that loose stone almost threw me. I'll work my way across the current, and get under the lee of that boulder, and try each side of the rift where it runs into the pool below the flat rock. Not a fish in the slack water on this side; they are looking for grub and larvae in the rift. Now, how would you like my coachman, by way of a change of diet? There's a chance for you—try it. Bosh! he missed it; but he is not pricked. Once more. Oh, ho! is it there you are, my beauty? Don't tear that dropper off. Hold him tight, O'Shaughnessy; you are the greatest hook ever invented. How he runs the line out, and plays off into the swift water! It would be rash to check him now; but I'll give him a few feet, and edge him over to the side of the rift where there is slack water. That's better; now tug away, while I recover some of my line. You are off into the current again, are you? but not so wicked. The click on this reel is too weak, by half—he gives in now, and is coming along, like an amiable, docile fish, as he is. Whiz! why, what's the matter, now? Has "the devil kicked him on end?" as my friend with the "tarry breeks" has it. He has taken but two or three yards of line, though. How he hugs the bottom, and keeps the main channel! Well, he can't last much longer. Here he comes now, with a heavy drag, and a distressing strain on my middle joint; and now I see him dimly, as I get him into the eddy; but there's something tugging at the tail-fly. Yes, I have a brace of them, and that accounts for the last dash, and the stubborn groping for the bottom. What a clever way of trolling! to get an obliging Trout to take your dropper, and go sailing around with four feet of gut, and a handsome stretcher at the end of it, setting all the fish in the pool crazy, until some unlucky fellow hooks himself in the side of his mouth. How shall I get the pair into my basket? There is no way but reeling close up, and getting the lower one into my net first, and then with another dip to secure the fish on the dropper; but it must be done gently. So—well done; three-quarters of a pound to be credited to the dropper, and a half-pound to the stretcher—total, one pound and a quarter. That will do for the present. So I'll sit down on that flat rock and light my dudeen, and try the remainder of the water presently. I'll not compromise for less than four half-pound fish before I leave the pool.

These are some of the incidents that the *lone* fly-fisher experiences on a favorable day, and the dreams and anticipations he has indulged in through the long gloomy winter are in part realized. "Real joy," some one has said, is "a serious thing," and the solitary angler proves it conclusively to himself. He is not troubled that some ardent young brother of the rod may fish ahead of him, and disturb the water without availing himself of all the chances; or that a more discreet companion may pass by some of the pools and rifts without bestowing the attention on them they deserve; but in perfect quietude, and confidence in his ability to meet every contingency that may occur, he patiently and leisurely tries all the places that offer fair. What if he does get hung up in a projecting branch of some old elm, that leans over the water? he does not swear and jerk his line away, and leave his flies dangling there – it is a difficulty that will bring into play his ingenuity, and perhaps his dexterity in climbing, and he sets about recovering his flies with the same patient steadiness of purpose that Caesar did in building his bridge, or that possessed Bonaparte in crossing the Alps, and feels as much satisfaction as either of those great generals, in accomplishing his ends.

If he takes "an extraordinary risk," as underwriters call it, in casting under boughs that hang within a few feet of the water, on the opposite side of some unwadeable rift or pool, and his stretcher should fasten itself in a tough twig, or his dropper grasp the stem of an obstinate leaf, he does not give it up in despair, or, consoling himself with the idea that he has plenty of flies and leaders in his book, pull away and leave his pet spinner and some favorite hackle to hang there as a memento of his temerity in casting so near the bushes. Far from it; he draws sufficient line off his reel and through the rings to give slack enough to lay his rod down, marking well where his flies have caught, and finds some place above or below where he can cross; then by twisting with a forked stick, or drawing in the limb with a hooked one, he releases his leader, and throws it clear off into the water, that he may regain it when he returns to his rod, and reels in his line; or he cuts it off and lays it carefully in his fly-book, and then recrosses the river. A fig for the clearing-ring and rod-scythe and all such cockney contrivances, he never cumbers his pockets with them. Suppose he does break his rod – he sits patiently down and splices it. If the fracture is a compound one, and it would shorten the piece too much to splice it, he resorts to a sailor's device, and *fishes the stick*, by binding a couple of flat pieces of hard wood on each side.

Captain Marryatt, in one of his books, says, a man's whole lifetime is spent in getting into scrapes and getting out of them. This is very much the case with the fly-fisher, and he should always curb any feeling of haste or undue excitement, remembering at such times, that if he loses his temper he is apt to lose his fish, and sometimes his tackle also.

My neighbor asked me once if Trout-fishing was not a very unhealthy amusement – he thought a man must frequently have damp feet. Well, it is, I answered; but if he gets wet up to his middle at the outset, and has reasonable luck, there is no healthier recreation. – But I have sat here long enough. I'll fill my pipe again and try the head of that swift water – If this confounded war lasts a year longer "Lynchburg" will go up to three dollars a pound, but it will be cheap then compared with those soaked and drugged segars that are imposed upon us for the "Simon-Pure," under so many captivating names. At all events *this* is what it professes to be, good homely tobac – Wh-e-euh! What a dash! and how strong and steady he pulls; some old fellow "with moss on his back," from under that log, no doubt of it. Is it line you want?—take it, eight—ten—fifteen feet—but no more if you please. How he keeps the middle of the rift! Don't tell me about the "grace of the curve," and all that sort of thing; if the bend of this rod isn't the line of beauty I never saw it before, except of course in the outline of a woman's drapery. Speaking of lines, I'll get a little of this in as I lead the fellow down stream, even at the risk of disturbing the swim below. It is the best plan with a large fish; I have Sir Humphrey Davy's authority for it, although I believe with Fisher, of the "Angler's Souvenir," that he was more of a philosopher than an angler. Talk of "dressing for dinner," when the fish are rising! Steady and slow, my boy, you are giving in at last—two pounds and a half or not an ounce! now I see you "as through a glass, darkly"—a little nearer, my beauty—Bah! what a fool I am! here a fish of a half-pound has hooked himself amidship, and of course offering five times the resistance he would if fairly hooked in the mouth, and no damage to his breathing apparatus while fighting, either; for he keeps his wind all the while. If he had been regularly harnessed, he could not have pulled with more advantage to himself and greater danger to my tackle in this rough water. I thought I had been deceived in this way often enough to know when a fish was hooked foul.

Now I call it strong wading coming down through that dark ravine; I must take a rest and put on a fresh dropper. And so my friend asked me if it was not very lonesome, fishing by myself. Why these little people of the woods are much better company than folks who continually bore you with the weather, and the state of their stomachs or livers, and what they ate for breakfast, or the price of gold, or the stock-market, when you have forgotten whether you have a liver or not, and don't care the toss of a penny what the price of gold is; or whether "Reading" is up or down. Lonesome!—It was only just now the red squirrel came down the limb of that birch, whisking his bushy tail, and chattering almost in my face. The mink, as he snuffed the fish-tainted air from my old creel, came out from his hole amongst the rocks and ran along within a few feet of me. Did he take my old coat to be part of this rock, covered with lichens and gray mosses? I recollect once in the dim twilight of evening, a doe with her fawns came down to the stream to drink; I had the wind of her, and could see into her great motherly eyes as she raised her head. A moment since the noisy king-fisher poised himself on the dead branch of the hemlock, over my left shoulder, as if he would peep into the hole of my fish-basket. The little warbler sang in the alders close by my old felt hat, as if he would burst his swelling throat with his loud glad song. Did either of them know that I am of a race whose first impulse is to throw a stone or shoot a gun at them? And the sparrow-hawk on that leafless spray extending over the water, sitting there as grave and dignified as a bank president when you ask him for a discount; is he aware that I can tap him on the head with the tip of my rod?—These are some of the simple incidents on the stream, which afterwards awaken memories.

"That like voices from afar off
Call to us to pause and listen,
Speak in tones so plain and childlike,
Scarcely can the ear distinguish
Whether they are sung or spoken."

But I must start for the open water below — What a glorious haze there is just now, and how demurely the world's great eye peeps through it! Trout are not very shy though, before the middle of May, even when the sun is bright. I have sometimes taken my best fish at high noon, at this season of the year. — I am as hungry as a horsefly, though it is only "a wee short hour ayont the twal." So I'll unsling my creel by that big sycamore, and build my fire in the hollow of it. If I burn it down there will be no action for trespass in a wooden country like this.

What boys are those crossing the foot-log? I'll press them into my service for awhile, and make them bring wood for my fire. I know them now; the larger one has cause to remember me "with tears of gratitude," for I bestowed on him last summer a score of old flies, a used-up leader, and a limp old rod. He offered me the liberal sum of two shillings for the very implement I have in my hand now; and to buy three flies from me *at four cents apiece.* — Halloo, Paul! what have you done with the rod I gave you — caught many Trout with it this season? Come over the creek, you and your brother, and get me some dry wood, and gather a handful or two of the furze from that old birch to light with. I'll give you a pair of flies — real gay ones.

Dining *alone* may be counted almost the only drawback to one's taking a day to himself, and you are glad of any stray native who is attracted by the smoke of your fire. Your whiskey is beyond a peradventure, better than he has in his cupboard at home; he is invariably out of tobacco — a chew or a pipeful, and a swig at your flask, will make him communicative. If he has not already dined, he will readily accept a roasted Trout and a piece of bread and butter, and while eating will post you as to all the Trout-streams within ten miles. It is, therefore, a matter of policy to cultivate the good feeling of the natives, the boys especially, as stones are of a very convenient size along the creek to throw at a surly fisherman. A few of "Conroy's journal-flies," which have occupied the back leaves of your fly-book for long years are profitable things to invest in this way, for three boys out of four you meet with, will ask you to sell them "a pair of fly-hooks," which of course results in your giving them a brace or so that are a little the worse for wear, or too gay for your own use.

If the fly-fisher, though, would have "society where none intrudes," or society that *won't* intrude, let him take a lad of ten or twelve along to carry his dinner, and to relieve him after the roast, by transferring part of the contents of his creel to the empty dinner-basket. The garrulity and queer questions of a country boy of this age are amusing, when you are disposed to talk. Any person who has sojourned at my friend Jim Henry's, and had his good-natured untiring boy Luther for his *gilly,* will acknowledge the advantage of such a "tail" even if it has not as many joints as a Highland laird's.

If there *is* an objection to a Trout-roast, it is that a man eats too much, and feels lazy after dinner. But what of that? it is a luxurious indolence, without care for the morrow — Care! why, he left that at home when he bought his railroad ticket, and shook off the dust of the city from his hob-nailed boots.

What pretty bright Trout there are in this bold rocky creek! it would be called a river in England, and so it is. We Americans have an ugly way of calling every stream not a hundred yards wide a creek. It is all well enough when the name is applied to some still sedgy water, which loses half of its depth, and three-fourths of its width, at low tide, and is bank-full on the flood. But speckled fellows like these don't live there. De Kay must have received some inspiration at a Trout-roast, when he gave them the specific name of "Fontinalis," and they are truly the Salmon of the fountain; for a stream like this and its little tributaries, whose fountains are everywhere amongst these rugged hills, are their proper home. What an ignorant fellow Poietes was to ask Halieus if the red spots on a Trout were not "marks of disease—a hectic kind of beauty?" Any boy along the creek knows better. And what a pedantic old theorist Sir Humphrey was, to tell him that the absence of these spots was a sign of high condition. Well, it may be in England, for the river Trout there, are a different species from ours. But I'll bet my old rod against a bob-fly that there is twice as much pluck and dash in our little fellows with the "hectic" spots. I don't wonder that Trout like these so inspired Mr. Barnwell, who wrote the "Game Fish of the North," when, with his fancy in high feather, he mounted his Pegasus and went off—"How splendid is the sport to deftly throw the long line and small fly, with the pliant single-handed rod, and with eye and nerve on the strain, to watch the loveliest darling of the wave, the spotted naiad, dart from her mossy bed, leap high into the air, carrying the strange deception in her mouth, and, turning in her flight, plunge back to her crystal home."

Julius Caesar! what "high-flying" Trout this gentleman must have met with in his time. Now, I never saw a Trout "dart from her mossy bed," because I never found Trout to lie on a bed of that sort; nor "leap high into the air, and turning in her flight plunge back," as a fish-hawk does. In fact, I may safely say I never saw a Trout *soar* more than eight or ten inches above its "crystal home." I honor "Barnwell" for the Anglomania which has seized him—he has been inoculated with a good scab, and the virus has penetrated his system: but I can't help being reminded by his description, of the eloquence of a member of a country debating society in Kentucky, who commenced—"Happiness, Mr. President, is like a crow situated on some far-distant mountain, which the eager sportsman endeavors in vain to no purpose to reproach." And concluded—"The poor man, Mr. President, reclines beneath the shade of some wide-spreading and umbrageous tree, and calling his wife and the rest of his little children around him, bids their thoughts inspire to scenes beyond the skies. He views Neptune, Plato, Venus, and Jupiter, the Lost Pleides, the Auroly Bolyallis, and other fixed stars, which it was the lot of the immoral Newton first to depreciate and then to deplore."

But a gray-headed man who cannot tie a decent knot in his casting-line without the aid of his spectacles, should forget such nonsense. There is one consolation, however, that this "decay of nature," which brings with it the necessity for glasses in seeing small objects within arm's length, gives in like ratio, the power of seeing one's flies at a distance on the water; there was old Uncle Peter Stewart who could knock a pheasant's head off at fifty yards with his rifle, and see a gnat across the Beaverkill, when he was past sixty.

Here is the sun shining as bright now as if he had not blinked at noon, and such weather, not too hot and not too cold; I must acknowledge, though, my teeth *did* chatter this morning when I waded across at the ford.

> "Sweet day, so cool, so calm, so bright,
> The bridal of the earth and sky;
> The dew shall weep thy fall to night,
>   For thou must die."

I'll start here, for it appears there is always luck in the pool or rift under the lee of the smoke where one cooks his Trout. It is strange, too, for it seems natural that the smoke would drive the flies away, and as a consequence the fish get out of the notion of rising. But no matter, here goes. Just as I supposed, and a brace of them at the first cast. Come ashore on the sloping gravel, my lively little fellows,—eight and nine inches—the very size for the pan; but who wants to eat fried Trout after cooking them under the ashes or on a forked stick?

There are no good fish here; the water is not much more than knee-deep, and they have no harbor amongst those small pebblestones. I have thrown in a dozen little fellows within the last ten minutes. I'll go to the tail of that strong rift below the saw mill. The last time I fished it was when that lean hungry-looking Scotchman came over here from Jim Henry's; he had been sneaking through the bushes and poaching all the little brooks around, where the fish had run up to spawn, with his confounded worm-bait. This stream was low then and the fish shy; I had approached the end of the rift carefully and was trying to raise them at long cast in the deep water, when he—without even saying "by your leave"—waded out within a few yards of where they were rising, and splashed his buck-shot sinker and wad of worms right amongst them. I said nothing, and he did not appear to think that interfering with my sport so rudely was any breach of good manners, or of the rules of fair fishing. A Scotchman, to catch Trout with a *worm*! Poor fellow! his piscatory education must have been neglected, or he belonged to that school who brag *only* on numbers. I know a party of that sort who come up here every summer from Easton and bring a *sauer-kraut stanner* to pack their Trout in, and salt down all they take without eating one, until they get home. They catch all they can, and keep *all* they catch, great and small. Bah! a poor little *salted* Trout—it tastes more like a piece of "yaller soap" than a fish. Such fishermen are but one remove from the bark peelers I found snaring and netting Trout in the still water below here, last August. I can just see their shanty from here. "Instruments of cruelty are in their habitations. O my soul, come not thou into their secret; unto their assembly mine honor, be not thou united!"

There is the sawyer's dog; if he comes much nearer I'll psychologize him with one of these "dunnicks"! But he turns tail as soon as I stoop to pick one up. Now for it—just at the end of the swift water—ah! my beauty—fifteen inches, by all that is lovely! He threw his whole length out of water—try it again—I can't raise him. This won't do. Am I cold, or am I nervous, that I should shake like a palsied old man because I missed that fish? Fie on you, Mr. Nestor, you who have run the rapids at the "Rough Waters" on the Nipissiguit, in a birch canoe, with a Salmon at the end of sixty yards of line, and your pipe in your mouth; I thought you had gotten past a weakness of this kind. But it will only make bad worse, and convince that Trout of the cheat to throw over him again; so I must leave him now, and get back to the log on that sunny bank and compose myself with a few whiffs, while I change my flies. It will be just fifteen minutes until I knock the ashes out of my pipe; by that time my vaulting friend will likely forget the counterfeit I tried to impose on him, if I offer him something else.

Now Dick gave me this for a meershaum, and I have no doubt Mr. Doll sold it for one in good faith; but it is a very "pale complected" pipe for one of that family. I have smoked it steadily for a year, and there is only the slightest possible tinge of orange about the root of the stem. It is hardly as dark as this ginger hackle in my hat-band. However, it is light, and carries a big charge for a pipe of its size, and the shortness of the stem brings the smoke so comfortably under the nose—a great desideratum in the open air. The pipe must have been instituted expressly for the fisherman; it is company when he is lonesome, and never talks when he wants to be quiet; it concentrates his ideas and assists his judgment when he discusses any important matter with himself, such as the selection of a killing stretcher. No wonder the Indians smoked at their council-fires; and, as for the nerves, I'll put it against Mrs. Winslow's soothing syrup. What a pity it is that infants are not taught to smoke! What shall my stretcher be; that fish refused Hofland's Fancy; now let me try one of my own fancy. Here is something a great deal prettier; a purple body in place of a snuff-brown, and light wings from a lead-colored pigeon instead of a sober woodcock feather. What a pretty fly—half sad, half gay in its attire, like an interesting young widow, when she decides on shedding her weeds, and "begins to take notice." I'll change my dropper also—here it is; body of copper-colored pea-cock hurl, wings of the feather of an old brown hen, mottled with yellow specks. What a plain homely look it has; it reminds me of "the Girl with the Calico Dress." You are not as showy, my dear miss, as the charming little widow, but certain individuals of my acquaintance are quite conscious of your worth. Let me see which of you will prove most attractive to my speckled friend. So here goes—two to one on the widow—lost, by jingo! He looked at her and sailed away. Has he ever heard of the warning that the sage Mr. Weller gave his son "Samivel?" Perhaps, then, he will take a notion to "the girl with the calico dress." Once more—now do take care! Ah ha! my old boy, you would be indiscreet, after all, and the widow has victimized you. Now she'll lead you a dance! Don't be travelling off with her as if you were on your wedding tour, for I know you would like to get rid of her already; but there is no divorce beneath the water,—you are mine, says she, "until death us do part!"

There you are, now! the three-minutes' fight has completely taken the wind out of you. That's the last flap of your tail; the widow has killed you "as dead as a mackerel." Acting the gay Lothario, were you? I know some scaly old fellows who play the same game ashore, stealthily patronizing Mrs. Allen, subsidizing the tailor, bootmaker, dentist, and barber, and slyly endeavoring to take off a discount of twenty-five per cent from old Father Time's bill. But that won't do, for folks of any discernment know at a glance those spavined, short-winded, shaky old fellows, who trot themselves out, as if they were done-up for the horse-market. Lie there, my Turveydrop, until I move down a little, and try under the bushes, on the opposite side.

With this length of line I can just come close enough to the alders to miss them. Dance lightly, O my brown girl, and follow in her wake, dear widow, as I draw you hitherward. Ah, ha! and so it is; there is one dashing fellow who sees charms in your homely dress. How he vaults!—nine rails, and a top rail! Did you ever know Turner Ashby? Not Beau Turner—I mean Black Turner. Did he ever straddle a bit of horse-flesh with more mettle? None of your Conestogas. There he goes again! How long have you belonged to the circus? But he can't run all day at that gait; he begins to flag, at last, and here he is now, coming in on the "quarter stretch." There you are, at last—died as game as a Dominica chicken. Once more, now. I knew it.—And again.

Three times my brace of beauties have come tripping home across the deep whirling rapid, and three bright Trout lie on the gravel behind me. I begin at last to long for the sound of some friendly voice, and the sight of a good-humored face. I must keep my appointment with Walter at the foot-bridge; so I am off. Some of the "Houseless" don't like this solitary sport. I know one of them who would as soon be guilty of drinking alone; but *he* is not a contemplative angler, and has never realized how hungry some folks get through the winter for a little fishing. May-be he has never read what William Howitt says, in his "Rural Life in England," about fishing alone. It will come home to every quiet fly-fisher. See what an unveiling of the heart it is, when the angler is alone with God and Nature.

"People that have not been inoculated with the true spirit may wonder at the infatuation of anglers—but true anglers leave them very contentedly to their wondering, and follow their diversions with a keen delight. Many old men there are of this class that have in them a world of science—not science of the book, or of regular tuition, but the science of actual experience. Science that lives, and will die with them; except it be dropped out piecemeal, and with the gravity becoming its importance, to some young neophyte who has won their good graces by his devotion to their beloved craft. All the mysteries of times and seasons, of baits, flies of every shape and hue; worms, gentles, beetles, compositions, or substances found by proof to possess singular charms. These are a possession which they hold with pride, and do not hold in vain. After a close day in the shop or factory, what a luxury is a fine summer evening to one of these men, following some rapid stream, or seated on a green bank, deep in grass and flowers, pulling out the spotted Trout, or resolutely but subtilely bringing some huge Pike or fair Grayling from its lurking place beneath the broad stump and spreading boughs of the alder. Or a day, a summer's day, to such a man, by the Dove or the Wye, amid the pleasant Derbyshire hills; by Yorkshire or Northumbrian stream; by Trent or Tweed; or the banks of Yarrow; by Teith or Leven, with the glorious hills and heaths of Scotland around him. Why, such a day to such a man, has in it a life and spirit of enjoyment to which the feelings of cities and palaces are dim. The heart of such a man—the power and passion of deep felicity that come breathing from mountains and moorlands; from clouds that sail above, and storms blustering and growling in the wind; from all the mighty magnificence, the solitude and antiquity of Nature upon him—Ebenezer Elliott only can unfold. The weight of the poor man's life—the cares of poverty—the striving of huge cities, visit him as he sits by the beautiful stream—beautiful as a dream of eternity, and translucent as the everlasting canopy of heaven above him;—they come, but he casts them off for the time, with the power of one who feels himself strong in the kindred spirit of all things around; strong in the knowledge that he is a man; an immortal—a child and pupil in the world-school of the Almighty. For that day he is more than a king—he has the heart of humanity, and faith and spirit of a saint. It is not the rod and line that floats before him—it is not the flowing water, or the captured prey that he perceives in those moments of admission to the heart of nature, so much as the law of the testimony of love and goodness written on everything around him with the pencil of Divine beauty. He is no longer the wearied and oppressed—the trodden and despised—walking in threadbare garments amid men, who scarcely deign to look upon him as a brother man—but he is reassured and recognised to him-

self in his own soul, as one of those puzzling, aspiring, and mysterious exis-
tences for whom all this splendid world was built, and for whom eternity opens
its expecting gates. These are magnificent speculations for a poor, angling carpenter or weaver; but Ebenezer Elliott can tell us that they are his legitimate
thoughts, when he can break for an instant the bonds of his toiling age, and escape to the open fields. Let us leave him dipping his line in the waters of
refreshing thought."

Thus writes William Howitt. But there is the foot-bridge, and here are my
little friends, the Sand-pipers. How often the fly-fisher sees them running
along the pebbly margin of the Trout stream (as Wilson truly says), "continually nodding their heads;" sometimes starting with their peculiar short
shrill note, from their nests in the wave-washed tufts of long grass, flapping
along the creek sideways, as if wounded in leg or wing, to decoy the fancied
destroyer from the nest of downy little snipelings. And there, where the waters
of the noisy rapid finds rest in the broad shallow below, is one perched on a big
gray boulder, as gray as herself. How lonely she seems there, like the last of
her race, were it not that her constant mate is on the strand below, busily
engaged picking up larva and seedling muscles for its little ones in the nest up
the creek.

And now for a slice of Prime:

The Major had been a week or two at the Profile House, living at his ease,
and rather content with the table, which was not by any means a poor one,
and solaced for any minor failures by his own wine. He did not wander much
among the mountains, but contented himself, book in hand, with the sunshine
on the broad piazza, and evenings in his own rooms, where his man, John, who
had been his personal servant more than thirty years, took care to make him
comfortable. His rooms were near mine, and that evening after Dupont and
myself had dined—for I make it dinner however late the coming home
occurs—I went to see the Major.

One can be very comfortable in a summer hotel if he will take a little trouble
and go to a little expense. One cannot be comfortable at any summer hotel in
America or the world without these. The rooms of my friend were two ordinary bed-rooms, one of which he used as a *salon;* and by a very little exertion it
had been made into a cozy and rather brilliant room. The table was literally
covered with books and periodicals, for the Major had a hunger for reading
which could never be satisfied, and every mail brought him packages. He was
tearing off the envelope from an Innspruck book-catalogue as I entered the
room, and I recognized the label of an old acquaintance.

"So you get catalogues from Carl Pfaundler, do you? I have picked up some
good things in his shop."

"Yes. I have a pretty extensive list of booksellers sending me their catalogues,
but it's getting to be rather a nuisance. I've about done with buying old books.
Come in; find a chair—John, a chair—help yourself to the claret. You dined
late, I fancy. Did you get me a good trout for breakfast?"

"Not a trout. I took a bat on the wing. Did you ever eat bat?"

"Never. I suppose it would be about the same thing as mice. Mice are not good; the flavour is musky. Rats are much better, and very decent eating, if they are properly fed. I don't know why bats might not be made eatable. They are carnivorous; but dogs are good food, if well cooked. However, we don't need to try experiments in this land, where the markets are better than in any other country on earth."

"I'm glad to hear you say that, Major. I have said it often, and it's pleasant to be backed by a man of your gastronomic taste."

"Who disputes it? Surely no one knows anything about eating. There are articles, of course, which are to be found in other countries superior to the same article here; but America is the only land for general good eating. One gets fearfully tired of an European kitchen, even with all the resources of Paris in the palmiest days of The Brothers. But here the varieties of fish and flesh are inexhaustible; and fruit — nowhere in the world is there a fruit-market comparable with that of New York. An English sole is not equal in flavour to a flounder taken in clear water at Stonington; and a turbot is no better than a tautog. Shad, sheepshead, Spanish mackerel, red snapper, bass, blue-fish — a fresh blue-fish is glorious — where will you stop in the list of fish that abound on our coast, every one of which is better than any salt-water fish known on the other side of the Atlantic?"

"Excepting sardines."

"Well, I may perhaps except sardines."

"May? None of your prejudices, old fellow. There's no dish of fish to be invented equal to sardines, fried and served as they used to do it in the old San Marco at Leghorn. I lament the closing of that house with profound regret. I have gone down from Florence more than once to pass a night there, just for the sake of the delicious breakfast I used to get on those sardines. No one else cooked or served them so in any town on the French or Italian coast."

"I remember, fifty years ago, seeing them catch sardines along the shore at Naples."

"Yes, I have sat many a morning in the window at the old Vittoria, looking out on the sea, and watching the sardine nets come in, glittering with diamonds; and I have taken them with a rod at Leghorn."

"I never found trout south of the Alps. Why is that?"

"Simply because you never looked for them yourself. The hotels rarely furnish them; but you can get them in Lombardy if you want them. I have taken trout in the Izak above Trent, and at Botzen."

"My dear boy, what a muddle your brain must be in about historic places. The idea of talking about trout-fishing at Trent, a place with which one never associated any idea but of profound ecclesiastical and theological significance."

"There's a charm in trout-fishing, Major, which you would have appreciated if your education had not been neglected. It has never failed me; and I have studied no small amount of history as I strolled along the bank of a trout stream. Were you ever at Salzburg?"

"There several times, and always fared well at the Hôtel de l'Europe."

"Ah yes, you think first of the hotel. So do many old travellers. So, I confess, do I sometimes. A poor inn is a fearful obstacle to the enjoyment of art or antiquity. But there are trout streams around Salzburg, and some fine trout in them; and I have passed some of the pleasantest days along those streams, looking up at the grand pile of the Untersberg, in whose caverns the two emperors sit face to face, sleeping, but now nearly ready to wake. I was fishing there in June, 1871, and wondering what could happen to rouse the mighty Charles, and a month later the thunders of Weissembourg must have shaken the imperial slumbers. But Ischl, Major, Ischl—were you ever at Ischl? It is the most lovely spot in Europe. Go there before you die, and don't go to the Hôtel Bauer on the hill, but to Sarsteiner's, The Kreutz, a capital inn, with old books in the halls, and pictures of all sorts of places, and large bed-rooms and saloons, and a kitchen that is not to be surpassed in or out of the Tyrol. It will suit you. The valley of the Traun is a glorious place, and the river is the only river my eyes ever saw which is indisputably superior in beauty of water to our White Mountain streams. The delicate apple-green tint does not harm its transparency. You can see the bottom in twenty feet of water. It flows like a liquid chrysoprase, and the trout and grayling in it are superb. Mr. Sarsteiner controls all the fishing in the valleys, and is himself an angler, a man of reading and extensive travel, and is interested in fish-breeding. The fishing is close at hand too. I went out of the house one evening about seven o'clock, and walked in five minutes to the other side of the Traun, just above the bridge and opposite the promenade, where the river glides swiftly down over a pebble bottom. It was nearly dark, but in fifteen minutes I had a half-dozen good trout, which the boy stowed safely in a barrel; for in Switzerland and the Tyrol, when you go a-fishing, you have always with you a boy, who carries a small barrel, in which it is his duty to keep the fish alive until they are transferred to the tank, which every inn keeps stocked with plenty of trout. It had gotten to be quite dark, and I was casting a large white moth across the swift current, when I got the heaviest strike, with one exception, that I ever felt from a trout in Europe. He made a splendid struggle; but the little Norris rod did its duty, and I brought him to barrel in a few minutes; that is to say, I landed and unhooked him, and handed him to the boy, while I hurried to cast again. I had made only one cast, when the boy shouted, 'He's too big for the barrel;' and I turned to laugh at his vain endeavours to crowd his tail into the hole. He was, in fact, two inches longer than the barrel, which had not been made in expectation of such fish. So I slipped him into his short quarters, and gave up the sport, and in five minutes he was the admiration of a crowd in the kitchen of the Golden Cross, swimming around in a small tank, into which cold spring water poured a steady stream. He weighed only two and three-quarter pounds English; but Mr. Sarsteiner told me that, though he had seen larger trout there, he was one of the largest, if not the largest, that he had ever known taken with a fly rod in the Tyrol. All the way up the river to Lake Haldstadt there are plenty of fine trout, and I have enjoyed many a day's sport along the beautiful stream."

"Now for the exception."

"What exception?"

"You said it was the heaviest strike, with one exception, that you ever felt in Europe."

"I'm a little ashamed of that other. You remember the Rhine above the falls, from Schaffhausen to the Chateau Laufen? I was fishing it one evening, years ago, in a boat, with a strong German boy to row. I had to keep a sharp lookout, for the current is wild, and it is not quite sure that, if you are careless, you may not go over the falls. By the bye, Major, with all our boasting, we haven't many cataracts in America as fine as the Rhine Falls. It's a grand piece of scenery. It looks better from below than above, however, if you happen to be in a heavy boat, with a stupid boy as oarsman. We were just on the edge of the swift water, and I told him to hold on by the bushes, and keep the craft steady while I cast. He obeyed, until a tremendous swirl and swash startled him as a trout struck the fly. The rush was so sudden that the boy was absolutely scared, so that he let go the bushes, and the boat swept right across the line at the same instant that the trout went down. My second joint broke close to the butt ferrule, and we went like lightning toward the falls. I dropped my rod to seize an oar, and threw my whole weight on it. The boat yielded, took the cant I intended, and plunged bow on into the bank, where I seized the bushes, and held on till the young Teuton came to his senses. Meantime, the second joint and tip had gone overboard, and the reel was paying out. I brought in line very gently, and grasping the lower end of the second joint, dropped the butt, and proceeded to try an old and difficult plan of using the hand instead of a reel. As soon as I got in slack enough, I felt the fish. He was at the bottom, and made a rush when he felt the first steady pressure of the tip. It took me twenty minutes, with second joint and tip, to kill that trout, well on to four pounds' weight, and the largest I ever killed east of the Atlantic. That same evening I took twenty more trout, and no one of them went over four ounces."

"I am one of the few," said the Major, sipping his claret appreciatively, and then tossing the full glass down his capacious throat, as if to wash a way out for talk—"I am one of the few who once loved angling, but have lost their taste for it. I've been latterly thinking the matter over, and—can you justify yourself in it? Isn't it cruelty to animals? You know these are days in which men are getting to have notions on that subject."

"I've no objection to their notions, and I have the highest opinion of the society for the prevention of cruelty to animals; but we must guard our sympathies that they do not go too far. No man of decency will be guilty of wanton cruelty to a beast. I have a warm love for some beasts. My dogs, my horses, have I not loved them? But there is much nonsense afloat on the subject. I rate the life of a beast somewhat lower than that of a man, and his comfort in the same ratio. I must often work even when I am sick. Rheumatism bothers me, and I have frequently to walk and even run when I am lame. Yes, perhaps it is gout. We won't discuss that; but lame or not I must work. Business requires it. I would drive a lame horse for the same reason. A poor carman cannot afford to let his horse rest, any more than he can afford to rest himself, on account of a slight ailment. It's an error therefore to suppose it always wrong to get work out of a suffering animal. So, too, I would kill a horse to accomplish a result which I valued at a higher rate than the life of the horse, if I could not accomplish it any other way. Some philanthropists, good men, but thoughtless, who would never dream of blaming a man for earning his bread and that of his children when he was sick and suffering, but would rather commend him, would fine and imprison him for working his sick horse with the same necessity impelling him.

"They should try to make a reasonable distinction in these matters between wanton cruelty and the necessary work that we must get out of a sick animal. I never saw a nobler beast, or one to which I was more thoroughly attached than my bay horse Mohammed; but great as he was and much as I loved him, do you not believe I would have ridden him through fire and tempest till he fell dead, if it were necessary to save his mistress, who loved him as well as I, a pain or a sorrow? Should I let her suffer to save a horse from suffering? Does your notion of charity extend so far as that? mine does not. I might give myself pain to save him pain; but her? — Never. Mohammed would have said so too if he could have spoken. I know he would.

"In war this whole subject is understood well, and no one thinks of finding fault with the destruction of the lives of beasts to accomplish the purposes of men; for in war human life is freely expended to purchase results. Who would blame an officer for using his lame, sick, dying mules and horses to the last moment to accomplish an object in the face of an enemy? It is then a mere question with beasts and with men, how much must be sacrificed to do the work. Would you require them to let sick mules rest in hospital, if they had no others?"

"Then you don't approve of stopping cars and omnibusses in New York, and compelling the passengers to dismount and find other conveyances, because the horses are lame?"

"Not at all. It is well meant, but it is bad in principle, and injures the society which does it. It would be right and proper to take a note of the horses and their owners and drivers, and make the necessary complaint in the police court, and if the animals were treated with wanton cruelty punish the guilty. But the time of a passenger is often worth thousands of dollars per minute, and the probability of such value outweighs all considerations of comfort to horses. In the days of the horse disease, when all the cities were suffering, it was both necessary and proper to use sick horses for transportation. It was a pure question of money value then. Shall a merchant allow ten thousand dollars' worth of perishable goods to decay for the sake of saving the health or the comfort of a cart-horse? Yet the absurd proposition was forced on the public that it was their duty to sacrifice their own comfort, property, and health to the comfort of the horses. Nonsense. If you had a sick child, would you hesitate to kill a horse if necessary to get a surgeon or a physician in time to save the child's life? If you had a loaded waggon full of perishable articles of great value, would you hesitate to use your lame horses, or kill them if necessary to save your property? Let us teach kindness to animals, men and beasts, and make it infamous to treat them with unnecessary or wanton cruelty; but don't let us get our ideas mixed up on the subject, so that we place the comfort of the beasts above that of the men. For all our purposes the comfort and the life of a beast have a measurable value. The owner is the judge of that value to him."

"But how about killing fish for sport?"

"In the name of sense, man, if God made fish to be eaten, what difference does it make if I enjoy the killing of them before I eat them? You would have none but a fisherman by trade do it, and then you would have him utter a sigh, a prayer, and a pious ejaculation at each cod or haddock that he killed; and if by chance the old fellow, sitting in the boat at his work, should for a moment think there was, after all, a little fun and a little pleasure in his business, you would have him take a round turn with his line, and drop on his knees to ask forgiveness for the sin of thinking there was sport in fishing.

"I can imagine the sad-faced, melancholy-eyed man, who makes it his business to supply game for the market as you would have him, sober as the sexton in Hamlet, and for ever moralizing over the gloomy necessity that has doomed him to a life of murder! Why, sir, he would frighten respectable fish, and the market would soon be destitute.

"The keenest day's *sport* in my journal of a great many years of sport was when, in company with some other gentlemen, I took three hundred blue-fish in three hours' fishing off Block Island, and those fish were eaten the same night or the next morning in Stonington, and supplied from fifty to a hundred different tables, as we threw them up on the dock for any one to help himself. I am unable to perceive that I committed any sin in taking them, or any sin in the excitement and pleasure of taking them.

"It is time moralists had done with this mistaken morality. If you eschew animal food entirely, then you may argue against killing animals, and I will not argue with you. But the logic of this business is simply this: The Creator made fish and flesh for the food of man, and as we can't eat them alive, or if we do we can't digest them alive, the result is we must kill them first, and (see the old rule for cooking a dolphin) it is sometimes a further necessity, since they won't come to be killed when we call them, that we must first catch them. Show first, then, that it is a painful necessity—a necessity to be avoided if possible—which a good man must shrink from and abhor, unless starved into it, to take fish or birds, and which he must do when he does it with regret, and with sobriety and seriousness, as he would whip his child, or shave himself when his beard is three days old, and you have your case. But till you show this, I will continue to think it great sport to supply my market with fish.

"Between ourselves, Major, I am of opinion that Peter himself chuckled a little when he took an extra large specimen of the Galilee carp, and I have no doubt that he and James, and even the gentle and beloved John, pulled with a will on the miraculous draught of fishes."

"Probably you are right; but I have lost my love for the sport. I can hardly say how it came about with me. I think it was the result of a long illness which I had in my middle life, and from which I recovered slowly, and in such strict confinement that the love of reading grew on me, and other employments lost the zest which I once found in them. I sometimes wonder now how you can read all winter and go a-fishing all summer as you do. I can't separate myself from my books."

"You are growing quite too bookish of late years, if you will pardon me for saying so, my old friend."

"As how?"

"I mean that you are getting to be dreamy in your manner, and you don't seem to realize the common events of life. You live so much among thoughts and imaginations that you're getting to be quite useless as a companion, except when one wants to talk or listen."

"I haven't lost my appreciation of claret."

"So I perceive."

"Your glass is empty. Help yourself."

"Thanks; I'm doing very well."

"Talking of books and fishing, Effendi, did you ever come across the 'Dyalogus Creaturarum?'"

"Yes, I have the Gouda edition of Leeu, 1482 I believe is the date."

"There's a comical little picture of a fisherman in it, illustrating a fabled talk between two fish. I don't know whether there is any older picture of the gentle art in existence, but that is worth noting as an historical illustration, for the angler there uses a float."

"The literature of angling is abundant, and art has always found ample range in its illustration. I have seen a score of pictures of fishing on ancient Egyptian monuments. Many modern artists are enthusiastic anglers. And in what kind of life could they find more of the beautiful?"

"Yes, a small rattlesnake."

"Gaudy, Major, and brilliant, but the brilliancy of the diamond and ruby compared with the soft glow of the pearl. Do you know these little Pemige-wasset trout are so exquisite in their pearl and rose colours that I didn't wonder the other day at the exclamation of a very pretty girl in the chariot on the way to the Flume, when they pulled up by me down the river and asked to see my basket. 'Oh, I want to kiss them,' she said."

"You didn't know her?"

"Never saw her before, or since."

"It was a fresh remark. I like it. I wonder who she was. It's a pleasant thing now and then to hear a bit of nature out of red lips."

"Your experience in the utterances of red lips is rather limited, Major. I was telling you just now that you live too much on books and too little on realities."

"On red lips, for instance?"

"Exactly. An old bachelor like you has great opportunities in life. You might take to fishing even, and perhaps some day, when you have a full basket, a pretty girl may ask you to let her look at the speckled beauties, and then—what might not happen as a consequence?"

"Bah! I've been through it all."

"You?"

"I."

"Fishing and —"

"Red lips—yes. Redder than this blood of the grape, and a thousand times as maddening. What do you boys of these late years fancy you can teach me, either in sports of the forest or loves of the town. I had drunk all the wine of that life up, and the cup was empty before you were born."

The Major was excited, and his dates were evidently confused. But it was refreshing to be called a boy, and I urged him on. He told stories of old sporting days, which proved that he was no idle boaster when he said he had gone through all that. He grew fairly brilliant as he talked.

"I remember," said he, "the very last night I ever passed in the forest. It had been some years then since I had given up my rifle and rod, but an old companion persuaded me to join him in November in Sullivan County, in New York, and I went up the Erie Railroad to Narrowsburg, and struck out into the woods for a ten-mile tramp to our appointed place of meeting. I knew the country as well as you know these mountains, but at evening I had loitered so that instead of being near the cabin of our old guide I was three miles away; darkness was settling down fast, and a heavy snowstorm was evidently coming on. I, who often said I would never camp out again so long as roofs remained among the inhabitants of earth, found myself wishing for the darkest hole in a rock or a hollow tree. Is it that the ground is not so soft a bed as it used to be, or have we grown harder?

"Night and gloom thickened around me. My eyes, from watching the clouds, retained vision of them longer than one who opened his suddenly at the place and time would have believed possible. The trees had passed through the various shapes and shadows which they assume in the twilight and first darkness. They were grim, tall giants, some standing, some leaning, some fallen prone and lying as they fell, dead and still; and some had gone to dust that lay in long mounds, like the graves of old kings. I kept on, pushing my way steadily, for there was no spot that I could find fit for a resting-place, and I had hope of reaching a good point for the night-halt by proceeding. I hit on it at length. There was a hill down which I went, tripping at every fourth step, and plunging into indescribable heaps of brush and leaves and stones, until I came out suddenly on the edge of a piece of burnt land, which a fire had gone over last summer. A pile of fallen trees lay on the very border of the unburned forest, and I sought shelter among them from a driving blast, which now brought snow with it in quantities. I faced the tempest a moment, and thought of that passage in which Festus described the angels thronging to Eden, and 'alighting like to snow-flakes.' I wished that there were more similarity, and that the flakes were fewer and farther between. But there was a terrible reality in the night and storm, which drove poetry from my brain. At this moment I discovered a pile of hemlock bark, gathered by some one to be carried to the tanneries. It was the first indication of this being an inhabited part of the world; but it was no proof that inhabitants were near, for these piles of bark are often gathered in remote parts of the forest. But it was a great discovery. There was enough of it to roof the City Hall; and in fifteen minutes there was as neat a cabin built among the fallen timber as any man could desire under the circumstances. It was artistically built, too, for I had built such before; and, by the bye, I recollect one which Joe Willis once constructed, in which the chimney arrangements proved unsafe, and we awoke at about daylight among the flames of our entire establishment. True, he laid it to my restlessness in the night, and actually charged me with getting my feet into the fire and scattering the coals, while I dreamed of the immortal—who was it that won immortality by setting fire to the Temple of Diana? But it was false, atrociously false. I was dreaming of _____, but let that pass.

"The wind grew furious, and the snow came thicker, finer, and faster, but none reached me as I sat in my shelter, open indeed on one side, but fully protected there by a fire built at a safe distance, which blazed as a pile should blaze that was the funeral pyre of more than one of the forest giants.

"And now the sound of the wind in the forest grew terrible in the grandeur of its harmonies. A lonesome man, far from my fellows, the sole human companion of the storm, the sole human witness of the fury of the tempest, I sat, or lay, half-reclined on the heap of brush that I had gathered for a bed, and with my hand screening my face from the intense heat of the fire, looked out into the abyss of darkness, and watched the snow-flakes driving from far up down toward the flames, as if they sought instantaneous and glad relief from cold and wretched wanderings; and I wondered whether, of intelligent creatures, I was alone in that wild, grand, and magnificent scene.

"Sometimes I thought I could hear human voices in the lull of the storm; but oftener I imagined that the inhabitants of other worlds were near, and that they were unearthly sounds which were so strange and abrupt and startling; and when I closed my eyes I was certain that, among all the confusion, I could hear the rushing wings of more than ten legions of angels; and in a moment of still calm, one of those awful pauses that occur in furious storms, in the deep, solemn silence I heard a cry, a faint but wild and mournful cry, and it seemed far off, farther than the forest, farther than the opposite mountain, beyond the confines of the world, and the cry grew into a wail—a wail of unutterable anguish, agony, and woe—such a wail as might have been Eve's when the flaming sword flashed between her and Abel; and it came nearer, nearer, nearer, and it filled the air, the sky, the universe it seemed, and thrilled through my soul till I sprang to my feet, and dashed out into the blinding, mad tempest. It was so long since I had heard it, that I had forgotten that voice of the mountain wind; but now I remembered it as the blasts swept by me, wailing, shouting, laughing, shrieking, and I retired to my warm nook, and laughed back at the storm, and slept and dreamed. I never slept better.

"I awoke at day-break, and the storm was over. A blue break in the clouds let through the light of a November moon, clear, soft, and exceedingly beautiful. Dawn drove the moonlight out of the forest, and I pushed on then and got my breakfast with old Steven in his cabin. I have never slept in the forest since that night. Help yourself to the claret, Effendi. It seems to me it's growing cold. Yes; I have led that life, and liked it well enough once."

"You've told me of your forest experiences, Major, but you rather fight shy of the subject of the red lips."

"I tell you I have tasted the wine of red lips to intoxication; but there were lips that I never touched whose utterances were more intoxicating."

The Major sat looking into the fire; for though it was August we had bright wood fires in the evenings, as we often do at the Profile House. He looked very steadily at the coals on the hearth, shivered once as if he were cold, bolted two glasses of claret in quick succession, and I waited, confident that I should hear his story at last, Soon he began to talk.

"Draw your chair close up. Light another pipe, and fill your glass. It is a cold night. My old bones shudder when I hear the wind wail over the house and through the trees. Capital claret, that! John, come in here. Open another bottle of claret, John. What, not another! Certainly, man, I must have it. This is only the second, and Mr. _____ has drank half, of course. Not drank any! You don't mean to say that he has been drinking nothing all the blessed evening? Effendi, I thought you knew my rules better than that. But you always would have your own way.

"One more bottle, John—but one. It shall be the last; and, John, get some Maraschino—one of the thick, black bottles with the small necks, and open it. But you know how, old fellow, and just do your best to make us comfortable.

"How the wind howls! My boy, I am seventy-three years old, and seven days over. My birthday was a week ago to-day.

"An old bachelor! Yea, verily. One of the oldest kind. But what is age? What is the paltry sum of seventy years? Do you think I am any older in my soul than I was half a century ago? Do you think, because my blood flows slower, that my mind thinks more slowly, my feelings spring up less freely, my hopes are less buoyant, less cheerful, if they look forward only weeks instead of years? I tell you, boy, that seventy years are a day in the sweep of memory; and 'once young for ever young' is the motto of an immortal soul. I know I am what men call old; I know my cheeks are wrinkled like parchment, and my lips are thin, and my head grey even to silver. But in my soul I feel that I am young, and I shall be young till the earthly ceases and the unearthly and eternal begins.

"I have not grown one day older than I was at thirty-two. I have never advanced a day since then. All my life long since that has been one day—one short day; no night, no rest, no succession of hours, events, or thoughts has marked any advance.

"I have been living forty years by the light of one memory—by the side of one grave.

"John, set the bottle down on the hearth. You may go. You need not sit up for me. We will see each other to bed to-night. Go, old fellow, and sleep soundly.

"She was the purest angel that flesh ever imprisoned, the most beautiful child of Eve. I can see her now. Her eyes raying the light of heaven—her brow white, calm, and holy—her lips wreathed with the blessing of her smile. She was as graceful as a form seen in dreams, and she moved through the scenes around her as you have seen the angelic visitors of your slumber move through crowded assemblies, without effort, apparently with some superhuman aid.

"She was fitted to adorn the splendid house in which she was born and grew to womanhood. It was a grand old place, built in the midst of a growth of oaks that might have been there when Columbus discovered America, and seemed likely to stand a century longer. They are standing yet, and the wind to-night makes a wild lament through their branches.

"I recall the scenery of the familiar spot. There was a stream of water that dashed down the rocks a hundred yards from the house, and which kept always full and fresh an acre of pond, over which hung willows and maples and other trees, while on the surface the white blossom of the lotus nodded lazily on the ripples with Egyptian sleepiness and languor.

"The old house was built of dark stone, and had a massive appearance, not relieved by the sombre shade in which it stood. The sunshine seldom penetrated to the ground in the summer months, except in one spot, just in front of the library windows, where it used to lie and sleep in the grass, as if it loved the old place. And if sunshine loved it, why should not I?

"General Lewis was one of the pleasant, old-fashioned men, now quite gone out of memory, as well as out of existence. He loved his horses, his dogs, his house, his punch. He loved his nephew Tom, uncouth, rough cub that he was; but above horses, dogs, house, or all together, he loved his daughter Sarah, and I loved her too.

"Yes, you may look at me as you will, I loved Sarah Lewis; and, by all the gods, I love her now as I loved her then, and as I shall love her if I meet her again.

"Call it folly, call it boyish, call it an old man's whim, an old man's second childhood, I care not by what name you call it; it is enough that to-night the image of that young girl stands before me splendidly beautiful in all the holiness of her young glad life, and I could bow down on my knees and worship her now again.

"Why did I say again? For forty years I have not ceased to worship her. If I kneel to pray in the morning, she passes between me and God. If I would read the prayers at evening twilight, she looks up at me from the page. If I would worship on a Sabbath morning in the church, she looks down on me from some unfathomable distance, some unapproachable height, and I pray to her as if she were my hope, my heaven.

"Sometimes in the winter nights I feel a coldness stealing over me, and icy fingers are feeling about my heart, as if to grasp and still it. I lie calmly, quietly, and I think my hour is at hand; and through the gloom, and through the mists and films that gather over my vision, I see her afar off, still the same angel in the distant heaven, and I reach out my arms to her, and I cry aloud on God to let me go find her, and on her to come to me, and then thick darkness settles on me.

"The doctor calls this apoplexy, and says I shall some day die in a fit of it. What do doctors know of the tremendous influences that are working on our souls? He, in his scientific stupidity, calls it a disease, and warns me against wine and high living, as if I did not understand what it is, and why my vision at such times reaches so very far into the deep unknown.

"I have spoken of Tom Lewis, her cousin. Rumour said he was the old man's heir in equal proportion with the daughter; for he had been brought up in the family, and had always been treated as a son. He was a good fellow, if he was rough, for he had the goodness that all who came within her influence must have.

"I have seen her look the devil out of him often. I remember once when the horses had behaved in a way not to suit him, and he had let an oath or two escape his lips preparatory to putting on the whip. We were riding together down the avenue, and he raised the lash. At the moment he caught her eye. She was walking up from the lodge, where she had been to see a sick child. She saw the raised whip, and her eye caught his. He did not strike. The horses escaped for that time. He drove them quietly through the gate, and three miles and back without a word of anger.

"Did I tell you I was her cousin also? A second cousin on her mother's side, not on the General's. We lived not far off, and I lived much of my time at his house. Tom and myself had been inseparable, and we did not conceal our rivalry from each other.

"'Tom,' said I, one morning, 'why can't you be content with half the General's fortune, and let me have the other half?'

"'Bah! Jerry,' said he, 'as if that would be any more even, when you want Sarah with it. In Heaven's name, take the half of the money, if that's all you want.'

"'Can't we fix it so as to make an even division, Tom? Take all the fortune, and let me have her, and I'll call it square.'

"'Just what I was going to propose to you. Be reasonable now, Jerry, and get out of the way. You must see she doesn't care a copper for you.'

"I twirled a rosebud in my fingers that she had given me that morning, and replied —

"'Poor devil! I did not think you could be so infatuated. Why, Tom, there is no chance for you under the sun. But go ahead; find it out as you will. I'm sorry for you.'

"A hundred such talks we used to have, and she never gave either of us one particle more of encouragement than the other. She was like a sister to us both, and neither dared to break the spell of our perfect happiness by asking her to be more.

"And so time passed on.

"One summer afternoon we were off together on horseback, all three of us, over the mountain and down the valley. We were returning toward sunset, sauntering along the road down the side of the hill.

"Philip, stir the fire a little. That bottle of claret is rather cold, it seems to me, or I am a little chilly myself. Perhaps it is the recollection of that day thats chills me.

"I had made up my mind, if opportunity occured, to tell her that day all that I had thought for years. I had determined to know, once for all, if she would love me or no.

"If not, I would go, I cared not where; the world was broad enough, and it should be to some place where I should never see her face again, never hear her voice again, never bow down and worship her magnificent beauty again. I would go to Russia and offer myself to the Czar, or to Syria and join the Druses, or to India, China, anywhere to fight. All my notions were military, I remember, and all my ideas were of war and death on the field.

"I rode by her side, and looked up at her occasionally, and thought she was looking splendid. I had never seen her more so. Every attitude was grace, every look was life and spirit.

"Tom clung close to her. One would have thought he was watching the very opportunity I was after myself. Now he rode a few paces forward, and as I was catching my breath to say 'Sarah,' he would rein up and fall back to his place, and I would make some flat remark that made me seem like a fool to myself, if not to her.

"'What's the matter with you, Jerry?' said she, at length.

"'Jerry's in love,' said Tom.

"I could have thrashed him on the spot.

"'In love! Jerry in love!' and she turned her large brown eyes toward me.

"In vain I sought to fathom them, and arrive at some conclusion whether or not the subject interested her with special force.

"The eyes remained fixed, till I blundered out the old saw—'Tom judges others by himself.'

"Then the eyes turned to Tom, and he pleaded guilty by his awkward looks, and half-blushes, and averted eyes, and forced laugh.

"'By Heaven!' thought I 'what would I not give for Tom's awkwardness now! The scoundrel is winning his way by it.'

"'Jerry, is Tom in love?'

"The *naïveté* of the question, the correctness of it, the very simplicity of the thing was irresistible and I could not repress a smile that grew into a broad laugh. Tom joined in it, and we made the woods ring with our merriment.

"'I say, Tom, isn't that your whip lying back yonder in the road?'

"'Confound it, yes; the cord has broken from my wrist;' and he rode back for it.

"'Jerry, whom does Tom love?' said she, quickly, turning to me.

"'You,' said I, bluntly.

"'Why, of course; but who is he in love with, I mean?'

"It was a curious way to get at it. Could I be justified? It was not asking what I had intended, but it was getting at it in another way, and just as well, perhaps. It was, at all events, asking Tom's question for him, and it saved me the embarrassment of putting it as my own. I determined this in an instant.

"'Sarah, could you love Tom well enough to marry him?'

"'I! Jerry; what do you mean?'

"'Suppose Tom wants you to be his wife, will you marry him?'

"'I don't know—I can't tell—I never thought of such a thing. You don't think he has any such idea, do you?'

"That was my answer. It was enough as far as it went, but I was no better off than before. She did not love Tom, or she would never have answered thus. But did she love me? Would she marry me? Wouldn't she receive the idea in just the same way?

"I looked back. Tom was on the ground, had picked up his whip, and had one foot in the stirrup, ready to mount again. I gulped down my heart that was up in my throat, and spoke out—

"'Sarah, will you marry me?'

"Philip, she turned her eyes again toward me—those large brown eyes, those holy eyes—and blessed me with their unutterably glorious gaze. To my dying hour I shall not forget that gaze; to all eternity it will remain in my soul. She looked at me one look; and whether it was pity, sorrow, surprise, or love, I cannot tell you, that filled them and overflowed toward me from out their immeasurable depths; but, Philip, it was the last light of those eyes I ever saw—the last, the last.

"Is there anything left in that bottle? Thank you. Just a glassful. You will not take any? Then, by your leave, I will finish it. My story is nearly ended, and I will not keep you up much longer.

"We had not noticed, so absorbed had we been in our pleasant talk, that a black cloud had risen in the west and obscured the sun, and covered the entire sky; and even the sultry air had not called our attention to the coming thunderstorm.

"As she looked at me, even as she fixed her eyes on mine, a flash, blinding and fierce, fell on the top of a pine-tree by the road-side, not fifty yards from us, and the crash of the thunder shook the foundations of the hills.

"For a moment all was dazzling, burning, blazing light; then sight was gone, and a momentary darkness settled on our eyes. The horses crouched to the ground in terror, and Sarah bowed her head as if in the presence of God.

"All this was the work of an instant, and the next, Tom's horse sprang by us on a furious gallop, dragging Tom by the stirrup. He had been in the act of mounting when the flash came, and his horse swerved and jumped so that his foot caught, and he was dragged with his head on the ground.

"There was a point in the road, about fifty yards ahead, where it divided into two. The one was the carriage-track, which wound down the mountain by easy descents; the other was a foot-path, which was a short, precipitous cut to a point on the carriage-road nearly a quarter of a mile below.

"Calling to Sarah to keep back and wait, I drove the spurs into my horse, and went down the steep path. Looking back, I saw her following, her horse making tremendous speed. She kept the carriage-road, following on after Tom, and I pressed on, thinking to intercept his horse below.

"The pace was terrible. I could hear them thundering down the track above. I looked up and caught sight of them through the trees. I looked down, and saw a gully before me full eighteen feet wide and as many deep.

"A great horse was that black horse Caesar, and he took the gully at a flying leap that landed us far over it, and a moment later I was at the point where the roads again met, but only in time to see the other two horses go by at a furious pace, Sarah's abreast of the grey, and she reaching her hand out, bravely trying to grasp the flying rein, as her horse went leap for leap with him.

"To ride close behind them was worse than useless in such a case. It would but serve to increase their speed; so I fell back a dozen rods and followed, watching the end.

"At the foot of the mountain the river ran, broad and deep, spanned by the bridge at the narrowest point. To reach the bridge, the road took a short turn up stream, directly on the bank.

"On swept the grey and the black horse, side by side, down the hill-side, not fifty leaps along the level ground, and then came the turn.

"She was on the off-side. At the sharp turn she pressed ahead a half-length and reined her horse across the grey's shoulder, if possible to turn him up toward the bridge.

"It was all over in an instant. The grey was the heavier horse. He pressed her close; the black horse yielded, gave way toward the fence, stumbled, and the fence, a light rail, broke with a crash, and they went over, all together into the deep black stream.

"Still, still the sound of that crash and plunge is in my ears. Still I can see them go headlong down that bank together into the black water!

"I never knew exactly what I did then. When I was conscious I found myself swimming around in a circle, diving occasionally to find them, but in vain. The grey horse swam ashore and stood on the bank by my black, with distended nostrils and trembling limbs, shaking from head to foot with terror. The other black horse was floating down the surface of the stream, drowned. His mistress was nowhere visible, and Tom was gone also.

"I found her at last.

"Yes, she was dead!

"Restore her? No. A glance at her face showed how vain all such hope was. Never was human face so angelic. She was already one of the saintly—one of the immortals—and the beauty and glory of her new life had left some faint likeness of itself on her dead form and face.

"I said I had never grown a day older since that time. You know now why. I have never ceased to think of her as on that day. I have never lost the blessing of those eyes as they looked on me in the forest on the mountain road. I have never left her, never grown away from her. If, in the resurrection we are to resume the bodies most exactly fitted to represent our whole lives; if, as I have sometimes thought, we shall rise in the forms we wore when some great event stamped our souls for ever, then I am certain that I shall awake in form and feature as I was that day, and no memorial will remain of an hour of my life after her burial.

"We buried her in the old vault close by the house, among the oaks. Beautiful to the very last.

"My voice is broken. I cannot talk any more. You have the story. That is the whole of it. God bless you, my boy. You have listened—patiently—to—my—talk.

"Good-night. Go to bed. I'll stay here in this chair awhile. I don't—exactly—feel—like—sleeping—just yet."

I left him sitting there; his head bowed on his breast, his eyes closed, his breathing heavy. My own eyes were misty.

In the hall I found John, sitting bolt upright in a large chair.

"Why, John, I thought the Major sent you to bed long ago?"

"Yes, sir; the Major always sends me to bed at the third bottle, sir, and I always doesn't go. He's been telling you the old story, now hasn't he, sir?"

"What old story, John?"

"Why, all about Miss Lewis, and Mister Tom, and the General?"

"Yes."

John laid his long black finger knowingly up by the side of his nose, and looked at me.

"Why, John—you don't mean to say—eh?"

"All the claret, sir?"

"John, my man, go in and take care of him. He is either asleep or drunk. Curious that! Why didn't I think a man was hardly to be believed after the second bottle, and perfectly incredible on the third. By Jove! he is a trump at a story, though."

It would be difficult to describe all that I dreamed about that night.

The evidence seems to me to speak for itself, and obviate the need for any comment. But I will concede that I can understand the basis for Prime's enormous popularity, because he is "a trump at a story."

10.
Halford and Purism

A lthough the first reference to dry-fly fishing in the sense that we know it today came in the 1851 third edition of G. P. R. Pulman's *Vade Mecum of Fly-Fishing for Trout,* there had been frequent mentions of the taking of trout with flies "on top of the water," going back over nearly two centuries to the time of Col. Robert Venables. But most of these citations of surface-takes of flies by trout were either as phenomena or desiderata, rather than to a recognized and purposive practice. But by the time of the Pulman mention that's what it had become. And by the time of Halford it had become, in Hills's phrase, "the common but not yet the universal practice." Hills is clear, in qualifying his famous pronouncement that "There are four names which stand above others in this history of the fly: the author of the *treatise,* who started it; Cotton who established it; Stewart who converted the world to upstream fishing; and Halford, who systematized the dry fly"; elsewhere he adds: "Halford is the historian of the dry fly. He did for it what Stewart did for upstream fishing. Neither were pioneers, for both described what they did not invent; but both, by practice and writing, made an unanswerable case for the system they advocated."

Hills, who had a marvelous flair for isolating the significant from a

198

plethora of confusing and sometimes apparently contradictory details, was never better than in defining and delimiting the significance of Halford and his helpers in establishing dry-fly practice, and in differentiating between the swimming of the fly on top of the water, as mentioned in angling writings back to the time of Mascall, and the conscious and repeated drying and floating of the fly that became common and purposive angling technique only in the middle of the nineteenth century.

The salient point that Hills makes between what is and isn't true dry-fly practice, in all that was said from the virtual dawn of angling about the desirability of keeping the fly on top of the water, is "the *intentional* drying of the fly." He thus awards the palm to Pulman for this passage in his 1851 edition:

Let a dry fly be substituted for the wet one, the line switched a few times through the air to throw off its superabundant moisture, a judicious cast made just above the rising fish, and the fly allowed to float towards and over them, and the chances are ten to one that it will be seized as readily as the living insect.

This then was the beginning of the dry-fly mania that was to become gospel before the century's end. Oddly enough, it was Francis Francis, and not Pulman, who gave it its first big push, at the very beginning of his long tenure as angling editor of *The Field*, in 1857, in an article which Hills quotes:

Francis, a celebrated writer, published an article on 12 December, 1857, in *The Field*, of which he had just become angling editor, on the Hampshire streams. Describing the Itchen, he says that however fine you fish, the motion of your line will at times startle the trout. "Accordingly I recommend the angler frequently to try a dry fly—*e.g.* suppose the angler sees a rising fish, let him allow his casting-line and fly to dry for a minute previous to making a cast,' and then throw over the fish and let it float down without motion. This is a killing plan when fishing with duns. On rough windy days they get drowned, and trout will take a wet fly as well as a dry one, or perhaps better, but on a fine day they sit on the water with wings upright, and then scarcely a fish will refuse a fly that floats, if its belly, legs and whisks be of the same colour as the natural and the wings not too heavy." Francis says that he had long had these thoughts in his mind, and had had abundant opportunities of proving the advantages of the dry fly, which shows that he knew and used it long before 1857. You must throw your fly like "thistle-down; do not let it dwell on the water too long, for many a fish will take it the second time, if you do not give him too long to look at it the first time." And you must float it right over his head.

Francis, ten years later, in *A Book of Angling*, formulated the case for the dry fly more sensibly than it was to be stated again for the next forty years, saying, first:

Now, there are two ways of fly-fishing, viz. with the dry fly and with the wet fly. Some fishermen always use one plan, others almost as pertinaciously use the other. To use either of them invariably is wrong. Sometimes the one will be found to kill fast and sometimes the other. In fine waters, particularly in the southern countries, where fly-fishing is certainly more of a systematic art than it is in the north, the dry fly is greatly used, and with very deadly effect at times. In very calm, bright and still weather, when a wet fly will often be useless, the dry fly will be taken most confidingly. In rough windy weather the wet fly is preferable, but I shall return to this subject presently.

Then, later, when he does, he continues:

I have mentioned fishing with the dry fly, and it is often an invaluable method. With the dry fly, fish may be killed on fine bright days, when the wet fly will be almost useless. If the angler on a bright calm day will notice the class of flies called duns, he will see how, when first hatched, they come floating down with wings upright and unsoiled, sitting lightly and cockily on the water—tempting morsels to the greedy fish. Few flies are then to be found in a wet, half-drowned condition, and therefore, if the angler sends one thus to the fish it will be frequently neglected. Taking, then, two or three turns of the fly in the air instead of one, so as to dry the tackle, let him deliver the fly straightly and well a yard above the fish, and merely raising his rod, as the line comes home, allow the fly, sustained by the dry hackle and wing and by the dry gut, to float down on the surface like the natural fly, without motion. If the gut be delivered in a wavy manner, the bends and turns in it will show a glitter and startle the fish; if the angler attempts to draw the fly towards him, it will 'make snakes,' and the dry gut will appear like a huge centipede crawling on the water. Perfect quiescence is required. It is quite wonderful at times what can be done under apparently adverse circumstances with a dry fly, no weather and no water being proof against it.

At this point, in my much later (1920) copy of *A Book of Angling*, Sir Herbert Maxwell appends the following editor's note:

Since this was written dry-fly fishing has become practically the exclusive method on chalk streams and is frequently practiced on northern waters only. The fly is usually anointed with a paraffin from a phial attached to a button of the angler's coat; but a far more convenient plan is to anoint the flies before going out. The oil dries very quickly on them and the flies are permanently waterproof.

Frederick M. Halford
*after a painting
by J. H. Amschewitz*

But hear Francis out, because the latter part of his 1867 statement on this subject is the most important, and it's a pity it wasn't listened to more attentively at the time:

The judicious and perfect application of dry, wet, and mid-water fly-fishing stamps the finished fly-fisher with the hallmark of efficiency. Generally, anglers pin their faith to the entire practice of either one or the other plan, and argue dry *versus* wet, just as they do upstream *versus* down, when all are right at times, and *per contra*, all wrong at times. It requires the reasoning faculties to be used to know these times and their application. As a rule rough weather is more favorable to a sunk or wet fly, while bright and calm weather favours the dry one. Indeed, if there be much ripple on, a dry fly can hardly be maintained.

Alas, the reasoning faculties Francis called upon were in momentarily short supply, and as Hills observed, paraphrasing this passage, ". . . already there were those who thought otherwise, for anglers pinned their faith to the entire practice of either the one or the other plan, and argued dry *versus* wet. The battle had already begun."

Since his chronicle of that battle is the best I know, let him continue the story:

With Halford was associated a band of enthusiasts who devoted themselves to perfecting the art and spreading the creed. Among them they systematised the practice; they dealt with and solved technical difficulties; they developed rod, line, hooks and flies to their present excellence; and all that they acquired or invented was told to the world in sober and convincing English. Never was a reform worked out with greater ability or presented with greater lucidity.

Halford's first book, *Floating Flies and How To Dress Them,* was published in 1886, followed three years later by *Dry-Fly Fishing in Theory and Practice.* He wrote five others, the last in 1913, shortly before his death. Two of the seven deal with special subjects, fishery management and entomology, and of the five that deal generally with fishing and fly dressing the first two are by far the best. His later books are less good.

Halford's place in the history of fishing is well marked. He is the historian of a far-reaching change, and as such it is probable that he will always be read. He was well-fitted for the task. He possessed a balanced temperament and a reasonable mind. He took nothing for granted, and proceeded by observation and experiment. He is the master too of a style suited to his theme, for while he never rises to great heights, he commands, in his earlier books, a prose which is apt and direct, and essentially his own. He established the dry fly as we know it. There have not been many changes since he wrote. Tackle has been refined still further, rod, reels and lines are if possible more excellent, flies are more closely copied and in particular the nymph and spent spinner are novelties. But the method of fishing is unchanged. You still have to find your trout rising or willing to rise, and to cast accurately and delicately. Halford's directions are as good and as useful as on the day when they were written.

If he is to be criticised it is because like most reformers he overstated his case. He considered that the dry fly had superseded for all time and in all places all other methods of fly fishing, and that those who thought otherwise were either ignorant or incompetent. He did not realise, and perhaps it is impossible that he should have realised, that the coming of the floating fly did not mean that previous experience and previous knowledge were as worthless as though they had never been; but that it meant that from then onwards fly fishing was divided into two streams. These streams are separate, but they run parallel, and there are many cross channels between them. Looking back more than a generation to Halford's first book, and taking note of what has happened, two tendencies are apparent. The floating fly has spread far beyond its original territory. When he first wrote it was the common but not yet the universal practice in a limited area; the chalk streams of Hampshire, Berkshire, Wiltshire and Kent, the Wandle, the Hertfordshire and Buckinghamshire streams, and the limestone streams of Derbyshire. Speaking generally, and without reckoning outlying areas such as Driffield Beck, Derbyshire was its northerly and Dorsetshire its westerly boundary. At his death, it had spread over all England, over Scotland, Ireland, and parts of France, Germany, Scandinavia, America and New Zealand; in fact, it was practised by some fishermen in most places where trout are to be found. It must not be imagined that wherever it went it conquered, for such was far from the case. But it won its way on rivers in which trout sometimes run large, such as Tweed or Don, and particularly in Irish rivers, of which the Suir is one. It has also come to be used more and more on lakes which hold big fish, such as Blagdon or Lough Arrow. And the new sport of fishing it for sea trout has been invented. Altogether Halford in the time between his first book and his death saw its empire spread over a large part of the earth.

   . . . In all the long history of fly fishing there has been no change so great as its introduction. Until it came we fished much as our ancestors did in the seventeenth century. Rods had been improved, certainly, but were in principle unaltered; the use of gut instead of hair had added a convenience: the invention of the reel modified the method of playing a fish; but the dry fly was more than all put together. It altered both the practice and the temperament of the angler. It called different qualities into request. It has a charm and an allurement which the older sport did not possess.

   In what does its charm lie? Partly in the fact that all the moves in the game are visible. Just as a stalk is much more interesting when you can see your stag and watch his slightest movement, so with a fish. If you see him your eyes never leave him: if not, you watch for his rise. If it does not occur with its accustomed regularity, you have put him down. If you can see him, you watch every motion. Then you see your fly too. Nothing is hid. When the fly comes over him, you see him prepare to take it—or treat it with stolid indifference. You see him rise and take. The whole drama is played out before your eyes.

   Then again you attack him when the odds are most in his favour. On a hot still day in June he is far more alert than on a blowing April morning. He has lost the exuberance of spring. The water is low and clear, and the surface unruffled. Weeds are thick and handy. Your gut must be the finest, your fly the smallest. He is hungry, it is true, but particular. Not only must your fly not fright him, it must please his lazy senses. When he pokes his nose at it and refuses, it may be that the reason is daintiness, not distrust.

   His size too is an added attraction. No dry fly fishing is good where fish do not run large, and a big fish is a prize. Shooting gives no such trophy. You do not find one grouse three times the size of another, and if you did he would be easier, not harder, to hit. But the trout gets craftier as he gets bigger: his cunning grows with his girth.

   The casting too has its fascination. On your day—and such days come to all of us, to make up for the many when we are either maddened or drugged and stupefied by our incurable ineptitude—how delicately and how surely you throw. You mean your fly to fall four inches above the fish, and sure enough it does, not an inch more or less. Nothing is too difficult: drag has no terrors: head wind is a friend, not an enemy, for does it not enable you to put a curve on your gut, which brings your fly over the fish first? You know exactly what to do, and you do it. Wherever the fish may be rising, your fly sails over him, hardly touching the water, wings up, floating like a cork, following every crinkle of the slow current. You gain an extraordinary sense of power. Your rod and line, right down to the fly, are part of yourself, moved by your nerves and answering to your brain.

But though Hills declares the debt of English anglers directly to Halford (and by indirection to Stewart and Ronalds on whose shoulders he stood) he tells only half the story, as far as American anglers are concerned, for Halford was the spark plug, on a trans-Atlantic scale, to Theodore Gordon, to whom his transmission of a paper of his patterns fathered the birth of dry fly fishing in America.

11.

Gordon
and Independence

J ust as I would not like to try to talk about Halford when the words of John Waller Hills are available, to do the job better, so I hesitate to venture to treat of Theodore Gordon when John McDonald's words are so ready hand. In *Quill Gordon* (1972) he has gathered together everything he ever wrote on Gordon, and nobody has ever written about him better.

We have seen, in the pre-Gordon era, how contemptuous Uncle Thad was of the imitationists, such as "Barnwell," and the extent to which the feeling was reciprocated, with a sort of patronizing indulgence for Norris's stubborn adherence to the age-old hackle flies, with which he took more pride in his presentation than in their intrinsic allure. Going on from that point, let us listen to McDonald:

FANCY FLIES

Skeptics where the wise trout is concerned often fish such as the Scarlet Ibis and Parmachene Belle, suggestive not of species or group but merely of fly life. One can get entangled here, however. The Parmachene Belle, for example, was created in the 1870's to imitate the fin of a brook trout; no one will ever know what the trout has been taking it for all this time. Fancy flies are fished without regard for the insects on the water. Both fancy and imitation flies take

trout, yet the reconciliation of the theories behind them would be the most revolutionary event in the history of fly-fishing. It would be easier to reconcile
Plato and Aristotle. Ray Bergman (*Trout*, 1938) takes the genial view that any
standard pattern will do. Another authority, Lee Wulff (*Leaping Silver*, c. 1940),
believes that the trout sees not color so much as a silhouette, and Wulff fishes
his flies accordingly. Charles M. Wetzel (*Practical Fly Fishing*, 1943) is a color
imitationist. The late Ray Camp of the *New York Times* used to like to try out
new flies. Charles Fox advises us to fish the fly that suits the conditions of time
and place. The fine Western flytier Dan Bailey prefers flies for streams. Jim
Deren fishes all the angles. By all accounts these master fishermen have taken
many fish. From this one ought to arrive at a skeptical conclusion. But be
careful: belief inspires confidence, and confidence inspires the angler.

Basically there are but two schools of fly-fishing—imitation and presentation,
both closed systems of thought. They work this way: The imitationist, making
due allowance for the fisherman's skill, believes that his trout rise to the nat-
uralness of his flies. He explains the basket of the presentationist as the result
of trout mistaking the fancy or unnatural fly for some known insect. In ex-
tremity, he will deny that there is any such thing as a fancy fly; all are imitations
in one way or another, and the basket would be fuller if the presentationist
paid more attention to the insects. The presentationist, on the other hand,
graciously attributes the basket of his adversary not to his flies but to his fishing
skill. The tallest tales of fishing experience will not crack the logic of these
views.

Regional fly practices defy all theory. Dry flies are predominant in the East
after the snow water and April freshets have run off, but toward the West flies
grow wetter and wetter. Imitation flies have prevailed for seventy-five years
from the Beaverkill in New York to the Brodhead in Pennsylvania. They turn
fancy north along the Seaboard to Maine and Canada. In the whole sweep of
the Rockies, flytiers are wonderfully enterprising and unorthodox. They often
abandon the delicacy of fur and feathers for the durability of hair, squirrel tail,
and bucktail. Large, rough, and radically spectacular, their flies express the
directness and enthusiasm of wild-country fishing.

THE OLD MASTER

The main tendencies of modern American flytying largely stem from Theodore Gordon, the old master of American fly-fishing, familiar to most
fishermen through his Quill Gordon fly. Gordon's influence was consciously
passed on by the generation immediately following him, the peerless school of
Sullivan County (New York) flytiers, standard-bearers of the imitation fly: Reub
Cross, who attributed his learning to Gordon's tutelage; Roy Steenrod, creator
of the Hendrickson fly, and Herman Christian (both Gordon's fishing companions); the Walt Dettes, man and wife; and the Harry Darbees. In delicacy,
precision, and style, the craft of the flytying masters is out of the old master,
Gordon. He died in 1915 and was swept from sight like a spent spinner. But we
know his work and his angling life from his surviving letters and numerous
"Little Talks on Fly-Fishing" in the files of *Forest and Stream* and the *Fishing
Gazette*, of which he was the American correspondent from 1890 (*The Complete
Fly Fisherman*, 1947).

Gordon was born in Pittsburgh in 1854 with a silver spoon in his mouth and fly-fished the limestone creeks of Pennsylvania from the age of fourteen. He lived a remarkable life, unheard-of in our day. A man of taste and intelligence, he was a good, restrained, yet warm and exciting fishing writer, a reader who knew Chaucer as well as Walton and Thoreau, Thad Norris (*The American Angler's Book,* 1864) as well as Frederic Halford (*Dry-Fly Fishing in Theory and Practice,* 1889), and a devoted follower of the great Francis Francis (*A Book on Angling,* 1867). When he fled civilization for his retreat on the Neversink, he put only one thing into his mind—the stream—and sustained it there unflaggingly for many years. An inexplicable performance, probably never duplicated by anyone anywhere. Gordon made an elegant backwoodsman. His one fishing photograph, taken around 1895, suggests a more than ordinary discrimination in clothing and equipment. He spit blood during his last three years and died presumably of TB. What we really know of him is that he lived a sweet, good life, and was perhaps the only man ever to express with his entire existence the ideal of the anglers' brotherhood.

Gordon did not entirely succeed in escaping the civilization from which he fled, and his early writing is more cheerful than his last. The destruction of forests, bringing ice jams and floods, and the pollution of streams, all of which killed the trout, bothered him more and more. He felt that the increasing purchase of riparian rights and the consequent closure of long stretches of streams for private use was a violation of the anglers' code. And although his fame brought him many invitations, he usually turned away from posted and specially stocked waters with the remark that they were too easy to fish and no test of skill. He respected the clubs for their role as trout preserves. But he loved difficult fishing, and he most enjoyed the days when the trout, especially the big ones whose lairs he knew, were elusive.

A FISH STORY

Gordon is the subject of many anecdotes. His small, slender figure was beloved by the people of Sullivan County, where he and his rod were most often seen bobbing along paths and streams. His haunts were the Neversink, the Beaverkill, the Willowemoc—the big three of Catskill trout streams—and the Esopus and Big Indian. But he had also fished in the dear Brodhead of Pennsylvania, and in streams south to Florida, north to Maine, and west to Ohio, Michigan, and Wisconsin. Gordon himself told a fishing story that reveals his stream manners. In the early spring of 1907, when the water was too high and roily for flies in the main stream, he turned off into a tributary (a useful hint for early-season fly-fishers) and soon came upon a little Negro girl fishing a pool with stick and string. He was stalking and she did not notice him. He intended to signal her: "I did not wish to poach upon her pool, but, as a matter of form, dropped my fly at the edge of the stone and not three feet from the small maiden's toes. It was seized at once by a half-pound native trout, which had been lurking under her pedestal, and I am not sure who was more surprised, the child or myself."

As a craftsman and an innovator, Gordon came upon the scene at an opportune time for a great man, and he lived up to the occasion. In 1890, two disparate traditions that today make up the central course of our flytying and fly-fishing were operating independently of each other. The first was the long tradition of English fly-fishing known since the fifteenth century, which was then undergoing its greatest turn with the development of the dry fly. The other was American fly-fishing, which was then still locked into the wet fly, used mainly either in indigenous fancy patterns or in imitation patterns tied on British models. Gordon brought about the juncture of these traditions.

On the English side, trout flies go back to the fifteenth century. We know from Hills's ingenious and masterful history that eleven of Berners's twelve flies, the first on record, can be traced down to the present time. They were wet, and strictly imitative. Other equipment consisted of long rods and twisted hair lines. From the early fifteenth century to Cotton in 1676 (Walton was not a fly-fisher) there was practically no change except for the addition of a number of flies. The seventeenth was a literary century, lit up by Walton, Cotton, Wotton, and other great fishing writers. Fly-fishers in the eighteenth century stopped writing, with the exception of occasional brilliant pieces such as Gay's verses, and got to work supplying the tackle essentially as we have it today: short rods, reels, silk lines, and drawn-gut leaders. It was a technical century; the artistry of flytying stood still.

ACTION UPSTREAM

The nineteenth century was the fly-fisher's epoch. Literature and fishing came together in the romantic appreciation of nature. The study of science led to the publication of fly-fishers' entomologies in color, notably Alfred Ronalds's monumental work, *The Fly Fisher's Entomology,* in 1836. Flytiers set to work with their models drawn in front of them and expanded their range with numerous species of insects. In 1851 George Pulman (*Vade Mecum of Fly-Fishing for Trout*) pulled the dry fly out of his hat complete, though for all anyone knew it might as well have been a rabbit. It was an extraordinary achievement, but a little ahead of its time.

Then came W. C. Stewart (*The Practical Angler,* 1857) and the first leap forward in fly-fishing history since its origin. Until Stewart, fly-fishers relied on the color and shape of flies to catch their fish. Stewart introduced *action.* How did he do this? By turning upstream. Some fly-fishers had been upstream men since Cotton's time, but Stewart went upstream and made an argument for it. Upstream fishing, wet or dry, is superior fishing for many reasons, but essentially for one: Facing upstream, the fisher controls the position of the fly; therefore the fishing is more precise and the element of luck greatly diminished.

THE DRY FLY

The effect on fly-fishing was profound, for upstream fishing was a prelude to the dry fly. The dry fly must float naturally, an effect almost impossible to obtain downstream. From Pulman, who first held it up, to Frederic Halford, who quit his business, took off his coat, and fought thirty-five years for its *exclusive* use, the dry fly had a rapid and spectacular development. During the late nineteenth century it came to maturity. Color and form were debated all over again. Halford wrote the second great entomology (*Dry-Fly Entomology*, 1897), with numbered color plates to identify tints and shadings. After Halford had done his work, a wet-fly fisher on a chalk stream in southern England "skulked like a poacher." Hills was a man of moderate judgment, yet here is his summation of the dry fly: "It altered both the practice and the temperament of the angler. It called different qualities into request. It has a charm and an allurement which the older sport did not possess. In what does its charm lie? Partly in the fact that all the moves in the game are visible."

The dry-fly rage was on in 1890 when Halford received a letter from Theodore Gordon inquiring about this new phenomenon. In his reply Halford enclosed a full set of his dry flies, each carefully identified in pen and ink; and the dry fly winged its way to the New World.

In the United States, sport fishing had been practically unknown before 1830. Fish was food. The fly was discussed in a few books—John J. Brown's, George Washington Bethune's, and Frank Forester's—in the 1840's, but was not widely used until the 1860's, when it suddenly bloomed. The Americans had learned most things from the English, who on their chalk streams lazily "fished the rise," that is, waited until the trout showed itself and then cast over the rise. But the Americans typically strode their fast-water streams and went after the trout wherever they lay, rise or no rise. The fishing was good—too good—and the fancy wet fly was often sufficient to the occasion until the 1870's, when the native brook trout of the East were suddenly fished out.

The great American fisher of the century was "Uncle" Thad Norris, learned in fishing literature and experienced in native practice. He knew about everything there was to know in his time, put it all down in 1864, and thereby equipped the school of early American fly-fishing with a rounded theory and practice. Like Stewart, from whom he may have learned it, he was fishing upstream, sometimes even drying his wet fly in an effort to make it float. That was the nearest an American came to getting in on early dry-fly development—a gesture.

By 1879 the brook trout were all but gone, and the hardier brown trout had not yet been transplanted from Europe. The editor of *Forest and Stream* threw in the sponge with a long editorial dirge, ending, "This is probably the last generation of trout fishers." Norris's crowd had got all the trout, and the following generations had to learn conservation. Eastern fishing, which was the larger part of early American fishing, increased in difficulty for more reasons than one. The immigrant brown trout was wiser than the native brook. Neither fancy flies nor wet flies were enough. Fly-fishers of the nineties faced upstream and waited for something to happen.

THE MODERN FLY

It was a historic moment, then, in 1890, when Gordon opened Halford's letter and fingered his flies. Gordon was already immersed in the brief tradition of American fly-fishing. The first practical book he had used was Norris's, from which he learned to tie his first flies. Like Norris and his predecessor Stewart, Gordon was an upstream man. He had fished through the decline of the brook trout and the rise of the brown, and so cherished the native species that he refused to accede to its scientific designation, charr. It was a *trout*. He had seen sights rarely seen by the modern Eastern angler: "water covered with dimples made by the rising trout as far as my view extended."

The significant thing is that Gordon had fished the wet fly dry, the natural outcome of an acute upstream man fishing over rising trout. Instinctively he had dried the fly, as Norris had done; but the construction of the fly was wrong. At best the wet fly keels over when dry and floats inert on the surface. It was natural that Gordon, a man consecrated to angling and a reader of English as well as American books, should have heard the echoes of Halford's crusading din across the water.

Gordon saved Halford's flies as models of construction for typing his own flies. But his job had just begun, for Halford's flies imitated English insects, which are different from ours. Gordon set out to correct this in his own way. Lacking any kind of formal fly-fisher's entomology, he studied what entomological information there was and began to observe duns and spinners on the water. It is thus owing in part to the lack of American color-printed entomologies that he observed flies under natural conditions and, tying imitations on the spot, initiated our contemporary style of American flies—cocky, pretty, subtle, and impressionistic.

He became for a time a strict imitationist—that is, he tried for an impression of individual species. Although he grew so well acquainted with insects in his long sojourn by the stream that he could carry hundreds of them in his memory, he gradually turned moderate—partly the effect of becoming a professional flytier. He came to believe that under all but the most difficult circumstances, an imitation covering a group of species was sufficient for good fishing. Gordon regarded his Quill Gordon as a pivotal fly that was subject to different dressings. This famous standard fly apparently was not meant to represent a single insect. "I can vary them to suit," he said.

A further contribution of Gordon's grew out of the fast stream: the English, fishing the rise in quiet water, can afford to use a softer hackle than Americans, whose flies are always being ducked by whitecaps, froth, converging currents, and other movements of the stream. Gordon sought a stiffer hackle, which was a matter of being more selective in cock necks, and tied it as sparsely as the conditions would allow. From this the fly developed greater delicacy and buoyancy. The key to the American dry fly today is still buoyancy, and assuming you start with a light wire hook, that means hackle. American flytiers now use stiff hackle in their flies even at the cost of departing from the exact color of natural insects.[1]

Other men in the early years of this century made important contributions to American fly-fishing. Since Gordon did not himself put his work between covers, the laurel for the first book on the dry fly went to Emlyn M. Gill, whose

---

[1] Only in two important instances is Gordon outdated: in the trend in the East away from his long, heavy rods, and in the trend away from the use of many bird feathers in flies. The crux of the materials problem, which to this day shows no hope of solution, is the difficulty of obtaining certain feathers. Dry flies fished in fast water must float on tiny, stiff strands of feather hackle obtained from rooster necks. But poultry raisers usually kill roosters before they are two years old, the age at which some of them might develop prized neck feathers; and flytiers generally cannot afford the cost of raising poultry exclusively for feathers. Rarest of necks is the blue dun; flytiers have made reputations on their blue-dun hackles.

Practical Dry-Fly Fishing hatched out the dry-fly cult in 1912. Here, as in England, the cult put on a great, if belated, campaign to sink the wet fly forever. Their titular leader was Gill's friend George La Branche, whose book *The Dry Fly in Fast Water* (1914) is regarded by many as the American classic. La Branche made a unique contribution to the technique of fast-water fishing: the decoy method of floating a fly many times over the supposed lair of a trout, for no less a purpose than to create *an entire artificial hatch*. His celebrated fly is the Pink Lady. Yet Gordon, who fished the dry fly from 1890, tied it, talked it, wrote about it, and preferred it when the conditions were right, never joined the cult or turned away from the art of the wet fly fished upstream. When the dry-fly rage came on, he resisted it. In England the "wet" man G. E. M. Skues (*Minor Tactics of the Chalk Stream*, 1910) had fought the "dry" man Halford, and together they produced a balance. Gordon's range was wider: he performed the joint services of a Halford and a Skues.

In brief, then, the classic American trout fly of today descended to us in the English line from Berners through Cotton (Walton's disciple) to Stewart, to Halford, to Gordon; and in the American line from Berners through Cotton to Stewart, to Norris, to Gordon. It continued down to us from Gordon through the creations of contemporary flytiers, some of whom have been mentioned here.

Whatever your preference in trout flies, take Gordon's advice and "cast your fly with confidence."

McDonald is concise, as Hills was, and has the gift of letting you see the forest without obscuring your view with the branches of sundry trees, so at the risk of some overlap, let's let him summarize some more:

The real work of the nineteenth century was in the creation of entomologies, the decisive shift to upstream fishing, and the invention of the dry fly, which together formed the greatest revolution in fly-fishing history since the sport has been known.

With the dry fly came a new brand of classicism, an effort led by Frederic Halford (*Floating Flies and How to Dress Them*, 1886, and other works) to create a definitive "scientific" set of imitation flies. . . . In the United States at about the turn of the century, Theodore Gordon introduced the dry fly, designed with an impressionism like Monet's and a streamside empiricism that altered forever the American weakness for imitating not our own natural flies but the established English artificials. He took his stand on mimesis as the ground of the art, but he was not a stickler for precise imitation: "If we have faith in the trout's ability to distinguish colors and shades of those colors, we have firm ground under our feet, a rational basis of action, and satisfactory explanations of many puzzles. Such a belief need not limit us to strict imitation of the natural in all cases."

Thus the luck factor, that Halford happened to send his patterns to as sweetly reasonable a man as ever lived, and not to an insistent dogmatist like himself, spared us over here the experience of quite such an insistent and insensate dry-fly mania as rigidified English fly fishing in the last decade of the nineteenth century.

That and the fact that the tumbling headlong rush of our freestone mountain streams, in contrast to the gentle flow of the placid English meadow streams, made it hard for our anglers ever to adopt, and successfully maintain, the English dry-fly habit of fishing only to the rise of a specific fish. It kept our angling from ever undergoing quite the stultification into a ballet-like ritualistic approach to stream fishing such as overtook English angling at that time and, to some degree, still hampers it with formalism.

It is in Gordon's own writings, as preserved in John McDonald's 1947 volume, *The Complete Fly Fisherman: The Notes and Letters of Theodore Gordon*, that we find the leaven of sense and sensibility which gave the American trout fisher that mastery of the dry fly which added a new dimension to his enjoyment of the sport without, in most cases, making him feel that he had to be enslaved by it, as much more generally became the lot of the English angler:

It seems to me that the addition of clear water to worm is sufficient to glorify the garden hackle and elevate it to a place above the artificial fly in the estimation of many fishermen on your side of the Atlantic. It is worming just the same, and no one can deny that it is death to small trout. There are so many fish that do not rise to the fly, and for which bait is legitimate, that the trout might easily be spared. Small mountain streams can be practically depopulated by bait fishing, never by fly alone. Our eastern brook trout *(fontinalis)* has a weakness for worm when small, and *fario* probably the same. I do not think that the rainbow trout cares much about worm, preferring flies and minnows. It seldom indulges in cannibalism as far as I can learn, being in this respect quite different from the other trout mentioned.

We can never repay the debt we owe to Mr. Frederic M. Halford, but I often wish that he would add to the burden by descending into personalities and giving more of his experiences in dry-fly fishing. There are so many of us who only get a few days on the water during the season, and must enjoy most of our sport by proxy. For many years I had at least two months with the trout, but this season my opportunities have been few and far between. The evening after the arrival of the *Fishing Gazette* is marked with a white stone, and I feel supremely grateful to those who write of their sport, particularly when the scene of action is pictured and one gets a glimpse of some skilful work with dry fly. There is really so much to be told if the narrator is a good observer. By the way, what a shock it was to learn that the alder fly is never on the water! What would Charles Kingsley have said to anyone who told him that his black or brown alder (I forget what he called it) never gave the trout a chance to gobble it. For years I thought it great medicine, when tied on a small hook, and it is only about ten years since it was displaced in my affections by certain dove-coloured insects. It is really dreadful to discover how little one knows, and the worst of it is that the older we get the more we realise how horribly ignorant we are. It is so pleasant to feel wise that after all is said it would certainly be better to die young.

The more I study the imitation of the natural fly and the various books on the subject (or which treat of it), the surer I am that trout have a wonderful eye for colour but a very indifferent notion of form. There is any quantity of evidence; but take your mayfly alone and note the curious buzzards that are mistaken for the natural, particularly hackle patterns that are deadly because so nearly right in colour. Shadows alarm trout greatly. Your shadow is more alarming than your bodily presence. But colour is another story altogether. How often have all anglers of experience had to acknowledge that the most trifling difference in colour made all the difference between a bad creel and a good one. Trout are wonderful animals, and their apparent vagaries might very well puzzle a Halford or a Marryat. Occasionally our faith in the art and science of fly-fishing is shaken, and we know not what to do. In the early spring sometimes it is quite useless to fish upstream or to use the dry fly. We must resort to salmon fishing tactics, cast across and down, and hang the fly over the lies of the fish. Sometimes thay take under water; again the only way to get fish

is to play a drop fly on the surface. This is one reason why I usually enjoy the later fishing more than the early days, when the biggest baskets are often made. The trout are well on the natural, they are in fine condition, and appreciate all the art and care we can devote to them.

. . . Thanks to the courtesy of Mr. Mills, of Leonard rod fame, I have been reading the fourth edition of "Dry Fly Fishing in Theory and Practice." I bought "Floating Flies" and "Dry Fly Fishing" when those books were first published, paying fifty cents on the shilling—just double the publisher's price—to procure them in the City of New York. These books were sources of much pleasure and profit to me, also of some pain, as for a time I tried to follow their teachings indiscriminately, without proper or due allowance for the different conditions under which my sport was pursued. For instance, I had a rod made to order which was as stiff as a poker—the manufacturer probably did not understand just what I was after—and used with it a very heavy tapered line. That rod nearly killed me before I summoned up courage enough to give it away. But the profit and the pleasure remained. In fact, I learned much that has been of permanent benefit in the matter of flies and fly-fishing. How much we owe to the good sportsmen who have condensed the practical experience of a lifetime in the printed pages of a book! I have learned to tie every kind of artificial fly, from the largest salmon fly to the smallest midge, from books. The modern writer (more particularly Mr. F. M. Halford), with aid of illustrations, makes the whole process so clear that anyone who really wishes to do so can learn. Uncle Thaddeus Norris' book, "The American Angler," taught me to tie wet flies; Mr. P. D. Malloch, in the *Fishing Gazette*, taught me to make salmon flies, and I also owe something to Captain Hale, whose book I read some years later.

I have read this (fourth) edition of "Dry Fly Fishing" with great interest, and feel inclined to jot down a few of the impressions it has made upon me. It seems absurd, yet I feel sadly discouraged over Mr. Halford's change of opinion in regard to the exact-shade-of-colour theory. If we have faith in the trout's ability to distinguish colours and the shades of those colours, we have firm ground under our feet, a rational basis of action, and satisfactory explanations of many puzzles. Such a belief need not limit us to strict imitation of the natural in all cases. We know that trout sometimes take flies because they resemble those upon which they are feeding; frequently they will take nothing except a good copy of a particular insect, but again they take the artificial for no such reason. It is alive (apparently), and they wish to kill it. It is red, red and white, or red and blue, and excites their predatory, ferocious instincts. In many wilderness streams and lakes, where natural water-born flies are extremely scarce, the fly-fisher must use his fly as a lure, not as an imitation. It must have life and attractive colours; it cannot be cast and allowed to rest where it falls; it must have movement—sometimes drawn along the surface, again, with short jerks, well sunk. One can move trout with a red and white fly in streams where they will rarely take it in, only dash at it. It excites them just as a red cloak excites a bull or a turkey-gobbler. In the days of the early settlers, a favourite bait was the ventral fins of the native brook trout, red and white, or red, yellow, and white, skittered on the surface of the water or even sunk. My extraordinary Bumble-puppy fly kills because it is wonderfully alive. It is just about as good for one game fish as another, showing that as a rule it is not taken as a fly at all. It was created to catch black bass in the first instance.

If I thought that trout were colour-blind, or nearly so, I am afraid that I would lose at least one-half of the delight I have in fly-fishing. While the snow-water was in the river and there was not a fly hatching last week, I could not take a trout until I tied up a thing intended to resemble a large larva or nymph, with a red tag. With that, in a few hours in two afternoons, I killed thirteen trout from 2½ lb. down. None of the native fly-fishers would go out, as they said it was useless; the trout would not rise. I could cover pages with instances where a slight difference in the shade of a Dun or other fly has made all the difference between taking trout and not taking them—an alteration, for instance, in the hackle in flies tied to same patterns. Another blow to me was to find that the Alder was never on the water. Many years ago I had a weakness for that fly, dressed very small—probably from reading Charles Kingsley's "Chalk Stream Studies." It is so long ago that I am not sure if this is the correct title of those charming sketches.

In Halford's "Dry Fly Fishing" I see that "Red Spinner" and "Detached Badger" were fishing together at the end of May, 1815—the year the Battle of Waterloo was fought—yet they are both active men in the world of affairs and fishing. However, this is probably a printer's error.

I was much interested in the fact—noted in "Dry-Fly Fishing"—that dry-fly fishers have taken to hand-lining trout when they go to weed, as that was the way I first learned to fish for trout.

Bear in mind that most of these notes, of the first decade of the century, were contributed by Gordon to the English *Fishing Gazette*, hence the frequent Anglicisms, doubtless supplied by the copy desk, such as "wading stockings," "fine cast" for fine leader, etc. But nothing can mar a fish story like this one:

I had one great day in June, 1901, and the sport was especially welcome, coming after a disappointment. Starting after midday, I reached the stream I was about to fish late in the afternoon with rain falling in torrents. I put on my waders during a lull, and found the water not only very high, but so much discolored that fishing was out of the question, at least with any prospect of success. There was no train to return that evening, or I would certainly have gone home. The rain ceased early in the evening, but I went disconsolately to bed and dropped off to sleep with the roar of the swollen stream sounding in my ears. The next day was Saturday, and when I went to breakfast, I was told that the water had cleared considerably. I soon found this to be the case; it was clear enough for fly, though still very high. The sky was overcast and it remained cloudy all day, constantly threatening rain; in fact, I believe that a few drops did fall from time to time.

Under these circumstances I was not long in getting under way. For some time I could do nothing. I could not reach the casts I knew, so as to fish them properly. At last I was encouraged by capturing a small trout of about a quarter of a pound. Proceeding downward I came to a place where the stream was greatly expanded over a wide rocky bed. Far out in the middle, near several large stones under water, was a kind of pool of fairly deep water, yet with a heavy current through it, while directly below was a large and dangerous rapid.

We knew the place above the rapid of old as the haunt of large trout. With great difficulty I succeeded in wading out far enough to fish this place properly, by casting a long line, although the water was within an inch or so of the tops of my stockings. I was fishing with only one fly, a kind of nondescript, tied by myself, with a light yellow body of wool on a No. 10 hook. At about the third cast, when the line was well extended and the fly over the lower end of the hole or depression, and just where the water probably began to shallow a trifle, I detected a very modest rise. I struck, and instantly an immense fish leaped from the water. The leap was diagonally across, not directly away from me, and really the trout appeared a perfect monster in this position, the curve of its broad back and wide spotted side, with the splendid propeller, a tail that to my excited eyes appeared as big as a palm-leaf fan, the fish cleared the water by many inches, and a desperate rush for liberty followed. I thought just then that I could not move (I changed my mind afterward), and had only thirty yards of line on my reel. Before I could curb this charge, only three or four turns were left me on the spool (you must remember that I had hooked the fish at the end of a long cast); in fact, I don't think that I really stopped the trout at all; he turned of his own will when he struck shallow water. I put on all the pull I dared, under which the fish gradually dropped back into the deepest part of the pool. I had recovered many yards of line when suddenly the trout rose toward the surface, a great swirl appeared, and then my reel screamed again. Before I could say Jack Robinson or even John, the fish had rushed down the stream and was in the heavy swift water at the head of the rapid. Nothing could stop him then; any attempt to butt him would have torn out the small hook, or caused a break in my fine cast. The line was quickly exhausted and I followed in water which for some yards was up to my waist. No thought of getting my wading stockings full then. The coarse rocks were cruel and the footing exceedingly bad, but I stumbled on, my legs like towers of lead. I was about winded when the fish took it into his head to stop in the rapid, probably behind some stone, but it appeared to be right in the middle of the rushing current. The check was but momentary, but it enabled me to get opposite the fish, and as he checked his wild career once more before reaching the shallows at the bottom, I managed better and felt that I had my good fellow in hand. I think that we were both pretty well played out by this time, and after many short rushes I stranded the fish where there was so little water that he fell over on his side. On getting him in hand I was greatly disappointed to find that instead of a five-pounder he was two pounds less.

Had this fish been lost, say, in running the rapid, he would have been remembered as that four- or five-pound trout that got away. Nevertheless, he was a noble trout and made a great fight.

Here is an illuminating note on the state of the dry fly in America as of 1906:

I see that a writer in the New York *Sun* states that dry-fly fishing is unknown in this country, or, if known to a few, is not practiced successfully. He is quite mistaken. The dry fly has been used on many streams in the Middle States for years. It was not unknown to Uncle Thaddeus Norris, who wrote the "American Angler's Book" about 1863. He gives an instance of great success with dry fly on the Willowemock, when wet fly was useless. In more recent years this method of fishing has been much resorted to by anglers of experience, where trout were shy and hard to take. The *Sun* man also says that no dry flies are tied in America. This is another error. I have seen beautiful work done by others, and tie all that I use myself. I have had a box of English dry flies for fifteen years, and used up some of them. I found out, however, that by following the colors of our own natural flies, which were on the water, I caught more trout, even when the work was rougher and less perfect to the eye. I believe that the entomology of American trout streams is much richer and more varied than anything known to fishermen in the United Kingdom.

English dry-fly anglers now often have a contempt for the wet fly, and seem to imagine that the only way to fish wet is with several flies cast downstream and dragging. This is absurd, as one constantly sees men casting upstream to rising fish. The only difference in method is that the fly is wet, not dry.

I admit that dry-fly fishing is most scientific, most difficult, particularly on such rivers as those in the south of England, or anywhere, where the water is still and flows very slowly. Even with fine-drawn gut and tiny flies, the cast which falls light as a snow flake, or feather upon the bosom of a quiet pool, is hard to accomplish, and with a burning sun high in the heavens, the gut no matter how fine it may be, is very conspicuous.

On many of our trout streams we have heavy rises of natural flies in the early part of the season, but if we joined the cult of the dry fly purist and cast only to a rising trout at all seasons, we would have a dull time of it. Not only this, but we would miss some of the most delightful and truly scientific fishing of the year, when the water is very low and clear and when a dry fly is often most successful. Our methods of fishing must vary with the season and locality. We cannot adopt one style in this big country and practice it everywhere and all the time. Fishing dry early in the season, on a roaring torrent, would be love's labor lost indeed, and in many wild regions the fly must be used as a lure, not as an insect floating upon the water.

Personally, I would rather fish the old streams which have been known to anglers for generations, where the trout are hard to take and where there are many natural flies. Here, whether we fish wet or dry, some little time devoted to the study of entomology is not wasted, but adds greatly to our pleasure, and often to our success. In America we can find the kind of fishing we prefer. We can even find a good imitation of the English chalk stream, if we wish. There are several such that I know of, and probably others. Yet I imagine that all fly-fishers would enjoy and profit by a visit to the Test and Itchen. There, if one is lucky, he may see some of the great past masters of the dry fly at work, men who think, talk and breathe feathers, quills, hackles and perfect dry flies, who can drive twenty-five yards of heavy line in the teeth of a gale of wind and place a tiny dun or spinner, floating and cocked, a few inches above a rising trout. It must be confessed that this is the perfection of the art.

And here, at the beginning of the last year of his life, is Gordon's review, for the *Fishing Gazette,* of George La Branche's *The Dry Fly and*

Fast Water. I don't know of any other single piece of his writing that gives a better feeling—a sense of "family," almost—for the angling heritage on this side of the water. Gordon gives the American angler a sense of pride, along with humility, that verges on reverence, for the fathomless mysteries of his sport:

The literature of angling is now very large, and upon the whole, America makes a very good showing. Since the time of J. J. Brown and his forgotten "Anglers' Guide," we have had a number of first-rate original writers. Frank Forester was among the first who wrote of field sports, but we are thinking of men native to this land. There was dear old Uncle Thad. Norris, Robert Barnwell Roosevelt, an uncle of Colonel Roosevelt, W. C. Prime, and many others. In recent years the out-of-doors', and sportsmen's magazines, have introduced a host of good men; sea fishing has been elevated to a science and we have such high authorities as Professor Holder, on the "Game Fishes of the World." Dr. Henshall was the recognized authority on the black bass, but, since he wrote, short casting rods, new methods, and a host of extraordinary artificial baits have come in. Many names occur to me, but it is unnecessary to mention them now.

For more than twenty years we were content to rely upon Englishmen as the supreme authorities on the use of the floating fly. Clever anglers began using this system regularly in the South of England about the year 1860; although we have records of the occasional use of the dry fly at an earlier date, in both countries. After the publication of Mr. F. M. Halford's "Dry Fly Fishing in Theory and Practice," 1889, the art was gradually adopted in this country, but it made no great stir. This we attribute to the fact that American anglers who had been in the habit of fishing upstream, with small flies, found the change from wet to dry comparatively easy. We have waters where conditions resembled those found in the South of England; but, for the most part, our anglers were accustomed to fishing the more turbulent mountain streams, on which the wet fly will always have its time and place. It was not until our sportsmen saw that the floater was frequently killing, when the wet fly failed, that the present vogue of the dry fly began. The first book on the subject appeared only two years ago. It was written by Mr. Emlyn M. Gill and undoubtedly caused a boom in dry-fly fishing in all parts of this country. But the demand for good works upon angling is inexhaustible. Thousands of anglers, old and young, experienced and inexperienced, welcome a new book by one of the fraternity and are delighted to invest a few shekels in its purchase. There are few things that give one more pleasure on a winter's night than a good work on fly-fishing.

I have just finished reading "The Dry Fly and Fast Water," by George M. L. La Branche (Charles Scribner's Sons), and expect to read it again. That, I fancy, is the test of a book or article. If we return to them with a relish they will surely please others.

Mr. La Branche is an old hand at the game; his style is direct and to the point. He is a close observer of the habits of the fish and loves to study the problems presented every day in the season on our rapid streams. They are always rising and falling; conditions are never quite the same from day to day.

Mr. La Branche gives many hints and wrinkles, and the leaves from the book of his experience will prove of value to many. His point of view is original, and there is not a dull page in this book. He has no great faith in the imitation of the natural insects and gives a very short list of artificial flies, dressed upon Nos. 10 to 16 (sized) hooks. Size is important at times, he thinks, but he is not bigoted in any way. His theories are his own, but he is quite willing to allow other folks to have their own notions. We all have our opinions, based on a great or limited experience, and may at times become a trifle warm when asserting our views. It is just as well to remember that angling is only a recreation, not a profession. We usually find that men of the greatest experience are most liberal and least dogmatic. I remember an old angler saying to me some time ago: "I have fished for trout for forty years; I have studied their habits and the methods of taking them. Formerly I was quite sure that I had nothing to learn; I knew it all. Nowadays I make no such claims. I know very little about trout and never expect to know very much in regard to them." It is often the man of limited experience who is most confident.

There is nothing dogmatic in "The Dry Fly and Fast Water." I know Mr. La Branche by reputation, and his ideals are high. He fishes the floating fly only, and kills a few of the largest trout. All others are returned to the water. What splendid sport we would enjoy on free water, if fly-fishing only was practiced, and the limit in size was raised to respectable proportions! I fancy that a trout should be big enough to take line from the reel before it is considered large enough to kill. The best of days is often the one when but three or four fish have been taken. The killing of large trout is remembered with a thrill of pleasure when heavy baskets of small trout are forgotten. If we reckoned our baskets in pounds instead of in numbers it would be better. The statement that a man has killed fifty or one hundred trout makes not the slightest impression on one's mind, except possibly a slight feeling of disgust. We have seen too many such creels. I am afraid that we envy the angler who reports that old four-pounder we have known for years. I believe that all anglers who fish streams of rapid descent will find pleasure and profit in this purely American work on dry-fly fishing. I do not think that I have done the author justice.

One indication of the unique veneration with which Gordon is regarded today by American anglers is afforded by Sparse Grey Hackle's account, in his 1971 volume, *Fishless Days, Angling Nights,* of a quest, that became a pilgrimage, for Gordon's grave:

THE QUEST FOR
THEODORE GORDON

First there was Theodore Gordon, the consumptive exiled to the Catskills, whose cosmopolitan personality and passion for angling enabled him to project his spirit across the ocean into kinship with the great figures of contemporary British angling; he was, in fact, the father of dry-fly angling in America. He died in 1915.

Then there was John McDonald, scholar, writing genius of *Fortune* magazine, and devoted angler, who more than thirty years later rescued Gordon from oblivion by the keenness of his discernment and the ardor of his research. His labors culminated in 1947 in the angling literary milestone THE COMPLETE FLY FISHERMAN: THE NOTES AND LETTERS OF THEODORE GORDON.

Then, some two years later, The Theodore Gordon Society (there is no connection with a conservation organization of similar name, which was formed some years later) was formed by four members of The Anglers' Club of New York: Lewis M. Hull (The Physicist), Guy R. Jenkins (The Underwriter), the late Edgar G. Wandless (The Attorney), and the present writer (The Reporter). Out of a chance conversation before the Club fireplace grew an expedition to the Catskills to photograph the house in which Gordon had died. On that occasion the four organized this most informal society, which eventually interviewed at length the surviving two of the three native fishermen who had been Gordon's only familiars in the Catskills, and later helped in solving the mystery of Gordon's last resting-place.

Finally, there was Virginia Kraft, then a talented writer-reporter and now an associate editor of *Sports Illustrated* magazine. In the course of authenticating Gordon's fly box for the then-new magazine, she formed a desire to know more about the man. Over the next several years she devoted several thousand miles of spare-time travel and investigation to finding and interviewing Gordon's few surviving, scattered family connections. In this manner she accumulated what meager information still was available about that little-known recluse and today undoubtedly knows more about him than any other living person. Ultimately this knowledge became the key which unlocked the mystery of Gordon's burial place.

THINGS OF THE SPIRIT

It was a most unseasonable pilgrimage for a late November weekend, a sentimental journey to find the Catskill farmhouse in which Theodore Gordon had lived his last years and died, and to see again, before a New York City reservoir should drown it, the lovely Neversink that he had fished. Unseasonable, yet it had crystallized instantly and urgently out of nowhere during a chance conversation among four angling friends. Why is not clear; but perhaps they had subconsciously in mind the news lately come from England of the death of Gordon's dear letter-friend, the great angler Skues.

They left the city that weekend in a drizzle that worsened into sleet, but they were warm and dry, and some sympathetic bond not only joined but uplifted their spirits. So while the station wagon slogged along, they sang the songs grave and gay that everyone holds in memory; and this was remarkable, for they were not a singing sort of men. Even when, at Napanoch, the sleet changed to a blinding white wall of snowflakes in the headlights and it seemed as if tire chains would be needed, they still sang, and when they came at last to Claryville, and carried their heavy lading into the frigid cabin, they sang though their teeth chattered.

Three roaring fires, a gallon of scalding coffee, and a mound of sandwiches soon made things comfortable, and they wound up smoking and chatting before the fireplace. But the first night of an expedition is nothing more, spiritually, than what the Arab caravan men call "the little start," a mere getting of the expedition on the road. So after nightcaps as tall as a cowboy's sombrero, they burrowed into heaps of five-point blankets and slept the night away.

Then it was morning, "the great start," the spiritual setting forth, with fires rekindled and the pungency of coffee summoning the sleepers to add to it the fragrance of that best smoke of the whole day, the pipe before breakfast. It was afternoon when the pilgrims finally took the road to Gordon's habitation. As the car picked its way through the deserted, ruined village of Neversink huddled amid slopes desolated by the dam builders, no reminder was needed that the shortest days of the year were at hand. The Physicist shook his head in despair as he read his light meter, and the others were depressed by the obvious approach of the day's end.

When they came to the spot, they were doubtful, for the house had been torn down, but a deer hunter who came by assured them that upon this foundation had stood the Anson Knight house, in which Gordon had lived out his last days. All this part of the valley had been condemned now for the reservoir, and the city had pulled down the dwellings at once to keep out squatters. Soon the place where Theodore Gordon had lived and died, as well as much of the river he had loved to fish, would sleep beneath a hundred feet of water.

The building site was across the road from the river and above it. A long knoll behind it was mantled with a dense windbreak of evergreens. A somber sky pressed down on the dark pines, and a pool in the river that had been bright crystal last summer now shone like black polished flint through the naked branches. The raw, wet air eddied in sullen gusts.

Sleet crunched underfoot as the pilgrims climbed the little pitch to the house and stood on the wall of a foundation filled with a mean, pathetic jumble of rubbish. Yonder still stood the rotting, unpainted barn and here were the weed-grown steps up which the weary angler must have plodded so often; but the spirit of Theodore Gordon had gone from the place and it was only a littered, dreary site.

Before they drove away, someone produced a flask and they stood together in the road looking back at the spot they had left, murmuring brief toasts to the greater angler as they sipped the spirits.

"Do you suppose Gordon took a drink, on occasion?" queried The Reporter.

"I am sure that he did, but Herman Christian and others who knew him agree that he was most temperate," replied The Physicist. "In one of his later letters to Steenrod, Gordon refers to 'my bottle of whiskey which I never use' but in an earlier article he recalls a weary walk home from fishing with a companion whose flask, 'a miserable caricature of a thing,' was so small that it provided no sustenance. Theodore Gordon was gently born and reared, and lived in many places, and I think we may safely assume that he knew how to enjoy the good things of life."

It was almost dark when they got back to their cabin. A conflagration was started in the outdoor fireplace, and while it burned down to a bed of embers, The Attorney made a salad. Then, muffled to the ears, he went out to the fire with a long-handled fork in one hand and a great steak in the other. He threw the latter on the embers and a rich aroma streamed down the wind so that a benighted hunter, a hundred yards away, stopped short and then struck out for home at a quickened pace. The Reporter brought the cook a drink, and they stood together looking at the river.

"The shades of all the great anglers who knew the Neversink must still frequent this place," said The Reporter. "They must be enjoying that savory scent, right now."

"'The gods of the place'—a pagan concept," replied The Attorney. "This steak is ready."

After dinner The Reporter went out to the woodpile, but before he carried in his load he paused to look and listen. Despite the snowy gleam of the ground, iron winter darkness lay on the land—an empty, desolate land unrelieved by even a point of light, from the peaks of Slide Mountain to the river gurgling half-frozen at his feet. But yellow lamplight streamed through the window; and inside the cozy cabin, redolent of good food and tobacco, they were singing an old college glee as they washed the dishes.

"Like a blackbird in the spring . . . " mourned the silvery tenor, the notes harmonizing sweetly.

"Oralee, Oralee, maid with golden hair," sobbed the counter tenor, and the baritone throbbed like a bronze bell. Soft and mellow, the music faded into the icy darkness, making it seem even more cold and empty. The Reporter gazed at the pool below him and imagined a frail little man casting with a nine-foot rod amid springtime greenery, placing a tiny dull-colored fly with consummate artistry. He carried in his wood, then mixed a stout drink and carried it back outdoors.

"The gods of the place," he quoted softly. "A libation to the gods of the place." He started to pour a libation in the manner of the ancients, then changed his mind and turned back to the cabin. He held the door wide and stood aside for a moment as if in invitation, then went inside and put the drink on the stone mantelshelf of the fireplace, in the shadows.

When the work was done the four sat smoking by the fire and their conversation was of Gordon, weaving into a varicolored fabric the threads of information gathered from the recollections of The Underwriter and several others of their acquaintance who had known Gordon, and from the collected letters which are almost our only record of him. They spoke of his frail physical aspect, his habit of rolling cigarettes between thumb and finger of one hand, of the mysterious "Fly Fishers" to which he several times refers in his writings as his club, and of Skues's coinage of the pen name Val Conson. It was getting late when the fire finally burned low and the room turned chilly.

"Throw on some wood," urged The Physicist with a shiver. "It's cold in here. How Gordon must have suffered, winters, in that primitive farmhouse."

"He did," affirmed The Underwriter. "It runs through his letters; he detested the cold. He was an outdoorsman, and loved the woods on a crisp, sunny winter's day, but he hated dark, raw weather like today's."

"Coldness and loneliness run through his writings," chimed in The Physicist. "Note how recurrently he says things like: 'It is too cold to work'; 'It is wild and lonely up here'; 'It is a dreary day'; 'This is a cold, raw day, damp and windy.' 'Now it is overcast, raw.' And in December 1905, he wrote in *The Fishing Gazette:* 'It is rather dreary in the country at this season. The birds have gone for the most part, the hum and buzz of insect life has ceased, the leaves, which recently were so beautiful, are on the ground, brown and withered. On a still day, Nature seems to be dead or at least in a comatose state. Even the light of day is hard and cold. As I write, the wind is shrieking and tearing at this frail wooden house as if determined to carry it off bodily.'

"The loneliness of this city-bred, cultured man imprisoned in a rude mountain settlement all winter was pathetic, and I think there was intense feeling in his remark to Skues: 'I am very lonely tonight and am writing to you for the feeling of companionship,'" concluded The Physicist.

"And now Skues is dead. What a reunion they must have had in Valhalla," mused The Reporter.

"A pagan concept," reiterated The Attorney. "It's getting late; let's turn in."

They wasted no time in their preparations for the night, but before he went to bed, The Reporter turned back to look at the glass on the mantelshelf. It was empty.

What the world knows of Theodore Gordon, the angler-epistolist, comes principally from his published letters to R. B. Marston and G. E. M. Skues in England, and the youthful Guy Jenkins; and from the recollections of his friends in the Catskills. Of these there were three; but one, Bruce Leroy, died long before without ever having recorded his impressions of Gordon. The other two were Herman Christian and Roy Steenrod, both living as this is written (1969). Herman Christian resides in Grahamsville, New York, and Roy Steenrod in his native community of Liberty, New York. Both are in retirement.

The nature of Gordon's friendship with each of his three Catskill friends differed in subtle ways. Christian and Steenrod agree that Gordon "thought a lot" of Bruce Leroy; Leroy named one of his sons after him. Yet, judging from Gordon's letters, he called him Bruce only occasionally. It is impossible to evaluate this friendship now because all we know of Leroy is that he inherited a prosperous farm at Leroy's Corners, two miles from Bradley, but preferred hunting and fishing to farming.

Herman Christian was Gordon's familiar; they lived only a quarter of a mile apart during Gordon's last years and saw a great deal of each other. Specifically, Christian fished with Gordon far more than did any other person. Gordon called him Christian, and Herman still refers to his friend as Mr. Gordon.

But Gordon never called Roy Steenrod anything but Mr. Steenrod and after ten years of correspondence still so addressed him in the salutations of his letters. Roy always refers to him as Gordon, but I think he addressed him as Mr. Gordon. Yet Roy feels that he was closer to Gordon than any of his other friends: "He told me more than anyone else in the world."

12.
Skues and a
Return to Reason

No one has better summarized the "return to reason" effected singlehanded by G. E. M. Skues than John Waller Hills in his 1924 volume *A Summer on the Test* (I quote from the 1930 second edition):

When, exactly twenty years ago, Mr. Skues wrote *Minor Tactics of the Chalk Stream,* he effected a revolution. The dry fly was at a height of its intolerant dictatorship, and the other method was discarded and ridiculed to such an extent that enthusiasts of the school of Halford regarded Mr. Skues as a dangerous heresiarch. Much water has flowed under bridges since then, and in that water many are the trout which have been caught on a sunk fly which would not have fallen to a dry. More and more each year does nymph fishing become a part of the modern angler's equipment, and he who does not possess the art is gravely handicapped. And at the same time has come the realization that this art is both difficult and delightful. It demands different qualities and it makes a different appeal, it opens a new field of observation and experiment, and it is as exacting a process as the other, for upon my word I find trout harder to catch under water than on the top.

Elsewhere in the same volume, Major Hills elaborates:

. . . At Whitchurch in 1890 no one dreamed of using anything but the dry fly ex-

224

cept occasionally when fishing still water on a windy day. But the curious point is that the Houghton *Chronicles* do not mention its introduction. When I think of the change which its use has made: how it has altered not only the fisherman's practice, but his temperament and outlook: when I run my eye over the vast literature to which it has given rise: I marvel that in what is its second home no one has recorded its adoption. Perhaps it is an example of the truth that we often overlook that which is nearest and describe worst what we know best.

Indeed, from the analogy of other rivers, I find it incredible that the dry fly had not captured the Test before 1882. It was common on the Itchen since the 'fifties. In the 'sixties James Ogden introduced it on the Derbyshire Wye, so successfully that the owner of the water prohibited the blow line. Halford found it in full swing on the Wandle in 1868. Francis Francis in 1867 says that it was greatly used on southern streams. The Test must have been one of these.

Wherever it was introduced, it conquered. The sunk fly was swept away, beaten and ridiculed. Perhaps the blow line, appealing as it did to human frailty, died harder. The Houghton *Chronicles* mention it in 1884; it lingered till the 'nineties here and there. I never saw it used. No, the dry fly came, and conquered both it and the sunk fly. Everyone thought it would rule for ever. Its advantages are so obvious. Its imaginative appeal is so powerful. If you had told any enthusiast of the 'eighties that within a generation the sunk fly would be back on the Test he would have laughed.

And yet it has returned, and the underwater fly or nymph is used more and more. Nymph fishing is no new thing. Marryat dressed artificial nymphs: and moreover many of the old flies, particularly hackle ones, are no doubt taken for them. But in the bright dawn of the floating fly's success the sunk counterpart was condemned. A large march brown or a large alder were sometimes fished downstream, sheepishly and shamefacedly. But nine fishers out of ten relied entirely on the fly which floats. Imitation got better. Spent spinners were dressed. Flies got smaller and smaller. But all were intended to float, and it was not until Mr. G. E. M. Skues produced *Minor Tactics of the Chalk Stream* in 1910 that underwater fishing was again systematised. He worked out several patterns, using the old dressings: but later both he and others have turned their attention to a more exact copy of the nymph than the old hackle or winged fly provided. Hence comes the modern school of nymph fishing. It is, no doubt, a return to the sunk fly. But it is an advance at the same time. It is the old problem in a new setting. It is a fresh and entrancing chapter in the ever moving history of trout fishing.

We would have to wade through some eight to ten books to refight the war, battle by battle, between Halford and Skues, as the opposing champions of dry fly and nymph, six by the former and four by the latter, and if you find the subject all that fascinating, you go ahead and read them. I've read them once, and there's other fishing I'd rather do in print than to wade them again. Besides, it really isn't necessary. To my mind, the whole story is adequately recapitulated, by Skues, in just two places: first, in the foreword to his 1910 volume, *Minor Tactics of the*

Chalk Stream, which you might liken to the original declaration of war, and second, in the summation of the subject he provided in his 1939 volume, *Nymph Fishing for Chalk Stream Trout,* which could be likened to the memoirs of the victor, or at any rate the survivor, of the struggle.

Here then, for the first item, and whattayaknow for once we do seem to have a first (1910) edition:

Rising from the perusal of "Dry-Fly Fishing in Theory and Practice," on its publication by Mr. F. M. Halford in 1889, I think I was at one with most anglers of the day in feeling that the last word had been written on the art of chalk-stream fishing — so sane, so clear, so comprehensive, is it; so just and so in accord with one's own experience. Twenty years have gone by since then without my having had either occasion or inclination to go back at all upon this view of that, the greatest work, in my opinion, which has ever seen the light on the subject of angling for trout and grayling; and it is still, as regards that side of the subject with which it deals, all that I then believed it. But one result of the triumph of the dry fly, of which that work was the crown and consummation, was the obliteration from the minds of men, in much less than a generation, of all the wet-fly lore which had served many generations of chalk-stream anglers well. The effect was stunning, hypnotic, submerging; and in these days, if one excepts a few eccentrics who have been nurtured on the wet fly on other waters, and have little experience of chalk streams, one would find few with any notion that anything but the dry fly could be effectively used upon Hampshire rivers, or that the wet fly was ever used there. I was for years myself under the spell, and it is the purpose of the ensuing pages to tell, for the benefit of the angling community, by what processes, by what stages, I have been led into a sustained effort to recover for this generation, and to transmute into forms suited to the modern conditions of sport on the chalk stream, the old wet-fly art, to be used as a supplement to, and in no sense to supplant or rival, the beautiful art of which Mr. F. M. Halford is the prophet. How far my effort has been successful I must leave my readers to judge. I myself feel that in making it I have widened my angling horizon, and that I have added enormously to the interest and charm of my angling days as well as to my chances of success, and that, too, by the use of no methods which the most rigid purist could rightly condemn, but by a difficult, delicate, fascinating, and entirely legitimate form of the art, well worthy of the naturalist sportsman.

In the course of my too rare excursions to the river-side, I have elaborated some devices, methods of attack and handling, which I have found of service, some applicable to wet-fly, some to dry-fly fishing, or to both. In the hope that these may be of interest or service, I have included papers upon them.

In conclusion I should like to express my gratitude to the proprietors of the *Field,* for permission to reprint a number of papers contributed by me to that journal over the signature "Seaforth and Soforth," which come within the scope of the work; and to Mr. H. T. Sheringham, for his invaluable advice and assistance in the arrangement of these papers.

— G.E.M. Skues

And here, twenty-nine years later, the summarizing look over the battle-grounds, after all the carnage:

A good many years ago I vowed by the Nine Gods—ineffectual beasts—that never again would I be guilty of a book. Years after, like a fool, I let myself be jockeyed against my better judgment into allowing the publication in book form of a collection of the angling oddments which from time to time I had committed to the periodical press. Some good man—I forget who it was—said *"Indignatio facit versus"*—and now in the beginning of my Eighties I find myself impelled by that same emotion to go back once more on my pledge to the Nine Gods.

In writing of the art of trout fishing with the fly, my contribution to knowledge has by degrees led, via the resuscitation of the use of the wet fly on chalk streams, to the practice of the use of life-like representations of the natural nymph. And while every fresh day's experience of the practice of nymph fishing has confirmed me in my conviction that I have been moving in the right direction, and while the practice appeared to find acceptance on almost every hand, I find in my latter days there seems to be a movement on foot designed to re-rivet on the chalk stream angler the fetters of dry-fly purism from which I thought common sense and the experience of the last quarter of a century had shaken him finally free.

Whether that movement be due to the revolt—in my opinion quite a legitimate revolt—on the part of a section of chalk stream anglers against the use by some anglers on chalk streams of lures supplied to them by—presumably ignorant—tackle dealers under the names of nymphs, but which bear no resemblance to the larval stage of the Ephemeroptera, to which alone the term "nymph" may legitimately be applied, or to some more obscure cause, I feel driven, in my old age, to attempt the task of describing fully and in detail what I conceive to be the true and proper practice of nymph fishing, and of establishing its justification. I shall no doubt fail to convince those who do not wish to be convinced, but at least I shall have done my best. If only I could persuade anglers to take out with them regularly a marrow scoop to extract the contents of the stomachs of their trout (without the dilatory and horrid mess of an autopsy), and a white-enamelled cup into which to wash out these contents, so as to analyse them and see what the trout are really eating, I might have some hope, for they would learn when the trout are taking winged flies and when nymphs and what nymphs are really like, and realise the justification of nymph fishing as a valuable branch of the chalk stream angler's art.

I am conscious that the volume contains a number of repetitions, but I have had to choose between making them and crippling my argument by innumerable cross-references. So I pray the forgiveness of my readers.

. . . Though I believe that the movement to reassert the exclusive dominance of the dry fly on chalk streams is largely due to the use by some anglers of the illegitimate lures sold as nymphs by many tackle dealers and ignorantly accepted as such by their customers, yet that is not the case put forward by the purists. The arguments adduced are based upon F. M. Halford, and I do not think therefore that the case for the nymph can be said to have been conclusively dealt with without an examination of the pronouncements thereon of Halford as its main and most authoritative opponent, both in his earlier work and also in his later works, when his doctrine had become less liberal and more and more pronouncedly purist. I am therefore inflicting on the reader a somewhat prolonged analysis of Halford's writings on this subject which I beg him not to skip, as it is vital to a correct understanding of how he came to assume his intolerant attitude on the question of fishing wet fly and nymph on chalk streams.

It is nothing but justice to say of Halford that the governing spirit of his purist doctrine was unselfishness, the desire to be fair at once to his brother angler and to the trout; and it is without any thought of imputing to him any less magnanimous motive that I feel bound to examine his pronouncements closely and to demonstrate how his failure to realise certain essential features of the situation led him, by the very fact of his magnanimity, to enunciate doctrines which experience has shown to be unsound.

I have already said that I have no quarrel whatever—on the contrary, I am in agreement with his objection to chalk stream anglers "fishing the water," searching it with a wet fly or a team of wet flies, thus catching or pricking and scaring unsizable fish, and incidentally covering as much water as would be enough for several anglers casting fly, dry or wet, or artificial nymph to individual selected feeding fish in position. But from first to last Halford never seems to have understood or believed that it was possible to direct the wet fly (or nymph) successfully to such fish when feeding subaqueously with as much

precision and with as much care for the feelings and interests of the brother
angler and as much consideration for unsizable fish as is displayed by the most
careful purist fishing the dry fly to surface feeders. He expressed his incredu-
lity in very definite terms at page 75 of his last work, *The Dry Fly Man's Handbook* (1913), in which he came down hard in favour of strict purism. He says:

> I am told that there is a school of fly fishermen who only fish the sunk
> fly over a feeding fish or one in position if it will not take a floating fly.
> This, they urge, is a third method of wet-fly fishing, the other two being
> the more ordinary of *fishing the water* with sunk fly either up-stream or
> down-stream. Candidly, I have never seen this method in practice, and I
> have grave doubts as to its efficacy.

Yet years of practice of this method have made me ever more and more convinced of its soundness, particularly in cases where in place of the wet fly an
appropriate pattern of nymph is presented to the feeding trout. This method,
moreover, is *not* "fishing the water."

Halford died in 1913, at a date when the practice of fishing the artificial
nymph was not much more than mooted, but the use of the wet fly fished upstream or up and across to selected individual fish had been put definitely on
the map; and though both in *Dry Fly Fishing in Theory and Practice* and in his
final volume he had authoritatively discredited the possibility of effective representation of the natural nymph, it was the wet fly that was the enemy in the
passage which I have quoted.

In the days preceding the advent of the dry fly there were no doubt exceptional fishermen who did some at least of their fishing to individual rising fish;
but, taking it by and large, I infer that most of the chalk stream wet-fly fishing
was done in rough windy weather with flies which searched the water, being
fished dragging across and down. The Diary of the Rev. Richard Durnford,
1809 to 1819, published in 1911 by Henry Nicoll under the title, *Diary of a Test
Fisherman*, speaks constantly of "a sufficient wind" and so on, and he used "a
bob fly to steady the cast." In those times the angler stayed at home on still
days. In his Autobiography (p. 83) Halford quotes Major Carlisle (South West)
writing of the Houghton Club water in the early 'seventies.

> Trout were far easier to catch, while of those who fished, perhaps only
> half—maybe fewer—had any idea of dry-fly fishing, and it was a common
> thing to see an angler flailing away with two big flies on the thickest of gut,
> downstream, and to hear his complaint of not catching anything.

Coming to the Test with his dry-fly experience of the Wandle, with the
restricted lengths there available for the individual angler, it is not unnatural
that Halford should resent the methods of the down-stream flailer. The heavy
and powerful dry-fly rods with their heavy tapered casting lines then in use by
dry-fly men were utterly unsuited to present a wet fly up-stream or up and
across to fish in position, and it is perhaps not unnatural that Halford should
have made little or no attempt to do so. When the light rod came in in the early
days of the present century, Halford fought against it and I doubt if he ever
possessed a rod and line capable of first-rate up-stream wet-fly work in still
weather on chalk streams. So, right through his work, whenever he speaks of
the use of the wet fly on chalk streams he invariably associates it with the prac-

tice of down-stream flogging and "fishing the water" as contrasted with fishing to individual fish.

As this statement has been challenged — notably in a debate on the subject of nymph fishing in chalk streams recently held at the Fly Fishers' Club — I feel bound to produce chapter and verse in justification of it. At page 36 of *Dry Fly Fishing in Theory and Practice* (1889), in a chapter headed "Floating Flies and Sunk Flies," Halford writes:

> In principle the two methods of fishing are totally and entirely distinct. With the dry or floating fly the angler has in the first instance to find a rising fish, to note accurately the position or what is technically called "spot the rise" and to cast to this fish to the exclusion of any chance work in other parts of the stream. With the sunk or wet-fly on the other hand he casts to a likely place whether he has or has not seen a rise there (more frequently he has not) and in fact his judgment should tell him where from his knowledge of the habits of the fish they are most likely to be found in position or ready to feed. Thus wet-fly fishing is often termed "fishing the water" in contradistinction to the expression "fishing the rise" which is applied to the method of dry-fly fisherman.

This is no doubt an excellent description of wet-fly fishing as practised on North Country and other rough rivers, but it does not seem ever to have occurred to Halford that the method of "fishing the rise" with the wet fly or nymph might be (as it has been) successfully adopted on chalk streams when the trout were seen to be feeding subaqueously.

I have already quoted at page 66 the passage from his last book, the *Handbook* (1913), in which, in spite of twenty-seven years' intervening experience, and in despite of testimony to the contrary he avowed his disbelief in such a method.

In his intervening work I have found no evidence whatever that he ever changed his mind on the subject. But his Autobiography (1903) contains a passage at pages 69 and 70 which I must quote for the sake of the comment it evokes.

> I was much interested, some years since, watching a first-rate wet-fly man, a Yorkshire fisherman, on a portion of the Upper Test. His flies were olive quills of various shades, iron blues, red quills, and such patterns, all of which he used on his native streams, and were dressed with peacock quill bodies, very meagre upright wings, and a single turn of hen hackle for legs. He did not in any way practise the "chuck and chance it" plan, but moved slowly up-stream, carefully studying the set of the current and quickly deciding where a feeding fish should be in each run. Sometimes it would be close under the bank, sometimes on the edge of a slack place, and sometimes on the margin of an eddy.
>
> Whenever he had made up his mind as to the most likely spot there, he would make one, or at most two light casts, placing his fly with great accuracy and letting it drift down without drag. Now this I take it was the best possible imitation of the work of a dry-fly fisherman, except that he had not spotted the fish and his fly was not floating in the dry-fly sense. His patterns were very similar in size, colour and form, to those of the ordi-

nary chalk stream fisherman. He used very fine drawn gut, and worked hard from morning to evening, never passing over a likely place without putting a fly into it, and very seldom losing a hooked fish.

It was in the early part of April, during strong westerly and south-westerly winds, when the hatch of duns was sparse, and when, in fact, all conditions were favourable to the sunk and unfavourable to the floating fly. He fished six days on a well-stocked reach of the river and killed in the aggregate seven trout weighing 9 lb. Candidly, I was somewhat surprised at the good result, and have often wondered whether he could repeat the performance. Of course the average weight of his fish, just over 1¼ lb., was very small for the Test, and two or three of them would have been returned by many dry-fly fishermen.

Let it be clearly understood, however, that this fisherman was most skilful and painstaking, and was a past master in the art of selecting the right spot, and in placing his fly accurately and delicately *there* at the first attempt. Had he merely fished the river up or down, or had he bungled his cast, or moved about rapidly, or, in fact, made any mistakes, I do not believe he would have killed a single trout, so that his bag represents the best possible result, under existing conditions, for a wet fly fisherman on a stream like the Upper Test.

Now on this passage I call my readers' attention to the words, "This I take it was the best possible imitation of the work of a dry-fly fisherman *except that he had not spotted the fish.*" The Yorkshire fisherman in question, a Mr. Reffit—a correspondent of my own—was therefore not fishing to an individual fish, but guessing, or judging if you prefer it, where the fish ought to be. He was fishing, moreover, in early April, a time of year when the rise is sparse and rarely extends over two hours, and though he fished "hard from morning to evening," we are not told that he fished to any rising fish or even saw any rise.

Halford says, "All conditions were favourable to the sunk and unfavourable to the floating fly." This brings me back to a passage in *Dry Fly Fishing* which shows pretty clearly that Halford did not know what conditions on chalk streams *were* favourable to the sunk fly. It occurs on page 39, where, after describing conditions favourable to the dry fly, Halford proceeds:

> On the other hand where no rising or bulging fish are to be seen, and whence it may be inferred that the fish are not taking surface food at all, the conditions are favourable for the use of the sunk fly.

This is quite wrong. Such conditions are *not* favourable for the use of the sunk fly. On chalk streams the fish must be as definitely feeding to take wet fly or nymph as to take the floater, with the difference that they are taking subaqueously; and they must be either bulging over weeds to the nymph emerging from the weeds, or taking the mature nymph on the verge of hatching. It is clear that the Rev. Richard Durnford knew this, though his most successful fishing was done in rough water.

There is another paragraph in the *Handbook* (at p. 68) in which Halford gives a description of wet-fly fishing, contrasting it with the dry fly. He says:

> The wet-fly fisherman does not as a general rule wait for a rising fish, but places his fly (he frequently uses two, three or even four) in a part of

the river where, from his experience of the habits of the trout he would expect a feeding fish to be located. Some fish up-stream, some down-stream and some across the stream. In the hands of a past master it is a most scientific and under favourable conditions a very deadly method of fishing.

Now this is an excellent description of the wet-fly method as practised on North Country and other rough rivers, but it is not fair argument to contrast it with the floating fly on chalk streams. Why did he not contrast the dry fly with the modern wet fly as applied to chalk streams? I suggest that the answer is to be found in the paragraph I have already quoted from page 75 of the *Handbook*. He had "grave doubts of its efficacy." In other words, he did not believe it.

Other sentences from the same volume illustrate Halford's attitude towards the wet fly. At page 74 he writes:

> Nothing more surely tends to develop further the increasing shyness of the fish than the presence of a few persistent down-stream floggers with the sunk fly.

True enough, but do we find anywhere a suspicion even that the wet fly or nymph can be fished to subaqueously feeding fish as precisely as the dry fly to surface feeders, and that there is no need for "persistent down-stream flogging"? No.

On the next page he proceeds:

> I will at once freely admit that up-stream wet-fly fishing is not so harmful on a chalk stream as the same method pursued down-stream. But in my view the continual flogging and the continual movements of the angler making his way along the bank too often in full view of the trout are however very nearly as destructive of the confidence of the fish as down-stream fishing. Then too the distance covered by the persistent flogger is so great that the limits of any ordinary length of water will be covered many times in a day's fishing.

If it be suggested that the methods there described are characteristic of the modern chalk stream angler with wet fly or nymph, I say they are unmitigated nonsense, intended by the writer to discredit a technique which he did not understand and disliked.

This brings me to the investigation of the question how it came about that a man of his high intelligence, ability and opportunities, so failed in understanding.

Let us turn back to *Dry Fly Fishing* at page 143. He is describing a cold day in May 1885.

> It was a day on which a fresh breeze from the north-west was blowing; and so cold was it that, to an idler on the river-bank, it was a difficult matter to keep his hands warm; and yet the number of flies hatching was, even to one accustomed to the plentiful supply on chalk streams, something astonishing. The trout seemed to have appetites which could not be appeased, rushing about in all directions, making heavy bulges under water as they took the larvae rising from the bed of the river, or here and there just breaking the surface as they seized the fly at the very instant of

its casting off the envelope in which it has passed pupa state. This should of itself indicate the fact that it was a most unsuccessful day, and that the trout could not be persuaded to look at any artificial fly, as their every movement was to secure the swiftly darting larvae when rising to the surface and before emerging from the shuck.

To dress an artificial representing the larva or pupa is difficult, but not an absolutely impossible task. Having overcome his natural repugnance to descend from what may be described as high art to the less scientific sunk-fly style of fishing, and having succeeded in turning out a fairly good imitation, the amateur is prone to imagine that he has at last solved the problem, and can, by fishing it under water, make sure of a respectable bag at a time when the fish are bulging incessantly at the natural larvae. Alas! how woefully he is *désillusionné. The fish will not look at this*, although it is an admirable representation, both in colour and shape, of the natural insect. And what is the reason? To elucidate this, take a handful of weed from the bed of the river and extract from it three or four specimens of the dun larvae with which it abounds; place these in a tumbler of clear water and patiently watch. Those that are nearly ready to hatch, or are rising to the surface for that purpose, seem positively electrified, every feeler or leg, and every fold or rib of their bodies, moving in an eccentric but continual motion. How is it to be expected that a timid, shy fish like a trout, who from painful daily, and even hourly, experience is warned to use the keenest of all the senses with which he has been endowed by nature, viz. his sight, for his protection, should mistake that motionless supine compound of dubbing, silk, quill, and hackle drifting helplessly and lifelessly like a log down the stream, for the active, ever-moving larva sparkling in the sunshine, and varying in colour at every motion as rays of light strike it at different angles?

Now just consider Halford's elucidation. He takes a handful of weed from the bed of the river and extracts dun larvae and finds them extremely active. I have already recounted how to the end he was in the habit of quoting G. S. Marryat's saying, "You can imitate the nymph, but you cannot imitate the wriggle," and there is a passage on page 122 of *Dry Fly Fishing* where, apropos of bulging, Halford writes:

> It is my opinion that the difficulty does not lie in dressing an artificial grub fairly resembling the dun's nymph but in imparting to that imitation the motion and direction taken by the natural insect at that stage of its existence.

It does not seem to have occurred to him that though a nymph—even a nymph nearing maturity—might be highly active when taken from his shelter in the weeds it did not follow that it was always active as the moment approached for it to put off its shuck. I have shown (with reasons), in the chapter on "The Way of a Trout with a Nymph," that in these conditions it is often practically inert and that, as well observed by Dr. Mottram, even when emerging from weeds on the occurrence of bulging, though it may move from side to side (possibly deflected by the changes in the current caused by the sway of the water) its motion is "quite slow and calm, not in the least fast or jerky."

I have so frequently caught bulging trout with an artificial nymph fished up-stream, and so much more frequently similarly taken trout feeding quietly under banks or in runs on the ascending nymph about to hatch, that I have no doubt whatever about the fact that there is nothing in the activity of the natural nymph to prevent the trout from taking an artificial nymph. A good imitation is in fact an excellent attraction for subaqueously feeding fish.

When however we come to examine what Halford has to say about trout feeding on nymphs in the latter conditions we find only one reference, viz. at page 125 of *Dry Fly Fishing* (1889):

> Sometimes fish, when feeding on larvae and nymphae, however, rise quietly, and do not move about much from place to place; and under these circumstances it is almost impossible to distinguish the apparent from the *bona fide* rises, except by watching intently the surface of the water with the view of making certain that the winged duns floating on the stream are being taken. One such case is brought prominently to my mind, when on a hot August evening a trout rose steadily under the bank until it was almost pitch dark. For an hour or more I kept on throwing steadily, and, I am vain enough to think, without making any glaring mistake, over this fish. Commencing with a very small pale yellow dun (Flight's Fancy), then trying in succession a blue-winged olive, red quill, ginger quill, hackled-winged red spinner, Jenny spinner, and detached badger, I at length, as a last resource, put up a small silver sedge on an O hook. The very first cast secured a trout upwards of 2 lb.; and knowing that fish feeding on *curses* will occasionally, for some occult reason, take this particular pattern, I fancied that I knew all about it, and made sure that it had been feeding on these annoying little insects. On my return home an autopsy of the contents of its stomach revealed an extraordinary conglomeration of shrimps, caddis, snails, larvae, and nymphae, but not a single winged fly.[1]

Here we have Halford hammering for hours a fish which was unquestionably nymphing, offering it in succession seven different patterns of floating dun, and ultimately getting it at dusk with a sedge. It never seems to have occurred to him, either during the incident *or at any subsequent time*, to fish a trout so feeding otherwise than with the floating fly: and the only credible explanation which occurs to me is that he always believed the nymphs on which the trout were feeding were too active to be successfully represented, and that therefore the sole hope that ultimately he might be led to make a mistake. I also infer that the only occasions on which he tried the artificial nymph must have been on bulging fish (I will not suggest with a dragging fly), and that he failed entirely, both then and thereafter, to realise that the fish rising quietly as described were not chasing active nymphs but were feeding on floating nymphs coming up so quietly as to be motionless, or in other words, "practically inert." I am no purist, but I must confess it seems to me at least as unethical to hammer a nymphing trout with a succession of floating flies as to offer a nymph to a trout which is exclusively taking hatched duns, a practice which I do not advocate.

---

[1] This statement is repeated at pp. 167–8 of the 1902 edition without comment or enlargement.

The incident quoted from page 125 of the first edition of *Dry Fly Fishing* is repeated, I believe, verbatim, in the subsequent editions—showing that Halford learned nothing from that or subsequent experience.

Before leaving this phase of the subject I have to refer to a passage on nymph fishing at pages 126–127 of the *Handbook,* where Halford writes:

> With respect to the question of dressing imitations of nymphs, I have always urged that any fly-dresser who sets his mind to it can do this easily. Years and years ago Marryat and I dressed most effective patterns to represent the nymphs of duns and mayflies by tying in a few fibres of black feather at the head, constructing the fly generally with a quill body, the colour of the abdomen of the natural nymph, hackle short and spare, and the whisks, which were also short, of gallina, were dyed to shade. When the body material had been tied in, the fibres of black feather were bent down into a shallow loop and fastened in at the shoulder to represent the wing cases of the natural nymph, the hackle was then turned, and the fly finished at the head.
>
> We killed a few fish with them, but discontinued their use for two reasons. The first, that in our opinion they were essentially wet flies, and the use of them on waters reserved for dry fly only, constituted a breach of the ethics of the dry fly. The second, which may possibly be a more cogent reason in the minds of many modern anglers, was that wherever and whenever we used them we found that the number of fish hooked and lost was out of all proportion to the total bag, and that the fish rapidly became inordinately shy and unapproachable. This, I think, sums up the position fairly from the dry-fly purist's point of view, and I can only advise my readers to abstain from trying bulging fish either on their own or their friends' fisheries in all cases where the use of the floating fly is considered *de rigueur.*

I find this statement hard to reconcile with the passage which I quoted at page 73 from page 144 of *Dry Fly Fishing,* where Halford says, "The fish will not look at this, although it is an admirable representation, both in colour and shape, of the natural insect." I have grounds for knowing that the date when Marryat was dressing artificial nymphs was before 1883, as he gave patterns to my friend, the late Rev. E. R. J. Nicolls, while he was fishing, during the tenancy of Marryat and Francis Francis, the same length of the Itchen which Mr. Irwin E. B. Cox took over at the beginning of 1883—and which I have been fishing ever since. I can only account for the statement by assuming a lapse of memory on Halford's part, since upwards of twenty-seven years had elapsed since the publication of *Dry Fly Fishing* and sixteen years since the death of Marryat. Assuming that he caught a few, the statement of the disproportionate number of fish hooked and lost would suggest that the experiments were made fishing downstream to bulgers with drag and not up-stream or up and across to trout quietly taking the hatching mature nymph.

Here again I must point out that Halford's advice is to abstain from trying *bulging fish,* once more ignoring the case of the trout taking the mature nymph quietly under banks and elsewhere which are the best trout to assail with the artificial nymph.

In further endeavour to understand Halford's mind on the subject let me quote some further passages—the first from page 239 of *Dry Fly Fishing* in the chapter on Autopsy:

> It has been clearly shown that by far the larger proportion of the contents of the stomach of a trout or grayling consists of larvae, nymphae, caddis, shrimps, etc. *which are normally in the middle or lower depths of the water.*

The italics are mine, and as regards nymphs, though most of their lives are spent in weeds and mud on the lower depths of the water, from the angler's point of view the times when they are being taken by trout, so as to give the angler a chance of interposing his imitation, are (1) when the trout are bulging to them over weeds, and (2) when the trout are taking them just under the surface on their way to hatch out. The numerous examinations which I have made of the contents of the stomachs of trout tell me that only a small proportion of the nymphs there found are taken in the middle and lower depths of the water.

At this point it may be convenient if I refer to another statement of Halford's from page 240 of the same chapter. He writes:

> In any case it must be remembered that the presence in an autopsy of nymphae just on the point of changing to the winged fly indicates that the fish, *although as a rule under such conditions looking downwards*, has yet followed the active nymph towards the surface.

This is another misapprehension on Halford's part. Apart from the fact that the nymph under such conditions is *not* active but in general practically inert, the trout, as clearly demonstrated by Colonel E. W. Harding in *The Fly Fisher and the Trout's Point of View*, is not looking downward, but lies with his gaze fixed upward and forward on the mirrorlike underside of the surface upstream of his window, and sees the approaching nymphs reflected in the surface, and rises gently to meet them, preferably near the point where reflection and reality are about to merge.

The paragraph at page 239 goes on:

> At the first glance a natural deduction from this would be that the sunk fly would be more likely to tempt than the floating ones. Very possibly many of the sparsely dressed patterns used more generally in the North for wet-fly fishing are taken for some forms of larvae . . . and it has been confidently said by North Country anglers of great experience that an adept of this style could work sad havoc on some of the well-stocked shallows of the chalk streams. Unfortunately very few of the disciples of the dry fly practice, even if they understand, the art of fishing the sunk fly, which may account for the fact that as a general rule when tried in the Hampshire streams it has not proved successful. It would be well for a first-rate performer to pay a visit to the Test or Itchen and thoroughly thrash out the point.

In this connection I may mention that I have had a good North Country angler on my own length of the Itchen (which the late William Senior described as the most difficult water he knew) and, fishing with nymphs lightly dressed according to my methods, and presenting them up-stream or across to trout

feeding on nymphs, he has made baskets which would have done any Hampshire angler credit.

Halford proceeds:

> I confess to feeling grave doubts as to the result. If it is to be judged by any attempt heard of up to the present time, it is foredoomed; if on the other hand previous failures have been due to want of knowledge and experience on the part of the fisherman, it is quite on the cards that it might revolutionise the whole art of fly fishing as practised in Hampshire.
>
> If, however, as I am inclined to predict, there should be a fiasco the natural question is to enquire whether it is possible to take these wary fish when feeding under water with an imitation of their natural food. The larva has been frequently imitated and has occasionally done well, but strange to relate on the days when it has done well, it has almost invariably turned out that other fishermen have done well with the dry fly.

That is a general statement which it is impossible to check. It is not my experience. I have known many occasions when the nymph alone was being taken, the hatched dun being wholly neglected, and but few occasions when trout feeding on the surface fly were wholly unattracted by the nymph.

Halford proceeds, "It has generally been in early spring when the trout are comparatively easy to catch." I do not agree. I have used the nymph successfully right through the season, even in the most difficult days of July and August, and have taken some of my largest trout on it.

Again Halford, misled no doubt by the contrast of dry-fly methods with the superseded wet-fly methods in use on chalk streams, was led to infer that still days and hot sun and clear water are fatal to the wet-fly (or nymph) fisher. He writes on page 29 of *Dry Fly Fishing*:

> As to conditions of weather, on the stillest days with the hottest sun and in the clearest water, the fish are generally on the surface where the wet-fly fisher would consider the conditions most unpropitious and unlikely on such days to kill fish is most gratifying to the angler's bump of self-esteem; and often the largest and most suspicious fish feeding under such conditions seem quite guileless and fall victims to the art of the dry-fly fisherman.

I would assure Halford, if he were here to receive my assurance, that on such days when the trout are taking the mature nymph rising to hatch, the like success may be predicated for the nymph fisher or the wet-fly fisher casting the right pattern of nymph or wet fly to selected individual feeding fish. In such conditions it is often the case that the trout are exclusively nymphing and are letting the floating natural dun go by; but they will take an appropriately dressed nymph where they would ignore the artificial floating dun.

In other places Halford suggests that only small (often unsizable) fish are taken with the sunk fly and that many are pricked and lost. On page 71 of the *Handbook* he pictures as typical an angler who

> will proceed to the upper limit of the fishery and flog it steadily down with wet fly. He will probably see some fish following his fly, occasionally even plucking at it and getting pricked; a few, but a very small proportion being landed, and of these the vast majority yearlings or two-year-olds. Perchance he may succeed in getting two or three killable trout, but these as a rule are only just up to or possibly under the legal limit of the fishery.

I need hardly say that this is not a method which is within my contemplation as legitimate wet-fly or nymph fishing. Fishing and searching the water with a dragging wet fly is undoubtedly apt to lead to the catching or pricking or scaring of unsizable fish. But the illegitimacy of such practices affords no reason for forbidding the use of the nymph or wet-fly cast up-stream or across to subaqueously feeding fish. And nowhere do I find in Halford's books any reference to such methods except the passage from the *Handbook*, quoted at page 66, in which Halford not only expresses his lack of belief in them but says he *had never seen the method in practice*. Nevertheless it is a great method and a fascinating one, and it has brought me the great bulk of my largest trout, and has greatly increased my score of 2-pounders on a river where 2-pounders are by no means everyday fish.

On page 45 of *Dry Fly Fishing* Halford says:

> On one point all must agree, viz. that fishing up-stream with the finest of gut and floating the tiniest of flies is far more exacting and requires in many respects more skill than the fishing of the water as practised by the wet-fly fisherman.

Exactly the same claim may be made for nymph fishing as defined and advocated by me.

The modern wet-fly fisher and the nymph fisher on chalk streams who know their business are *not* "fishing the water" but casting to individual selected subaqueously feeding fish in position.

On the question of comparative skill as between that method and the dry fly I do not wish to dogmatise. I do not pretend to be an exceptionally skilful fisherman. My practice, like that perhaps of many other anglers, often falls short of my theoretical knowledge. But I may say I have heard not a few skilled dry-fly fishermen confess that to fish the artificial nymph according to my method was beyond them.

I do not think it necessary to pitch my case for fishing the artificial nymph to nymphing trout so high as to say that it revolutionises the entire practice of Hampshire trout fishing. In fact it leaves the correct practice of dry-fly fishing intact for all occasions where it is applicable, but it *does* fill a gap in the armament of the chalk stream angler, in providing him with a clean and sportsmanlike method of meeting those hours (and it is often those days) when trout are nymphing and letting the upwinged dun go by disregarded.

My claim therefore for nymph fishing is that it enables the angler to approach a nymph-taking trout with success in bright weather and smooth water in conditions which authority had hitherto held to be almost impossible, that it enables an angler to deal with a nymph-feeding trout, which would either be hammered in vain by the dry-fly fisherman, or else, if he were a real understanding purist, be left despairingly alone; and that thus the method of nymph fishing which my good friend the late H. T. Sheringham called "exact wet-fly fishing" constitutes as real if not as great an advance in the art of fly fishing as the dry fly indubitably did. It has the merit of superseding or getting over serious difficulties and limitations of the dry fly and so adding to the angler's chances of sport.

Though I have subjected the works of Halford to so critical an analysis, it is only because he has been beyond question the dominant writer on chalk stream fishing, and it is only just to say that no other writers on that subject ever seem to have suspected the propensity of chalk stream trout to feed largely on nymphs (outside the practice of bulging) prior to my calling attention to the subject—or even (apart from Dr. J. C. Mottram, Eric Taverner and Colonel E. W. Harding) since.

H. S. Hall, who was Halford's contemporary and wrote of the dry fly in the Badminton Library just before *Floating Flies and How to Dress Them* appeared and took the angling world by storm, is silent on the subject. Viscount Grey seems to have had no suspicion of the state of the case, not had Major Fisher (*Rod and River*, 1892), nor Lord Buxton. Earl Hodgson, though he mocked at the pretensions of the dry-fly purist, gives no reason for the faith that was in him. Passing outside the chalk stream area we find nothing on the subject in Stewart's *Practical Angler*, nothing in David Foster's *Scientific Angler*, nothing in E. M. Tod and nothing in any of the wet-fly authorities. The subject is in fact relatively a new one, and that must be my justification for inflicting yet another book on the patient fly-fishing public.

But let's not leave Skues without stopping for one good fish story, just for fun, such as "The Undoing of Aunt Sally," in *Minor Tactics of the Chalk Stream.*

There are places in most rivers—generally, I think, about the spots most frequented by man—where trout establish themselves, which seem, though willing enough to take duns as they come, to be independent of them as a staple food, and to take gaily every day and all day long, and often far into the night, whatever fly-food comes along, always excepting, *bien entendu*, the angler's flies, however delicately offered. Such trout are readily put off their feed, but not for long, and the angler, returning to the spot after a short absence, may make up his mind to find his friend back in position, pegging away as freely as ever. Everyone has a chuck at these fish—no one can resist them; but it is a rare thing for one to be caught—and the Coachman may account for a few. A strong ruffle in the water *may* enable you to take one unaware, but, generally speaking, the ordinary tactics, whether dry-fly or wet, are thrown away on such fish, and the only chance is to fall back on something exceptional either in lure or in method of attack, or both.

Followeth the example of

THE UNDOING OF AUNT SALLY

She was called Aunt Sally because everyone felt bound to have a shy at her. Her coign of vantage was near the bottom of the water, where the fishery begins, and her irritating "pip, pip," as she took fly after fly in the culvert that was her home was too much for the nerves of nine anglers out of ten, so that the absurdest efforts to circumvent her were made daily—efforts to float a dry upwinged dun down the culvert from the top: result, immediate and irremediable drag; efforts to flick a fly upstream to her in the culvert from below: result, broken rod-tops, barbless hooks, flies flicked off against the brickwork, and other disasters, leading to profanity.

The *locus in quo* was a stream in the South of England, flowing some fifteen yards or so wide at a good even pace, with a nice purl on it, down to and past a deep hole used for bathing by the farmers' lads. From this hole, a culvert in the left bank, a yard wide and, say, four yards long, diverts a considerable body of the stream into a new channel, to drive a mill in the town below. This was the fastness in which Aunt Sally had taken up her abode, and throughout the spring and summer had defied all efforts to dislodge her.

It was my first visit to the stream that year, and from 9 a.m. till 3 p.m. on an August day I had worked away for meagre results. There was no rise of fly after ten o'clock, and a strong rise of water-rats. Three trout had I turned over, and one of one pound two ounces reposed in my bag. I had not seen a rising fish for hours, when, weary and disappointed, I drifted down the right bank to the bottom of the fishery, and sat down to rest on the steps which are set in the hole to assist bathers in clambering out.

"Pip!" I heard coming from somewhere. I looked up-stream, I looked under my own bank, but not a sign of a ring was to be seen. "Pip, pip!" again. At last, leaning low and looking through the culvert, I saw, some two yards down, what I took to be a dimple of a rising fish. Watching a few moments, I saw it repeated, and my spirits revived. My point was fine, so I took it off and knotted on a yard of sound Refina gut, and ended it with a brown beetle with peacock's herl body and red legs. I soaked him well, so that there should be no drag on the surface, and then, getting my length for the other side, let the fly and gut drag in the stream till the moment I made my cast. Fly and gut together struck the brick face of the culvert, and fell in a heap at the mouth. Instantly the current caught the fly and gut, and extended it down the culvert. Almost at the same moment the current of the main stream, across which my reel-line lay, began to drag upon it, and completed the extension of the gut by the time the beetle had run a short two yards down the culvert. At once it began to drag back. This was too much for Aunt Sally—to have that beetle scuttling from her when it was almost in her mouth. She came at it, and in a flash secured it ere it could escape from the culvert; and before she could turn she was skull-dragged out of her fastness and turned down into the stream below. She made a determined fight for it, but she was very soundly hooked, and I gave no needless law, so that her fifteen inches were soon laid out upon the grass. Not knowing of her fame, I was quite content with her one pound eleven ounces; but an angler who told me of her reputation said she had always been put down as a much bigger fish. An hour later I looked down the culvert again, but the water had dropped some inches, and there was not enough current through the culvert to make it fishable. I had hit the happy moment for the undoing of Aunt Sally.

I think we can go now, but here, just in case you should want to come back, are the books in question:

FREDERIC M. HALFORD, *Floating Flies and How to Dress Them,* 1886.

————, *Dry-Fly Fishing in Theory and Practice,* 1889.

————, *Dry-Fly Entomology,* 1897.

————, *An Angler's Autobiography,* 1903.

————, *Modern Development of the Dry Fly,* 1911.

————, *The Dry-Fly Man's Handbook,* 1913.

G. E. M. SKUES, *Minor Tactics of the Chalk Stream,* 1910.

————, *The Way of a Trout with a Fly,* 1921.

————, *Side-lines, Side-lights and Reflections,* 1932.

————, *Nymph Fishing for Chalk Stream Trout,* 1939.

13.
Mottram
and the Mysteries

I must confess that I'd forgotten that Skues twice cites Mottram, in that passage from his last book, and both times with respect. Conditioned by the cavalier dismissal of Mottram with a sentence of faint praise by both Hills and Robb, I had come to think of him as the completely unsung genius of English angling literature. And from the blank looks I've elicited, even from some pretty keen angling bibliophiles, at every mention of his name for the past decade, I had come to the conclusion that Mottram was angling's Invisible Man. Hence my surprise now, at coming across this double mention of him by Skues in 1939. The J. C. stood for John Cecil, and he lived from 1880 to 1945. I've never found him listed in any of the English biographical dictionaries I've come across, nor in places like *Who Was Who,* though I invariably look, whenever I have access to a reference book that might conceivably be expected to list him. I had somewhere got the impression that he was a surgeon, but Skues's reference to him as "Dr." J. C. Mottram is unsettling to that assumption, as one of the peculiarities of British English is that while they call their physicians Doctor, they call their surgeons Mister.

In any case, I don't know and will never understand why Mottram's first book, published when he was thirty-five, *Fly-Fishing, Some New Arts and Mysteries,* didn't have the same sort of impact that had been registered five years earlier by Skues's *Minor Tactics of the Chalk Stream.* True, it can't be maintained that it was overlooked, since it did enjoy a second printing in 1921, but I would have thought that by now, over a half century later, his name would have become a modern angler's household word. Both the 1915 and the 1921 editions (printings, I should say, since they are identical) seem extremely hard to come by, and it is only his later books that crop up with any regularity in book dealers' lists. They are far less outstanding than the first one, which I consider one of the most innovative fishing books ever written, and I'm not as surprised to see them settle into that gray middle-distance filled by the chorus-like line-up of "other titles" that form the bulk of dealers' listings.

But his last book, *Thoughts on Angling,* undated but seeming from interior indications to date from the early days or months after the Second World War's end, or around the time of his death in 1945, seemed to me to be considerably superior to the interim volumes, and to represent a more than partial comeback to the stunning show of form of his first book. Yet apart from routine listings I've never seen a reference to it in print.

Mottram died young, for an angler, his sixty-five years missing by one even the middling mark reached by Uncle Thad Norris in the previous century. But Norris is a towering figure, looming larger as his centennial approaches, whereas Mottram languishes in near obscurity, a third as long after his lifetime. Yet in his first book alone, you would think there would be enough to keep his memory green and assure him a lasting place on a level with, if not quite Skues, then certainly Hewitt and La Branche.

I used to speculate on the possibility that since Mottram's thought processes seem radical, and his whole approach to the tradition-laden English practice of angling somewhat less than worshipful, he might be the victim of a conspiracy of silence, based simply on his auspices not being quite right, and he himself being from "the wrong side of the tracks." But I was on a wrong scent, as I could have told myself, on second thought, merely from the circumstance that his book was published by that arch-symbol of British sporting respectability and rectitude, "England's country newspaper," *The Field.* That, and the fact that some of the material in the book had appeared in *The Field,* and some in *Salmon and Trout* magazine and the *Flyfisher's Journal* effectively quieted that suspicion.

Besides, I happened upon a bound volume of the *Fishing Gazette* for

1921, and looking through the index to see if any mention of Mottram was made, I found a most respectful notice of the second printing of *Fly-Fishing, Some New Arts and Mysteries.*

So obviously the ensuing silence was in no way conspiratorial, and I was wrong in suspecting that Mottram might not be in good standing as one of the old boys. Indeed, he had an angling press pseudonym, "Jim Jam," the standard appurtenance of the time, like Skues's "Seaforth and Soforth" and "Val Conson," and Theodore Gordon's "Badger Hackle." (The once common use of pseudonyms survives into our day only in the unique persona of Alfred W. Miller's "Sparse Grey Hackle"—or can you think of another? John Voelker's "Robert Traver" doesn't count, because that's just a pen-name, which is a different matter.)

But R. B. Marston himself endorsed Mottram in unequivocal terms, in the *Fishing Gazette* notice in 1921, and in British fly fishing as of that era that was the direct word from Mt. Olympus. He referred back to his original review of the first edition of *Fly-Fishing, Some New Arts and Mysteries,* in which he had said, "It is a book by a very keen and clever fly-fisher, too broad-minded to think that only absolute dry-fly fishing counts; it is a book which the fly fisher with years of experience will enjoy, because it often challenges views which are founded on the results of experience." He then concludes "I can endorse what I said in 1915 and recommend the new edition to all fly fishers—wet or dry."

Right below this notice Marston has another, headed "A New Work by Mr. G. E. M. Skues," which reads:

"Messrs. A. & C. Black will publish shortly a work which is certain of a hearty reception from trout anglers, entitled 'The Way of a Trout with a Fly,' by Mr. G. E. M. Skues ('Val Conson'), author of 'Minor Tactics of the Chalk Stream,' which is now in a second edition; it will contain three full-page plates, two of them in colours. In a prefatory note we are very aptly reminded that 'the way of a man with a maid, and the way of a trout with a fly, remain with us to be a delight and a torment to thousands of generations yet unborn.' From the table of 'Contents' it is pretty certain that our author has a great variety of notes from personal experience as to the way of a trout with a fly—notes which will prove of great assistance in getting a trout into the creel."

Both notices include the legend that the book in question can be had, post free—for 7s. and 18s.9d., respectively—from the Manager of the Book Department, *Fishing Gazette.*

Why, then, under such equal auspices, did the angling readers of the time flock to the second, which shortly became one of the best-known titles in all angling literature, and stay away from the first, in numbers that amount to, as the saying is, droves?

And what are Mottram's "Mysteries," that were fated to remain so well kept?

Well, some of them were to be revealed all over again, within the decade after Mottram first put them down in unquibbling black and white, notably by E. R. Hewitt in America and by J. W. Dunne in England, while others had to wait for their rediscovery over three decades, to the time of Vincent Marinaro's *A Modern Dry Fly Code*. In each instance, the "second coming" of the mystery's revelation was received with awe, and discussed with wonder, by the angling fraternity as a whole.

It was only when Mottram first propounded them, and offered their solutions, that they couldn't seem to get a rise out of anybody. In simple justice, some part of the luster today surrounding the names of Hewitt, Dunne and Marinaro should be reflected back on the name of Mottram.

This is not to say that these three later writers ever consciously aped or copied him, but it is to say that he anticipated all of them.

Let's get out the Mottram and see how the case stands, as Major Hills would say. For once, we seem to have both first and second editions on hand, but I don't think it matters which one we quote from, as except for the notation of "second edition" on the title page of one, they appear to be identical in both their text and their diagrams. Correction: I do find one small difference, after all. Here's a sentence, on page 179 (the page numbers are identical in the two copies) which reads:

May 1921 bring for us many a still, sultry day or evening when, but for the devouring insect world, all is quiet; may this silence many a time be suddenly broken by trout jumping and splashing in the water in the endeavor to free himself from my wee smut or yours.

Turning to the same page in the other copy, the sentence reads the same, except for the date:

May 1914 bring us many a . . .

What interests me about this latter sentence, aside from the obvious reflection that the silence in 1914 was more notably broken by gunfire than by the jumping and splashing of trout, is the consideration that the two printings of Mottram's first book have usually been dated, in dealers' listings (the books are themselves undated) as 1915 and 1921, and indeed they are so indicated in the *Fishing Gazette* notice just quoted. But this indicates that Mottram wrote the chapter a year earlier. Small matter, because in both cases the chapter on "Smutting Fish" begins with the identical sentence about the season of 1913 and remains identical except for the change of dates already noted in the concluding sentence.

The season of 1913 was remarkable for the dearth of Ephemeroptera and abundance of smuts, and on referring to my log I find that almost as many chalk-stream fish were killed on smuts as on duns.

It seems, therefore, that smutting fish deserve serious consideration, for they call forth the fisherman's highest art, they require for their capture his greatest skill. Fine tackle, the smallest of hooks, and most accurate casting are necessary. Although the hook be small and the tackle fine, the fish may, nevertheless, be large and powerful, and thus require delicate handling before it can be guided into the landing net.

Many advise the use of large flies and correspondingly thick gut for smutting fish, a medium-sized sedge, for instance, and thus at once overcome all difficulties; but it is only when night has almost begun that the smutting fish can, as a rule, be persuaded to look at large flies; during the day and in the early part of the evening this plan is generally a failure, except with fish of little or no education, who will, of course, take anything. It is the smutting fish of open or club waters that are now referred to; fish that know the angler's shadow, the fall of his gut on the water, the contents of his flybox, the sharpness of his hooks, the strength of his gut, the length of his landing-net handle, the size of the fish he is allowed to kill, and the length of his membership.

There are a few circumstances which favour the angler when attacking smutting fish. The weather is usually favourable, the air is calm, facilitating accurate casting; the half-light of evening, which helps to hide the angler, is often the time when smuts are thick on the water. Further, smutting fish are not very readily put down, because their attention appears to be fully occupied with the collection of these minute insects. Lying, as the fish do, just beneath the surface, they view things above the surface of the water through a very small hole, and for this reason a bad cast, if only a little inaccurate, will pass unnoticed because not seen. Although in this respect an advantage, in another way it is the reverse, for, unless the fish be accurately covered, the angler's fly will pass by unseen; his fly must pass right over the nose of the fish, and this necessitates extremely accurate casting. Smutting fish will often rise at very short intervals, perhaps once every second. The rings thus made, as well as the high position of the fish in the water, will to some extent conceal the angler. Smutting fish always rise in exactly the same spot, and will not deviate to one side in order to take the angler's fly, because the fish cannot see the fly unless it passes directly overhead.

When smuts are on the water, sometimes all the fish in the water, large and small, will be found rising; even when only a few are feeding, it does not follow that these will all be small fish: large fish are as fond of smuts as small ones. I have seen 3 lb. and 4 lb. fish taking smuts at a time when only quite a few fish were rising. The hatch of smuts may be very local. Under the shelter of trees or waterside herbage, when they are swarming, i.e., buzzing, round a particular spot, selecting mates or egg-laying, no more than a single fish, or perhaps half a dozen, may be found taking them; much time may be wasted over such local smutting fish by attempting to take them with duns, spinners, or other flies, as a result of failing to recognise that the fish are taking smuts.

Mottram goes on to give five tyings for the true smutting fish — as opposed to those taking flotsam:

Flies must now be considered, and, first, the natural. Many suppose that the number of different kinds of smuts found on our rivers is very great, but this is not so. This error may be the result of examining spiders' webs close to the water and taking for granted that all, or most of, the flies found therein have come off the water. In reality most of these are land flies. Even those belonging to the water vary much in colour, according to the length of time they have been in the web, and thus one species will have the appearance of many.

On the other hand, there is a kind of smutting fish that is not truly a smutting fish. Very often one hears the angler say, "The fish were smutting the whole day long." This occurs especially in still, thundery weather, and in September; examination of the water shows it to be covered with all manner of small insects, green fly, tiny ichneumons, hoppers, minute beetles, gnats, midges, smuts, and a host of other unnamed, unknown minute insects which have fallen or flown upon the water. It is the fish which are feeding on this flotsam that are likely to be taken with a small sedge, or, better still, a green fly. A small sedge is of little use for a *true* smutting fish. There have been recognised only three kinds of smuts which cause definite rises of fish; others there probably are, but they cannot be common.

Mottram addressed himself only to the "true smuts," saying:

These, then, are the flies which have proved themselves successful with smutting fish; as is the kind of smut, so must be the kind of fly. Care must be taken to distinguish between truly smutting fish and fish taking flotsam.

For me, smutting fish make the most interesting fishing; is there a fishing enjoyment more delightful, more satisfying, or more satisfactory than to take a goodly two-pounder from a weedy stream, with a little smut on fine gut? It seems to me that there is the same difference between taking a fish on Mayfly and on an olive dun as there is between taking him on an olive dun and a smut.

It remained, for a long time, a separate problem to take fish on the "other unnamed, unknown minute insects" — the *minutae* in other words, those hoppers, beetles, gnats and midges that much later became the chosen territory of Marinaro, Fox and Grove and Schwiebert, but he did point the way.

He did more than point the way, however, in many other instances, where he not only named the mystery, but clearly indicated its solution.

But before we hunt them out, I'd like to slip in first this deft little characterization of some different kinds of anglers, in his introduction:

It is useless to argue the question as to whether, or no, fly-fishing is worthy of serious thought. A definite conclusion can never be arrived at because so much can be said for and against. Nevertheless, many will agree that to fishing can be applied the axiom, "That which is worth doing at all is worth doing as well as one is able." At any rate, it is in this spirit that fly-fishing is here approached. There are many ways of regarding the sport. It may be looked upon as a strife between hunter and hunted, brain against brain, skill v. skill, cunning v. cunning; thus it appeals to the hunter born. Others there are who cannot help associating fishing with pot-filling: it is well to regard these, as criminals are now regarded, as objects for pity. The savage is in all of us, in some more than in others.

There is the scientific angler. For him fishing is a series of experiments: facts are noted, conclusions drawn, laws made; and because fishing is an eternal enigma, so is he eternally a slave to it. First he goes a-fishing on a clear, frosty day and returns with many fish; therefore he says "frosty days are the best." Next he fills his basket on a sultry day of rain, thus confusing his first conclusion. He turns to the wind; he notes that the S.W. winds are favourable until a biting nor'easter shatters the theory. Then he tries temperature, humidity, conditions of the water, or of the insect life, and so on; he even tries himself, with alcohol and without alcohol, with much tobacco and with little tobacco. Thus he wanders from experiment to experiment. Flies, gut, rods, are all tested in this way, and yet the solution, instead of coming nearer, seems, like the mirage, to keep ever receding before him as time passes by, until at last he must leave the problem unsolved, fortunately for the everlasting pleasure of those who follow.

The naturalist-angler is a common species; he says, "I never saw a rise the whole morning." He spent all the time searching for a grey wagtail's nest near the upper fall. Fishing takes him bird's-nesting, insect-watching, flower-gathering, into places where otherwise he would be a trespasser.

The jolly angler is now sadly rare. When fish require long hours for their capture there is no time for much good fellowship, as there was when a basket could be filled more quickly, as of yore.

The poacher is frequently a fisherman; he is both fearless and adventurous. For him fishing alone is too tame a sport; he must have more excitement; his one eye must be on the fish, the other on its guardian; one ear must be listening for a rise, the other for a twig broken under foot. Every sense must be on the look-out, every muscle ready, his whole body and mind must be fully occupied. Whilst others in his place would shake with fear he is full of delight.

The poetic angler is by no means rare. He is a lone man, drawn to the silent places by the water, and carries a rod that may linger there with good excuse.

Fishing has given rise to the fish-breeder, a born angler whose enthusiasm has carried him further than mere angling, into being the foster-father of many little fish; he cares for and nurtures them; he tends to their pastures, guards their breeding grounds. He regulates their numbers, mixes their blood, destroys the bad, conserves the good, protects them from enemies, and gives them friends. He, too, carries the rod, but seldom has the heart to slay.

Did you find yourself sharply in focus in one of those six mirrors? I did. I'm that last one, the fish-babier. But whichever one you are, that or one of the other five, we'll both find plenty to chew on in *Some New Arts and Mysteries.*

In any case, we both enjoy fish stories, so here's one, early on, to swallow while I scout on up ahead for something more substantial:

. . . Here is a true story from my log: Joey was a goodly fish of 2½ lb., somewhat black, 'tis true, but age will tell. He was named after a certain angler because of a cunning look common to both. Joey lived in a rather narrow deepish stream and fed on a small gravel patch just below a willow tree spreading over the water; when he was hooked, as not uncommonly he was, for he was a bold fellow, instead of running off under the willow tree, as would be expected, he always ran down and disappeared into a bed of rushes about five yards downstream; there he either freed himself from the hook or broke the gut. He was particular about gut. Anything thicker than 3X, even when offered with every civility and with the greatest delicacy, was never accepted. Now, we all loved Joey, and he never created any bad feeling or jealousy among us because he never allowed himself to be caught. Until the day of his death we loved him, and then we were sorry for him and loved him the more.

He was foully murdered. It had been noted several times that Joey, when hooked, always entered the reed bed by a particular gap in the reeds called Joey's Front Door. Mr. _____ said therefore to himself, "If I trap the front door Joey will be mine." So one day, whilst Joey was busy sucking down black gnats, a landing net was quietly fixed across his front door, and so arranged that the bag of the net projected inwards among the reed stems, the handle of the net stuck out of the water among the reeds. Mr. _____ then put on some 6X gut and a good black gnat; Joey paid no attention to the 6X gut and chanced the gnat, arguing, "If it is gut I can easily break that thin stuff at home." Mr. _____ then pulled the hook into Joey and at the same time made a dash at the landing net. Joey, on feeling the hook, bolted for home, and entering by the front door banged into the net, thus telling Mr. _____ that he had come in. Mr. _____ gently raised the net out of the water, with Joey in it, and walked ashore.

Joey had not broken anything, the connecting chain was intact.

Joey, fly, 6X point, gut cast, line, rod, reel, angler, there was through connection, and all was fair, or so at least it seemed to a brother angler who appeared on the scene at the moment. "Bravo," he said, "how did you manage it on that fine gut?"

Mr. _____: "I reeled in the line as fast as I could, got a pull on the fish before he turned to go to the rushes, held him outside, then pulled him downstream, and landed him twenty yards below by that willow herb."

Bro.: "How then, sir, do you account for all that mud by the reed bed?"

Mr. _____, hesitating: "Oh, that must have been a dab-chick, there was one about."

Bro.: "And I'm a dab-chick too, I suppose," and off he went.

Further cross-examination at the club-house resulted in the conviction of wilful murder of poor Joey by Mr. _____; afterwards the culprit made a full confession, and was granted a reprieve.

A rather similar story is told of X. and Y. X. and Y. had no fish, the day was far advanced, only a few pence were left of the ten-shilling tickets, the eve was cold and heartless. X. and Y. must each have a fish.

X.: "Now, there are two nice fellows up this little ditch; how are we to get them?"

Y.: "I know. You see the narrow place close to that rock? Well, go in above it and make the water muddy for about ten yards above it. Then place your landing-net on the bottom and facing upstream, and wait there while I go up and drive the beggars down . . . Look out, they're off."

Bang, bang, right and left, plumb into the net, a quick heave, and two fine fellows are kicking on the grass.

Enter the keeper. "Rather a fine brace you've got, sir."

Y. (hastily): "Yes, it was a most extraordinary thing. I had them both on at once [and so he had], and when my friend very cleverly got them both into the net [so he did] we found that neither of them were on the hook [neither were they]," which proves that there is nothing more valuable than half a truth.

Well, here's something. Ten years before J. W. Dunne's epochal *Sunshine and the Dry Fly,* which for the first time introduced the factor of transparency as virtually a Fourth Dimension of dry-fly tying, here's Mottram on dry flies of the future:

It is not surprising that the present-day dry flies are delicate works of art, and in many respects excellent imitations of Nature, seeing that they are the result of the work of many hands and brains for many years. Nevertheless, practically all anglers who have compared artificial with natural flies agree that there is still much room for improvement. Fly-tiers, too, are rightly not satisfied with their results, and are aware that finality has by no means been reached, and that fly-tying is still enjoying its youth. He who has closely looked at dun or spinner will be for ever convinced that man can never make a complete copy of the insects, but must be content with only caricatures, so delicate in form and modelling, so subtle in colour, so varying in transparency are their parts.

As the rate of evolution of the dry fly seems at the present time, and for no apparent reason, to be somewhat slow, an attempt is here made to show along what lines hopes for better things may be realised. As a preliminary, it is necessary to examine very closely those qualities which characterise a fly, or for that matter any object, in order that note can be made of the more important.

COLOUR. The colour of an object is an evasive character, because it changes under different conditions of lighting and, further, the colour of animals is subject to considerable variation (this has often been observed in the Ephemeroptera). For these reasons no man of science, when describing an animal, lays much stress on this quality. Moreover, suppose a fly be tied that exactly matches in colour a natural insect, it will be found that when both are moved to another condition of lighting they will now not match, this because the materials composing the natural and the artificial, being different, react differently to a change of lighting.

Furthermore, the colour of an object is best seen when light is reflected from it and worst seen when lit from behind.

The illumination a fly has when seen by a fish is against the sky, when all opaque objects look black, even a snowflake. Colour, therefore, is not a quality the dry-fly tier need very seriously consider except under a few comparatively rare conditions, of which mention will be made later.

TRANSPARENCY. — This quality, that an object may possess, is not a common quality, and even when present is taken little note of, because its demonstration requires a special and unusual lighting. The object must be lit by a bright light from behind. People do not as a rule examine objects against a bright sky, yet this is how a fish must view a floating fly. It follows, therefore, that the fly-tier must by no means neglect this quality; he must examine the natural flies against the sky, take note of those parts which are opaque and those that are transparent, and further, of the transparent parts he must note the colour, for whilst traversing the fly's body the sun's white light becomes coloured. If, then, the fly-tier thinks colour of importance, here is a type of colour which is of far greater value than any that is reflected.

FORM. It may be said that objects are almost without exception recognised by their shape. This is by far their most distinctive character — insects by their having six legs, spiders by their having eight, ants by their long waists, wasps by their narrow ones. Suppose an ant, a wasp, a spider to be all of the same colour, yet by a single glance we should know them — by their shapes. Birds fly across the setting sun; they all look black, but we can easily recognise them — a heron, a duck, a plover, a gull, a pigeon — even when planing on poised wings. The form of an object includes its size, the amount of space it occupies; by it we distinguish between a wood ant and a red ant. But size is of much less importance than the relative size of the parts, the creature's silhouette against its surroundings, and its internal drawing. We recognise a sedge fly neither by its colour nor by its size, but by the length of its wings compared to the rest of its body, its general outline, and the modelling of its surface. It is unnecessary to give further proof that form is a quality of vast importance. Nearly all objects can be recognised by their silhouette; those of our grandfathers had much to recommend them. The silhouette of an object is best seen when it is viewed against a bright light. Now, as before noted, it is in this way that fish see floating flies, so it follows that the dry-fly dresser who is striving to imitate form must pay most attention to the insect's silhouette, its outline against the sky.

WEIGHT. Flies built for aerial life are light, and so must the angler's flies be light and buoyant. So highly characteristic is this quality of flies that to copy it must be one of the fly-tier's first aims.

MOVEMENT. — Because the majority of flies when on the water keep quite still, it is only in exceptional cases that this quality need be considered.

Having thus briefly examined these qualities, and gained the conviction that it is impossible to combine them all in one complete imitation, it now becomes necessary to compare them in order to decide to which most attention must be paid.

I think I have shown that colour, except the colour of the transparent parts, need not be faithfully copied. By this I mean that other more important qualities must not be sacrificed whilst striving to reproduce correct colour. Transparency and form must be considered side by side; I have endeavoured to prove that the fly's silhouette is by far the most important character to be imitated, and in reality the silhouette is the outline of the non-transparent parts. If, while this is being copied, the shape, size, and colour of the transparent or relatively transparent parts can at the same time be indicated, so much the better; but care must be taken not to mask the outline of the far more important, because more apparent, opaque parts.

Lightness and buoyancy go hand in hand and are important. A dry fly must, above all things, float. Some difficulty is usually experienced when endeavours are made to keep the true form of fat-bodied flies and at the same time make them light and buoyant. I would place the qualities in this order of importance, the most important first: Form, buoyancy, lightness, transparency, transparent colour, reflected colour, and movement.

Passing from the theoretical to the practical, Mottram then gives several different tyings of one fly, each copying one or more, but never all, of those dominant qualities which, at one time or another, characterize the natural. One strives only for buoyancy, another for transparency, another — and this for most frequent use, in the absence of special conditions, puts special emphasis on silhouette ("silhouette flies of gnats, midges and smuts are particularly deadly") and still another stressing especially the element of color as seen in reflected light.

Here is the prescription for their use:

. . . I would use the colour fly early in the morning or late in the evening, casting it so that the fish would see it lit by the sun. I would use it for fish rising close to the bank, casting it close in shore so that the fish would see it against a dark background. For similar reasons, I would use it under overhanging trees. The transparent fly I would especially use on very bright days or against a sunset, knowing that then transparency is of much importance. The buoyant fly I would use where the water was covered with scum, as it is just above a mill, and where it is difficult to keep other patterns afloat. I would use it on very calm days, when it is important to drop the fly lightly. I would use it in very rough water because it is not easily swamped. The silhouette fly I would use at any time, knowing that the fish rarely see more than the floating flies' silhouettes.

In conclusion, I may say that fishing in this way adds an immense interest to the sport. A fish that has refused one type need not be despaired of; give him a rest, and then try another. If he has refused a silhouette, try him with a transparent one against the sun, or the colour fly lit by it, or drop the buoyant fly softly before his nose.

As for wet flies, Mottram says—and what heresy in 1914—"The wet-fly fisherman had better forget about the flies he tied to imitate flies." Let him instead copy the following "moderately comprehensive" list of creatures, duplicated more correctly by lures than flies as such: "Alloins, fry, little fish, shrimps, and possibly young crayfish, ephemeral nymphs, dragon fly larvae, stone fly larvae, water beetles, water boatmen, caddis nymphs, and dipterous larvae." For some of these, not previously attempted, he gives tyings, and refers to others, described elsewhere by himself or others, concluding:

Of this nature are the new wet flies; their use entails a new kind of fishing, an art the practice of which requires much skill, and wherein rules are logical, a science based on true observation rather than myth, a craft requiring diverse tools for various uses, a sport immensely interesting, and which all gentle anglers should honour.

One Mottram heresy is not shocking to us today, nor would it have been to Skues, even then, but must have seemed horrifying, in 1914, to every proper fisher south of London, and that is what he called "fishing on sight"—in other words, to the sight of a fish, rather than circumspectly waiting for its rise. He not only suggests it, he even includes the possibility of dapping ("that despised art"), and concludes with a confession that must have seemed tantamount to Bernard Shaw's use of the unspeakable word "bloody," spoken right out loud on the London stage, in *Mrs. Warren's Profession*, for the first time.

Looking back, I am not sure that I have not had more real enjoyment, more true sport, and more keen excitement when fishing on sight than when angling for the shyest and most timid of rising fish.

At such a passage I still can't help harboring the stubborn suspicion that, despite all the respectable character witnesses I cited earlier on his behalf, an admission like that—not merely of doing the undoable, but thinking the unthinkable and saying the unsayable, that it was quite

frankly fun at the time—might alone have been enough to get him drummed out of the corps.

But it is in the chapter "A Defect in Modern Dry-Fly Tackle" that Mottram seems to me to make his longest leap forward, and ahead of his time. The studies and tests represented by the diagrams, for example, are virtually identical with those that E. R. Hewitt worked out on his own some seven years later, in *Secrets of the Salmon*. And although Mottram's primary aim in these tests was to show the need for a stronger check on the reel, he reached the conclusion, later shared by Hewitt, but never really exploited until many decades later, that a short rod has considerable advantage over a longer one:

The modern dry-fly rod is such a very perfect piece of mechanism that it is almost a sacrilege to use with it any imperfect tackle; and yet it seems to me that offence is being daily committed. For this reason an attempt is here made to show that the reel has not followed the progress of the rod, but has rather, in some respects, retrogressed. In this attempt it is necessary to consider first, along certain lines, the mechanics of a single-handed rod.

A single-handed rod is one which can be comfortably manipulated by one hand. Thus used, the power that can be applied to it is the turning power of the wrist, which I have found to be about equivalent to a force of six pounds acting at a distance of one foot. It will, of course, vary somewhat with the individual. The result of the application of this power will not always be the same, but depend on how it is applied. First, proof will be given that, when playing a fish, less strain can be put on a fishing line when the rod is held vertically, than when it is held at an angle to the horizon. In order to simplify this proof, the rod will, in the first place, be assumed to be perfectly rigid.

Referring to Fig. 1, AB is a rigid rod 6 ft. long; at the end A is depicted the power of the wrist, 6 lb. acting at 1 ft., this power will produce a strain on the line L of 1 lb. at B, when the rod is held vertically.

Now consider the arrangement of forces when the rod is held at an angle of 45 degrees to the horizon AC. The wrist power will produce, as before, a force of 1 lb. CD; but the equalising strain or tension CF on the line is not acting at right angles to the rod, but at an angle of 45 degrees, so that only a portion of CF, CE, will be available for counteracting the force CD. The rest of this force CF, CH will act along the rod and will be counteracted by the angler pulling the rods towards him with the force CN equal to CH. Thus it follows that under these conditions the tension on the line must be greater than when the rod is held vertically, namely, 1.5 lb. as against 1 lb.

Similarly it can be shown that when the rod is held at an angle of 67.5 degrees to the horizon, the tension on the line will be 1.15 lb.; and when at an angle of 22.5 degrees, 2.8 lb.; in the latter case the angler will have to pull the rod towards him with a force of 2.5 lb.

Having come to this conclusion with regard to a rigid rod, it is easy to see that the same laws hold good for a pliant one. Referring to Fig. 2 AB is the 6 ft. rod held vertically, when the wrist power (6 lb. at 1 ft.) is applied at A, instead of producing, as before, a tension of 1 lb. on the line L at B, it now bends the rod into a curve AC; thus the length of the rod, considered as a lever, is shortened, instead of being 6 ft. long it is now reduced to AD, 5¼ ft. long. With this shortened rod the wrist power produces a strain of 1.14 lb. on the line.

Now consider the play of the forces when this pliant rod is held at 45 degrees AE. In this case the effective length of the rod is reduced to AF, 4 ft. long. The wrist power will produce on this 4 ft. rod a force FH of 1.5 lb.; this force will be balanced by a tension on the line FK of 2 lb.; also, as shown in the figure, when the rod is held at 67.5 degrees a strain of 1.35 lb. is placed on the line, and when at 22.5 degrees a strain of 5.8 lb. Therefore, the nearer to the horizontal a single-handed rod is held, the more strain can one put on the line. In fact, if an angler were to hook an immensely powerful fish on very strong tackle, his rod would be gradually pulled down to the horizontal, and then, if he still refused to give line, he himself would be pulled into the water.

The two following conclusions will next be arrived at:

(1) A short rod is more powerful than a long one.
(2) A whippy rod is more powerful than a stiff one.

In Fig. 3 are shown two rigid rods, AB 6 ft. long and AC 8 ft. long; to both at A is applied the wrist power; in the case of AB this will result in a force of 1 lb. at B, but in the case of AC of only .75 lb. at C, because AC is a longer lever than AB.

Now suppose they are both equally pliant, that is, that the wrist power will reduce their length in the same proportion, say by 10 per cent. or by 20 per cent. Referring to the figures, we see that when the long rod is reduced in length by 10 per cent, .8 lb., can be put on the line; when the short rod is reduced by 10 per cent., 1.1 lb. Similarly, a reduction of 20 per cent. results in a strain of .9 lb. in the case of the long rod and 1.25 lb. in that of the short. Now compare rods of the same length, but of different pliability. With the more whippy a greater strain can be put on the line, as is illustrated in Fig. 3; with AF, the more pliant 8 ft. rod, a strain of 1.25 lb. can be put on the line, whereas with the less pliant 6 ft. rod AE only a strain of 1.1 lb.

From these several conclusions some practical deductions can now be made:

1. A short rod has an advantage over a long one in that with it a greater strain can be placed on the line.

2. In the same respect a whippy one is better than a stiff one. Of course, the disadvantages of the long and stiff rods can be overcome by holding them at a smaller angle to the horizon than the short and whippy ones, but this in itself is detrimental, as will appear later.

3. In order to obtain the full power of a single-handed rod when playing a fish, it should be held not vertically, but at an angle to the horizon. At what angle? If at a small angle, say under 45 degrees, then the natural elasticity of the rod, by which the tackle is protected from sudden great strain, is thrown out of play; on the other hand, as has been shown, the smaller the angle the greater the power obtained. Probably the best angle lies between 50 degrees and 60 degrees, then enough of the rod's elasticity remains to protect the tackle.

Let examination now be made of the dry-fly fisherman's tackle in the light of these deductions. Take any rod, reel, and line as they are found at the water-side, hold the rod at an angle of 55 degrees to the horizon, and then determine what force is required to pull line off the reel. It will be found to be no more than a few ounces. This means that the pulling power of the rod is not being utilised owing to a defective reel. Instead of a few ounces, the force required should be such that the tackle can quite safely stand, which may be anything from 1/2 lb. to 3/4 lb. upwards.

First, let us consider a tackle which can stand a maximum of 4 lb. to 5 lb., such a tackle as would be used for large brown trout, sea trout, or for Mayfly fishing. At no time will the angler wish to put this full strain on his tackle, but when the fish is running he will want to put on a strain of at least 1 lb. By exerting all his strength he may be able to do this with an 8 ft. rod held vertically, but he would most certainly unduly strain his rod; he can, however, easily put on this strain if he hold the rod at 33 degrees to the horizon, but, as has been found, the check on the reel will give long before such a strain on the line is reached.

What is required is a reel with a much more powerful adjustable check than any at present on the market. Many reels by slight structural alterations can be made to fulfil these requirements: with such a one the angler should adjust his tackle in this way: First place the reel-drag full on; next, holding the rod at 55 degrees, exert a strain of 1 lb. on the line; then gradually reduce the drag until the line begins to unwind freely. A reel so adjusted, full of line, will be much more strongly checked when nearly empty; it is well, therefore, to make the adjustment on an empty reel. Thus I am of opinion that at present anglers are using the modern dry-fly rod with an unsuitable reel. The old rod did not require this powerfully checked reel for several reasons; it was whippy and had small flying rings, both of which gave rise to a large amount of friction (the snake rings and the stiffness of the modern rod counteract this). Further, the old reel's hub was a pencil of metal from which the last of the line could only be unwound with difficulty (most modern reels have a large barrel).

Another collateral benefit of that demonstration is that it affords a rationale for the ancient practice of pointing the rod at a jumping fish. This approach to the horizontal, instinctively indulged in to avoid giving the jumping fish something solid to pull against, can now also be seen to be giving the low angle at which the rod can absorb the maximum strain exerted by the thrashing contortions of a fish in the air, which so often produce sudden quick jerks on the line.

But Mottram is full of unsuspected insights, all along the way, as in this instance where he is discussing leaders (called of course "casts" in British angling terminology), and although he is talking of gut, decades before the introduction of our synthetics, still the basic truth of some of the things he says has survived and triumphed over many faddish attempts to prove otherwise in the intervening years.

For instance:

The fly-fisherman's success, although he is often unaware of it, depends to a large extent upon his gut cast. Nevertheless, he goes to his tackle merchant, buys the routine three-yard tapered cast, and thinks no more about this part of his equipment. Then he goes a-fishing. If he is successful, all must be well; if unsuccessful, reasons can be readily found—the fish were not feeding, there was a dearth of fly, he had not the right fly, the sun was too bright, the wind too furious, the day too cold, or the fates were otherwise unkind. Seldom, if ever, does he ascribe the fault to his gut cast. Three yards of carefully tested and selected tapered gut, this at least cannot be wrong. Besides, was it not stained a delicate blue? Have not the authorities recommended such a cast? And did not his trusted tackle merchant guarantee its great resisting power to fracture, and describe it as an "all-round cast" and name it adamantine?

A ready-made cast is like a ready-made suit, suitable only for fine weather. Just as a shower of rain or a few days' sun will ruin the suit, so a strong wind or a glassy water may make the cast useless. According to the fishing, so must be the cast. An "all-round" cast is like an "all-round rod," bad all round. Even the colours that gut should be stained cannot be standardised; moreover, it is an open question as to whether gut should be stained at all. Its invisibility depends to a large extent on its transparency, which even the faintest stain must destroy to some extent.

Would that I, for one, had read that and believed it, before wasting countless hours staining spools of nylon, and myself and the kitchen sink, with a dozen different kinds of dyes, culminating in the purple Tintex that Preston Jennings so insistently advocated. I was a long time coming to the realization that when fish wanted my fly they would take it, and when they didn't they wouldn't, no matter what I had done to the leader.

The only other thing of Mottram's that I remember, and would like to look at before we leave him, is the last chapter of his last book, written just before his death, *Thoughts on Angling*. It's called "My Gaff," and it seems a most suitable leave-taking from a formidable fisherman, in many ways the most extraordinary I ever encountered in print:

I do not write about the gaff, but of some notches upon it, made during a lifetime whenever I was lucky enough to catch fish of unusually large size. All the fish were taken by fly-fishing, and they are here recorded to show what a keen fly fisherman was likely to take during about forty years, 1905–1945.

During the previous generation the fly fisherman probably had opportunities a little more favourable, although transport was not quite so easy nor rapid; in the coming generation air transport will give the wealthy fly fisherman command of the best fishing over great distances, his hunting-ground will be greatly expanded and his prospects greatly increased. One foresees long week-ends in Finland after the great grayling there, or in Sweden after huge sea trout.

The first notch in the gaff records a trout. There are no notches for grayling because one larger than 2½ lb. was never caught, and I had set myself 3 lb. as the lowest limit worthy of record. Many years ago, on the Kennet at grannon time, I caught a great grayling which must have weighed close upon 4 lb.; it was from a Society's water and, according to their rules, out of season—I put it back regretfully. I hooked and played one above 3 lb. in August, at the bottom end of the marsh at Hungerford. There was a fall of red ants; hurriedly I tied one by the waterside, and with it rose and hooked the monster. I played it fearfully and very lightly; this was a mistake, because grayling when not quickly landed are liable to gain a second wind and rush wildly about, even jumping out of the water. This one did and so broke away.

The first notch is at 19 inches, for a trout of 5 lb. 2 oz. I have caught four trout over 5 lb. on the Kennet, but this one was not on May-fly but an olive nymph on 4X gut. I had been fishing the Lambourne during the morning and was walking down the canal after tea to fish the Kennet at Thatcham when I saw a great trout swimming slowly up the canal near the surface. I hurriedly released the nymph and switched out some line and, bending down as the fish came opposite me, I cast out the nymph and drew it across its nose. The trout turned and followed it, slowly opened its great mouth and swallowed it; I waited until the fish had turned back before tightening. The fish was not very perturbed, allowing me to walk quickly beside it, guiding the cast now on one side, now on the other of the many weed beds which were passed. The fish was not scared by my presence on the bank, probably because it was used to pedestrians. Presently the fish turned around and we walked down a long way, then we again walked up, arriving close to where it was hooked. By this time signs of fatigue were apparent, so choosing a place clear of weeds, I held the fish firmly, played it out and landed it. I did not really enjoy playing that fish, all the time fearing the 4X gut.

The next notch is at 20 inches, for a Kennet trout of 6 lb. 1/16 oz., on a May-fly, the taking of which has already been described.

The third notch, at 21½ inches, represents a trout of 6¼ lb. caught from Butcombe Bay, on Blagdon, on a No. I Wickham fished dry on a calm evening, when many trout were rising. This fish made one long sustained run, straight down into the abysmal depths of the reservoir; in spite of hard braking he went on and on until 30 yards of line and 70 to 80 yards of backing were out. I began to be very fearful that he would take my all, but at long last he slowed up and stopped; then I was allowed to reel him in with hardly a struggle, though a long job. After he was on a short line he made a few circles round me, then came quietly into the net: a curious battle. The fish was the record Blagdon trout for that year.

Beyond this notch and before coming to those for sea trout, there could have been notches for large brown and rainbow trout in New Zealand, but I was there at the peak of big fish, when trout in their teens were of no particular account.

The next notch, at 30 inches, represents a 12¾-lb. sea trout taken from the River Dovey; it was caught on the last day of a holiday. I was fishing for salmon and thought it was one, but after reaching home I took some scales and was astounded, on looking down the microscope, to see that it was a sea trout about nine years old, which had spawned five times. It was the second fly-caught sea trout for the British Isles of the year.

A second sea trout notch is at 31 inches, the weight 14 lb. An account of the great battle this Norwegian fish fought is given elsewhere.

The salmon notches begin with a little fish of 32 lb., at 42½ inches; it was my first 30 pounder, and for the River Stordal a big fish.

The next was at 43 inches, weighing 35 lb. I recorded her because, in killing her, she nearly killed me; she died on the River Eira. The upper beat of this short river between River Eira and the sea, when the snow first melts, is a terrifying sight of tumbling, spouting, roaring white water. Until the water falls not many fish reach the upper beat. The going is too bad for ascending fish; he would be in for a very rough time. After fishing two days blank, this fish was hooked on a large fly on very thick gut, in a small flat close inshore. I tried to hold him there, but steadily lost ground, and, when it became obvious that he must go down, I yelled for the boat. A little distance below was a wooden trestle bridge with trestles only about 10 yards apart. The boat had to shoot these and care taken to choose the arch which the fish would be most likely to use; it seemed doubtful which of two the fish would make for, so I gave a tremendous heave to pull him over to the arch more favourable to us. Then I had to let everything go whilst I kept the point of the rod down to avoid the bridge. We shot through, boiling water tossing the boat about alarmingly. The gillie quickly put out the oars, which had been shipped, and I lifted the rod, finding the fish still with us below the bridge. We edged shoreward and about 200 yards down went ashore, where there was a little slack water; there I had to hold the fish with the rod pointing almost directly at him, but step by step I lost ground, and when the fish sidled off into white water I had again hurriedly to enter the boat which the gillie had kept handy. Over a distance of three miles we did this six times, only occasionally could I walk the fish a few yards up-stream, quickly to lose this advantage as soon as ever the fish willed it. During the passage down-stream we had to pass through some dreadful places of rocks and spouting waters, where, in cold blood, I would have been paralysed with fear. We now came to the site of an old fish-trap, where a number of piles and stakes pro-truded from the angry water; among these was only one small gap where the trap itself was located, the piles were the remains of a pallisade directing the fish into the trap. The gillie told me to reel in the salmon close to the boat, for by this time the fish was very tired and little more than a dead weight in the water. Shooting this gap was a clever feat of water-lore and boatmanship; there was no room for error, or rather the speed gave no time for any error to be corrected. It was a place where some years previously there had been a total wreck; happily I did not know this at the time. Having shot the gap, we entered an enormous whirlpool lying behind the piles which had diverted most of the river to the far side. Here I went ashore and for the first time gained control over the fish, which was carried round and round the whirl of water; whenever it passed near the main current I pulled hard to keep it out of this, and when-ever it came near the shore I pulled hard to try to bring it to gaff. After three or four times round the pool it came to the top. The first sight of the fish was a disappointment: I had hoped for a 50-pounder—a by no means uncommon size for the Eira, but it was not in this class. The next time round brought the fish just within reach of a long gaff and the fight ended.

After a long rest I went to look at the fish; the gillie had carried her far inland. She was a brilliant block of silver, gracefully streamlined, but with a huge wound in the side of her face so large that I could put my hand through it. The gillie told me that nearly all the big fish hooked when the river was at its full height were lost through the hook tearing out—sometimes a piece of flesh is found impaled on the fly; he also said that he had taken out anglers too timid to pull hard, with the result that they were carried down another four miles to the sea.

The next notch is at 48 inches, for a 42-lb. fish. Apart from knowing that this was my first 40-pounder, I can remember nothing about it; evidently it was an uneventful capture.

The last notch records my largest salmon, 45 lb., at 56 inches. It was on Sand River. The gillie and I had finished lunch, so I asked him to make a fire and brew some coffee whilst I walked down to a small pool beyond a little pine wood. I fished it down with a 3/4-inch Thunder, killed a 15-pounder half-way down and had made the very last cast at the bottom when bang! she went. The fish went right across to the far side and kept there, 80 yards away, for a long time coursing up and down. All I could do was to hold the rod above my head to prevent drowned line. After working up a long way, she started across and I was able to pull her over to my side; then she backed down and looked like going into a backwater below, full of water-logged trees, so I had to keep walking her up. She refrained from gymnastics, but seemed stubborn and heavy; at last I had a sight of her and was astounded at her great size. It seemed possible that she was a 50-pounder, and I had no gaff and the edge sloped too quickly for breaching, the gillie was beyond call—he had fallen asleep. She had to be tailed. Dozens of times I drew her nose to the edge and, sneaking up behind, tried to grab her tail: she was out in the river again. At last stepping into the water, I was able to grab her tail with my right hand. Of course she struggled, and I felt I could not hold her with one hand, so I threw the rod on the shore and grabbed with both hands. She then gave a violent flop which knocked me off my feet and, having no hands, I went full length into the water. The salmon and I drifted down in a sort of rough-and-tumble fight, the salmon struggling to be free, I to regain my feet; thus we drifted down about twenty yards, getting into water up to my middle, but at last I regained my feet and carried my fish a long way inland: connection with the rod had long since been severed. When I waked the gillie and told him of the two fish without a gaff, one a 50-pounder, he would not believe me. He was right; it was 5 pounds short of every angler's wish.

14.
Hewitt
and the Nymphs

About the best thing you and I could wish each other would be to live as long, and enjoy fishing as much, and keep as fit for it, as E. R. Hewitt.

He had passed eighty-eight when I first knew him, as a member for only a couple of seasons of the Big Bend Club, which leased his water on the Neversink. But I'll never forget his slight silhouette, outlined against a twilight sky, as he peered up to put on one of his size sixteen nymphs, without glasses, and did it in one deft quick motion. Those little nymphs of his had the most diabolically small eyeholes—about half the size of the eye on Paul Young's size twenty midges—and I used to have a hell of a time threading them onto 5X or 6X tippets, even with glasses, and I was just a bit more than half his age at the time.

A small man, and of the wiry, jumpy, nervous type, he was as over-endowed with ego as so many little men seem to be. But he had the clear eye and the smooth skin, even as he was rounding ninety, that you always find surprising even in an apple-cheeked schoolboy, and hence seemed almost beyond belief in a man entering his tenth decade.

He wasn't as much fun to talk to as he might have been, because he tended to run on, to a degree verging on boredom (though you could kick yourself for entertaining such a thought in his presence) with the result that you never got quick answers to any of the dozens of questions you were dying to ask, but rather a long lecture on the topic that enthralled his fancy at the moment. You might hear more than you were panting to know about lecithin, for instance, which he crammed into every corner of his diet—I must be wrong, but I swear I got the impression he even ate it in ice cream—and as he went on you had to admonish yourself, as you would a restless child, to shut up and listen, reminding yourself of what a privilege it was to be talking face to face to one of the angling great—and that *you* would become a bore if you tried too pertinaciously to turn the talk back to angling.

But I wrote about Mr. Hewitt in both my other fishing books, so I'm the one that must stifle the tendency to go on and on. I suppose the tendency is natural enough, since of the twelve main pillars of my fisherman's Pantheon, he's one of the only two I could have known personally. But that can get in the way, too, since our present purpose is fishing in print, rather than with, or for, people.

I have all his books on my shelves—except one, which I must have just borrowed and returned after reading it, that he wrote about Ringwood, the Cooper-Hewitt ancestral estate, now largely a park—and the chief reason my collection is so complete is that Mills were always marvelous about keeping his titles in stock—even the little pamphlets about nymphs and stream improvement, etc.—long after all the normal and expected sources had dried up. They also stocked his silver nitrate-treated leaders, long after there could have been any still perceptible demand for them. I remember seeing them, down there on Park Place, well over a decade after his death, and I feel sure they still had some up to the day they closed their doors in the fall of '72.

But since it's like a retrospective exhibition of an artist's work, I think his last book, *A Trout and Salmon Fisherman for Seventy-five Years,* is the best place to start. With the help of that unique midwife of our angling literature Sparse Grey Hackle, Mr. Hewitt redigested both his 1922 volume, *Secrets of the Salmon* and his 1926 *Telling on the Trout,* and various other basic elements from his collateral writings, with much new material added during the rewriting.

The book's premise is beautifully expressed in its Preface:

The Ancients wrote of the three ages of man; I propose to write of the three ages of the fisherman.

When he wants to catch all the fish he can.

When he strives to catch the largest fish.

When he studies to catch the most difficult fish he can find, requiring the greatest skill and most refined tackle, caring more for the sport than the fish.

The first age is always true of the beginner, the second during the most vigorous part of life, while the third occurs in the more mature years. The pleasures derived at this later age may be even greater than during earlier life. Unfortunately few fish long enough to reach and enjoy this last age. I have known many of ripe years who have never passed the first two ages of the fisherman.

This book deals with the three ages of one fisherman and tells what he has learned in three-quarters of a century about the arts of angling for trout and salmon, the tackle, baits, the biology of these fish, their habits, their natural foods and habitat conditions.

Few have been granted so long a fishing life, with so many opportunities to find out so much about trout and salmon. I hope I may be able to hand this knowledge on to others so that they may continue on the pleasant path after I have been obliged to stop.

Starting to flip pages, just to see what the passages are that I dog-eared when I first read the book, my finger caught at random this lovely little fish story:

One day, along Popolopen Creek, a number of good-sized fish had been seen, and I anticipated there were likely to be more. This branch of the creek was a small stream where larger fish run up at times from the bigger water below. The part where I was fishing was about fifteen feet wide, wandering down through rocky pools. I came to one pool of fair size; it was gravelly, about two feet deep in the middle, with a swift run in the top, and a large boulder partly under water on one side. After fishing the tail of the pool, a good look at the deeper water in the middle disclosed a brook trout, about a pound in weight, perfectly motionless. Casting over it for some time in every way, I was unable to make it move, as it seemed petrified. Moving up closer and touching it with the tip of the rod did not make it move or pay any attention. This seemed quite out of the ordinary. I wondered what could be the matter, but fortunately guessed what must be happening.

The brook trout was evidently at home in this pool and did not want to leave it. It was badly frightened at something and watching it intently. I looked for a snake and could see none, and then it suddenly occurred to me that there must be a large brown trout which had lately come into the pool that the brook trout thought it owned, and that it was probably under the rock at the head of the pool, and may have been chasing the brook trout out of its favorite hiding place before I came. If so, it was possible that I might get it.

I put on a large fly and looked well at the leader to see that everything was in good shape, and cast several times near the large boulder. The fly was sucked under in the current and was fast to a good-sized fish, which refused to come out from under the rock. I stood still and kept up the strain; after a while it came out and ran around the pool and jumped. I finally landed it after it had gone under the boulder again, a fine brown trout nearly three pounds, with the large sharp teeth of the cannibal. This was a very large fish for this small stream. If the brook trout had not disclosed the secret by its peculiar action, I do not believe I should ever have taken this fish, as it might easily have broken my light tackle by surprise.

The brookie as a damsel in distress, saved from the fell clutch of a villainous big brown by the timely intervention of Hewitt's chivalrous rod — could he have forgotten this story, with its reference to the "large sharp teeth of the cannibal" when he assured me, one night in 1955, five years after the book came out, that he had never known a brown trout to be cannibalistic? Maybe he was pulling my leg, though when Charlie Kerlee and I both cited instances where we had surprised them in the act, he stubbornly maintained his position, once he had taken it, with such an ex cathedra attitude of "I have spoken" that we both thought it politic to change the subject.

But that little story leads right into a passage that is one of my long-ago thumb-indexed favorites:

If a fisherman is a good sportsman he can play a delightful game of solitaire with himself, of the most interesting kind. I have made a practice of doing this for years on the stream by keeping score of the number of fish seen rising, and the percentage of these which are raised to the fly and the number hooked. My temper ebbs and flows with the results. When the great day comes when 90% to 95% of the fish I see rising are raised and hooked, I feel like the golfer who has beaten the best previous score.

Years ago the point was passed where the number or weight of the fish taken counted much with me, as I generally return to the stream by far the larger number of fish taken. The skill of playing the game is the real interest and the real sport. If more fishermen would play the game for sport and return the fish to the stream, we would all have better fishing.

One evening at Henryville, lying in bed with the window open toward the porch, I listened to two brother anglers talking below. One remarked:

"That fellow Hewitt is a damned liar. I don't believe he puts the fish back as he says he does, because he rarely brings back many."

The other replied:

"I thought so for years until yesterday, when I went with him to the Brod-head and watched him put back twenty-six good trout before he put a single one in his basket. I have been thinking this over. Why should we kill all the fish we take on a fly? I am not going to do it in future."

Let us all play the game as a high-class sport, and not as a means of securing food. Most of us have enough to eat tomorrow, and the streams can never produce enough trout for the fishermen. You need not be alarmed about fish dying if they are returned to the water. If they do not bleed and are not bruised by the fingers deep into the flesh, they rarely die. Rubbing the slime off a fish does not do any harm, as is generally thought. I caught 760 trout one season for our hatchery with a fly, and only lost two from injury. A few fish for your own use, or for friends, is all right, but no angler ought to take home all he can catch when fishing is good.

It's so easy to poke fun at Mr. Hewitt, because he *was* dogmatic and opinionated and always inclined to make his every last and least pronouncement with what Ernest Schwiebert calls "the typical Hewitt posture of complete expertise in all facets of the subject." But within pages of some of his sweeping statements that seem redolent of arrant braggadocio he could let his guard down and tell on himself the way he liked to think he was telling on the trout. An instance is the passage about losing a big fish on the Test when he was fishing the Stockbridge water of the Houghton Club with Major Hills:

One evening the piece of water allotted to me was that at the mill just above Stockbridge. Here the river forms a large round pool, just below the mill dam, which is perhaps one hundred and fifty feet across. The water flows in several channels separated by water weeds. On the west side, from which the pool must be fished, there is a bank perhaps six feet above the water. The gillie who accompanied me for this evening told me, on the way there, that a very large trout had lately been seen in this mill pool but no one had been able to raise it as it seemed too wise, and always fed in the center lane among the weeds. When we approached the pool we looked carefully and there was the large trout rising regularly in its favorite place. It looked to me like a most difficult long cast to make, but one which was possible with some luck.

I inspected my leader carefully, and put on a sedge fly, which seemed the right thing for this time in the evening, on this water. I made several practice casts below the fish and then risked all to make the long cast into the center lane among the weeds. The fly alighted just right above the place where the fish had been rising, and floated down with some loose leader near the fly. As it passed over the place where the fish was, it disappeared, being sucked down quietly. I struck and was fast to the fish. Fortunately it did not go into the weeds, but made for the open water below. Evidently it was confident it could easily get rid of the fly.

I moved down the river bank below the fish so that I could tire it out from below. Luckily in all its efforts it never got fast to any weeds, so that I was finally able to work it over to the bank where we stood and swim it around so that the gillie could slip his long-handled net under it. I heaved a great sigh of relief when I saw it lifted from the water. When it was above it about four feet, it made a desperate struggle. It was too heavy and strong for the old net, which broke, letting the fish splash back into the water so that I still held it with the line passing through the hoop of the net. It was thoroughly frightened by this time, and made a straight dash for a weed bed, where it parted the leader in one rush. I must say I did not want to lose this big fish, as I hoped to have one large one to my credit in the Club book.

A year later when I again visited the Houghton Club I had a look at the Club record book and found the following entry dated a week later than my loss of the big fish: "Trout, five and one-half pounds, from Mill Pond. Disdained by Hewitt."

But maybe, on second thought, that tells at least as much about Major Hills as it does about Mr. Hewitt.

By the way, that passage followed by a page one in which Hewitt said, "It is quite probable that most brown trout feed largely on fish and bottom food after four years of age. This means in our country that the sixteen-inch fish are about the age when they cease to take the fly in the daytime, while the English fish may have two years, or perhaps three years, before they become cannibal feeders."

But perhaps a better sample of Mr. Hewitt's occasional ability and willingness to tell on himself is afforded by this charming vignette:

One would never have thought that a beautiful day on the Beauly would be fraught with such lasting consequences, yet so it was.

My friends had arranged for me to fish for a day for salmon with the priest of the village because he was universally regarded as the best and most enthusiastic fisherman in the neighborhood and they wanted me to have the advantage of his great skill in my day's sport. They little realized that his skill was equally great in quite another direction.

We arrived at the water about nine and at once began to try for elusive salmon. I was to show what I could do by the methods successfully developed in American waters and had every confidence that I could do the same in Scotland. But the Scotch salmon thought otherwise and came up and looked at my dry flies and, as an old Indian once said to me: "They say, 'Go to hell.'" In fact, I made a sorry exhibition of American fishing. It simply did not work, though I tried all the tricks learned in long years of fishing in our waters. I became more and more dejected and was placed in just the right frame of mind for the priest to get in his professional services. They are most successful with the downtrodden and hopeless.

At last luncheon time came and I crawled from the stream. The priest opened the basket and produced both food and wine. Even so, my spirits did not revive and I was in just the frame of mind to become desperate. That is, to ask for advice.

After a long silence the father asked: "My son, have you always been true to the art of angling?"

I knew only too well what he meant, but parried the question, which meant the searching of the heart for long memories of years of misdeeds. He came to the point and insisted on a direct answer to his question. Had I always fished honestly with proper sporting tackle and in a legal way, or had I broken the faith and poached, or fished in unseemly and wicked ways? My conscience smote me as thoughts of many misdeeds flooded over the memories of the past. It was almost more than I could bear, to think of all my evil ways. The kindly old man inspired confidence, as he had to generations of his parishioners, and the desire surged up to unburden my mind of all my piscatorial sin and receive absolution and direction for my future life. I fell on my knees and called out, "Father, I will confess all if only you will show me the true way to salvation."

"My son," he replied, "only by full and free confession can salvation be reached. You must lay all your sins bare and I may be able to point out the road. Tell me all."

"I used to fish with worms for years," I confessed, "and used all sorts of means to get my worms. They were dug with a spade."

"That is allowable and no more than any novice will do, and not a real crime against the law of sport."

"But, Father, I picked up nightwalkers at night in people's gardens, using a light."

"In old times, my son, this was not considered wrong."

"But, Father, I used an electric torch."

"This begins to look serious."

"Later I used mustard to bring them to the surface."

"Worse and worse."

"Latterly I have even used an electric current to make them come up."

"This is indeed a crime. The poor worms have no chance against modern science. Applications of science to worm catching have been excommunicated long since."

"Father, I have used a lead with a worm and raked the bottom for trout."

"This is against all laws of sport, and indeed is a crime."

"But, Father, there is another way of fishing for trout, using the belly fin and jerking it through the water. I practiced this for years and caused the death of endless trout; and I have both jigged and snared trout and salmon."

"My son, I must confess that I, myself, have hooked salmon foul on a fly, but never with more than one hook, and never with a lead. This partly condones my offense, for which I ask forgiveness, and hope that I may never be so tempted again, as I feel that my will may not be strong enough to resist in my old age. Even my bishop once tried to jig a salmon on the Shin—and I had to show him how to do it."

"But I have tickled trout and taken them without any tackle at all. I have even tickled and gotten them out after they have escaped from the hook."

"This, my son, is a real crime after one passes the age of ten years. Of course, we all have to pass through our apprenticeship."

"Father, I have refrained from using carbide or dynamite, but I have one serious crime of this nature to confess. I was led into it by a greater sinner. My own tutor showed me how he used to get trout in England. He brought out some Indian fish berries which he threw in the water of a still pool. These caused all the trout to swim to the surface and turn on their sides so that they were easily lifted out. I did this only once."

"My son, this is only one single offense, and can be overlooked. We all slip once in a while."

"Father, I never used nets or set lines to get trout, but I have one more crime to confess. I have speared at night, but only with an old-fashioned tin spear light with candles and never with a flashlight."

"That makes a great difference if you did not use any of the modern contraptions and used only the time-honored methods. I hope, my son, you will do this no more. Are these all the crimes in your calendar?"

"No, not all. I have let the water from a pond and then closed the gate and picked up the trout below in the low water. The only extenuating circumstance is that they were not killed but used for stocking."

"My son, this is allowable, and any other thing is allowable which is used to increase the fish in the stream. Now, if this is all, I will give you the law of sport and my blessing if you will swear not to transgress again. Always fish in the legal season and fish with a fly and not with coarse lures and bait, for this is not sport, but murder. Do all you can to increase the fish in the streams and make good sport for others, and never take more than a few fish for your day's sport. Always be kind and courteous to other fishermen. If you do these things your fishing sins will be forgiven. Place your hands on this book, which is my fishing Bible, and swear that you will henceforward be true to the laws of sport."

I did as directed, and felt my burden of angling sin lifted. With a kindly smile and a genial twinkle in his eye he opened the book at the title page. It was my own:
Secrets of the Salmon.

I love Mr. Hewitt's story of how he invented the Neversink Skater:

A few years ago I developed a new way of dry fly fishing in order to be able to catch large brown trout which I had seen rising at times in large, still pools after white or yellow butterflies, when they would pay no attention to any ordinary fly. When this new fly fishing method was worked out I wrote it up for *The Sportsman* magazine and it was published in August, 1937. I will give the substance of this article here, as I am sure it will interest many trout fishermen.

Many anglers have seen large trout leap for small white or yellow butterflies and have been unable to interest these trout in any fly they could present to them. It became evident to me that large winged flies in some way did not appear like butterflies to the trout, and they therefore ignored them. I studied this problem carefully and came to the following conclusions. The butterflies did not rest on the water; they sometimes touched it but were always moving. When they did touch the water they only did so very lightly and were away again. I could not imitate this procedure with any flies I had in my box. How was I to do this? I went back to my camp and tied several flies, finally making what is known now as the Neversink Skater. This was tied on a No. 16 light Model Perfect hook, which is the lightest hook I know that will hold a big trout. The big fly was tied as a hackle and not a winged fly because large winged flies do not cast well on the fine leaders which it is necessary to use in large, still pools. The fly had no tail, because this would interfere with its movement over the surface of the water. It was tied sparsely because I wanted it to cast easily and not have too much air resistance. It was made as large in diameter as possible, with the longest hackles I had. The outside diameter of some of these

flies was two inches while some were slightly smaller. Even then, they were really not as large as the butterflies the fish were taking.

When I had completed some flies which I thought worth trying, I went down to the river to a pool where I knew there were a number of large trout. I wanted to make a fly which would take them at any time of day because I had seen them jump for butterflies at all times, and I knew they would take the right fly if I could make one. My first attempts were made right in the middle of a sunny day in July. I found it most difficult to cast these large flies until I used enough line to supply sufficient energy in the cast to propel the fly forward when the line was checked in the air. As soon as I got out about forty feet of line the fly cast easily and well, and could be made to alight on the water like a feather and be jumped and dragged over the surface without getting wet or going under. It ought, therefore, to make an impression on the fish similar to a butterfly.

When I had perfected my casting so that I thought I could manage the fly reasonably well, I tried the pool in which the large fish were concealed under a ripple of current among larger stones, where the water was perhaps thirty inches deep. When the fly had made only two jumps over the water, a large trout of about four pounds leaped out of water right over the fly like a porpoise and missed it entirely, and before it had time to come again a smaller trout repeated the maneuver. Neither fish touched the fly at all. I had enough sense to rest these fish and move lower down where there should be other fish. This time another big trout jumped for the fly, and I just touched it without hooking it. This showed they were not playing but wanted the fly. If the fly were fished well, it was evident they could be caught.

I wanted someone else to see this sport, so I left my rod and returned to my camp to get my son, who was taking a midday nap. The fly was then cast in the same place as at first, but drawn more slowly to give the fish more time. This time, when the trout rose, it took the fly solidly and was landed after the usual playing. Then my son claimed a try, as he was sure he could do this stunt. He also jumped two fish before he landed one. We kept on in this same run for an hour, to see if this method of surface fishing would put these trout down, or whether they would fail to be scared by this kind of fishing. The latter proved to be the case, and only bungled casts scared the fish. We caught six large trout in this run, right in the middle of the day, and hooked one more. Next day these same fish rose again as if nothing had happened. This would certainly not be the case with any other method of trout fishing I know. After fishing out this run we tried under my dams and found that the big trout would come out from under them and even take these flies in the white water. We also found that this type of fishing is effective in big, still pools, although it is much harder here to make the fly move properly on the surface than where there is a slight current. I had developed a way of dry fly fishing which would raise and hook large trout in all kinds of water at almost any time of day. This seemed to me to be a real advance in fly fishing.

One will ask, why not use this way of fishing all the time? The answer to this question is simple. Only the larger trout are effectively caught by this method, and in most streams there are so few large trout that one might fish long distances without raising or seeing a fish. Besides, casting a long line with upraised rod and jumping the fly is very tiring to the arm and one cannot do it for long together. Also, this method requires at all times a fairly long cast and many places in a stream are only suitable for short casting. I only use this type of fishing where the water is right and where I have good reason to think there are larger trout. Ten- or twelve-inch trout will jump at this fly, but it is so large that it is difficult to hook them. Another reason for not using this method of fishing continually is that these Skater flies become damp after a time, and when this occurs they will not stay on top of the water and move properly, and have to be carefully dried and set right or a new fly put on. They certainly are not a durable fly.

I use these Skater flies of several colors and find that one kind is better at one time and place, and at another time a different pattern is better. I carry them tied as a Bivisible, brown with white wisp at the head, white, cream-colored, and badger, gray with black center, and all brown. I think I prefer the cream color and the Bivisible to the others.

I find that few fishermen can cast well enough to fish this fly properly although I have taught a number of people to do it, and some of my friends swear by this fly and believe it is the best ever made. It certainly will raise more large fish than any other dry fly. You won't find it on sale in any tackle stores, as few suitable feathers are available.

Even in Europe this Skater fishing can be most effective, as the following story will prove.

I rented a moor in Scotland at Pitlochry, in Perthshire, for several years. As we only shot three days a week on the moor, I wanted to get some salmon fishing to fill in the spare time. Hearing that the Duke of Athol had a river where there were many salmon, I inquired of his agent and rented it for the season. I ought to have been suspicious, as the price was very low, but I was green about Scotch rentals and felt sure I could catch salmon in any river where they were. I went over to the Tilt and fished hard without raising a single salmon. After a week or so of this I became discouraged, although I saw numbers of salmon in many of the pools. Finally, in talking with the garage man in the village, I learned that salmon had never been taken in the Tilt on a fly in summer. A few had been caught on worms or minnows or spoons, but never on a fly. I do not care for this so I abandoned the salmon fishing as a bad job.

One afternoon I happened to meet the Duke of Athol at a tea, and he asked me how I was making out with the salmon on the Tilt. I told him the fishing was impossible with a fly. Evidently his conscience smote him for letting a stranger in for fishing which was hopeless, for he offered to let me fish his own private loch, which was reported to be the finest trout fishing in Scotland, and he said he would send me the key to the road gate. Next day the great key arrived, about six inches long and weighing a pound. At that time I had an English friend stopping with me for the shooting, so we drove the car down to Loch Ordie the next day, arriving there about noon. The gillie in charge of the boat was enthusiastic about the numbers of large trout there were in the loch, but said that there was no chance of raising any until evening and perhaps not then, at this season.

I thought we had better give the loch a try, as we were there, so we put up our rods and rowed out. My friend put on the regular Scotch loch flies they all use, three at a time on the leader. I thought that the gillie probably knew his business and that such fishing would be hopeless, so I put on one of my Neversink Skaters of a cream color. The gillie looked at it and remarked. "Ye will catch no fush with yon feather duster." I told him my friend was getting nothing with his Scotch flies and I would be as well off as he was.

I had only been casting the Skater a few minutes when there was an explosion under the fly and a great trout leaped high in the air with the fly in its mouth. It was easy to hook it and it was soon in the boat, a four-and-a-half-pound fish. The gillie remarked sullenly, "That war an accident." I soon began casting again with a new fly, as this fish had bedraggled the first one badly. In a little while the same thing happened again. These large fish were coming up so fast from deep water that they could not stop at the surface, but went high in the air when they reached the fly. After the second fish my friend wanted to know if I had any more "feather dusters." I gave him one, but, not being used to this type of fishing, he only got one rise, which he missed. My good fishing continued, and I caught large trout every little while until we had taken a dozen of from four to five and a half pounds. I thought the Duke owed me something to make up for the salmon fishing. I went home satisfied that the Neversink Skater was as good in Scotland as it was here.

Next day I returned the key to the Duke with thanks, and enclosed several of my flies in the note, telling him what I had done to his loch. He immediately began to fish the loch with my flies, and he did raise a few fish, but failed to hook any of them. He thought that this failure was due to the small hooks so he sent one of my flies to Hardy and had some tied with treble hooks at the head of the fly to hook the fish. Of course this made the fly heavy and he raised no trout. He never did get any of his big trout from his loch with my flies. The story of what the crank American had done to the Duke was the joke of all the gillies in the countryside.

Even on the Test these flies work. I got fish there with them against the protest of old Lunn, the keeper of the water. He was most astonished at seeing trout caught in this way.

Several years ago I taught a California man to use these flies and he reported to me that they worked well on the Snake River in Idaho, and that he also had raised steelhead with them on the Rogue in Oregon. I am quite sure they are effective anywhere trout come to the surface for butterflies or large flies of any kind. One of my friends took eighty landlocked salmon from the Grand Lake Stream in Maine with these flies, when no others were being caught at all by other fishermen.

My old Cahill Bivisible Spider, the most versatile fly I ever found for stream fishing, was a near twin of Mr. Hewitt's Bivisible Neversink Skater. I used to get them from Mills three and four dozen at a time, and once used nothing else for an entire season. So far be it from me to pooh-pooh Mr. Hewitt's entirely justifiable pride in his creation of this "new way of dry fly fishing." But, really, doesn't he make it sound just a little more important than man's discovery of the means of making fire, or the invention of the wheel?

Well, that's the way Mr. Hewitt was. Not content to let it go that the Neversink Skater was a pretty damn good fly, which nobody will deny—oh no, he has to make claims for it that would earn it canonization as one of the miracle-workers of all time.

I also took scores of trout on the Upper Beaverkill on Mr. Hewitt's nymph. But back in the early thirties when he was first telling the world about the wonders of nymph fishing he expressed the fear that his nymphs might empty the streams where they were used. Some of the streams where his nymphs were first used are indeed empty of trout today, but from other causes than the use of his nymphs.

Still, in spite of all the bombast, some of his statements which seemed so preposterous when he first advanced them, now seem with the passage of time to be merely sensible. This was heresy when he first propounded it, in the days of the over-worshipful awe with which the use of the dry fly was regarded:

The really expert fly fisherman desires to take his quarry by fooling him with the imitation he offers and is not satisfied if he gets his trout in any other way.

This is perhaps the reason why real sportsmen look down on methods of fishing which are at variance with their ideas of the proper way trout fishing should be done. If this is so, then nymph fly fishing ought to have a very high place in the estimation of the true sportsman.

I often hear it remarked that nymph fly fishing is like worm fishing and requires no skill. Such remarks only show the entire ignorance of the speaker of the whole art of underwater angling. A nymph fly dangled still in the water would have no more attraction to a trout than a small stick. No trout would take it. It is only when the fly looks like the insect and also behaves like it in the water that it becomes really attractive to fish. The purist, if there is such a person, can be a purist in nymph fly fishing just as well as with a dry fly.

The knowledge required to fish nymphs properly is far greater than that needed for any other kind of trout fishing and can only be acquired after long practice. Any one who can cast at all can easily place a dry fly on the water and let it float and take trout if they will rise to the surface, and it is this ease of getting trout in this way, when they are feeding, which is one of the great attractions of dry fly fishing. Little knowledge of the habits of the fish and no knowledge at all of fly life and habits are needed for dry fly fishing, and any one who can cast can take many trout by this method. It is quite different with the nymph. One may have the right nymph for the water and one on which the trout are living at the time, and yet, by placing it wrongly and making it travel in the water in ways in which real nymphs do not swim, or by having an unsuitable leader too visible to the trout, one may fail to get any fish at all, when the same tackle in the hands of one who knows how to use it would get many more than any dry fly.

Again there is usually little difficulty in hooking trout rising to a dry fly, the main trouble being that fishermen strike too fast; otherwise, they get a large proportion of the fish rising to the fly. They can see just what they are doing. With the nymph it is far different. Even when trout take the nymph it is most difficult to time the strike so as to hook them, as most of the time the nymph is invisible and one must acquire that sixth sense of when to tighten the line which the experienced fisherman gets after years of practice. Besides, it is always necessary in nymph fly fishing to use a long fine leader and this greatly increases the difficulty of taking trout, particularly the large ones, as these light leaders will part readily if they are used to strike a fish hard. This cannot be tolerated at all in nymph fly fishing, and most men have to learn to fish all over again if they ever become at all successful with this method.

I regard nymph fly fishing as a more skilful way of taking trout than the dry fly, and one requiring infinitely more knowledge and technique. I can teach any one to be a fairly good dry fly fisherman in a few days but I would not undertake to make a good nymph fly fisherman in a year, and it might take several seasons before he would show a really good performance, for it must be remembered that by far the larger part of trouts' food consists of nymphs and therefore the nymph is the best method of taking large numbers of fish. It is only because nymphs are not used properly that our streams are not depleted of trout. It is fortunate that few have acquired the necessary skill and knowledge to fish in this way well, and that those who have are men who never take many trout from streams.

The irony is that the two things for which Mr. Hewitt will be best remembered, in the long annals of angling, concern both the nymph and the dry fly. He was indubitably the first angler to take a salmon on a dry fly with a one-and-a-half-ounce rod—some thirty years before Lee Wulff began to make that seem like par for the course—even though his difficulties in playing it made the guides refer to it as "the salmon that caught Mr. Hewitt" and left him disinclined to try it again. And just as indubitably, he was the conduit from Skues, in the establishment of nymph fishing in America, as Theodore Gordon had been from Halford, in the establishment of the dry fly.

I still find him great fun to read again, and take a few pages of Hewitt, almost like a pep pill, every so often when a protracted spell of fishlessness gets me down. He was a happy man, whose fishing helped him grow old gracefully. He said it well himself:

Although now over eighty-one, I am still able to fish streams and find it most pleasant to have tea at five o'clock at my house on the hill and then drive down to the Neversink and fish until dark. There are always plenty of trout, but it is not every evening they will rise well. It is these hard fishing times which I enjoy most. I try to find out how to take these difficult trout and almost always return them to the water when I have done so. I am certain I caught one individual trout, which I called "Tubby," seventeen times last year without injuring him at all. It is delightful to have my old friends visit me and to watch them have a good time fishing. It is wonderful to watch the evening light come on and the night finally take the place of day. This is what is happening to me; the evening is coming on pleasantly, and the night will soon take its place according to the order of nature.

While I have no doubt killed more fish than I should at times, as has been told in the foregoing pages, I hope I have made some amends by what I have been able to do for my friends the fish, and also for my friends the fishermen.

May we meet along the stream, and if not there, then in the happy fishing grounds of the Micmac Indians in the hereafter. I only hope it may aid you, if only in some small way, to have as much pleasure as I have had on the rivers. On parting with one of our guides, as we left for home, he remarked: "When you die, Charon will have to stop the boat on the Styx and let you fish; he could never get you across the river." I only hope I may have one last chance to see if I can raise one there also.

And now with Walton, "*Blessings upon all that hate contentions, and love quietnesse, and vertue, and Angling.*"

And I like the paragraph that Ernie Schwiebert has in *Nymphs*:

Both Hewitt and his fishing camp are gone now, like Bergman and John Atherton as well, men whose fishing was strongly influenced by the old master and his river. The ancient Buick with the rod holes cut in its roof no longer traverses the rough twin-cut trails along the Neversink. Change is still inevitably erasing the pastoral beauty of the region, although its sense of the past still survives in the white clapboard church at Claryville, with its wooden trout weathervane.

15.
Jennings and the Future

Preston Jennings stands in the same relationship to American angling as Ronalds does to British; each of them was, if not the first to think of serving as a link between angling and entomology, at least the first to approach the role properly, and do it right.

Neither was encyclopedic; they both left a lot of room for future work. But each was willing to tackle the job at which others had boggled, and each left a solid foundation on which others could build.

As Major Hills pointed out in *A History of Fly Fishing for Trout,* it took a Ronalds to father the breed of the naturalist-angler, or angler-naturalist, that characterizes the modern era of fly fishing. And as English artificial flies became increasingly representative of the natural insects, now observed and classified more and more closely, that served as their models, they became less and less effective over here, as American insects differ basically from their British counterparts in nature. Hence a Jennings became as needed to us as a Ronalds had been, almost exactly a century earlier, to them. Like all broad generalizations, it is an oversimplification, yet basically true, to say that in both instances all that was needed, and all that was awaited, for modern fly fishing to enter its new era, was somebody who could speak both languages, the inexact and colorful English of fly-fishing tradition and the precise and rigid Latin of entomology, and was willing to tackle a formidable task. Ronalds and Jennings, in their respective times and circumstances, just happened to qualify. Both had been anticipated, but both made the needed fresh start, and had the patience and persistence and above all skill to follow through.

Louis Rhead, by a full nineteen years, had preceded Jennings, with a volume called *American Trout Stream Insects,* but he missed the connection. He failed to make the identification clear between the individual fishing-fly pattern—the one thing the fly fisherman knew—and the specific category in the broad genus of insect subdivisions that only the scientific entomologist could supply. Instead, Rhead gave his drawings, which were excellent, fanciful names of his own devising, which only created added confusion, to any attempt to relate the old colloquial fly names with their respective Latin labels. Thus Rhead's work had the effect of a divisive third force, to set back instead of advance, the correlation of the two sets of terminology. That, and the fact that he was overawed by Halford and La Branche, kept his work from getting off on the right foot, and himself from the role of pioneer trailblazer that all who came after would have to follow.

Preston Jennings gave Rhead due credit, while at the same time diagnosing the nature of his work's faults, and the net effect was to decrease Rhead's stature. It had already been diminished by neglect, as Rhead was nine years dead, and virtually in obloquy, by the time Jennings wrote. Ironically, fate was to play something of the same dirty trick on Preston Jennings in turn, as he was himself almost nine years dead before the belated "rediscovery" of his *A Book of Trout Flies* brought him his long overdue recognition. Since I've written extensively about him in the chapter called "Preston Jennings for President" in *The Well-Tempered Angler,* and in the entries both on him and on Louis Rhead in "The Angler's Best Companions" section of *The Joys of Trout,* there's no point in holding us up here to go over all that ground again, so long as I put him in his proper perspective in relation to other major angling figures we have occasion to encounter.

But before I forget, I do think we could take about a cigarette's worth of time out—or say a pipeful's—to consider this whole strange business of neglect and discovery of some very important angling writings.

You know, up to about a dozen years ago, you could state with all the assurety of an axiom the proposition that the better the angling book the more certain it will be remaindered for a dollar.

I've forgotten now whether it was '61, the year before I was sick, or '63, the year after, that I bought two dozen copies of *The Salmon* by J. W. Jones, in a Marboro Books clearance sale, to give to everybody I could get to promise to read it, but I'll never forget my first excited sight of it, by the dim light of a spring Sunday night in 1959, in Hardy's window on St. James's Place in London. The store was closed, of course, on a Sunday night. I'd been in there just two days before, and the book hadn't been in the window or anywhere in sight inside, or I'd have bought it. As it was, my plane back to the States was leaving later that night, so I had to write back to Hardy's to get a copy. I'd forgotten the author's name, so I had to ask for the new book called, I thought, just *The Salmon* by somebody with a short common name, like Smith, Jones or Robinson. Well, bingo, I'd hit it smack in the middle with Jones, and back came the book, no more than some six or seven weeks after I'd spotted it in Hardy's window.

After going to all that trouble to get it, and after reading it like a bible for a couple of years, and lending it only to people I knew I could trust to return it (or could get it back from if I suddenly needed it), do you wonder that I twice grabbed up copies by the dozen when the American edition was being remaindered for a buck?

And did you know that the same thing could have happened with some of the most important angling books of our time, like Vince Marinaro's *A Modern Dry Fly Code,* Preston Jennings's *A Book of Trout Flies* and, at one wobbly moment before it went on to become a certified modern classic, even Ernie Schwiebert's *Matching the Hatch?* Well, it could and did, and those are by no means the only instances that could be cited in support of the melancholy truism with which I began this little detour. Fred Everett's *Fun with Trout,* which is a perfect love of a book, suffered the same fate, going into that limbo in which it still awaits rescue. In fact, I almost wanted to go into hiding when I heard that *The Well-Tempered Angler* had gone into a second printing in the spring of '66, after its original appearance in the fall of '65, because I felt pretty sure that knowledgeable fishing book collectors would take that as a sign that it couldn't be very good.

Only the most hard-core blue-collar how-to books could be sold in any quantity to anglers in America, before the sudden resurgence of interest in fly fishing that began just a few years back. The only exceptions

I can think of, before 1970, are Bergman's *Trout,* and *McClane's Standard Fishing Encyclopedia.* All the rest of the good ones had to become scarce before they began to be appreciated. Now, one by one, they're being rediscovered.

And that's what happened, over a span of thirty-five years, to *A Book of Trout Flies,* after Eugene Connett published it as a Derrydale Press item in 1935, and Crown issued it in reprint very shortly thereafter. In no time, it seemed, the Crown reprint was nearly as hard to lay hands on as the original Derrydale, and there was to come a time when this book that once went begging on the bargain counter commanded an average figure of a hundred dollars for the original edition and fifteen to twenty for the first Crown reprint, as a collector's item in book dealers' lists.

Reissued in 1970, once again as a Crown reprint, but this time with a new introduction by Ernest Schwiebert, and a suitable launching by Nick Lyons as one of his first selections in the Crown Sportsmen's Classics series, it ran through seven printings within three years. Riding the crest of the wave of new interest in fly fishing, the same enthusiastic reception was now attained by other reprintings of books long out of print, such as the legendarily scarce Marinaro's *A Modern Dry Fly Code,* the hard-to-find, but uniquely valuable Hills's *A History of Fly Fishing for Trout,* and even such a recondite item as John Dennys's joyous pastoral of the year 1613, *The Secrets of Angling.* Within a year there was a veritable spate of newly available classics, from Crown, Freshet, Winchester, Van Cortlandt and Stone Wall presses. But though I rubbed my eyes at the illusion that the millenium was here, I wasn't really ready to concede the complete repeal of my old law about the inverse ratio of quality to sales, as applied to angling books, until I saw the runaway success of a brand new title like Swisher's and Richards's *Selective Trout,* surely the most innovative fishing book in over a decade. When a book as good as that one could ring up a sale of over forty thousand copies, which it did virtually overnight, then it was clear that a new day had indeed dawned, and my old rule was a dodo.

I only wish that Preston Jennings could have lived to see the second career of *A Book of Trout Flies,* a work that was truly a labor of love, and as far as he knew, when he died too soon in February of 1962, represented love's labor lost. That was the time when Charlie Fox was trying in vain to find a publisher for *This Wonderful World of Trout,* and the next year, having failed to find one, decided to publish it himself. That was the low point. But by the decade's end, a publisher was to come to him, and bring out not one new edition of *This Wonderful World of Trout* but two. The wheel had come full circle.

Since Preston Jennings's work has been restored to active currency, after decades of neglect, I will not quote from *A Book of Trout Flies* as much as I would have wanted to if the book were still hard to come by, but will confine myself to Schwiebert's Introduction to the 1970 edition, and one small excerpt from the book itself. Then I'd like to move over to two samples of his work that have not been heretofore collected, the two articles he wrote for *Esquire* in 1956.

Here is how Schwiebert focuses on Jennings, bringing him into close-up out of the panoramic picture of fly-fishing entomology:

The vacuum was filled in 1836, with the disciplined scientific identification and accurate color plates that became available to anglers when Alfred Ronalds completed his *Fly-Fisher's Entomology,* the first classic work on trout-stream insects. Ronalds is the full flowering of fly-fishing development since its genesis in Aelian, the logical result of more than two thousand years of sport. There have been more than a dozen editions, although it catalogs only the hatches of Staffordshire and Derbyshire; and its thoroughness became the yardstick for all subsequent work on fly hatches.

That example was equaled in the nineteenth-century chalk-stream studies made by Frederic M. Halford on the rivers of Hampshire. Halford codified the sum of fly-fishing knowledge before his time into a rational philosophy, and with the help of brilliant fishermen like Hall and Marryat, his work identified the principal hatches of southern England; books like *Floating Flies and How to Dress Them* and *Dry-Fly Entomology* are classics of angling literature.

Halford has been followed by stream entomologists like Moseley, whose *Dry-Fly Fisherman's Entomology* appeared in 1920, several years after Halford's death. Moseley continued his work with exhaustive studies of British caddis hatches, and the Halford tradition is still alive today. Subsequent books on the fly hatches of Britain have been compiled by writers like Theakston and West and Walker, and the compendium of stream insects thus far is perhaps the *Angler's Entomology,* published by J. R. Harris in recent years, with excellent color photographs of hatches collected and recorded at streamside.

The example of these British writers migrated to America in the years after Halford, and first emerged again in the work of Louis Rhead. His book *American Trout Stream Insects* was printed in 1920, and attempted to catalog the hatches of Catskill rivers, although there was no effort to identify the species with the technical precision of his British counterparts.

The first American work on fly hatches that included modern fly-dressings as well as accurate identification of the insects was the first edition of *A Book of Trout Flies,* completed in 1935 by Preston J. Jennings. Like the appearance of Ronalds in 1836, the work of Jennings a century later set the standard of excellence that has measured all subsequent American work on fly-fishing entomology.

Since its initial Derrydale edition first appeared, covering principal hatches from the Raritan and the Brodheads to the Catskills and their sister rivers farther north, there have been other books on American hatches. Knowledgeable fly-fishermen are familiar with Charles Wetzel and his *Practical Fly-Fishing.* Art Flick and his classic little *Streamside Guide,* and my own *Matching the Hatch,* which appeared in 1955. Each of these later books had its principal inspiration in the work of Jennings, and the exquisite watercolors and drawings in *A Book of Trout Flies* set the standard for illustrations of fly hatches in this country.

And now for one tidbit out of *A Book of Trout Flies,* which comes at the very end of the Jennings text, just before the Afterword by Eugene V. Connett, 3rd:

. . . It is said that one small dog can put a mountain lion up a tree, not because the lion is afraid of the dog but because the lion reasons that if such a small and insignificant animal has the temerity to chase him it must be mad, and so the lion climbs the tree to let the mad dog go by.

The trout probably feel the same way about any fly which does not act naturally, and leave it severely alone.

There is a delightful Frenchman by the name of Charley, who, with his bustling little wife, Amelia, runs a small hotel at Analomink, Pa., on the Brodhead. Delightful food, cooked by Charley himself, and comfortable beds make the place a veritable oasis for the fly-fisher visiting the famous trout-stream. In addition, Charley had a free-rising trout in the pool just in front of the hotel.

I had heard a great deal of the beauties of the stream and the week previous to my visit had been shown four Brown Trout of noble proportions which had come from it. I had been assured that there were lots more where they came from, but that they were hard to get. I was not taking my hat off to any fly-fisher, especially as the four fish I had seen had been taken on a fly of my own design, so without ado I set out for Analomink. Charley informed me that I could have my meals whenever I wanted them, and, as there were still a couple of hours of daylight left, I decided to have a try at the fish and eat later.

Charley told me that he thought the fish were feeding, and it was with some haste that I got into my waders and hurried downstairs. Despite Charley's duties as chef, bartender and host, he seems to have time to show strangers the stream which, in my case, did not take very long as we simply went across the railroad tracks in front of the hotel, where Charley pointed to the stream and said, "That's a good stretch for a dry-fly." Even as he spoke one of the free risers sucked in a natural. That was enough for me. As I scrambled down the hill to the stream I called to Charley to ask how many fish he wanted for breakfast, and he replied that a brace would be ample.

I waded into what I considered to be an ideal position for casting to a good fish that was rising below a rock at the middle of the run, and with the utmost confidence placed a Hendrickson over the fish. The Hendrickson had been selected because the natural fly, *Ephemerella invaria,* was on the water and was being taken by this fish as they floated past the feeding location.

Nothing happened except that Mr. Trout rose again and gulped in a natural within a few inches of my fly. This performance was repeated a number of times before I came to the conclusion that the leader must be too short or too heavy; so I changed to a sixteen foot 3X leader. But this did not induce a rise. Various flies were then tried, March Brown, Fan-wing Royal Coachman, and finally Quill Gordon in small sizes, but none of these flies was any more successful than the Hendrickson which, by all indications, should be the killing fly at this time.

During the time I was changing flies, native fishermen using wet-flies would come by on the way downstream and several of them tried for this fish at my invitation, but "no soap." When it got so dark that I could no longer see my fly on the water I returned to the hotel beaten. Charley was setting up beer for a couple of natives in the bar, when I dragged myself upon a stool to drown my disgust. He, of course, wanted to know how I had made out and it was with some reluctance that I had to admit that I had fished over one fish for two hours and had failed to get it; in fact, had not "put it down."

Charley made some remark of condolence and then turning to his beer patrons remarked that the year previous there had been a fish occupying that same position and that two guests who had been spending a week at his hotel had taken turns fishing for it. Finally, the day before they were to leave, they came into the bar and offered to lay a wager that this fish could not be taken on a fly. Charley said that he slipped on a pair of boots, the stream being then low, took his rod, and, without even removing his white bartender's jacket, waded across the stream to the *far side* and sneaked up under the alders to cast his fly over the "Constant Feeder." He took the fish on the first cast. He had said enough!

The first thing the following morning I, too, waded across the stream. All previous casting to this fish had been from the near side of the stream, and I took this "free riser," this "constant feeder," on my first cast, on a Hendrickson fly, the same fly which had been refused perhaps a hundred times the evening before. But, it was the first time that any fly had been delivered without drag!

Apparently, no one but Charley, who had fished the stream for many years, knew of the almost imperceptible drag which protected this trout's feeding position. However, it was there, and this trout had grown old and fat under its protection. Not a big fish, as Brown Trout go, but an excellent fish for any stream and right in Charley's door yard.

I hope there will be another one there next year, and I hope, also, that Charley will be a little discreet in making suggestions to other guests at his hotel.

So much for Jennings the practical and pragmatic fisherman; now for Jennings the theorist, as revealed in those two pieces he contributed to *Esquire,* the one about the *Isonychia bicolor* being "the nymph phase of the Royal Coachman," and the other his tenaciously held theory that, despite all evidence to the contrary, salmon do feed after their return to fresh water from the sea.

Both articles were illustrated in color, with drawings of insects and photographs of the flies tied to imitate the naturals, which I am unable to reproduce, since the original color copy was returned after the articles appeared, and is not recoverable. Since Jennings supplied the dressings for the flies he tied for these two articles, the lack of illustration does not vitiate their value.

Here is the first one, from the July 1956 issue:

THERE *IS* A ROYAL COACHMAN
NATURE HAS A MATCH FOR "THE FLY THAT NEVER WAS"
By Preston J. Jennings

It might be almost anywhere; it could be in Michigan, in Montana, or along the Pacific Coast, just so long as it is a place where fly-fishers congregate. Nor is the time important; it might be July or August or, if it's on the Pacific Coast, it might be October. Let's make it right now at Dick Kahil's Rainbow Lodge at Mt. Tremper in the Catskill Mountains of New York State.

We're in a dimly lit room beclouded with pipe and cigarette smoke. In the far corner is a small bar where Dick Kahil, the genial host, is mixing the third round of vodka and tonic. It has been a long hot day, with no fish moving except an occasional fingerling rising to the knots in the leader, and the boys, having communed with Nature in sweat-filled waders all day and more recently with the spirits, are just about ready to turn in when, suddenly, the door opens and in walks one of those persistent fishermen who do not know any better than to keep on fishing after dark. He makes his way to the only vacant stool at the bar, eases his weary frame on the leather and asks for vermouth on the rocks.

After the first libation has been stored away and the second one mixed, Dick cautiously asks, "How did you make out?"

The late arrival strokes a three weeks' growth of beard and says, "Well, son, didn't do too badly; picked up a couple of good fish just at dark, right at that spot you told me about, and both fish took a Fanwing Royal Coachman. Matter of fact, there were quite a few natural Royal Coachman flies in the air tonight. It seems there were more of them than I have seen since that little high water we had back in '51." Then he displays as pretty a pair of rainbows as you could expect to see in these parts and exits.

After his departure the room is filled with loud guffaws.

"Who does that old windbag think he is trying to kid with that story of a hatch of Royal Coachmans?" one of the boys remarks. "I began fishing before that guy was born. I know the English chalk streams, I've fished all over America, and have taken a few side trips to Chile and New Zealand, and I've never seen a natural insect that looks like a Royal Coachman. The fellow was just pulling our leg, but he didn't fool me. Come to think of it, though, there was one time when I was almost positive I saw a lot of Royal Coachman flies flying around. We had a kind of picnic over on the Beaverkill. We were sitting around Bill's place in the dark—there was a power failure—and I can almost swear I saw a swarm of Royal Coachmans flying around, but when the lights came on the swarm had disappeared . . . so I can't be sure."

Well, the amusing part of it all is that both men could have been right in their statements. The natural insect *does* exist, and in considerable numbers, over a wide area of both Coastal Ranges of the United States and in the Central States; but since it is present over streams just at dark and is such a strong flier, fly-fishers seldom have the opportunity to see it at all, much less collect it for close examination. The green egg mass, which characterizes the Royal Coachman, is loosely held by the insect, ready for instant dropping at the selected part of the stream, so that if you happen to be fortunate enough to catch one in your hand the chances are that the egg mass would be instantly released. It was only with the help of a butterfly net and a cyanide quick-killing bottle that the writer was able to collect specimens.

The Royal Coachman family is represented in Nature by a group of May flies consisting of about twenty-five slightly varying species under a generic name of *Isonychia*. The word means "two pads of equal size," which the nymph has on four of its six feet.

May flies are aquatic insects, spending the greater part of their life span in the water in the form of a nymph, where their chief purpose seems to be to serve as food for fish. In the winged stage they are of particular interest to the fly-fisher as they are generally in evidence during the daylight hours, while other types of aquatics seem to prefer the nighthours.

They begin life as an egg which, having been deposited on the surface of the water by the mature winged fly, sinks to the bottom where it ultimately hatches into a tiny creature called a nymph. As soon as this nymph begins to feed it develops a hard shuck or shell which is cast off at successive intervals as growth increases. As maturity nears, wings develop within the nymphal case, eggs develop in the females, and sperm in the males and, finally, when everything has become ready, the nymph rises to the surface or crawls up on the lee side of a partially submerged stone, splits open the case and emerges as a winged fly. Such emergence is called a "hatch." In this stage the fly is known as a subimago or in the fisherman's language, because of its dull appearance, a "dun." It then flies upward to the woods, where for the next twenty-four or more hours it shelters on the undersides of foliage. During this period it sheds a complete skin or membrane, emerging with glassy, crystal-clear wings and a more generally brilliant body. In this final stage of life it is called an imago and, due to the rapidity of the wings when in flight, by fishermen a "spinner." The return to the stream is referred to as a "brush hatch."

Why has the May fly been equipped with a skin which it can shuck off? The answer lies in the balance which Nature maintains. The voracious trout has little equipment for controlling the volume of light entering its eyes. It has no eyelids, and the iris, or pupil, has little or no power of contraction; hence during the daylight hours its range of comfortable vision is *away from* the source of light and it sees the subimago, or dull-colored dun of the May fly, by light which is reflected from it, so that when viewed against a background or foliage the fly is relatively inconspicuous. When daylight fades, the trout has to shift the direction of its range of vision *to* the source of light, which is the sky, and transparent objects such as the imago or spinner of the May fly, seen as a silhouette, are not so readily visible. This balance is of course delicate, for if the flies were completely invisible the fish would starve; on the other hand, if the flies were readily visible they would all be eaten in a short period of time.

The distribution of various members of the *Isonychia* group is very wide, ranging from North Carolina into Canada, through Michigan, Arizona and presumably Colorado, through California and Oregon and perhaps farther north. Here in the East emergence begins about the middle of May, reaching its peak about June 15, with occasional flies emerging throughout the summer and sometimes as late as October. On the West Coast they appear to be abundant during October. They are large flies with a wingspread of approximately one inch or slightly more; Eastern, *Isonychia bicolor* (recently called "albomanicata"); Western, *Isonychia velma*.

The hour of emergence is usually late afternoon, but on a dark day it may be early afternoon, while the egg-laying spinners operate just at dark.

The nymph is free-swimming and, incidentally, is the only one of this type found in our trout streams. It ranges about the gravel of the stream bed, sometimes poised or anchored on the tips of four legs, its two front legs being equipped with bristlelike filaments which are so arranged that they form a kind of dip net. This net is used by the nymph to collect food as it sweeps by in the current. Being constantly exposed to enemies its only means of escape is speed, and it has plenty of that. As the time of maturity and emergence as a winged fly arrives, the nymph generally swims toward the shallower portions of the stream, which is the bank. Here it climbs up on the downstream side of a partially submerged stone, splits its nymphal shuck and flies away.

During this journey the nymph is exposed in open water and is highly vulnerable. An artificial nymph following the course of the natural should be cast toward the middle of the stream and, as it begins to drift with the current, retrieved slowly by gradually weaving in the line with the fingers of the left hand. This is very important for, if the artificial is allowed to drift free in the current, the fish would pass it by as an empty shuck rather than a living, swimming nymph.

My own dressing of the artificial Coachman Nymph is as follows:

Tail: Brown partridge
Body: A mixture of claret and dark-red seal's fur
Thorax: Peacock herl
Ribbing: Round gold tinsel
Hackle: A few turns of red or furnace cock's hackle
Hook: A No. 8 or 9 Sproat.

For Steelhead in Western streams the writer has been assured that a nymph of this type in sizes as large as No. 4 is highly successful.

There are, however, a number of natural nymphs which seem to misjudge the distance to a haven and, therefore, have to emerge directly from the surface of the stream. If there is much of a breeze, especially in a downstream direction, many winged flies capsize before getting off the water. At such a time the Wet Leadwing Coachman is very effective and perhaps the Governor occupies a similar position on the West Coast.

If there is little or no abnormal breeze the winged flies get off the water fairly well. In such instances a dry fly of the Dark Variant type works well. Incidentally, the writer introduced this fly to the Catskill Mountain streams in the Spring of 1932, where it killed very well, but it was not until 1936 that he was able to associate this artificial with the subimago or dun stage of the May fly Isonychia. However, as early as 1932 one friend reported taking fifty-four trout on a single fly of this pattern! Later it resulted in the capture of one of the largest brown trout—a seven-and-a-half-pounder—to be taken on a dry fly; Walter Squires did it with the assistance of Mead Schaeffer on the Battenkill at Arlington, Vermont.

The dressing of the Dark Variant is as follows:

Tail: Rusty-blue dun cock's hackle
Body: Stripped peacock herl
Hackle: Rusty-blue dun cock's hackle
Hook: No. 12 or 14, depending upon the quality of the hackle.

The finest hackle for this fly comes from a breed of birds called the Old English Blue Game, but there are only a few such birds in this country.

The diameter of the artificial should approximate the wingspread of the natural insect, which is about one inch.

With this type of fly the hackle is the most important part, as it suggests the wings of the natural insect in motion, that rapid fluttering which precedes the actual take-off and poses the problem of now or never, which the trout has a hard time resisting. The original fly can actually be attributed to an Englishman, Doctor Baigent, although the American version is heavier hackled. Dr. Baigent worked on a problem of fly design which he called "altered refraction." The writer corresponded with the doctor, but did not grasp the import of what Dr. Baigent was trying to do until some time later. Apparently, Dr. Baigent knew that light reflected from, or passing around, narrow filaments such as the wing veins legs and tail of a natural insect, and subsequently being bent or refracted as it entered the water, would show tiny bands of colored light, i.e., red or blue on either side of the filaments. Undoubtedly what Baigent was trying to do was to reduce the visibility and therefore the falsity of the artificial by using a hackle that contained pigments which would neutralize the effects of this particular lighting. In other words, red pigment neutralizes a red light, and blue pigment neutralizes a blue light.

This principle has been applied to the staining of leader material with a red/blue dye (purple Tintex), resulting in the use of heavier and therefore safer leaders than usual. For instance, within the past few weeks a friend landed a three-and-three-quarter-pound brown trout taken on a dry fly under extreme low-water conditions, using a 2X leader, test 4½ pounds, stained as above, a feat he would not have been able to accomplish with finer material and lower test strength.

For late-evening fishing, tie on a Royal Coachman Wet or Dry, and the chances are you will take fish; besides, you will be a purist of the first water, for the natural insect *does* exist.

Both the Coachman and the Governor are nineteenth-century imports from England, and the association of the "Coachman" with Tom Bosworth is too well-known to bear repeating here. The "Royal" Coachman is strictly American, the wet version being more or less of an accident. A New York City flytier who wanted to make a more durable Coachman tied a few strands of red floss around the middle of the body, hence the "Royal" Coachman. At a much later date this wet fly was converted into a dry fly, probably by the late Theodore Gordon.

In America the Royal Coachman takes precedence because it conforms to Nature while the original Coachman has the body of the dun or subimago stage with the wing of the spinner or imago stage. In other words, it is not just right.

As the natural insect has rapid water for a habitat it follows that the artificials are especially attractive to rainbow trout. For the steelhead of the West Coast, which is a sea-run rainbow, there are at least two killing patterns of wet flies which seem to the writer to be closely identified with the West Coast natural, *Isonychia velma*. They are the "Cummings" and the "Carson." The colors in both patterns are of course exaggerated, but this would be neutralized by the low visibility in high and roily water. A further study of the natural flies will bring forth still better patterns.

That same year, 1956, in the October issue, Preston Jennings furnished his salmon article with drawings of the Stone fly (*Perla capitata*), May fly (*Hexagenia occulta*) and Sedge fly (*Stenophylax*) by the late Alma

W. Froderstrom of the staff of New York's Museum of Natural History, and of a Minnow (Black-nosed Dace) by Charles de Feo, along with two sets of flies, the first in each instance representing the insect as it appears in strong light, and the second fly representing the same insect's appearance in low light; also of his own devising was a color absorption chart, drawn on a spectrum, to show how much more sensitive fish are to the red end of the spectrum than we are. Thus, to the fish-view, red becomes increasingly important with decreasing light. To the caption for this chart he appended the following footnote, in contrast to the greater sensitivity of fish to the spectrum's red end:

Human visibility is so much greater at the blue end, that French flag (tricolor) had to be adjusted because first reaction when blue and red were equal, was that there was too much blue.

The dressings for the strong-light and low-light patterns of the four flies he devised in imitation of the three insects and the minnow follow at the end of the text. A box, which was inset midway through the article, summarized its points:

1. Salmon do feed in fresh water after their return from the sea.
2. Salmon can distinguish colors, are especially sensitive to red.
3. Salmon take artificial flies which suggest the natural food produced by their native river.

Here is the article itself:

THREE SECRETS OF THE SALMON
*Why the salmon mistakes an artificial fly
for food, and why he eats it.*

by Preston J. Jennings

If you will stop for a moment to consider the human animal you will almost immediately recognize a characteristic trait which seems to be peculiar to man alone, and that is an inborn desire for mastery. Old historians called this thing dominion and, for reasons of their own, described it as something which set man apart from the rest of the animals of Creation. In other words, man was given dominion not only over other animals but over the fish of the sea as well.

Anyone who has handled a fly rod knows that the fish he seeks to master is not sought for economic reasons, but is merely a means of satisfying or expressing that God-given thing which is called dominion.

During the fly-fisher's early years, this desire for mastery is satisfied by the capture of trout, which in itself is no mean feat as the trout is both cautious and wary, requiring delicate tackle as well as some knowledge of the types of natural insects upon which it is accustomed to feed, so that appropriate artificial flies, imitating or suggesting these insects, may be presented. After a while, however, this desire for mastery is no longer satisfied by the trout, which is relatively small, and a larger and perhaps more elusive fish must be sought if man is to exercise to the full his birthright of dominion. This search must of necessity lead him in the end to the Atlantic salmon, the king of all fish taken by means of fly tackle.

The Atlantic salmon at one time was abundant along the Atlantic seaboard, perhaps as far south as the Delaware River. As an instance of this abundance, the Connecticut River, when it was first dammed in the late eighteenth century, had such an accumulation of fish below the dam that for the ensuing three years farmers hauled them away by the wagonload, presumably for use as fertilizer.

As civilization expanded and the need for water power grew, more and more dams were constructed which barred the salmon from their normal breeding grounds. Then industrial pollution increased and there were changes in climate, with the result that the Atlantic salmon almost disappeared from our waters (they still can be found in a few minor streams in the state of Maine) and must be sought in the rivers of our neighbor to the north, Canada.

During the early years of our nation the customary dinner celebrating the

Fourth of July consisted of Atlantic salmon, new garden peas and freshly dug potatoes. New Englanders still try to preserve this tradition, but in most cases the salmon which graces the table is the product of a commercial fisherman's net operating in the coastal water adjacent to the mouths of Canadian rivers; the new garden peas are from the frozen-food locker; and the potato is the only product produced locally.

Yes, about the only thing left to remind us of those good days of yore, when rivers and streams of New England literally boiled with the run of July salmon, is the hot potato!

And, speaking of hot potatoes, if you want to handle some really hot verbal ones, all you have to do is to visit a fishing camp on almost any Canadian salmon river and listen to what goes on during the course of an evening around the fireplace. The boys are home from a long and hard day on the river and, with the help of a few bottles of that good Canadian ale and a warm fire, spirits revive and tongues wag.

An old friend of the author, Charles Phair, repeatedly claimed that there was one hot potato for which he had not been able to find a satisfactory answer, even though he had fished for and caught salmon all of his life. This very simple question, for which a simple answer should be forthcoming, is: why does the Atlantic salmon take an artificial lure, commonly called a salmon fly?

Before we can arrive at a simple answer we have to clear up several misconceptions about salmon.

Perhaps the reason for so much argument as to why a salmon is caught on an artificial fly is due, first, to the general belief that this fish does not feed when it returns to fresh water; second, that fish in general are color-blind; third, that the artificial salmon fly does not have any counterpart in Nature, in that it is not a plausible imitation of anything which the fish may have previously taken as food.

Unfortunately, many books written by fishermen are merely interesting diaries or journals recounting their own experiences at actual fishing. A fisherman learns very little while actually engaged in fishing; here he is only putting into practice those things which he has already been told by a more experienced angler, or those things he has acquired by reading and study. One learns very little on the stream unless one has a preconceived idea of what to look for and what to do. However, if the fly-fisher happens to be a woman, Lady Luck seems to play an important part. To illustrate: while fishing a Gaspé river a celebrated Broadway actress stopped for lunch and left her salmon fly trailing in the water from the beached canoe. Before the pre-luncheon cocktails were consumed the canoe was yanked off the beach by a salmon which, when landed, weighed thirty-six pounds! Truly a prize for which more experienced anglers had sweated and labored for years without avail.

Let's take up the question of the salmon feeding, or at least taking food upon its return to the river, a journey concerned primarily with seeking a suitable spawning ground and, later, a nursery for its young. For many years salmon have been taken in Scotland on natural bait, such as minnows and prawns. These natural baits, however, are not allowed on Canadian rivers, and American fishermen are not familiar with their use. The Britisher, Arthur Wood, the master of the greased or floating-line fly-fishing, noted that salmon often would feed on the natural British March Brown (a May fly, *Rithrogena haarupi*), and that during one entire season he fished his water on the River Dee with an artificial March Brown and accounted for as many fish as usual.

If the salmon does take food in the river, why is it then that food is never found in its stomach? This may be due to two things. First, the salmon has a tremendous capacity for digesting and assimilating food: it grows from a weight of a few ounces when it runs to sea to three to five pounds in one year of sea feeding, to ten or twelve pounds in two years, and from twelve to twenty-five pounds in three years. Second, a salmon is seldom gutted until some hours or days after it is caught and by that time the digestive acids have completely obliterated any traces of food. In this connection it might be stated that Doctor William McFarland, a New York surgeon, decided to gut salmon *immediately* after capture, and found that some 50.2 per cent of the fish examined contained identifiable food—minnows in the case of the large fish and aquatic insects in the small fish or grilse.

Thus it would seem that salmon do feed in fresh water, but, as they are seldom seen actively seeking food, it would appear logical to conclude that they take only such food as can be obtained with a minimum of effort. From a standpoint of economy it would hardly pay for so large a fish to spend more energy in going after food than the food so obtained would replace. The types of artificial flies, which we will shortly discuss, are predicated upon an illusion of being nearer—and, therefore, reached with a minimum of effort—than they actually are.

This leads us to the consideration of the next phase of the question as to why the salmon is caught on a fly: *are fish color-blind?*

The general belief persists that fish are color-blind, notwithstanding the colored flies and lures fishermen use to catch them! While fishermen do not have the equipment, time and curiosity to go into experiments covering this field, much work has been done in the scientific field by men with both the equipment and the urge to find out the facts.

Vision depends upon two things: light and the receiving apparatus, or eye, for the reception of light. Light, as we understand it, is a form of energy liberated by chemical reactions taking place in the planet we call the sun. This energy reaches the eye, which contains within the screen or retina a substance which reacts to or is bleached by light. This substance is called rhodopsin or, more commonly, visual purple, and it has the peculiar capacity to recover immediately after bleaching, perhaps within a small fraction of a second. The reaction caused by the action of light is then transmitted by the optic nerve to the brain centers which control voluntary action.

A comparative analysis of rhodopsin from both the human eye and the eyes of a variety of fresh-water fish, including members of the salmonid group, has been reported by Dr. A. C. Krause in *The Biochemistry of the Eye* and the chart on page 72 shows this comparison. It will be noted that in the case of the fish the eye is more sensitive to the long wave or red end of the spectrum, while the human eye is more sensitive to the short wave or blue end.

The finding agrees with another experiment, this one conducted by Frank A. Brown, Jr. of the State of Illinois Natural History Survey, in which he trained a number of bass to respond to various colors by a process of reward or punishment. He sums up his findings: "My own results indicate that the vision of light-adapted bass would more closely resemble that of a human being with perfectly normal color vision, looking through a pair of yellowish glasses." This second experiment only serves to confirm the findings of Dr. Krause, the biochemist, that fish can distinguish colors and are especially sensitive to the red end of the spectrum.

Two things then have been established: salmon *do* feed in fresh water and they *can* distinguish colors. It is entirely possible that the surface-feeding fish sees and is familiar with more color than the average human being for the reason that all angular light striking the surface of the water is split in such a way that the individual rays which produce the reactions of color are seen separately; in other words, they are not parallel to each other, but fan out at varying angles which result in bands of colored light, such as those in a rainbow in the sky. This process, which is called refraction, at first glance may seem mysterious. It is, however, mechanically quite simple. Light or energy from the sun travels through the intervening space or vacuum at a terrific rate of speed; this rate of speed is much reduced in water, since water acts as a brake, slowing down the rate of speed. Mechanically, light acts as though each ray or wave advanced with a flat face at right angles to its direction, so that if the ray struck the surface of water vertically the entire face of the ray would be retarded equally. Conversely, if the light struck at an angle, only one side would be retarded while the other side would still be moving through air which offers little appreciable resistance. Hence, light entering water from a vertical position remains daylight, or white light, as the individual rays are still parallel, while light striking at any other angle (the various rays with their individual faces) would be diverging at varying angles under water.

It is this divergence of the individual rays making up white light, or daylight, that allows us to appreciate the particular effect of the separate reactions in the retina and which result in our seeing the various colors that collectively form the solar spectrum.

A practical illustration of this action may be made with an ordinary table fork. Here the tines are parallel. Insert the fork vertically into a roast of meat and all of the tines will penetrate, but try impaling the same roast with the fork held at an angle and you will find that only a few tines will enter and, unless you are careful, you will end up with a few badly bent tines.

Another point worth considering is that all of the light striking the surface of water does not penetrate it; some of it is caromed or reflected off the surface. Vertical light has about ninety-five per cent penetration. Light from the lowest angle of about three degrees has only five per cent penetration. This means that the light reaching the eye of the fish looking out of water is of varying intensity, depending upon the angle. As the fish has no mechanical means of adjusting its eye, such as an eyelid or contractible opening of the iris, it seems to make great use of this natural condition by looking in the direction where the volume of light is most comfortable for its vision. It is also interesting to note that, in the case of the fish, *each eye operates independently of the other*. The optic nerves which connect the retina with the brain cross each other on their course to the side of the brain opposite the individual eye; but, unlike the human optic nerves, which are interwoven or fused, these remain free of each other. This independence allows one eye to be blinded by too much light while the other eye enjoys good vision in a lower light. Incidentally, the eye of the fish is in some ways similar to the eye of the owl, which is adapted for vision in very weak light.

Most objects which we call colored contain substances known as pigments.

These have the property of reflecting light on a selective basis, in that they reflect only a part of the spectrum and absorb or convert the remainder into a longer wave length, or heat. This means that the volume or intensity of reflected light is lower than the full or direct light from the sky. Therefore, it seems logical to assume that during the daylight hours a surface-feeding fish uses the low-angle *reflected* light from the object, and during the late afternoon or evening hours it reverses the direction of vision towards the low-angle *direct* light from the sky. During the night it would in all probability look up vertically and thereby utilize the maximum amount of light available at that time. This, however, would be white light, since it strikes the surface vertically and the individual rays remain parallel. Under this latter condition a black artificial fly, seen as a silhouette, would be the most visible and is, perhaps, the reason why black flies are so successful in places where night fishing is practiced, as in New Zealand.

Many fishermen with inquiring frames of mind have experimented with tanks of water, usually constructed with one glass side set at an angle of about 48°, which is the angle of refraction of light striking the surface at the lowest angle of, say, three degrees. This glass side permits the observation of the split, or refracted, light without further distortion. In every case with which the author is familiar, beginning with the American, H. P. Wells, 1885, all of these experimenters were interested in the appearance of an artificial fly, both the submerged or wet fly and the surface or dry fly. The author's interest, however, is not with the artificial fly, but with the natural aquatic insect which forms the common food on which the fish is accustomed to feed, both in its early years as a parr and in its mature stage as a salmon. With this in mind two slightly different tanks were constructed, one considerably larger than the other. With the larger tank it was found that objects on the surface, at the edge of what is called the "fish's window," when seen by light reflected *from* them, were lighted by a series of colored lights ranging from blue at the top, through green and yellow, and ending with red at the bottom. Conversely, if the object was lighted by light from behind, it appeared as a silhouette surrounded by bands of colored light, with yellow and red on top, with blue and green bordering the lower margin. This phenomenon, to the author's knowledge, had not been recorded up to that time. The problem then became one of applying this method of lighting to the natural insects. As the tank proved to be unwieldy, a small glass prism, such as is used in binoculars, replaced it. Glass, incidentally, is slightly more resistant to the passage of light than water, hence the individual rays which make up daylight are split at slightly wider angles, but for all practical purposes the prism proved to be the solution of the problem.

From a large collection of natural insects, many of which are common to the Appalachian Mountain Range as far north as Newfoundland, it was a simple matter for the author to select one of each of the three types of aquatic insects generally associated with fly-fishing (a Stone fly, a May fly, and a Sedge fly), view them through the prism, and then design an artificial fly which would in some way suggest the size and coloration of each natural fly as it might appear to the fish when seen resting or laying its eggs on the surface of the stream. Two types of lighting were used for each fly. The first was by light reflected *from* it; the second by light from *behind* it, so that the fly would appear as a silhouette. This was done on the theory that during periods of strong daylight the fish would be looking away *from* the source of light and that in times of poor light it would be looking *into* the source of light. The Stone fly, incidentally, is in season early, the May fly is prevalent in midseason, perhaps as late as September, while the Sedge is more common in the fall.

These artificial flies are wet flies and are fished just beneath the surface; their value lies in the creation of an illusion of proximity. A natural insect on the surface at the edge of the fish's window must of necessity be close to the fish, while the artificial creates the same illusion even though it is still a great distance away. In other words, with flies of this type you get greater coverage of the water in which you hope a salmon may be resting. It has been suggested by students of the salmon that while at sea it ranges along the continental shelf where food is plentiful, but where landmarks by which it can determine distance are very few. It is this weakness, then, of judging distance which causes it to move great distances to take an artificial fly that appears to be only a few feet away.

In the case of flies which suggest minnows, the problem is slightly different. Here the natural minnow is well protected by its normal coloration, being dark on the topside and white or light below. If it gets off balance, however, so that the angular split light strikes the bottom or white side, colored lights are reflected. These rays are then caromed off the mirrorlike undersurface of the water and are seen by larger fish which take them as food. During the spring, which is the breeding time of the dace, or common stream minnow, the male has to turn on its side to fertilize the eggs being extruded by the female, who remains in a normal position. During this period red pigment is deposited over the sides and belly of the male dace, which is one of the ways nature has devised to prevent the broadcasting of the highly visible split light. In other words, the red pigment neutralizes the red end of the spectrum to which fish, as we have seen, are particularly sensitive.

Artificial flies which suggest minnows are necessarily quite large and should be used only under conditions of poor visibility, such as turbid or high water, or low light. Under proper conditions they kill well not only for salmon, but for trout and steelhead. The two patterns of minnow-type flies are necessary because of the variations in the spectrum. Under full light, say during June, yellow light is predominant. As the intensity of light diminishes, during the fall months, yellow is replaced by orange.

Artificial flies for salmon are by no means something new, as they have been tied and used in Scotland for at least one hundred forty years. One early writer suggests that the maker of gaudy flies for salmon may exercise his fancy as he pleases, for it is impossible for him to be too extravagant in his ideas. Following this line of reasoning, literally hundreds, perhaps thousands, of different salmon-fly patterns have been devised on what might be called a tie-and-try basis, and it is not the wish of the author to detract from them in any way. As a matter of fact, if it hadn't been for the author's curiosity as to *why* a salmon would take some of the more common standard patterns, the underlying principles of fly design, based upon the natural insect, would not have been sought.

It is to be noted that both the bodies and wings of the artificial flies are quite thin, much smaller than indicated by the natural insect. The reason for this is that the light illuminating the window of the fish originates in an arc of approximately 174°, but, by refraction or bending as it enters the water, this arc is compressed to approximately 97°. This compression of the light causes objects illuminated by it to also appear compressed.

The artificial flies illustrated are strictly amateur patterns developed by the author over the past twenty years and, as they are not tied commercially, the dressings are given. Incidentally, they have proved to be killing patterns on a great many Canadian rivers in New Brunswick, Nova Scotia, Cape Breton and Newfoundland. They have also been tried with good results in Iceland and Norway, and worked well in British Columbia for steelheads, a close relative of the Atlantic salmon.

In view of the existing evidence it seems reasonable to conclude that the Atlantic salmon does take food in fresh water and that the artificial fly, which it mistakes for food, *is* related to and suggestive of that food. It is the author's hope that other fly-fishers will pursue this line of reasoning and thereby add to their own enjoyment as well as to the sum total of the knowledge of nature, which is the beginning and end of all things.

STONE FLY
(PERLA CAPITATA)
YELLOW STONE
(STRONG LIGHT)

Tag . . . Flat red tinsel
Tail . . . G. P. crest and Indian crow
Body . . . ½ flat gold tinsel, ½ black floss ribbed with gold oval tinsel
Hackle . . . Dark-blue dun cock's hackle and brown partridge
Wings . . . G. P. crest, dyed red and yellow, veiled with widgeon and brown mallard, G. P. crest dyed green and blue on top
Cheeks . . . Jungle cock
Hook . . . #4 and #6 low-water salmon
Head . . . Black

STONE FLY
(PERLA CAPITATA)
YELLOW STONE #2
(LOW LIGHT)

Tag . . . Flat green tinsel
Tail . . . G. P. crest, dyed green, and kingfisher
Body . . . ½ flat silver tinsel, ½ black floss ribbed with silver oval tinsel

Hackle . . . Medium-blue dun cock's hackle, and grey partridge
Wings . . . G. P. crest, dyed green and blue, veiled with widgeon; G. P. crest, dyed red and yellow over-all
Hook . . . #4 and #6 low-water salmon
Head . . . Red

MAY FLY
(HEXAGENIA OCCULTA)
IRIS DUN
(STRONG LIGHT)

Tag . . . Gold oval tinsel
Tail . . . Blue dun and claret cock's hackle
Body . . . Green floss (radiant), ribbed with gold oval tinsel
Hackle . . . Blue dun cock's hackle, and claret cock's hackle
Wings . . . G. P. crest, dyed red and yellow, green, and blue, veiled with unbarred mandarin or wood duck
Hook . . . #6 and #8 low-water salmon
Head . . . Red

MAY FLY
(HEXAGENIA OCCULTA)
IRIS SPINNER
(LOW LIGHT)

Tag . . . Flat green tinsel
Tail . . . Blue dun and magenta cock's hackle
Body . . . Flat red tinsel, ribbed with gold oval tinsel
Hackle . . . Light-blue dun and magenta cock's hackle
Wings . . . G. P. crest, dyed green and blue, veiled with unbarred mandarin or wood duck, with G. P. crest dyed red and yellow over-all
Hook . . . #6 and #8 low-water salmon
Head . . . Red

SEDGE FLY
(STENOPHYLAX)
IRIS SEDGE
(STRONG LIGHT)

Tag . . . Flat green tinsel
Tail . . . G. P. crest and Indian crow
Body . . . Black floss, ribbed with gold oval tinsel
Hackle . . . Medium blue and claret cock's hackle
Wings . . . G. P. crest, dyed red and yellow, veiled with barred mandarin or wood duck and brown mallard, G. P. crest dyed green and blue over top
Hook . . . #2 and #4 Dee salmon
Head . . . Black

SEDGE FLY
(STENOPHYLAX)
IRIS SEDGE #2
(LOW LIGHT)

Tag . . . Flat red tinsel
Tail . . . G. P. crest, dyed green, and kingfisher
Body . . . ½ flat silver tinsel, ½ light-blue floss, ribbed with silver oval tinsel
Hackle . . . Light-blue and magenta cock's hackle
Wings . . . G. P. crest, dyed green and blue, veiled with unbarred mandarin or wood duck, with G. P. crest dyed red and yellow over top
Cheeks . . . Kingfisher
Hook . . . #2 and #4 Dee salmon
Head . . . Red

MINNOW
(BLACK-NOSED DACE)
LADY IRIS
(STRONG LIGHT)

Tag . . . Silver oval tinsel
Tail . . . G. P. crest and Indian crow
Body . . . Flat silver tinsel ribbed with silver oval tinsel
Hackle . . . Yellow cock's hackle
Wings . . . Pair of yellow cock's hackle, swan, dyed red, yellow, green and blue, veiled with badger cock's hackle
Cheeks . . . Jungle cock
Hook . . . #2 low-water salmon
Head . . . Red

MINNOW
(BLACK-NOSED DACE)
LORD IRIS
(LOW LIGHT)

Tag . . . Silver oval tinsel
Tail . . . G. P. tippet
Body . . . Embossed silver tinsel, ribbed with silver oval tinsel
Hackle . . . Orange cock's hackle
Wings . . . Pair of orange cock's hackle, swan, dyed red, orange, green and blue, veiled with badger cock's hackle
Cheeks . . . Jungle cock
Hook . . . #2 low-water salmon
Head . . . Red

16.

The
Latter-Day Elect

Tell you what. With Jennings, I feel that we really finished the trip we set out to take, and that any time and/or space we have left could be put to better use for some listings rather than for any more samplings.

You may think this is reneging, but it really isn't. It's not a case of "one thought for you and two for me," either. Travel is supposed to be such an acid test of friendship, and I figure if I didn't lose you after the first forty or fifty pages, you and I are good for the distance.

And as for the supply of books, there must be at least as many—no, looking them over I see there are even more—that we haven't dipped into as there are that we have sampled up to here.

But now it's not really so much a matter of your time and attention span I'm worried about (on that score I'd be glad to give you a testimonial if you have any use for one), but two entirely different problems that I feel we're up against at this point.

First, among the many shortages that now beleaguer our beloved but obviously benighted country, one of the first to be bruited about, before anybody said anything concerning gasoline, was a paper shortage. And I'm just scared that if we try to go on too unconscionably long beyond where we are now, we might get rudely interrupted by the news that "the paper is all."

Second, when we get past Preston Jennings, who died only a little over a decade back, we're getting uncomfortably close to today, and that brings up another question. What do we do about living authors?

It's a hell of a time to bring this up, I realize, since the meandering path we've taken up to here is strewn with references to them. But except for a couple of cases where I deferred to guys I deemed better qualified than I am to talk about specific junctures of angling history (both John McDonald and Sparse Grey Hackle on the subject of Theodore Gordon, for instance), we've so far confined our attention to living authors to citations of them, in one connection or another, without actually dipping into their pages.

I think we ought to leave it that way. You know I've never been timid or coy about admitting, both personally and professionally, that some of my best friends are authors. And the pages of both *The Well-Tempered Angler* and *The Joys of Trout* are peppered with them. But I think there's a point beyond which even friendship shouldn't be strained, and I'm afraid we're approaching it now.

So from here on, where we have occasion to refer to a book by a living author, we'll just leave it at that; I'll refer you to it, without directly dipping into it. After all, books by people still living are easy to come by. All the best ones, that proved their worth by going out of print, are now being reprinted right and left. And those that aren't currently in print are pretty generally to be found in libraries.

I may be oversensitive on this score, but we've been going along, following the mainstream of angling literature, making random casts wherever we felt like it, as if all the fishing in print were in the public domain. And indeed most of what we've covered up to now has been. But we're beginning to get to what I can only liken to posted waters. Living authors have rights, and as a longtime editor I of all people ought to be the last to treat them cavalierly.

For instance, there's a book I'm practically drooling to dip into right now, called *Through the Fish's Eye*, but it's a 1973 book. The authors, Mark Sosin and John Clark, are very much around. I don't know John Clark, but I know Mark Sosin, and I know it'd be perfectly all right with him if we waded right into *Through the Fish's Eye* and I pointed out a half dozen passages that I'll bet anything would raise your eyebrows right up to your hairline.

Still, you don't need me to lead you to a book like that, which has been widely publicized and displayed and reviewed, including by me, in *The Flyfisher,* where I put it right up on the select and still uncrowded shelf occupied by Brian Curtis, whose book *The Life Story of the Fish, His Manners and Morals* I've so long touted as the one book every angler owes it to himself to read. In *The Joys of Trout* I quoted Curtis at great length, but Curtis is long dead, and his book has been unaccountably neglected. Quite the contrary is the case with *Through the Fish's Eye,* which I hailed as a welcome newcomer to "angling literature's least crowded category."

I was making the point that most current offerings in this field are classifiable as Instructional or Inspirational—describable either as "Gee, fellas, wait'll you've tried this new wrinkle," on the one hand, or "Come fish and invite your soul with genial ol' me," on the other, and in between there is only the very rare and much to be prized fishing book that tries to get you, if not to think like a fish (because it can be argued that fish can't really think), then at least to see the fish's world from his point of view. It's not an easy trick, by any means, and it's been only seldom attempted, but it's been brought off beautifully in *Through the Fish's Eye.*

So get it, by all means, and read it, if you haven't already, because I'm morally certain you'll enjoy it. But speaking of "seldom attempted," it occurs to me to wonder now, as it didn't then, at the moment when I was carried away by my enthusiasm for this new book, just how long it has been since this far from easy trick was last brought off, except by Brian Curtis, who died in 1960.

Well, I don't have long to wonder, because here, practically within arm's reach in the orderly chaos of my jumbled shelves of fishing books, is a bright and shining answer, in the form of a slender volume called *My Friend the Trout,* by Eugene V. Connett.

Yes, he of the Derrydale Press, whom we last encountered in the little afterword he appended to the original Derrydale 1935 edition of Preston Jennings's *A Book of Trout Flies.*

To pick up *My Friend the Trout* now, after reading Brian Curtis and the new Sosin-Clark *Angler's Guide to Gamefish Behavior* is to experience that thrill of recognition—that authentic little chill of the hair's rising on the back of your neck—that you get whenever you realize how some angling author in the past has foreshadowed another's discoveries of much later on.

It's the way I felt when I first read Mottram, long after I'd read Hewitt and even Marinaro, and realized what extraordinary perception he had had in 1915, to anticipate the "mysteries" they were solving, to our wide-eyed astonishment and delight, in the middle of the century.

It's the way I felt on rereading Al McClane's chapter on the dry fly "upstream and down" in his 1953 volume, *The Practical Fly Fisherman*, at that very moment in the nineteen seventies when the applause was still ringing in the rafters over the heterodox innovations of those Young Turks, Swisher and Richards, and the magician of the "sudden inch," the new master of the "worked" dry fly, Leonard Wright.

Sure, I joined in the applause for the new wizards, and I still applaud them, because they're keeping things moving in the right direction, but it still doesn't keep me from coming to my senses, late or soon, with the realization that indeed in this field, as in so many others, there is truly nothing new under the sun.

As witness, in the light of all this new scientific knowledge we're now all agog with, some of the fundamental truths that Gene Connett hit upon, by the simple process of ratiocination, as long ago as the beginning of the sixties, when *My Friend the Trout* was first published.

Says Connett, on page 93 of *My Friend the Trout*, "As far as I can see it works just about as well without the hackle as with it."

Tossed off just like that, almost as an aside, isn't that a startlingly prophetic remark, when recalled after more than a dozen years, just when we are all in prayer-meeting saying Amen to the "new" gospel of the no-hackle fly, as propounded by those radical evangelists, Swisher and Richards?

Connett's rationale of writing *My Friend the Trout* in 1961, his fifth fishing book since 1924, was "to make clear the difference in fishing with one's own point of view in control, rather than that of the trout." He had fished for fifty years, assuming like all the right-thinking young men in the years just before World War I that the dry fly was "the proper way" to take trout. His observation was that the fisherman's equipment had changed a lot in those fifty years, whereas the equipment of the trout hadn't changed an iota. The logic of "progress" would lead you to expect that with all the improved equipment and knowledge on the one side, the odds would have shifted correspondingly in the angler's favor, but if anything trout had become over the course of that fifty years harder than ever to catch. This was the dilemma to which Connett addressed himself in *My Friend the Trout*, and that is what makes this little book one of the most valuable, for rereading every so often, that an angler can have.

Books like that are all too rare. Every season sees the advent of new wonder guides to everything that concerns the angler, from knots to nits, and how to pick them—all calculated to refine still further even the most sophisticated trouter's approach to his quarry. The knowledge-content of some of these new books is awesome. But the wisdom-quotient that may be expected to be distilled out of all that knowledge is minimal.

Connett, in effect, gets us to forget for a moment how much we know about trout fishing, and concentrate instead on what the trout knows. The trout knows nothing about trout fishing, or there wouldn't be any. He doesn't even know what a hook is. The trout, indeed, is very like that ignoramus, for whom we all have such lofty contempt, who "doesn't know anything about art but knows what he likes."

The trout likes what he recognizes as familiar and accustomed, in all his surroundings, and by the same token, being a creature governed by instinct and unable to reason, dislikes anything and everything that is unfamiliar and unrecognizable. Unlike us, trout are not looking for something new and different, to eat or to do. Unlike us, trout are not bored by the constant repetition of eating and doing the same things over and over again. Trout, being animals, are perfectly content with just more of the same, as long as they live, and unlike us, are in no way concerned with changing or bettering their lot. They are not adventurous, as we are, because adventure to them, as indeed to all animals, is something they don't have to seek, that comes looking for them when they least expect it. The only adventures that trout like and seek were summed up in three words long ago by David Grayson in a book title: *Adventures in Contentment.*

The wonder of a book like *My Friend the Trout* is that, at least while you're reading it, it gets you to concentrate totally upon what's important, not to you, but to the trout. One of its key sentences is, "We all see what we're looking for and don't notice other things." A trout isn't looking for your waders, for instance, and won't notice them, unless and until you move. Stand still long enough to smoke a cigarette, and you're as much a part of his underwater scenery as a log or a piling.

Maybe I sound as if I were oversimplifying, and of course to a degree I am, but so is Connett. He simplifies to the extent of including only significant detail, and skips the rest, but all the better for his purpose which is to get you to concentrate on the essentials. In his chapter on the trout's vision, which is nowhere nearly as detailed and comprehensive as Sosin and Clark's in *Through the Fish's Eye*, Connett tells you about as much concerning the role of the rods and the cones in the trout's retina as you'll probably remember no matter how much you may read about it—that trout have both, whereas bats have only the rods, and snakes and lizards only the cones; that the rods are withdrawn from the image plate in the retina by day, and contact it by night, whereas the cones work the day shift and are withdrawn at night, with the consequence that trout see color by day and only form (and ultraviolet rays) at night. Connett and a friend found that a wet mole fly, apparently tied of materials luminous to ultraviolet rays, was the only thing they could get some wise old browns to take in the pitch-black darkness of a moonless night.

My Friend the Trout is full of things like that. If I'd read it better and oftener I'd have saved ten years in coming to the use of Preston Jennings's *Isonychia bicolor* nymph whenever I find myself fishing in only partial light or complete darkness.

Maybe the title is off-putting. Perhaps *My Friend the Trout* has too much of a Pollyanna or Goody Two-Shoes sound for the modern sophisticated angling reader to feel impelled to look it up or even pick it out on a shelf among other fishing books.

I know titles can work against books, most unfairly. I feel sure that if Odell Shepard had given his one fishing book almost any other title than *Thy Rod and Thy Creel*, his name would be venerated by this generation of fly fishermen. But the combination of the two archaic possessives and the word "creel," plus the holiness of the title's pun on the phrase from the Lord's Prayer about "thy rod and thy staff," must have done a lot to earn it one of the swiftest passages to oblivion ever meted out to an angling book.

I've never seen a printed reference to it, and Howard Walden, in *Angler's Choice*, is the only anthologist who ever quoted it. It was published as far back as 1930, by Edwin Valentine Mitchell, an almost-private printing by a Hartford publisher, in Connecticut where Shepard lived at the time. But it was produced by the Vail-Ballou Press, like many well-known books before and since, and its distribution was handled, according to the title page, by Dodd, Mead in New York, who were never to my knowledge accused of sneaking the likes of Rudyard Kipling into American print. Nor was its author exactly unknown; at least in academic circles Odell Shepard was pretty well known, and this was his *seventh* book.

I've been going through fishing books like a termite, at least since 1950, but I have never to this day come across a listing of Odell Shepard's *Thy Rod and Thy Creel,* even in the New York Public Library, which I've infested the last nine summers, and where I thought they had everything. It took William Humphrey, author of that modern salmon-angling classic *The Spawning Run,* to call it to my attention, which he did in a letter after he had read *The Joys of Trout,* saying that he liked no other angling book better than Shepard's, not even excepting Walton's.

It was only after he had lent me his copy, and I had read it at a gulp, that I recognized a passage as having been anthologized somewhere, and it took Nick Lyons, who had just finished serving Howard Walden as editor for the Crown Classics reissue of the Derrydale volumes, *Upstream and Down* and *Big Stony,* to tell me where. Apparently even that taste of Odell Shepard's prose, above the unfamiliar by-line and the unenticing title, had not been enough to send me off in panting search

for a copy of the book, and if Bill Humphrey hadn't written me about it, I would undoubtedly have missed it entirely.

Today I can think of nobody who has written about angling more beautifully than Odell Shepard, at least since Walton, and I have almost the same feeling about Shepard's book that I have about Walton's, that it is almost a disservice to quote from it, because like *The Compleat Angler* itself, it should be swallowed whole, and then savored again at leisure.

Shepard himself called Walton's "the best book about fishing ever written," and with that, as with every other word Shepard wrote, I fully agree. But Shepard also forecast his own book's immediate future with uncanny accuracy, saying as early as the third page of his introductory chapter, "A Trial Cast":

There is of course no "public demand" for such a book as I am shadowing forth—but then, all fishermen know what the public is, else they would not show such eagerness to get away from it. Speaking among friends, the general public does not know how to demand any good thing; it does not really want good things until they are provided; and if all writers had paid strict attention to the law of supply and demand we should now have exactly no literature whatever. Consider furthermore, that there is no great public demand for brook trout, and that what demand there is might be supplied by hatcheries at a huge saving in effort and expense. This book, like fishing itself, is either a luxury or else it is nothing. . . .

A few brothers of the angle who see this book may take it a little hard that I seem to speak of fishing for trout as though there were no other kind of fishing. My title should have indicated to them that I have not tried to cover the whole range of angling in all its kinds, for one does not put a tarpon or a sword-fish into a creel, and even the larger salmon and bass are seldom so disposed. Angling, like any other thing, is best defined in its purest and finest examples.

Maybe, like the selection that Howard Walden made in his 1947 anthology, I have not given you enough of Odell Shepard in those two paragraphs to give you more than a hint of the redolence of the book's "perfume and charm," but I'll make you any suitable small wager you like that once you've inhaled the verbal magic of that first short chapter, "A Trial Cast," you'll be as drugged by it as the swine before Circe, and you won't want to be snapped out of it when you come to the last paragraph:

And now to all good anglers who have read to the end of this book—the patience elsewhere learned standing them here in good stead—I wish as good a day as that, and a larger catch, when next they go a-fishing. May they cast their flies into beauty and draw them back over the waters of peace.

God. Who but a poet would have had the sense to leave those three "goods" serenely alone in their place—good anglers, and good stead and good day—and not give the second and third "goods" some the-saurus-spawned synonymous alternatives? Sure enough, looking over to the left of the title page, the listing of other books by Odell Shepard shows that the first one, *A Lonely Flute,* was a book of verse. The rest, which preceded this one on fishing, were *Shakespeare Questions,* which has a test-bookish sound, *Bliss Carman* (the Western poet, and *Thy Rod and Thy Creel* mentions that Shepard's own fishing began in the West, though it came to its zenith in England), *The Harvest of a Quiet Eye, The Joys of Forgetting* (a nice title, from which I unwittingly stole in part myself), and *The Lore of the Unicorn.* None sounds like a best seller rampant, but I do seem to remember hearing from either William Humphrey or Nick Lyons, the only two people I ever discussed him with (everybody else saying O'Dell Who?) that he won some sort of prize for another biography, and I think it was of Bronson Alcott. That would indicate that he had at least a measure of appreciation and a

modicum of fame before he died, though he certainly never won any appreciable amount of either from *Thy Rod and Thy Creel.*

Doesn't it make you want to see the book given another chance, under a new title? Of course, that's a silly question if you haven't read it at all. But that's the way it makes me feel. It's too late for our belated amends to do him any good, I know, because he's been dead these twenty years or more, but that's as the wink of an eye in the long annals of this sport, and I'm not thinking so much of making it up to him for our neglect as to the oncoming generations of fisherman-readers. If ever there was a book of our century that I'd like to see commended to the anglers of the next, this would have to be it.

I could be wrong about the title for that matter. Probably titles alone neither make books sell nor keep them from selling, any more than covers do. (Still, magazine covers are the most favored explanation, in hindsight, for the success or failure of given issues.) But I had one book with what everybody agreed was a really good title, *Toys of a Lifetime,* about a lot of things I felt wouldn't warrant a whole book each, and its sale was catastrophic. Naturally, the way a parent dotes on a backward or handicapped child, it was my favorite, of all my books, but Max Schuster of Simon and Schuster made me see why it failed. He said people don't want to read about a lot of things, they want to read about one thing; at least one thing at a time. "Arnold, you're suffering from hardening of the categories."

But if that satisfies me about my own favorite failure, it doesn't begin to explain Odell Shepard's, because he proclaimed his intention to stick to one thing right from the outset, and did it, and beautifully. The book as a whole is of a sustained loveliness that I find downright drenching, and I'd rather read it again tonight than catch a four-pound brown tomorrow morning. So maybe it was the title, at that.

Robert Traver, who made enough of a killing, both book and movie, from *Anatomy of a Murder* that he could retire from his longtime Upper Michigan judgeship and devote himself to fishing spring and summer and thinking and writing about it fall and winter, first celebrated his newly earned leisure with a book called *Trout Madness.* Having mellowed, though not too much, since then he wanted to call his new book *The Joys of Trout.* When he heard I'd beat him to that one he was disappointed, though I feel sure it couldn't have mattered to him very long. If I'd written one book called *Trout Madness,* I'd consider *Trout Magic* virtually heaven-sent as the title for another, and that's the title he got on the rebound.

Thought we weren't going to mess around with living authors. Thought we'd settled that — thought we'd settled it with flowers, so to speak.

Quiet, please. Can't you see I'm thinking? And if it helps at all to know what I'm thinking — I'm thinking we're lost.

All right, I'll think out loud. I know I said after we left Jennings, and we were getting on up pretty close to today, we'd have to figure out some way to cover the rest of the water, as it were, without any more of this protracted fishing around in print.

But then I thought of Connett and Shepard and after all they *are* both dead. For that matter, Joe Brooks is dead now, too, and I thought *Trout Fishing* was the best thing of its kind since Bergman. Still, that's virtually a current book, as angling works are reckoned. A title's hardly broken in until it's been around a season or two, and acquired its listing in all the tackle catalogs. In fact, with the spate of angling books there's been in recent years, you almost need a guide to the listings.

And maybe that's our cue, to find the best way to use the time and space we've got left together on this trip. About all we've got to lose, at this point, is your patience, and you're a better judge of that than I am. We can at least give it a try.

Annotated List of
SOME CHOICE FISHING IN PRINT
Since 1935

The date is arbitrary, of course, but 1935 was the year of the original Derrydale edition of *A Book of Trout Flies,* and I did say we'd try to take off from Preston Jennings and come on down to date. And since we'll really have to pack it in after this, I'll try very hard not to pass up anything good.

ATHERTON, JOHN. *The Fly and the Fish*

This is a classic, or the term is without meaning. Originally a private printing by the Anglers Club of New York, it was issued in a trade edition by Macmillan in 1951, but that too soon became scarce and *The Fly and the Fish* suffered that temporary eclipse that I always used to think was the inevitable fate of all the best fishing books of our time. In this case, rescue from oblivion came with a boxed reprint by Freshet Press, Rockville Centre, New York, in 1971. Atherton was as much artist with the flyrod as with the brush, and while there's almost a tactile pleasure in looking at the drawings he made for this book, there's no less artistry in the text. Atherton is particularly good on getting you to treat the wet fly and the nymph with the same respect that in his day was commonly reserved only for the dry fly. This is a book that no fisherman will ever really outgrow, and we all owe a debt to Freshet Press for keeping his memory green. He was buried beside his beloved Battenkill, and William Herrick contributed a poem about that streamside scene to *The Gordon Garland* in 1965. A fitting tribute to a great angler and a rare spirit.

BAKER, R. PALMER, JR. *The Sweet of the Year*

This is a sleeper, that will someday be discovered all over again. One section of it was published in *The Gordon Garland,* and the book itself came out in the fall of that same year, 1965. It was just ahead of the great wave of resurgent interest in fly fishing that has since carried lesser books to greater prominence. This book has all the surprise charm of an inadvertent stumbling upon a secret stream, somewhere back of beyond, on a day when you didn't expect to get in any fishing at all, that turns into a day you remember the rest of your life. Actually, I have "remembered" a stream, nights between waking and sleeping when I was thinking back over past fishing scenes, only to realize that it wasn't a stream I ever actually fished at all, but was only recalling from reading about it in that little book of Baker's. Has that ever happened to you? I swear, outside of Haig-Brown's pages, it has hardly ever happened to me. So *The Sweet of the Year* is a book to look up and cherish. It won't be all that easy to find, but it's worth the effort.

BASHLINE, L. JAMES. *Night Fishing for Trout*

No thing of beauty, despite the 1973 Freshet Press imprint and the Joan Stoliar credit line for the book and jacket design. The illustrations are sheer road-company Webster, as cartoons, and the whole thing has a sleazy look. But try not to be put off by that, because this book comes in the special category, *hors concours,* that around magazines we always term "great even if it's bad." So much of my own trout fishing is done in the dark that I'm probably overprejudiced in its favor, but I really don't know of anything else like this, and Jim Bashline is "the one that can do it." He's a "just the facts" sort of writer, so don't look for any Connett-Jennings subtleties about rods and cones or ultraviolet perception, and don't be turned off by how astonishingly old-fashioned a lot of his fly-pattern recommendations are. Night fishing is a whole separate world of trout madness, and Bashline is one of its maniacs of the first magnitude. He's taken some whopping fish by what you and I would probably consider the least likely means. But this is a crazy realm where it's fatal to try to talk sense, so it behooves us to shut up and listen. I know, from my own experience, that nothing you'd expect to work at night ever does, and vice versa. And Bashline has the endorsement, in the introduction, of that fisherman's fisherman, Charles K. Fox.

BATES, JOSEPH D., JR. *Atlantic Salmon Flies and Fishing*

Color me prejudiced, if you will, but this is the first book by Col. Bates in over a score of years that I could really embrace with unqualified enthusiasm. Even forgetting the 1947 volume on spinning, I felt through a subsequent run of books that Colonel Joe was a sort of Tom Sawyer of angling authors, getting all the rest of the gang to whitewash the fence for him. Collections of flies by this guy and that, and — oh, I don't know, shaving off other people's beards I guess is how you'd put it — so admitting and knowing of my prejudice, I came to this one all set to scoff, and remained to cheer, if not pray. Because this book has that old true magic — the unique thrill that can only be experienced when you're on one end of a line and an Atlantic salmon is on the other.

There are about forty books on trout for each one on salmon, and by no means does every book on salmon give you that authentic spine-tingling feel, but this one does. It's not cheap, but it's a beautifully made, and boxed, book published in Harrisburg, Pa., by Stackpole Books in 1970. Besides, what's a mere fifteen dollars or so, compared to the cost of practically anything pertaining to salmon fishing nowadays? As the Guide Michelin would put it, this book is "worth the journey."

BERGMAN, RAY. *Trout*

To paraphrase a beer slogan, this was for a whole generation considered the one fishing book to have when you're not having more than one. Or, as I've said before, this can be likened to Dr. Spock's baby book, for quite literally a whole generation of fishermen grew up on it, from 1938 when it was first published by Penn Publishing Co. in Philadelphia, and 1944 and 1952 when it was brought out in new editions by Knopf in New York, and kept constantly in print ever since. A hardy perennial.

BROOKS, JOE. *Trout Fishing*

His swan song, published by Harper & Row in New York just before his death in Montana in the summer of 1972. Here again, as with the other Joe, Col. Bates, after twenty years of books that left me feeling vaguely so-whattish, came one that I fell for all the way. I rate it right alongside Bergman's *Trout*, which it supplements if not supplants. Since comparisons are invidious, let's just leave it that between them these two books tell the trout fisherman everything that he needs to know, or can ever learn from books.

CROWE, JOHN. *A Book of Trout Lore*

This is an A. S. Barnes title, dating back to 1947, and it deserves reprinting. This is another of those underestimated books that came out at the dark moment when too many ex-fly fishermen were out chasing after the false gods of the fixed spool, and this must have seemed more quaintly outdated at that time than it ever would again. But it's the kind of homey, warm, almost folksy book that makes me think we really ought to have a third category in angling books. To the "instructional" and "inspirational" into which they've always been divided, we ought to put a buffer between, called simply "devotional." This would qualify.

CURTIS, BRIAN. *The Life Story of the Fish: His Manners and Morals*

Oh god. What can I say about this one that I haven't already said, every which way I could say it? This is the book I found in, of all places, my own library, where it was stuck away in the bottom of a magazine rack, and had either forgotten or never realized that I had it, and then one day when I came across it in the course of an attic to cellar search for another book, read it with a sustained shout of Eureka and began telling all and sundry about it, in the biblical manner, that is, shouted from the house tops. It's not a fishing book, of course, but a layman's outline of ichthyology. Still, I don't see how anybody could read it without becoming a better, and more understanding, angler. First published in 1938, *The Life Story of the Fish* was published again in 1949 in a revised edition, and then reissued in a Dover reprint in 1961, just shortly after the author's death. One of the most idiosyncratic books this side of *Alice in Wonderland,* it is lit up by the author's droll and quiet wit in a way that makes even the most detailed passages a sustained delight. Surely there can be few more delectable tales in print, on any subject, than the Brian Curtis account of the spawning migration of "a little smeltlike fish six inches long" punctuated at one point by the author's sly aside that "I would rather be a grunion than an eel." This book is one of the rarest treats in all the literature open to what Walton called "the perusal of most anglers."

EVERETT, FRED. *Fun with Trout*

Aside from the felicitous title, which I think of as lighting up any bookshelf with a ruminatory smile, I don't suppose there's any great crying need for this 1952 Harrisburg title to be reprinted, at least as long as so many more significant angling volumes are still waiting their turn to be retrieved from undeserved neglect. But it is one of those books you look back on with a warm feeling, even though on taking it down from a relatively little-visited shelf you aren't suddenly smitten with any very shattering revelations. Still, I'd save a small corner for this, in that third category, between instructional and inspirational, that I class as devotional.

FARSON, NEGLEY. *Going Fishing*

I had this 1943 Harcourt Brace title as one of six "underestimated books" in *The Joys of Trout,* though the list wasn't my own and I hadn't laid hands on a copy of this at the time, though I had read and highly recommended the other five. Since then I've made up the deficiency, and now I can add, with the poet, "and oh 'tis true, 'tis true." It gives off the authentic scent, and you know it from the very first page, with its deprecatory beginning—"This is just the story of some rods and the places they take you to"—but the self-deprecation is almost immediately given the lie by such luminous sentences as "I love rods, I suppose, with the same passion that a carpenter, a violinist, or a Monaco pigeon shot love their implements" and a related reference to a rod as "This magic wand has revealed to me some of the loveliest places on earth." Just go along, and enjoy, as Hank Siegel says, some of the grandest reading in all angling literature.

FENNELLY, JOHN F. *Steelhead Paradise*

Another out-of-the-way item, published in Vancouver, B.C., by Mitchell Press in 1963, but printed again in 1970, and worth looking up. The author is a retired Chicago investment banker, but no literary accreditation is really relevant—you either get the real feel of steelhead and salmon or you don't, and in this little book of 114 pages you do, whereas in some bigger and more pretentious works you don't.

FLICK, ART. *Streamside Guide to Naturals and Their Imitations*

Just because Preston Jennings "poisoned" me on this one is no reason to go on nursing a grudge against it. It's a major work, and I'd be a fool to say otherwise. Published by Putnam's in 1947, it had a revised reissue by Crown in 1969 and the new life it deserves. Obviously one of the most valuable and useful pocket books a fly fisher can have.

FOX, CHARLES K. *Rising Trout*

Here's a note I found in my copy. (Whether Charlie asked me for this, or indeed if I ever sent it, I have no idea, but if I said it then I'll say it again.): The Chaucer of the Le Tort has taken a great step forward, from *This Wonderful World of Trout*. That was a fascinating book, and one that deserves a permanent place in every fly fisher's library. (Freshet Press has since agreed with me on that point, at least, with a reissue of that 1963 work in 1971.) But *Rising Trout* is even better, for it combines the lore and the beauties of days spent astream on flowing trout waters with an element of "how-to" that is on the postgraduate level. You may think you're a thinking angler, but don't be too sure, until you have subjected yourself to the solution of your most persistent and difficult angling problems in the way Charlie Fox outlines in *Rising Trout.* You could almost call this book "the thinking man's streamside guide to the ultimate in trout tactics."

Charlie Fox not only tells you his way with heavy trout on light terminal tackle, and his way will stack up with the very best, but he also documents his every judgment with a wealth of fishing wisdom from the great minds of angling's past. The result is that you enjoy as you learn, and to your surprise you find that thinking can be fun, when it is applied to some of the most persistent problems of our sport.

GORDON, SID. *How to Fish from Top to Bottom*

There are books, like Walton, that you can read and reread all your life. There are many others that seem to you, once you've read them, empty as a nutshell when you try to come back to them. There have been books that I read and remembered, from when I was a kid in high school or college, with near-ecstasy of savored general remembrance, that I couldn't wade through when I picked them up again in eager anticipation of renewing their delights, a decade later. *South Wind,* by Norman Douglas, was one, and *The Brook Kerith,* by George Moore, was another. I had thought of them both as favorites, until I found that I couldn't get through thirty pages of either of them without being bored blind. By contrast, I was "underwhelmed" by *Alice in Wonderland* and *Through the Looking Glass* when I read them first at what would have been generally considered the appropriate age, the onset of the teens, and then "discovered" them with delighted whoops about a dozen years later.

I can pick up Theodore Gordon, as represented in *The Complete Fly Fisherman,* John McDonald's collection of Gordon's Notes and Letters, intending only to check something, and find myself immediately immersed, and soon in need of a loud alarm to snap me out of it, and get me to go back to whatever I was supposed to be doing before I goofed off with Gordon instead. But try as I will, I can't read the other Gordon, Sid, who wrote *How to Fish from Top to Bottom,* straight through again to win a bet. I read it when it came out, in 1955, and found it most informative. It was stuffed with so much firsthand observation, and tips and suggestions, that I could well see how it might serve some people as a virtual bible, and I wasn't surprised that Charlie Fox gave it a thumping endorsement ("Best Book on Fishing I've Ever Read") on the jacket, though I was not unaware that Charlie was working at Stackpole, its publisher, at the time. But though I remembered being impressed by its chapters on nymphs and on stream improvement, I found I hadn't dog-eared a single page, either there or anywhere else in the book. Charlie's a better fisherman than I am, which we've proved every time I've fished his water on the Little Southwest Miramichi, so I'm quite ready to concede he may be a better reader, too. And Sid Gordon was a veteran of more than sixty years of fishing when he wrote the book. It stands to reason I must be wrong on this one. You'd better see for yourself on this one, and not let me put you off it.

GORDON, THEODORE (AND A COMPANY OF ANGLERS). *American Trout Fishing* (1965)

It's hard for me to say anything about this without sounding like the headwaiter pushing the roast duck, because I edited it, but I still want to register my impressions that this book, steady as its sale has been since 1965, is nonetheless underappreciated. It's the first American edition of the only sizable essay on fishing Theodore Gordon ever had published, and may well be the only survivor of his legendary lost manuscript that nobody could ever find after his death in 1915. This, the title essay of the volume, was published in London, in a huge handsome book called *Fishing at Home and Abroad,* limited to seven hundred and fifty copies, edited by Sir Herbert Maxwell, and its inclusion in this American book, fifty-three years later, was a sublime accident.

We were getting together, as the first publication of the then fledgling Theodore Gordon Flyfishers, a memorial volume called *The Gordon Garland,* to come out on the fiftieth anniversary of Gordon's death, and the more literate members had been asked to contribute something that was either directly about Gordon or could be interpreted as paying tribute to his memory. Ed Zern, who had turned in a lovely little piece called *A Day's Fishing,* had gone off to England, and promptly found this forgotten 1912 book with a piece in it by Gordon himself.

Thus at the very last minute our "round of devotions" to the memory of Theodore Gordon was enlarged to include a major piece of writing under Gordon's own by-line. So we had no compunction about re-titling *The Gordon Garland,* once our privately printed memorial edition had been published in 1965, for its issuance in a trade edition the next year, as *American Trout Fishing,* by Theodore Gordon "and a company of anglers"—all of us being delighted to reappear in print as so many accompanists to his solo performance. When the star attraction is a legendary figure like Theodore Gordon, brought back alive, so to speak, after more than half a century, we latter-day fishers could consider ourselves honored to appear in his presence as a train of his spear-carriers, or as coolies pulling his carriage.

Anyway, if you can't conveniently lay hands on a copy of *The Gordon Garland* itself, and they are scarce now, then you really ought to get a copy of its trade edition, *American Trout Fishing*, while they're still around. There's no better certificate of literacy, for any angler who wants to make even the minimum gesture toward being observant of the amenities of his sport. In fact, I would consider cover to cover reading of this and *The Complete Fly Fisherman: The Notes and Letters of Theodore Gordon* as the best short cut to obtaining the equivalent of a diploma as being, after a mere two books, a really well-read fisherman. I have little empathy for a bluffer's guide to any subject, but it does occur to me that anybody who has a reasonably retentive memory could make a very presentable showing, even among the scholars and gentlemen of the fly-fishing world, if all he had read in *American Trout Fishing* (or *The Gordon Garland*) was Ernie Schwiebert's "Homage to Henryville" and Ted Rogowski's "Cracker Barrel Discourse." He could talk such a good game, as it were, that even the experts would be bound to be impressed.

GROVE, ALVIN R., JR. *The Lure and Lore of Trout Fishing*

Having missed no chance to tout this book since its original appearance in 1951, I'm damned if I'll pass up another chance here, even at the risk of sounding like a stuck phonograph needle. I'll content myself with repeating just a bit of the last words I've said on the subject lately:

There are only a handful of books that are as basic as freshman English—that is, absolute prerequisites to being anything like well-read, by today's sophisticated angling standards. This is one of them.

And thanks to the 1971 Freshet Press reprint, copies of *The Lure and Lore of Trout Fishing* are no longer scarce as the proverbial gallinaceous dentures—so scarce in fact that I had to dig up my copy to lend to Freshet so they could copy it, mistakes and all, with a facsimile edition to relieve the shortage.

HACKLE, SPARSE GREY. *Fishless Days, Angling Nights*

One of the best of the many fine things Nick Lyons has done for fly fishing was to get Alfred Miller to expand and amplify his classic *Fishless Days,* which had long been available only as a private publication of the Anglers Club of New York, tantamount to saying that for most people it was simply unavailable. The act can only be compared to the preservation of some national treasure, as Sparse constitutes the last literary link to the glorious past, the golden days of Gordon, Hewitt and La Branche. The new material on Gordon alone made the book precious. Since Sparse Grey Hackle was nearing his ninth decade at the time (1971), it was prudent and sagacious of Lyons to nursemaid its completion with the gentle persistence that he devoted to the project. I only hope anglers a hundred years hence will have some way of knowing how much they owe Nick Lyons for his rescue of this and so many other worthy works from what surely would have been oblivion.

HAIG-BROWN, RODERICK. *Fisherman's Spring, Winter, Summer, Fall* (and a half dozen other classics)

What can I say, that you don't already know? In terms of literary value, Haig-Brown's work is the surest lasting contribution that our time has made to the mainstream of angling literature. English by birth, Canadian by residence, he's all-American in affectionate acceptance by literate anglers everywhere. All I can say is cherish his every word, because, certain as sun-up, it will be cherished by future generations of anglers after you.

HALL, JOHN INGLIS. *How to Fish a Highland Stream*

You certainly don't need me to tell you about Haig-Brown or Sparse Grey Hackle, or Grove either, for that matter, but on this one you do. So please sit up and pay attention, or you'll go right on missing a treat that I know you'd thank me for, if you ever find it. Make a note, or something.

The stream is the Truim in Scotland, and this book was published in 1960 by G. P. Putman's Sons, but in London, not here. I suppose because the author is British, and not otherwise well known, and the stream isn't famous either, the book was considered to be of only limited and regional appeal, and thus not a good commercial risk for simultaneous American publication. (Poor reasoning, really: who ever heard of Oz, before they read about it in the pages of L. Frank Baum, and who ever heard of *him,* before he wrote about Oz?)

Well, of course I exaggerate, because obviously this book doesn't have the universal appeal of *The Wizard of Oz,* or I wouldn't have to be telling you about it now. But I do regard it as an absolutely unique work in angling literature. For one thing, nobody but an angler could possibly read it. Anybody else would consider it an exhibit of the author's certifiable lunacy.

All it is, it's a trip you take to the Truim, and a relentless blow-by-blow account of your experience fishing it with John Inglis Hall, and it's as deadpanly factual as a news story in *The New York Times.* It's not a long book, either. But if you're even half as suggestible as I am, it'll leave you limp. Never in my reading experience has so much frustration been compressed into so few pages. Nor could anybody but an inveterate fly fisherman possibly get the *einfuhlung* of the almost ecstatic rage that the trip's successive and seemingly unending foul-ups induces. Any prudent reader would take the book's message as a fair warning that the Truim is a stream to stay away from at all costs. Naturally, what I got out of it — and I'm pretty sure you would too — is a twelve-year itch to fish the Truim before I die. Nowhere in print have I ever encountered such a vividly vicarious sensation of the frustration that is inherent in fly fishing. Nor do I know of any even remotely comparable example of the glorious truth that Robert Traver was hinting at when he characterized fly fishing as "one of the few pursuits left to man that it is fun even to fail at."

HUMPHREY, WILLIAM. *The Spawning Run*

I wish this could have been included, as it was originally meant to be, in *Fisherman's Bounty,* the best angling anthology to date. It was first printed as a short story in *Esquire* in June 1970 and was promised at the time to Nick Lyons for inclusion in the anthology, which was just then nearing its press date. But at the last minute somebody at Knopf got the idea of issuing it in book form all by itself, so it had to be pulled out of the collection. (How Nick Lyons can be so nice and still be so successful surpasses my understanding, but he relinquished it without a murmur.) Even in pocket size hard cover format it made a book of only 80 pages, including ample illustration, and at four fifty a copy that brought the reading cost per page of Humphrey's text up close to a dime — high even for an age as rampantly inflationary as ours. And it sold an astonishing number of copies — especially for a bad year like 1970 — around ten thousand, the last I heard. But the cost of joy has always been an infinite variable, and when you consider that this book celebrates, as well as any ever has, the joys of salmon fishing, which is not for nothing known as the sport of kings, I suppose the traffic will bear any cost. (After all, I do know salmon fishermen who paid a hundred dollars a copy for Ernie Schwiebert's *Salmon of the World* and that's only 54 pages, though they're many times the size of Humphrey's and 30 of them are in full color. Salmon fishing is rapidly approaching parity with the cost of yachting, which Morgan defined for all time as being more than you can afford if you have to ask how much it is.)

But even if vicarious salmon fishing is the only kind in your foreseeable future, if you've ever done any, or so much as wanted to, you'll have a high old time reading *The Spawning Run.* For one thing, it's as unabashedly American as anything written about Britain since *A Connecticut Yankee in King Arthur's Court,* and for another it's about as painless a primer of salmon fishing, its traditional techniques and mores, as I know in print.

KOLLER, LAWRENCE R. *Taking Larger Trout*

This was published by Little Brown in Boston as long ago as 1950 but it stands up very well today, despite the many newer bags of tricks that so widely we've hailed every few years ever since. It's worth going back to look at, even now. Some of his wrinkles will still surprise you, in terms of size of trout evoked, even though you are a confirmed disciple of such later evangelists as Swisher-Richards and Wright. (Nor should his 1963 coffee-table effort, *The Treasury of Angling* be completely forgotten either; it was a nicely nostalgic volume, with some lovely things in it.) Larry was always too gun-happy to live up to my ideal of the complete angler, but he was a dedicated fisherman, and his last wish was to be laid to rest beside his beloved Neversink, which he was, not long after *The Treasury of Angling* was published, though not before it was remaindered. Still, in those days, before the current renascence, it was still a badge of honor for a fishing book to be remaindered, so it seems to me that Larry at the very least deserves what they used to term, at Harvard football games, "a short cheer."

LAMPMAN, BEN HUR. *A Leaf from French Eddy*

A gem of purest ray serene. On this one, I inhale like an incense the very words on its dust jacket: To all men who seek to fathom the mystery and preserve the beauty created by sweet waters flowing towards the sea . . .

By then I'm gone, like the susceptible subject who hears the hypnotist saying only those first words, "You are now feeling sleepy, very, ve-ry, sleep . . ." Swoosh.

If I can get you to read only Brian Curtis, Ben Hur Lampman and Odell Shepard, I will count myself a success and you a soul forever saved for the greater glory of trout. Talk about "the perfume and the charm" that suffuses the best pages of angling literature; immerse yourself in these and you will be truly anointed, even baptized.

Hear Lampman on why men fish:

People try to explain it, although this is unnecessary, but nobody ever has been quite able to do so, not even Walton. But most fishermen are agreed there is a quality in trout fishing that approaches the ideal. It is like the pursuit and realization of a pleasing dream. The trout is its symbol of abundant reward. It is something like this: We know, of necessity, that we can never have all to which we aspire, and we realize, too, that the dreams of aspiration have a way of fading, and yielding, until they are gone beyond recovery, and we have but memories of them. Is it sad? No. That isn't it. This is the common experience of mankind. We are reconciled to it, or nearly so. Yet men must dream of a time, if it be no more than a single day, when their dreams shall come true, even as they dreamed them. Now the virtue of trout fishing is that it, of all pursuits, rewards the dreamer with realization of his dream. The trout are more beautiful than he remembered them as being, and the day, the scene and the occupation are at harmony. That is why men go trout fishing.

It has often been remarked by trout fishermen that, when they are about the affairs of stream and rod, the events of yesterday and the necessities of tomorrow are singularly dwarfed in importance. They seem somehow to lack for real significance. The beauty of stream and forest, the beauty of the fish, the agreeable nature of the employment—these are real. All else appears to be of little moment, and to wear an aspect of trickery, as though men were both betrayed into and by it. It is for this reason that men go trout fishing, vowing that they prefer it to other recreations. Physically weary as they are before the sun is high, the truth is they are resting. They have rediscovered the escape. The stream they fish is running through their hearts to bear away the frets and worries of yesterday and tomorrow. All fishermen will know how it is, though it is uncommonly difficult to explain.

But I despair of saying anything of Lampman half as good as every least and last thing he says on every one of the mere 100 pages allotted to his text in the precious little book compiled from his papers by Vernon S. Hidy. It was published in 1965, nine years after Lampman's death, in an edition limited to 950 numbered copies, under the salubrious title *A Leaf from French Eddy*, by the Touchstone Press,

Portland, Ore., and was characterized on the title page as Volume One of The Lampman Papers. But I understand this was followed by a trade edition, which is also seemingly out of print by now. It is worth waiting for, and surely it will be reissued sometime somehow or there is no justice at all in this purportedly free country.

LEISENRING, JAMES, AND HIDY, VERNON S. *The Art of Tying the Wet Fly and Fishing the "Flymph"*

Dial me for Leisenring and I'm afraid you'll get the answering service. I'm sorry, but with the best will in the world I've just never been able to get anything out of the Leisenring book that I felt was worth remembering, or wanted to put into practice on the stream. I felt that way with the original edition, that came out in '44, and I still felt that way when I tried again, after Nick Lyons put it back in print with a revised 1970 reprint, one of his first selections for the Crown Sportsmen's Classics series, with three new chapters added by Pete Hidy. I must be wrong. Maybe it's just because I haven't fished a wet fly, except in salmon patterns, since the early fifties, but somehow nothing Jim Leisenring could say or do or show in *The Art of Tying the Wet Fly* ever turned me on the least bit. Remembering Ernie Schwiebert's almost worshipful treatment of him, in "Homage to Henryville" and other places in his books, I feel it isn't fair to leave big Jim out of any even selective and subjective sort of honors list, with both Schwiebert and Nick Lyons so obviously ready and willing to outvote me on him. So all right, I'll grant what everybody already knows anyway, that he was a substantial and significant figure in early twentieth-century American angling practice. (That still doesn't make me like him as a writer. So was John Alden Knight.)

Tell you what, though, I will vote for Vernon S. Hidy with real enthusiasm. Now there's somebody I feel has been underappreciated, in his own right. He's been such a great proselytizer for Leisenring, it moves me to want to say "Speak for yourself, Pete." For my money, there's more of "the perfume and the charm" on almost any page of Hidy's *The Pleasures of Fly Fishing,* issued by Winchester Press in 1972, with a foreword by Sparse Grey Hackle, than I've ever been able to discern in all of Leisenring. And even as far back as a couple of decades before that, as editor of the *Creel,* the beautiful and distinctive organ of the McKenzie Fly Fishers out in Oregon, Pete Hidy was a trailblazer, in bringing a civilizing overlay of appreciation of the traditional and historic lore to the then generally rough and ready state of Western fly fishing in general. To my mind, V. S. Hidy can never be praised enough, for he showed the way, like a lantern in the dark, long before such journals as *The Flyfisher, Trout, Fly Fisherman Magazine,* and *The American Fly Fisher* were ever dreamed of. He is one of those rare spirits who could, almost single-handedly, give a sport a good name.

LEOPOLD, ALDO. *A Sand County Almanac*

You could look farther and do worse than settle on this 1949 volume as the dawn of the great awakening to the crucial significance of ecology and environment that became headline news some twenty years later. Aldo Leopold was concerned with both these matters long before Being Concerned became chic. If you didn't happen to get a free copy a few years back when Arthur Godfrey was giving them away by the hundreds, then it would still be worth your while, even now, to go out of your way to pick one up.

MARINARO, VINCENT; MCCLANE, A. J.; MCDONALD, JOHN.

Three of the elect. When the saints go marching in—that is, when the roll is called of the angling immortals of our time—these three will be of their number. And since our present purpose is rather to dwell on the things you might conceivably miss, there's obviously no point in my making any extended mention of them here. No fisherman above the literacy level of our sport can possibly be unaware of Marinaro's *A Modern Dry Fly Code*, McClane's *Standard Fishing Encyclopedia* or McDonald's *The Complete Fly Fisherman: The Notes and Letters of Theodore Gordon*. We need pause here no longer than it takes to genuflect.

MIGEL, J. MICHAEL (editor). *The Stream Conservation Handbook*

Now here, on the other hand, is the kind of book for which all available bells should be rung and every possible drum beaten. A book like this warrants the revival of the town crier's employment contract—its importance cannot be sufficiently impressed on every passerby short of taking to the rooftops.

Such a book doesn't make the coziest kind of read, like curling up in the inglenook with pipe and slippers for some nostalgic inhalation of Waltonian lore; in fact, quite the contrary is bound to be the case, for unless your complacency is of the density of an armadillo's shell, you will find it a most uncomfortable read, because its inescapable message is that unless you get off your duff and find some way of getting involved, pretty soon there isn't going to be any more fishing, for trout or anything else.

Maybe your threshold of personal involvement is so high that your reaction to the stimulus of books like this can be likened to Robert Maynard Hutchins's memorable solution to the occasional urge to exercise—"just lie down until it goes away." But otherwise it's hard to see how anybody could read a book that shows and tells, as vividly as this one does, what the despoilers are going to go right on doing to our sport, without wanting to do something about it. That too is made equally plain, for this book is as detailed and specific as a blueprint, in its answers to the question of "What can any one person do?"

(You could well feel that this is none of my business, that you and I never signed up for anything more than a projected walking tour of angling literature, and that I'm presuming on the nature of our acquaintance. Well, true, I feel an implied obligation to limit our discourse to matters concerning trout or the members of their more or less immediate family. But perhaps that ought to include concern for trout, in the sense of recognizing the not impossible contingency that the always pleasant pastime of fishing for them in print may yet be transformed, like the hunting of dinosaurs, into an activity that can be conducted only in print. In the light of that dire possibility, we would both be better served if I used the next three lines or so, not to tell you about some charming book that could conceivably enhance your leisure time, but to tell you how and where to join the newly formed American League of Anglers. I'll take a chance and cover that bet: it's ten dollars and it should be sent to 810 18th Street, N.W., Washington, D.C. 20006.)

As for *The Stream Conservation Handbook,* I will content myself with telling you what Nelson Bryant said about it in *The New York Times:* "Those who have watched the degradation of a treasured stream with frustration and sadness will learn from this little handbook that they need not stand idly by while what is loved is lost. If only a tiny fraction of the nation's thirty-nine million fishermen buy this book and follow its suggestions, much will be accomplished."

NEEDHAM, PAUL R. *Trout Streams*

This 1938 classic of stream biology, reissued by Winchester Press in 1969 with updating annotations by Carl E. Bond, is one of the keystones of angling wisdom. Sometimes I think that if we were as intelligent about our angling reading as we are at least supposed to try to be about our eating habits—that is, try anyway for a balanced diet—we would have to divide our books into another two categories: those we gobble down, like dessert, and those we consume with more measured enthusiasm, "because they are good for us," like spinach. I could read Odell Shepard practically daily, for instance, and some passages, like some in Walton, almost have down by heart, whereas I know that if I were to devote equal reading time to an almost rosary-like meditation of the pages of Dr. Needham's *Trout Streams* I'd be a much better angler in consequence. It's like trying to pay equal attention to your high school teacher who is the worthiest of creatures and has your best interests at heart, who happens to be plain, and a slip of a girl who happens to be beguiling. Dr. Needham could remedy a lot of my stupidities on stream, I know, if I would only pay enough retentive attention to what he tells me, whereas Odell Shepard is so nice he only confirms me in them. It's not that *Trout Streams* is boring, because a lot of it is really fascinating, but just that it doesn't happen to be the kind of book that has the pizzazz that Shepard has, at least for me, and that Walton has so obviously had for so many, that makes return visits seem a form of self-indulgence.

RAYMOND, STEVE. *The Year of the Angler*

This has it. Good as his first book was, I can't imagine going back to the pages of *Kamloops* at least once a year, unless to bone up immediately before going on a trip that might involve encounters with Kamloops trout, but I can readily conceive of reading *The Year of the Angler* again and again. It's as the Pennsylvania Dutch say, some things you want to keep around "just for pretty." Such books, and such authors, are rare, and Raymond is somebody simply not to be missed. If you missed this one, it merits going back for. Its worth warrants a long life, and therefore many printings. (I hope the next will correct two mistakes on page viii, where Fox, Grove and Marinaro are called not "the masters of the minutae," which they are, but of the minutiae, which they aren't, and the publication year of *A Leaf from French Eddy*, which was not 1968 but 1965. But neither of these was Steve Raymond's fault.)

RIGHYNI, R. V. *Salmon Taking Times*

If you've ever fished for salmon, and/or ever expect to fish for them, then this book is worth going out of your way for. Doesn't the very title make your mouth water? What else about salmon—remembering that one fish can ignore ninety-seven casts you make to him, and then grab the ninety-eighth as if it were the first one he'd seen—what else can possibly be as important as their taking times? We all have our favorite theories or superstitions about this, mostly wrong, but Righyni delves into the mystery deeper than anybody else has. The book was issued by Macdonald in London in 1965, and I bugged a dozen publishers about it, to try to get them to import the English sheets, while they were still new, to make a small American edition of it, but couldn't find one who would take a chance on it. They all gave me the same story—that fly fishing is itself a minority activity and that salmon fishing is therefore a rarity of a rarity (an enigma wrapped up inside a dilemma, so to speak) and nothing for a commercial publisher in his right mind to risk publishing unless somebody's willing to subsidize it. Well, hell, I couldn't go that far, so the matter died aborning. But that was before the great boom in fly-fishing books, that began only about three years later, so maybe today it would have a chance. Trouble is, now I can't find it myself—I've turned the house upside down looking for it—and can only conclude that maybe some umpteenth publisher I tried with it simply never bothered to return it. But I remember it well, as a stimulating and even exciting book for any salmon fisher to read. (I do find a copy of a later Righyni book, on grayling, and called just that, which was also published by Macdonald in 1968. But my god, if publishers think a salmon book is a poor risk, unless the author is as well known as say Lee Wulff, then what chance has a book on grayling, when we have only one state where there are any grayling to be found? Two, I guess, with Alaska in the Union, but otherwise Montana is the last redoubt of this lovely fish that was once Michigan's glory.) A pity on both counts—because Righyni's a good man, and I wish he were better known over here. His newest book (Macdonald, 1974) is *Advanced Salmon Fishing*.

RITZ, CHARLES; SCHALDACH, WM. J.; SCHWIEBERT, ERNEST.

Certified, all three, as purveyors of wines that need no bush. Certainly not from the likes of me, who could use some lessons from each of them. The current edition of the one and only book by the one and only Charles, *A Flyfisher's Life*, carries an introduction by me; so does Bill Schaldach's *The Wind on Your Cheek*, and Schwiebert's *Salmon of the World*, though the latter, at a hundred dollars a throw, must be a fairly well-kept secret. All three, despite a wealth and diversity of other fishing experience, are still faithful to trout as the fish they love to come home to, and to me that's a sign that a man's heart is still in the right place.

328 THE FISHING IN PRINT

STEWART, GEORGE R. *Not So Rich As You Think*

Not a book concerning trout, but very central to a deep concern for the future of trout, though nowhere does it say so in so many words. But books about trout preach only to the converted, whereas books like this have a better chance to stir up the passions of those not already concerned about conservation through an interest in sport. I honestly think Rachel Carson's *Silent Spring* did more to arouse the citizenry than any two dozen fishing books you could name. This book, by the widely known author of *Storm, Fire, Earth Abides* and *Names on the Land*, could almost better be called *Air*, because it's the best account I know of the worldwide problem of air pollution, and the environmental crisis that it symbolizes. Published by Houghton Mifflin in 1968 it was one of the first of a spate of books on "the effluent society," but it was not matched or even approached by any of them, to my mind, until the publication of Barry Commoner's *The Closing Circle* (Knopf, 1972) which supplements it without supplanting it. Between them, I should think, these two books constitute a liberal education for any concerned angler, to comprehend the extent and nature of the threats to the future of fishing. There isn't so much as a paragraph about trout in either of them, but that's all right, because what's good for the country will ultimately be good for trout, whereas the obverse of that proposition is very hard to sell to non-anglers, who are after all about a four to one majority. The importance of clean water and fresh air can be impressed on almost everybody, including politicians. The latter cannot be impressed about fish, except by the purely negative consideration that fish can't vote. It's fine to talk among ourselves about the future of fishing as if it mattered, but when we try to talk to politicians it will always have to be on the basis of getting them to do things, or prevent things being done, in spite of the fact that it will benefit fishing and fishermen rather than because it will.

TRAVER, ROBERT. *Trout Madness, Trout Magic*
(and many happy returns of the theme)

Somewhere in *The Fly and the Fish* I remember John Atherton musing on his idea of the ideal rod, and saying that if he ever got around to getting it made, he'd have Pinky Gillum make it for him. Of course he never did, and if he had, he wouldn't have had very long to enjoy it. But it seems to me, thinking back on it, that it's almost an absurdity. For to a truly involved fisherman, isn't any one rod almost a contradiction in terms? I don't think there's any such thing as one rod, any more than there's such a thing as one peanut. Either you're eating peanuts or you aren't. I prefer not to know how many rods I have, because of some vague guilt feeling about having too many. I know I keep four one-piece rods strung up, with flies on them, in the rod rack in the ladies' room at the club. And there are three more like that in a coat closet near the front door at home, kept in that same readiness just in case I should find something going on at the club that would keep me from getting into the ladies' room. But these are only the front line troops, so to speak. How many more there are in reserve, I'd rather not say, on the ground that confessing and bragging can easily be confused. But I suspect most really devoted fishermen feel the same way, and given their druthers, would enjoy being "varietists at heart" (as Dreiser said he was about women), rather than cleaving only and always to one rod, however admirable.

Jack Atherton is long beyond reach for questioning, but I think what he really was saying, in unwitting echo of the old time Buick ads, was that when better rods were built, Gillum would build them.

Well, in a way I've answered my own question, because when I thought of that line in *The Fly and the Fish*, what crossed my mind was that I felt about Robert Traver's books the way John Atherton felt about Pinky Gillum's rods. And of course I realize that this *is* an absurdity. If there were such a thing, or had to be, as one fishing book then of course it would have to be Walton, by over three centuries of common concert, but there doesn't have to be, thank goodness. So I guess all I'm saying is that to me in my time, and nobody can speak for more than that, when better fishing books are written, Robert Traver will write them.

Maybe this isn't as silly as it seems. I think of Odell Shepard, setting out to write the kind of fishing book he'd like to read. Well, that's really what he was saying, wasn't it? Yes, here's the passage: "I shall be content to write the rambling, idle, quite unpractical sort of book about fishing that I myself like to read" and then he goes on about being "by the fire in winter when the brooks are sealed, or by the stream on drowsy noons"—language as lovely as I can recall since Rupert Brooke's own "fish, fly-replete in depth of June, dawdling away their wat'ry noon" or however the poem went (god, it's been almost sixty years since I read it) that ended with "There shall be no more land, say fish"—well, anyway, if that's the formula, and I think it's a pretty good one, then there's nobody I'd rather trust with it than Robert Traver.

If I'd been alive a hundred-odd years ago, I'm sure I'd have felt the same way about Thad Norris—"there's the one I'll let speak for me"—and he was far from the only one writing at that time.

All it boils down to, I suppose, is that if I had to pick an odds-on favorite, for my money, in the great American fishing book sweepstakes that seems to have begun growing so fast in just these past few years—if I had to bet on somebody to come up with a book that I'd not only want to read but to reread early and often—well, I'd have to go with Traver. I'm talking about a book to read for fun, of course—a book that may harbor, around the turn of the next page, a thigh-slapping rouser of a sentence like Uncle Thad's "what a pity that infants aren't taught to smoke" or Traver's own about trout fishing being so enjoyable that it "really ought to be done in bed"—books so captivating to read that you really feel there should be some way to learn to hum or whistle them. McClane is more knowledgeable, and Lee Wulff is a far more determined perfectionist, obsessed with rod lengths and fly sizes and hell bent for efficiency as a fishing machine—well, that's part of why I settle on Traver, I suppose—he gives you that wonderful relaxed, lazy, unhurried and unflustered, comfortable "old shoe" feeling, page after page.

On the other hand . . .

WACKETT, L. J. *Studies of an Angler*

The farthest remove from Robert Traver, in every sense, including the geographical, this man hails from Melbourne, where his book was published in 1950. And he's as intent as Traver is casual. Wackett wants to know the reason why, when trout don't behave according to the form chart, whereas Traver would obviously prefer not to find out, rather savoring their unpredictability. The world of fly fishing is big enough for both of them, of course, and if it weren't for worry-warts like Wackett the art would have stood still since Walton's day. Wackett is a true original, of the little Tommy Horner persuasion—like Dunne, and Col. Harding, and Mottram and Hewitt—always poking a thumb in, probing around to at least lift a corner of the curtain veiling the mysteries of our subject.

Before I say another word about Wackett, though, let me be quick to disavow any knowledge of him—all I know is that he is a Wing Commander with a string of initials after his name—and I would never have heard his name if that canny bookfinder Col. Henry Siegel of The

Anglers and Shooters Bookshelf in Goshen, Conn., hadn't called *Studies of an Angler* to my attention.

One chapter in Wackett's *Studies of an Angler* has a higher revelation quotient, I should think, than any one chapter in any of the hundreds of fishing books that have come out anywhere since 1950. Tall claim, I know, and I can't support it, because who can possibly profess to have read them all? But I can at least say that I haven't seen anything like it in all the hundreds of fishing books I have read in the last twenty-five to thirty years. It's called "The Effect of Temperature and Pressure on Trout" and it's 36 pages long. Together with the following chapter, "The Practical Aspects of the Reactions of Trout to Meteorological Factors," which is the application to practical angling of the pure theories developed in the preceding chapter, you have the equivalent of a handbook of some 54 pages. But I feel pretty sure you would find yourself devoting more reading time to those relatively few pages than you would be likely to spend on ten times that many of pages of ordinary angling book reading. First of all, you have to read them twice to get settled down from the discombobulation of reading them the first time. The first time you read them, you'll find yourself so constantly saying "poor fish" that it will be hard to take in more than a fraction of their instructive value. If you're half as suggestible to print as I am you will not be able to read these pages without acute discomfort, as you mentally enact the contortions you would have to go through, if you were a fish, just to keep yourself on an even keel, so to speak, and keep from being literally blown up out of the water, by changes of temperature and pressure to which fish are very frequently obliged to accommodate. After you have absorbed these pages you will never again marvel that fish occasionally go off their feed — you will on the contrary wonder how they ever find time to do anything but "navigate," as it were, to maintain the proper level and position at which they can breathe comfortably. This alone seems such a full-time job (granted, they are built better for it than we are) that it seems an occasion of wonder that they can ever divert their attention from it long enough to look for something to eat.

Anyway, Wackett shows you, with words and pictures (diagrams) both what trout must go through in their swimming motions and in their bodily adaptation, to the changing pressures caused by the rise and fall of the temperature and the barometer, and while it may to a degree lessen for you the unpredictability of their behavior, it will certainly to a much greater degree increase your understanding of them and your sympathy for their problems. You may decide that life is not half as tough as you always thought it was, and take back any idle thoughts you may ever have entertained about coming back in another incarnation as a fish.

There is no publisher's imprint on the title page of *Studies of an Angler*, beyond the notation of "Melbourne 1950," and on the verso there is merely the mention that the book was registered at the Melbourne General Post Office for transmission through the post as a book. There is the designation of the printer's name and address (J. T. Picken & Sons Pty, Ltd., 265-275 Franklin Street, Melbourne). I presume the "Pty" stands for "Printery" and the span of the street numbers suggests that it's hardly a hole in the wall, but generally it's not very satisfactory to try to get information about a twenty-four or twenty-five-year-old book from a printer when you don't even know the name of the publisher for whom it was printed.

I'd say the situation calls for the services of a bookfinder, and since Hank Siegel is the only one I know who ever heard of it, he would seem to me to be your last best hope of getting a copy. The rest of the book is not the most regaling read ever offered an angler, except one who has immediate or future plans to fish in Australia, but I know a lot of serious fishermen who would go out of their way to get the information that's in those two chapters.

WALDEN, HOWARD T., 2ND. *The Last Pool, Upstream and Down* and *Big Stony*

An acknowledged classic, so why doesn't it turn me on? Or what is it that, once turned on, turns me off? Doesn't the very name, Howard T. Walden 2nd, give you the impulse to step right up and call him Mister? It sounds so very top drawer. "William T. Tilden 2nd" reverberates in my memory, triggered by the echo of Walden's resounding name. And the two names are of very nearly the same vintage, I should imagine. Walden is old enough to have seen service in the First World War. I wonder that his very venerability doesn't warm me up, as it contributes in large measure to the affectionate regard that predisposes me towards Sparse Grey Hackle every time he reaches for his pen instead of his rod.

Fifty years ago, when I was just getting started in what was then termed, with a straight face, the business world, I simply assumed that everybody around me was older than I. Nowadays, when I hear of anybody who is still around and is older than I am, I jump to the conclusion that he must be crowding Methuselah.

But this volume, though published in its author's sunset years, is a combined reissue of two Derrydale Press books he wrote in his relative youth, back in the thirties, and except for a few second thoughts he added for the edition of 1972 in the Crown Sportsmen's Classics series, it represents the outlook of an angler at high noon of his fishing life. So maybe the thing that sticks in my craw is that, after taking advantage of the chance to make changes and additions here and there throughout the book — presumably in the light of some forty years of further reflection — Walden still says, as he said in his original Derrydale Press printings, that the kill is the core of trout fishing. He says, in effect, that to give up the killing of the fish is to give up the sport entirely, since to him the kill is the heart of the matter.

How can anybody say that, in this day of the spread throughout the states of stretches of streams reserved for Fishing for Fun Only, and the steady proliferation of Catch and Release Clubs?

I remember Mencken, in the early days of flying, saying "Give me the kind of accident I have a chance to walk away from." I feel the same kind of line should be drawn, within which to confine our sports. I simply can't regard as sporting any sort of game or contest where I don't have to play for keeps but my opponent does. To me the essence of sport is doing something I don't have to do. If I have to do it, it's work. But equally of the essence is the equity of the activity. If sport is something I don't have to do, it should be something I can stop and walk away from, to come back and do again. If whoever or whatever else may be engaged in the activity can't have the same option, then to my mind it ceases to be sport. It can't be a sporting relationship, it seems to me, unless it's reciprocal. How can it be one-sided and still be sporting?

Granted, my concept of sport may be narrow. It seems to afford only a very tight fit for such sports as mountain-climbing and auto-racing, where there are many moments when you can't just stop and walk away. But for that matter, so are there in stream fishing, or we'd have no need for such a thing as a wading staff.

Paradoxically, some of the loveliest pages in *The Last Pool* have to do with the return of gallant fish to the waters from which they've been taken, so it's obviously not fair to say that Walden has the heart of a pirate, simply because of his insistence on the classification of trout fishing as a blood sport. But it does mar my enjoyment of what is otherwise a beautiful book.

Another giant plus for Walden, in my book, is that he alone, of all anthologists, commentators, critics and the like, ever paid any attention to that "darling book" (to use the term Bethune applied to Walton) Odell Shepard's *Thy Rod and Thy Creel,* from which he excerpted passages in his 1947 volume *Angler's Choice,* the first American anthology devoted exclusively to trout fishing. That alone marks him for me as a man of rare discernment.

WULFF, LEE, *The Atlantic Salmon*

We've got to pack it in sometime, so what better way to quit winner than to wind up with our champion angler and our finest fish? If Paris be, as sometime alleged, the place where all good Americans go when they die, then Atlantic salmon fishing is the ultimate destination of all good trout fishermen. Salmon fishing is the only logical supplement to trout fishing, though I am not of those who would equate "supplement" with "supplant." Once a trouter always a trouter, if you've really applied yourself to the pursuit for all there is in it. But for the postgraduate course beyond trouting, I still know no better school to attend than Lee Wulff's 1958 classic *The Atlantic Salmon.* He makes the progression from trout tactics and equipment more painless than anybody else.

There's a lot more learning about the fish itself, in readily available print, since 1958, notably J. W. Jones's *The Salmon,* of the very next year, and the two Anthony Netboy books, *Atlantic Salmon, A Vanishing Species?* (1970) and *The Salmon: Their Fight for Survival* (1973). All three are essential, to anybody with more than the most casual of interest in this noble fish. But as far as the fishing is concerned, Lee Wulff's book can still stand as the last word. And apart from its absolutely certifiable instructional value (what it doesn't tell you about fishing for salmon you can get along without) it still stands as one of the all-time great vicarious fishing trips in angling literature. In that passage in the book where he puts the small light rod in your hand and then begins calling the casts, as you go on trying one thing after another to an incredible total number of tries before the supreme moment when the salmon finally takes, you've been over an emotional roller coaster ride for which I know no reasonable facsimile in print.

For wrongly transposed picture captions and typographic mishandling the book should have been declared a disaster area from the day it came out, and as for the purportedly deluxe edition, I always felt that was an arrant gyp (I gave my copy of that version away, to serve as a duty present I didn't feel much like giving somebody I didn't like very much), but with all its faults as an example of bookmaking, *The Atlantic Salmon* is still the one salmon fishing book to have, even if, and indeed especially if, you're not having more than one.

I've called him our champion angler and with reason, as he has set up the records to be broken, sooner or later, one by one in his ten-year campaign to explore and demonstrate the broadening of the fly rod's range, after pioneering the extended versatility of light tackle. As a succession of individual exploits it is beyond comparison and certainly warrants the application of the title "champion" in a half dozen different directions.

In the development of tackle, tactics, techniques and equipment, his record has been brilliant, and in the philosophic aspects and conservational applications of the whole concept of Catch and Release his example has been beyond reproach. Certainly nobody has ever better expressed the whole idea of enlightened modern angling than Lee Wulff in his original one-sentence summation: "These fish are too valuable to be caught only once." Almost equally the great national angling organizations, such as TU and FFF, and the forensic action units, such as CASE and subsequently RASA and the newly formed American League of Anglers, are indebted to his efforts.

There is only one possibly deplorable side-effect of the virtuoso stature of his individual exploits, and that is the tendency in recent years toward an increasing emphasis on the competitive side of angling. This could be a dark cloud on the horizon of our sport. One of the glories of angling over the ages has been its contemplative and uniquely noncompetitive recreational nature. This despite the fact that fishing matches, party boat pools, casting tournaments, and the carnival underside of some overcommercialized camping-and-outdoor sports shows have been, like the poor, almost always with us. None of this has ever been anything the likes of Lee Wulff could have been blamed for, but there is the ever-present possibility that an unwitting and almost inadvertent consequence of his influence could endow this side of angling with a degree of respectability and prominence that it has never had before. At this late date, in the long history of angling, that would be a regrettable development. It is to be hoped that, as an omen, it will remain tiny and insignificant, and soon be averted.

Meanwhile, you and I can go our separate ways, secure in the knowledge that whatever may befall in the future of fishing in water, we can always beat a strategic retreat to the snug harbor that is afforded by the now teeming shelves and stacks of the fishing in print.

A BIBLIOGRAPHICAL NOTE

Readers who are minded to take other fishing trips in print, of a less dilatory and discursive nature than the one just concluded, and are willing or even eager to dispense with the services of an opinionated and talkative guide, are directed to the following sources. (You don't need a guide, but you may need a bookfinder, because the books about the books about fishing are notoriously hard to come by. Except for Hills, all of them are out of print. Anglers and Shooters Bookshelf, Goshen, Conn., is recommended. In England, try R. J. W. Colby, 15 Mapperly Hall Drive, Nottingham NG3 5EP.)

These sources may also be consulted for confirmation or denial of your suspicions of your present guide. You may have harbored the feeling that, guidelike, he has skipped all the best spots, and/or, at the very least, saved some of them for himself. This list is a good place to check such feelings, too.

BARTLETT, JOHN. *Catalogue of Books on Angling, including Ichthyology, Pisciculture, Fisheries and Fishing Laws.* Cambridge, Mass: J. W. Wilson & Son, 1882. (With supplement, 1886.)

BETHUNE, GEORGE WASHINGTON. "A Waltonian Library" (in the first American edition of *The Compleat Angler*). New York: Wiley & Putnam, 1847.

BLAKEY, ROBERT. *Historical Sketches of the Angling Literature of All Nations.* London: John Russell Smith, 1856.

GOODSPEED, CHARLES ELIOT. *Angling in America; Its Early History and Literature.* Boston: Houghton Mifflin, 1939.

HAMPTON, J. FITZGERALD. *Modern Angling Bibliography.* London: Herbert Jenkins, Ltd., 1947.

HILLS, JOHN WALLER. *A History of Fly Fishing for Trout.* London: Philip Allen & Co., 1921. New York: Henry Holt & Co., 1921. (Rockville Centre, N.Y.: Freshet Press, 1971).

HORNE, BERNARD S. *The Compleat Angler 1653-1967: A New Bibliography.* Pittsburgh: Univ. of Pittsburgh Press, 1970.

MARSTON, ROBERT BRIGHT. *Walton and Some Earlier Writers on Fish and Fishing.* London: Elliott Stock, 1894. (Reissued in 1903.)

OLIVER, PETER. *A New Chronicle of The Compleat Angler.* New York: The Paisley Press, Inc., 1936. London: Williams & Norgate Ltd., 1936.

PICKERING, WILLIAM. *Bibliotheca Piscatoria* (in Thomas Boosey's *Piscatorial Reminiscences*). London: Wm. Pickering, 1836.

RADCLIFFE, WILLIAM. *Fishing from the Earliest Times.* London: Murray, 1921.

ROBB, JAMES. *Notable Angling Literature.* London: Herbert Jenkins Ltd., 1945.

SATCHELL, THOMAS, AND WESTWOOD, THOMAS. *Bibliotheca Piscatoria. A catalogue of books on angling, with bibliographical notes.* London: W. Satchell, 1883; Dawsons of Pall Mall, 1966.

————— AND —————. *A Supplement to the Bibliotheca Piscatoria.* London: Sampson, Low, Marston & Co., 1901. (Included in Dawsons' reprint.)

SPARROW, WALTER SHAW. *Angling in British Art Through Five Centuries: Prints, Pictures, Books.* London: John Lane, 1923.

TURRELL, W. J. *Ancient Angling Authors.* London: Gurney & Jackson, 1910.

WETZEL, CHARLES MCKINLEY. *American Fishing Books. A bibliography from the earliest times up to 1948, together with a history of angling and angling literature in America.* Newark, Delaware: Privately printed, 1950.

WOOD, ARNOLD. *A Bibliography of The Complete Angler (up to 1900).* New York: Charles Scribner's Sons, 1900. (Edition of 128 copies.)

Index